THE WORLD'S GREAT
MILITARY
HELICOPTERS

GALLERY BOOKS
An Imprint of W. H. Smith Publishers Inc.
112 Madison Avenue
New York City 10016

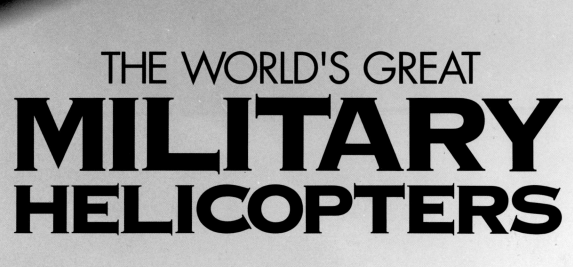

THE WORLD'S GREAT
MILITARY
HELICOPTERS

First published in the United States in 1990 by Gallery Books,
an imprint of W. H. Smith Publishers, Inc.,
112 Madison Avenue, New York, New York 10016

Gallery Books are available for bulk purchase for sales
promotions and premium use. For details write or telephone
the Manager of Special Sales, W. H. Smith Publishers, Inc.,
112 Madison Avenue, New York, New York 10016. (212) 532-
6600

Printed in Hong Kong

ISBN: 0-8317-9679-0

Pictures were supplied by:

Aerospatiale, Paul Beaver, Bell Helicopters, Flt Sgt J. K. Bell,
British Aerospace, Peter R. Foster, Sgt Green, Denis Hughes,
IDF/AF, Imperial War Museum, Paul A. Jackson, Jon Lake,
Laphot North, McDonnell Douglas, P. R. March, MBB,
Militarverlag des Deutschen Demokratischen Republik, Bob
Munro, No 814 Sqn FAA, No 820 Sqn FAA, No 28 Sqn RAF, No
202 Sqn RAF, Lindsay Peacock, Flt Lt Chris Perkins, Herman
Potgieter, Royal Australian Air Force, Royal Marines, Royal
Navy, Royal Netherlands Navy, Sikorsky, John W. R. Taylor, US
Air Force, US Army, US Navy, Mark Wagner, Roger P. Wasley,
West German Navy, Westland Helicopters

Special thanks to TRH Pictures

Production controller: Alastair Gourlay
Production editor: Chris Marshall
Design: Brown Packaging

Previous page: US CH-47 Chinooks show their lifting capacity as
they bring forward cargo vehicles.

CONTENTS

The WESTLAND AEROSPATIALE ARMY LYNX

Westland Army Lynx: British tank-blaster

*Eight **TOW** missiles, a simple but highly accurate tactical navigation system, superb maneouvrability and high speed make the Lynx a powerful anti-tank weapon, and a major element in **NATO**'s ability to meet any hostile thrust. That the aircraft has not been widely exported is more due to politics than to capability.*

From the earliest days of military flying, manufacturers have appreciated that to make an aircraft capable of performing two duties is to double one's potential market. In the fixed-wing world it has long been the case that true multi-role aircraft are extremely difficult to develop, but the same is not true of the younger helicopter: only comparatively recently have there emerged heavily armoured, tandem-seat helicopters whose dedication to the attack role is complete. Most of Europe's combat helicopters still have light transport capability, and in a coat of (say) red and white could pass almost unnoticed on a civil airfield. A few are equally at home on land or at sea, one of the leaders of that field being the Westland WG.13 Lynx.

Though based on a common airframe and dynamic system, the Navy Lynx and Army Lynx are sufficiently dissimilar in their avionics and weaponry for the former to be treated separately. However, it was the British army which was primarily responsible for the genesis of the Lynx, even though purchases of the land model have totalled only 132 of the 334 Lynxes firmly ordered by mid-1986.

Many factors were responsible for shaping today's Lynx, one of the most important being a requirement for air transportability in the Lockheed C-130 Hercules after minimal dismantling. Thus the helicopter has emerged as a squat though not unattractive machine,

with engines mounted atop the cabin, behind the short rotor shaft. During the mid-1960s, when design work was under way, the early lessons of US involvement in Vietnam indicated that two engines were a key requirement for battle zone operations so long as one could provide enough emergency power to get a damaged machine back to base.

Rolls-Royce powerplants

A pair of Pratt & Whitney Canada PT6A turboshaft engines driving a 13.41-m (44-ft) diameter rotor appeared to be the answer until the 1967 Anglo-French helicopter agreement forced a change of plans. France was to buy Lynxes for its navy (and its industry have a 30 per cent share in the programme), but a rotor size of 13.00 m (42 ft 7.8 in) was the French limit, for hangarage reasons. The PT6A could not then be sufficiently uprated to accommodate the change, but Rolls-Royce came to the rescue with its BS.360 turboshaft, which was initially rated at 671 kW (900 shp). Later known as the Gem, this engine was combined in a paired installation with a rotor of the then new semi-rigid design, together with a new gearbox. The result was a compact power unit which was both simple to maintain and reduced power losses to a minimum.

As such, the helicopter met Ground Staff Operational Requirement (GSOR) 3335, which was issued in June 1966 for a

*This Army Air Corps Lynx carries an unusual weapon load for trials or evaluation, consisting of 24 unguided **SURA** rockets. Front-line Lynxes rarely carry anything other than eight **TOW** wire-guided anti-tank missiles.*

machine able to lift 12 troops; or three stretchers and three walking wounded; or 1242 kg (2,738 lb) of freight. A further version was schemed to meet a French army specification for a tandem-seat gunship with chin-mounted turret sporting two 20-mm cannon, plus other weapons on stub wings. This latter variant failed to materialize, and armament for British army aircraft was initially restricted to theoretical provision of a general-purpose machine-gun or 20-mm cannon in the cabin doorway. It was to be a further decade before more lethal equipment was added.

The prototype Lynx first flew on 21 March 1971, followed on 12 April 1972 by a development aircraft for the army's utility model. After some changes of detail, the Lynx AH.Mk 1 was finalized, and the initial example (the eighth production Lynx) flew on 11 February 1977. Immediately identifying the Army Lynx

*The combination of speed, manoeuvrability and firepower makes the Lynx an ideal tank-buster. Its roof-mounted sight and sophisticated **TOW** missiles allow the Lynx to observe the enemy from the safety of cover.*

Main rotor blades
The all-metal, fully articulated main rotor has the provision for power folding to facilitate shipboard operations

Winch spotlight
To facilitate operations in low light and night conditions, the winch is fitted with a spotlight which is adjustable; controls are immediately adjacent to the winch controls

Radar radome
The helicopter carries the MEL AW 391 search radar antenna in a thimble radome; the display is situated in the helicopter's main cabin. This system may be upgraded to the Sea Searcher set in due course

Life raft stowage
In the helicopter's main cabin, there is stowage for the air-droppable MS10 (10-person) liferaft in its special container

Main cabin door
These sliding doors give access to the capacious cabin. The Sea King has only one main cabin door, located on the starboard side, with a two-section airstair door well forward on the port side. All cabin windows can be jettisoned in emergency. Up to 22 survivors may be accommodated

Upper U/VHF aerial
The standard air-to-ground and air-to-air communications set is a dual UHF and VHF radio, controlled from the rear cabin and/or the cockpit

Intermediate angle gearbox

ILS aerial
Mounted on the rear end of the fuselage is the ILS localizer aerial, which is part of the same landing and approach system

Keith Fretwell

Observation window
Most Sea Kings are fitted with bubble observation aerial, which can be used during search and rescue operations

Fuel jettison pipe
To reduce weight during specific flying operations such as mountain rescue, there is provision for the jettison of aviation fuel

Antenna
This antenna serves the VHF communications radio used for working with naval and coastguard vessels

Tailwheel
The fixed tailwheel assembly uses either Goodyear or BTR Dunlop Aviation tyres

ADF loop
The automatically tuned/steered ADF loop is carried under the fuselage

tems remained unchanged. The improvement concerned an increase of 227 kg (500 lb) in gross weight, to a new level of 9526 kg (21,000 lb) or, if some operational restrictions were accepted, 9707 kg (21,400 lb). Engines changed to the uprated Gnome 1400-1, a modified gearbox was fitted and the tail rotor design changed from five to six blades. Production contracts covered 21 new HAS.Mk 2s and conversion of 46 surviving Mk 1s to HAS.Mk 2A standard.

First steps towards providing an improved detection system were taken in 1978 when Sea Kings of one squadron (No. 814) were fitted with the American Jezebel passive sonobuoy system, complete with onboard signal processor. There was then a change of direction, and instead of updating the whole fleet in this way, the FAA opted for a new British system in the forthcoming Sea King HAS.Mk 5.

Whilst retaining Plessey 195 sonar, the revised aircraft gains in detection capability through installation of the Marconi/GEC AQS-902 LAPADS and provision for Ultra Electronics mini-sonobuoys. AQS-902, originally a private venture, was developed for helicopter use from the larger and more sophisticated AQS-901 equipment installed in the BAe Nimrod MR.Mk 2. The AQS-902 console, including a moving pen recorder, is located in the rear of the cabin, to port, room having been made by moving the rear bulkhead back 1.73 m (5 ft 8 in). Manning of the new equipment is assigned to the sonar operator, who now has a powerful computer at his disposal to elicit the tell-tale sounds of a submarine from the ocean's background 'mush'.

Farther forward and also on the left (sonobuoy stowage racks cover the starboard side of the cabin) is the radar position. Sea King HAS.Mk 5s have an enlarged, square-topped spine radome associated with the change to MEL ARI 5991 Sea Searcher radar, which is an I-band (3-cm) unit with double the search range of its predecessor. All-digital, with 360° coverage, it has multiple track-while-scan ability and also a steerable sector 'width', a sector-scan facility and a

rolling ball control to position the marker on its 43-cm (17-in) display screen. The radar operator may select display modes in which the helicopter occupies a fixed position on the screen (centre or offset), or appears to move over a stationary surface map.

Other changes in the HAS.Mk 5 include a new sonobuoy launch tube in the rear of the cabin, a strengthened floor and new navigation equipment (replacing the AW 96) in the form of Decca 71 Doppler and Decca TANS. In 1981, four Sea King HAS.Mk 5s of 'B' Flight, No. 824 Squadron, began operational trials with AQS-81 towed MAD equipment installed in the starboard float. The fitment, similar to that of the US Navy SH-3s, remains an option. Aircraft have also been equipped in service with the four sensor 'boxes', on the nose and rear fuselage sides, associated with Racal MIR-2 'Orange Crop' ESM equipment for pinpointing the origin of radar and radio transmissions.

Orders for new-build Sea King HAS.Mk 5s currently total 30, of which the first was delivered in October 1980, but all other available HAS.Mk 2/2As are being converted to this standard in a programme near to completion. Sea King HAS.Mk 5s of Nos 820 and 826 Squadrons flew continuously in all weathers to protect the British Task Force which liberated the Falkland Islands in the 1982 war with Argentina. They generated 6,489.5 hours and 3,421 deck landings in 2,253 sorties, yet serviceability was consistently over 90 per cent in spite of atrocious weather.

In Mk 5 form, the Sea King can operate

Norwegian Sea King Mk 43s are used primarily for search and rescue duties by four detached flights of Skvadron 330, based at Bodo, Banak, Orland, and Stavanger-Sola. This gives a good, even coverage of the whole country.

up to 160 km (100 miles) from its parent vessel for extended periods, and detect submarines at unprecedented distances using its own buoys, and those dropped by an RAF Nimrod MR.Mk 2. Having identified its target by a combination of buoys and 'dunking' sonar (plus possibly radar, ESM and MAD) it can destroy the quarry with Mk 11 depth charges or Mk 46 and newer Marconi Sting Ray homing torpedoes. An anti-shipping option will become available later in the 1980s when the HAS.Mk 6 version (exported as the Advanced Sea King) enters service with provision for two highly capable BAe Sea Eagle missiles. Based on the Mk 5, the Sea King HAS.Mk 6 is to have improved, integrated ASW acoustic processing systems for even more efficient submarine detection; a strengthened fuselage and uprated transmission; and a further increase in maximum weight to 9752 kg (21,500 lb). The main rotor blades are to be made in composite materials, for a fourfold increase in life and improved damage resistance, following their introduction on the production line in 1985

This Sea King HAS.Mk 5 of No. 814 Squadron carries two Marconi Sting Ray torpedoes and a pair of BAe Mk 11 depth charges. A towed Magnetic Anomaly Detector is carried on the starboard undercarriage sponson.

Sea King: Westland's Warhorse

The Sea King is in service with a large number of customers in four continents, fulfilling a variety of front-line and support duties. Sea Kings were used in action in the Falklands, proving themselves to be rugged and dependable and capable of operating in the most primitive conditions with minimal support.

Seen dipping its Plessey Type 195 sonar, this Westland Sea King HAS.Mk 5 belongs to No. 820 Squadron, a Culdrose-based anti-submarine warfare unit.

When the Royal Navy began the search for a new ASW helicopter to replace its Westland Wessex, it was not unnatural that its interest centred on the Sikorsky SH-3 Sea King. First flown in 1959, this American helicopter clearly possessed great promise for the role not only by reason of its installed detection equipment, but also because it was capable of accepting the more advanced ASW aids expected to become available in the years to come. The initial RN order for Sea Kings, placed in June 1966, thus proved to be a beneficial move both for the Fleet Air Arm and for Sikorsky's UK licensee, Westland. Assigned the vital task of defending RN vessels from submarine attack, the British-built Sea King is now into its third avionics update, whilst Westland has secured considerable overseas sales from as far afield as Australia.

Central to this success has been Westland's long-established relationship with Sikorsky, stretching back through the WS-58 Wessex, WS-55 Whirlwind and WS-51 Dragonfly/Widgeon. The UK firm secured the right to build, develop and modify the Sea King and sell it in Europe and the British Commonwealth, resulting in the broad range of variants now in service. Apart from the continually updated ASW model, versions are operated in the anti-ship, AEW and SAR roles, and a further strain is optimized for troop carrying, fire-support and ECM. Firmly established in service, with production now

close to 300, the Westland Sea King family will be a central feature of naval helicopter operations until the end of the century.

Sea King anatomy

The basic Sea King is an amphibious helicopter with a single-step boat hull incorporated in its all-metal, semi-monocoque fuselage. Two stabilizing floats, or sponsons, are mounted one on each side of the cabin, these also acting as stowage for the retractable, twin-wheel main landing gear units. The remaining single wheel of the reverse tricycle gear is at the extreme rear of the boat hull and is non-retracting. Sea landings are made only in an emergency, however, aided by inflatable bags mounted in the floats. Shipboard stowage is assisted by a folding tail boom and main rotor blades which fold backward under hydraulic power to positions close to the fuselage sides. Export Sea Kings intended to operate from vessels of frigate size may be fitted with a harpoon type haul-down device, such as the Dominion Aluminium Fabricating system employed by the Sea Kings of the Indian Navy.

In the ASW role, the Sea King is flown by a crew of four, including two pilots for all-weather operation. Above the cockpit is normally fitted a foreign object deflector to protect the two Rolls-Royce Gnome engines. These turboshafts required little adaptation to the heliocopter, as they are

licence-built versions of the General Electric T58 installed in the American SH-3. Behind the main rotor is the spine radome (an easy recognition feature of British-built Sea Kings), this having changed shape in line with progressive improvement of the installed search radar. The cabin houses two ASW/radar crew members and a retractable 'dunking' sonar, whilst attachments on the lower fuselage side are available for up to four homing torpedoes or depth charges.

Many of the Sea Kings in current FAA service began their lives to HAS.Mk 1 standard as part of the first batch of 56 aircraft which followed four Sikorsky-built pattern and development helicopters. Delivered from 1969 onwards, they represented a minimal change from the American model, the more significant modifications including Ekco AW 391 search radar, Plessey 195 'dunking' sonar, Marconi AW 96 'Blue Orchid' Doppler and a Louis Newmark Mk 31 automatic flight-control and stabilization system. In the first stage of updating, to produce the Sea King HAS.Mk 2, the detection sys-

The British Ministry of Defence (Procurement Executive) operates a small number of Sea Kings for radar and equipment trials and experimental work. This aircraft is a Mk 4X, basically a Commando with search radar.

The WESTLAND SEA KING

Westland Naval Lynx variants

Lynx HAS.Mk 2: original RN version with Gem 2 engines of 671 kW (900 shp), 4309-kg (9,500-lb) initial maximum weight limit and Ferranti Seaspray radar for Sea Skua missiles; optional MAD; MIR-2 ESM later added; 60 built
Lynx HAS.Mk 2(FN): French version of HAS.Mk 2, but ORB-31-W radar, AS.12 missiles, French avionics and Alcatel 'dunking' sonar; 26 built
Lynx HAS.Mk 3: uprated RN version with 835-kW (1,120-shp) Gem 41-1 engines; 31 being delivered
Lynx HAS.Mk 4(FN): French version of HAS.Mk 3 with Gem 41-1 engines, uprated transmission and 4763-kg (10,500-lb) maximum weight; ORB-31 and sonar; 14 built
Lynx Mk 21: Brazilian version of HAS.Mk 2; nine built
Lynx Mk 23: Argentine version of HAS.Mk 2; two built
Lynx Mk 25: Netherlands SAR and utility version, lacking ASW equipment; Gem 2 engines; local designation **UH-14A**; six built
Lynx Mk 27: initial Netherlands ASW version with Gem 41-1 engines and Alcatel 'dunking' sonar; local designation **SH-14B**; 10 built
Lynx Mk 80: Danish ASW version of HAS.Mk 2 with Gem 41-1 engines; eight built
Lynx Mk 81: second Netherlands ASW version; MAD instead of Alcatel sonar; Gem 41-1 engines; eight built
Lynx Mk 86: Norwegian SAR version of HAS.Mk 2I but with Gem 41-2 engines of 835 kW (1,120 shp) and non-folding tail; six built
Lynx Mk 87: uprated Argentine ASW version with Gem 41-2 engins; eight ordered; one completed, but not delivered; became company demonstrator
Lynx Mk 88: West German ASW version with Gem 41-2 engines; Bendix AQS-18 sonar; non-folding tailboom; 14 built
Lynx Mk 89: Nigerian ASW version with Gem 43-1 engines; RCA 500 Primus radar; three built
Lynx 3: under development; navalized version of second-generation Lynx, with revised rear cabin/boom contours, advanced-technology rotor blade design and 1004-kW (1,346-shp) Gem 60s, chin-mounted 360° search radar, target-acquisition systems, standard 'dunking' sonar and MAD

Westland Naval Lynx warload

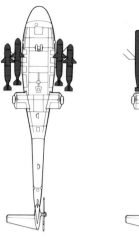  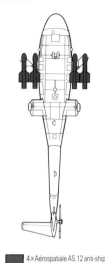 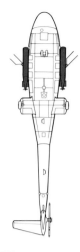

4 × BAe Sea Skua anti-ship missiles

2 × Marconi Sting Ray homing torpedoes

4 × Aérospatiale AS.12 anti-ship missiles

2 × Aerojet Mk 46 homing torpedoes

Royal Navy ASV
Sea Skua, a new sea-skimming missile with a range in excess of 15 km (9.3 miles), is the Lynx's principal weapon against surface vessels. Prematurely brought into service for the Falklands war, its debut (on 3 May 1982) saw one ship sunk and another damaged. Additional optional armament can include a 7.62-mm (0.3-in) GP machine-gun in either cabin doorway.

Royal Navy ASW
A further new weapon employed by Lynx, Sting Ray, is entering service as the standard anti-submarine homing torpedo. With an endurance of eight minutes, Sting Ray has an advanced guidance system and warhead, effective against the latest type of reinforced hulls. Deployed in the Falklands war, Sting Ray was officially given limited service clearance on September 1983 and a full production contract was placed in January 1986.

French Navy ASV
Lynx of the Aéronavale do not have the all-weather ASV potential of their British counterparts with the Seapray radar/Sea Skua missile combination. Instead, ORB-31-W radar is used for surveillance, whilst wire-guided AS.12 misiles are directed onto their targets optically via a SFIM APX M335 gyro-stabilized sight on the cockpit roof. Range is limited to 600 m/6,562 yards.

French Navy ASW
The widely-used Mk 46 is a homing torpedo with a speed of 40 kts, and contains 44 kg (97 lb) of explosive within its total weight of 230 kg (507 lb). A US weapon designed and developed by Aerojet, its manufacture is currently assigned to Honeywell Inc., which has built over 9,000 examples.

Specification: Westland Lynx HAS.Mk 3

Rotors
Main rotor diameter	12.80 m	(42 ft 0 in)
Main rotor disc area	128.7 m²	(1,385 sq ft)
Tail rotor diameter	2.21 m	(7 ft 3 in)

Fuselage and tail unit
Accommodation	pilot and observer	
Length overall, rotors turning	15.163 m	(49 ft 10 in)
Length, fuselage	11.92 m	(39 ft 1.3 in)
Length folded	10.62 m	(34 ft 10 in)
Height overall	3.48 m	(11 ft 5 in)
Tailplane half span	1.776 m	(5 ft 9.9 in)

Landing gear
Fixed tricycle landing gear with single mainwheels and steerable twin nosewheels
Wheelbase	2.94 m	(9 ft 7.75 in)
Wheel track	2.78 m	(9 ft 1.4 in)

Weights
Empty	2740 kg	(6,040 lb)
Maximum take-off	4763 kg	(10,500 lb)
Internal fuel load	733 kg	(1,616 lb)

Powerplant
Two Rolls-Royce Gem Mk 41-1 turboshafts
Maximum contingency rating, each	835 kW	(1,120 shp)

Navy Lynx recognition features

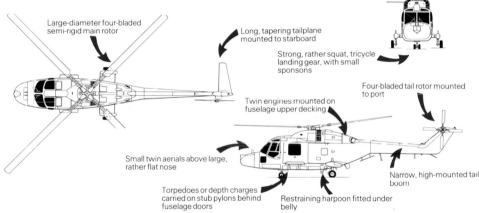

Large-diameter four-bladed semi-rigid main rotor

Long, tapering tailplane mounted to starboard

Strong, rather squat, tricycle landing gear, with small sponsons

Four-bladed tail rotor mounted to port

Twin engines mounted on fuselage upper decking

Small twin aerials above large, rather flat nose

Narrow, high-mounted tail boom

Torpedoes or depth charges carried on stub pylons behind fuselage doors

Restraining harpoon fitted under belly

Performance:

Maximum speed at sea level	125 kts/232 km/h	(144 mph)
Hovering ceiling out of ground effect	8,450 ft	(2575 m)
Maximum range at 4763-kg (10,500-lb) TOW	593 km	(368 miles)

Time on station 93 km (58 miles) out with two torpedoes on ASW mission 2 hours 29 minutes
Same mission parameters but with 'dunking' sonar 1 hour 5 minutes
Initial rate of climb	2,170 ft	(661 m) per minute

Payload/weapon load
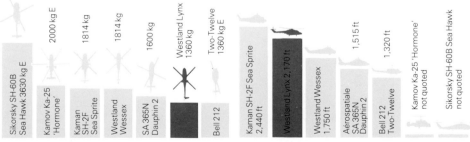

- Sikorsky SH-60B Sea Hawk 3630 kg E
- Kamov Ka-25 'Hormone' 2000 kg E
- Kaman SH-2F Sea Sprite 1814 kg
- Westland Wessex 1814 kg
- SA 365N Dauphin 2 1600 kg
- Westland Lynx 1360 kg
- Bell Two-Twelve 1360 kg E

Maximum rate of climb per minute
- Kaman SH-2F Sea Sprite 2,440 ft
- Westland Lynx 2,170 ft
- Westland Wessex 1,750 ft
- Aérospatiale SA 365N Dauphin 2 1,515 ft
- Bell 212 Two-Twelve 1,320 ft
- Kamov Ka-25 'Hormone' not quoted
- Sikorsky SH-60B Sea Hawk not quoted

Speed at sea level
- Sikorsky SH-60B Sea Hawk 160 kts E
- Aérospatiale SA 365N Dauphin 2 151 kts
- Kaman SH-2F Sea Sprite 130 kts
- Westland Lynx 125 kts
- Kamov Ka-25 'Hormone' 119 kts
- Westland Wessex 117 kts
- Bell 212 Two-Twelve 100 kts

Range with maximum standard fuel
- Aérospatiale SA 365N Dauphin 2 880 km
- Kaman SH-2F Sea Sprite 661 km
- Westland Wessex 628 km
- Sikorsky SH-60B Sea Hawk 600 km E
- Westland Lynx 593 km
- Bell 212 Two-Twelve 420 km
- Kamov Ka-25 'Hormone' 400 km

Service ceiling
- Kaman SH-2F Sea Sprite 22,500 ft
- Sikorsky SH-60B Sea Hawk 19,000 ft E
- Aérospatiale SA 365N Dauphin 2 15,000 ft
- Westland Wessex 14,100 ft
- Bell 212 Two-Twelve 13,000 ft
- Westland Lynx 12,000 ft
- Kamov Ka-25 'Hormone' 11,500 ft

Nigerian Navy

Nigerian Lynx Mk 89s are similar to the aircraft delivered to Argentina and Brazil, but are equipped with RCA 500 Primus radar in place of the more usual Seaspray. The aircraft operate from shore bases and from the frigate *Aradu*. Three aircraft were delivered, and equip No. 101 Squadron.

No. 101 Squadron

Formed: April 1985
Base: Ojo-Navytown (and JNS *Aradu*)

Task: ASW
Aircraft: Lynx Mk 89 01-F89, 02-F89, 03-F89

Lynx Mk 89s formed the initial equipment of the Nigerian navy air component when it formed in 1984.

Norwegian coastguard (Kystvakt)

Norway's Lynx Mk 86s operate from Sola/Stavanger with Skvadron 337, and are operated mainly on behalf of the coast guard for fishery protection, offshore oil rig security, and search and rescue duties. They wear 'Kystvakt' titles on the fuselage sides.

Skvadron 337

Formed: October 1981
Base: Sola/Stavanger
Task: Surveillance/SAR
Aircraft: Lynx Mk 86 216, 228, 232, 235, 237

Norway's Lynx are operated by the air force on fishery protection and SAR tasks, and carry 'Kystvakt' (coast guard) titles.

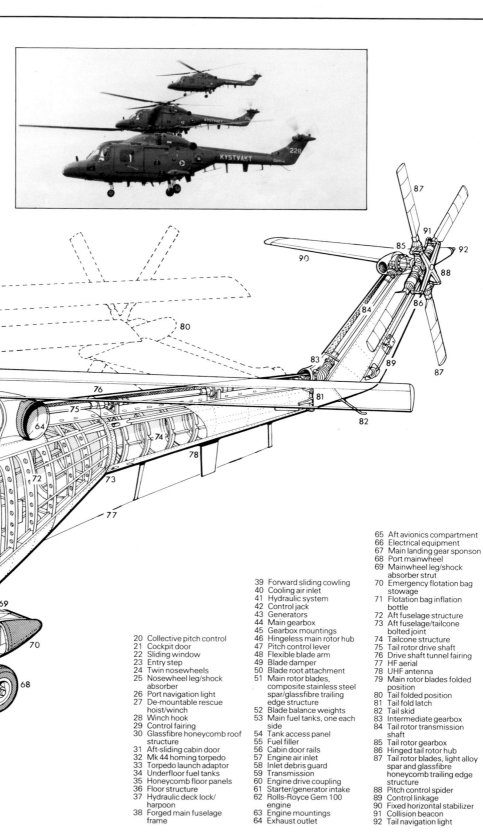

20 Collective pitch control
21 Cockpit door
22 Sliding window
23 Entry step
24 Twin nosewheels
25 Nosewheel leg/shock absorber
26 Port navigation light
27 De-mountable rescue hoist/winch
28 Winch hook
29 Control fairing
30 Glassfibre honeycomb roof structure
31 Aft-sliding cabin door
32 Mk 44 homing torpedo
33 Torpedo launch adaptor
34 Underfloor fuel tanks
35 Honeycomb floor panels
36 Floor structure
37 Hydraulic deck lock/harpoon
38 Forged main fuselage frame
39 Forward sliding cowling
40 Cooling air inlet
41 Hydraulic system
42 Control jack
43 Generators
44 Main gearbox
45 Gearbox mountings
46 Hingeless main rotor hub
47 Pitch control lever
48 Flexible blade arm
49 Blade damper
50 Blade root attachment
51 Main rotor blades, composite stainless steel spar/glassfibre trailing edge structure
52 Blade balance weights
53 Main fuel tanks, one each side
54 Tank access panel
55 Fuel filler
56 Cabin door rails
57 Engine air inlet
58 Inlet debris guard
59 Transmission
60 Engine drive coupling
61 Starter/generator intake
62 Rolls-Royce Gem 100 engine
63 Engine mountings
64 Exhaust outlet
65 Aft avionics compartment
66 Electrical equipment
67 Main landing gear sponson
68 Port mainwheel
69 Mainwheel leg/shock absorber strut
70 Emergency flotation bag stowage
71 Flotation bag inflation bottle
72 Aft fuselage structure
73 Aft fuselage/tailcone bolted joint
74 Tailcone structure
75 Tail rotor drive shaft
76 Drive shaft tunnel fairing
77 HF aerial
78 UHF antenna
79 Main rotor blades folded position
80 Tail folded position
81 Tail fold latch
82 Tail skid
83 Intermediate gearbox
84 Tail rotor transmission shaft
85 Tail rotor gearbox
86 Hinged tail rotor hub
87 Tail rotor blades, light alloy spar and glassfibre honeycomb trailing edge structure
88 Pitch control spider
89 Control linkage
90 Fixed horizontal stabilizer
91 Collision beacon
92 Tail navigation light

French naval aviation (Aeronavale)

The French navy received only 40 of the 80 Lynx HAS.Mk 2(FN) and HAS.Mk 4(FN) helicopters originally ordered. They are equipped with French radar and sonar systems, and are armed with wire-guided AS.12 missiles, aimed using a rather primitive roof-mounted sight. They are operated from aircraft carriers and destroyers, and occasionally from frigates.

This Westland Lynx HAS.Mk 2(FN) wears the markings of 31 Flotille, based at Lanvéoc Poulmic.

31 Flotille
Re-equipped: September 1978
Base: Lanvéoc-Poulmic (and aircraft-carriers)
Task: ASW/ASV
Aircraft: Lynx HAS.Mk 2(FN) 263, 264, 266; Lynx HAS.Mk 4(FN) 811

34 Flotille
Re-equipped: November 1979
Base: Lanvéoc-Poulmic (and destroyers)
Task: ASW/ASV
Aircraft: Lynx HAS.Mk 2(FN) 269, 278, 622, 624, 626

35 Flottille
Formed: 11 June 1979
Base: Lanvéoc-Poulmic (and *Jeanne d'Arc*)
Task: ASW/ASV
Aircraft: Lynx HAS.Mk 2(FN) 271, 627; Lynx HAS.Mk 4(FN) 814

20 Escadrille de Servitude
Equipped: (partially only) May 1978
Base: St Raphaël
Task: Development and trials
Aircraft: Lynx HAS.Mk 2(FN) 260, 272; Lynx HAS.Mk 4(FN) 803

Early French Lynx had white cabin roofs, but most have now received an overall grey colour scheme.

German naval aviation (Marineflieger)

Marineflieger Lynx Mk 88s are equipped with Bendix AQS-18 Sonar, and do not have folding tailbooms; they are otherwise broadly similar to RN aircraft. Twelve were originally delivered and a further pair are on order. They are based on Type 122 and 'Bremen' class frigates.

3.Staffel/ Marineflieger- geschwader 3
Formed: 1 October 1981
Base: Nordholz (and 'Bremen' class ships)
Task: ASW
Aircraft: Lynx Mk 88 8301, 8304, 8307, 8309, 8312

Marineflieger Lynx can be operated from 'Bremen' class and Type 122 frigates used by the Bundesmarine.

Netherlands naval aviation
(Marine Luchtvaartdienst)

Dutch navy Lynx SH-14Bs are equipped with a French Alcatel DUAV-4 'dunking' sonar, while the SH-14Cs have an AQS-81 MAD, which is also available to RN Lynx crews. These two variants operate from de Kooij, with No. 860 Squadron. Unarmed UH-14As are used for SAR and support duties by No. 7 Squadron, also at de Kooij.

7 Squadron
Re-equipped: August 1977
Base: de Kooij
Task: SAR/support
Aircraft: UH-14A (Lynx Mk 25) 260, 261, 262, 264, 265

860 Squadron
Re-equipped: September 1979
Base: de Kooij (and frigates)
Task: ASW
Aircraft: SH-14B (Lynx Mk 27) 266, 269, 270; SH-14C (Lynx Mk 81) 276, 283

A Lynx Mk 27, locally designated SH-14B, of No. 860 Squadron, Dutch navy.

Westland/Aérospatiale Lynx HAS.Mk 2 cutaway drawing key

1 Hinged radome
2 Ferranti Seaspray radar
3 UHF antennae
4 Air inlet
5 Radar equipment
6 Front bulkhead
7 Windscreen
8 Windscreen wipers
9 Instrument panel shroud
10 Downward vision window
11 Rudder/yaw pedals
12 Pitot head
13 Temperature probe
14 Engine controls
15 Cockpit eyebrow window
16 Pilot's seat
17 Centre console
18 Co-pilot's seat
19 Control column/cyclic pitch control

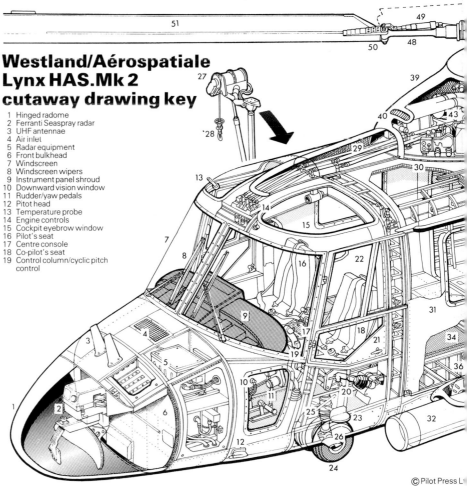

© Pilot Press L

Engine air intake
A particle separator is provided for the twin engine intakes for the Gem engines. The wire mesh foreign object damage (FOD) guard prevents any potentially damaging object from being re-cycled into the turbines

Main rotor system
The naval Lynx is one of the few helicopters with a semi-rigid rotor system, carrying four main rotor blades. For use aboard ship, the rotor system allows negative pitch to be applied. The hub and arms are built as a complete unit using titanium worked from a single forging

Main rotor blades
Until refitted in the next few years, naval Lynx are flown with conventional stainless steel sparred main rotor blades which are capable of being folded for hangar stowage. The blade is covered with moulded glass reinforced plastic and the blade tips are plastic in construction

Inspection ports
To facilitate pre-flight inspections, the Lynx is fitted with Plexiglas inspection ports to show fluid levels in the main gearbox

RESCUE

335

Harpoon
The naval Lynx uses a Fairey Harpoon deck connector for launch and recover in bad weather. The Harpoon holds the helicopter to a grille mounted in the frigate flight deck and is released on launch; immediately after landing, the helicopter's pilot releases the Harpoon into the deck grille to secure the helicopter

Cargo hook
In a limited way, the naval Lynx can be used for Vertrep (vertical replenishment), using cargo nets to carry loads. For exercises, the Lynx HAS.Mk 2/3 can recover its own drill torpedoes using a long line from the hook

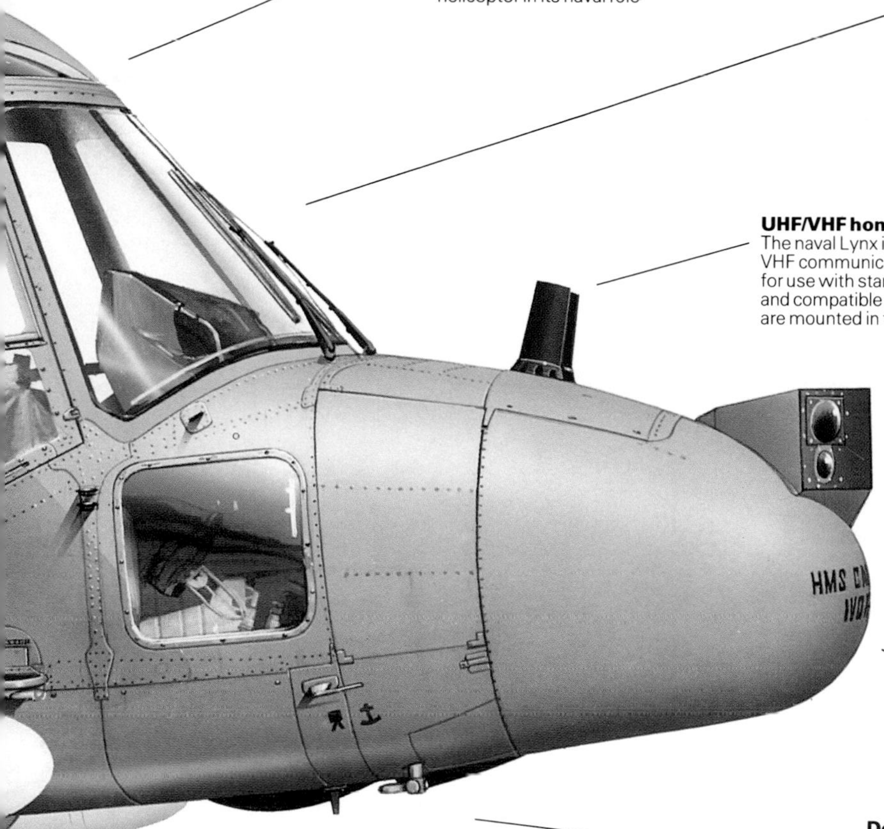

Main cabin
Behind the two main cabin doors, there is provision to carry a rescue winch, door-mounted machine-gun or up to nine passengers (or their equivalent weight in stores). In the Sea Skua role, the helicopter is kept as clean of additional equipment as possible

Cockpit
The naval Lynx is usually flown by a single pilot from the right-hand seat (although dual-control training helicopters are on strength), with the observer (the tactical commander) in the left-hand seat. The cockpit contains various displays, instruments and controls for the operation of the helicopter in its naval role

Aircrew
The Lynx aircrew (which can also include an aircrewman/winchman for SAR and other non-tactical tasks) is made up of pilot and observer, either of whom can be the flight commander, but the observer is usually the tactical commander, irrespective of rank. In operational flying, the aircrew wear flight suits, immersion coveralls, the Helmets Mk 4A flying helmet and could be required to carry NBC kit. The helicopter is soon to be updated with the GEC Avionics passive identification system for long-range, night/bad weather surface searches

UHF/VHF homer
The naval Lynx is fitted with twin UHF/VHF communications and homing radios for use with standard NATO frequencies and compatible equipment. The controls are mounted in the cockpit

Orange Crop forward sensor
There is a forward antenna box for the MIR-2 Orange Crop system, which will be replaced by PIDS in due course

Sea Spray radar
Contained in the nose radome of the Lynx HAS.Mk 2/3 is the Ferranti Sea Spray monopulse radar which is used for surface search, identification, navigation, homing and Sea Skua missile illumination. The Mk 1 set is being updated with either the Mk 3 or the MEL Super Searcher radar systems

Doppler aerial
On the underside of the naval Lynx, there is a radar altimeter, Doppler 91 aerial and various other sensors which allow for deck landings in the worst conditions flyable. The Doppler system feeds information to the TANS (Tactical Air Navigation System) which is the primary navigational aid for the observer

Identification number
During peacetime operations, naval aircraft are coded to allow easy recognition and visual identification. 335 is the individual code for HMS Cardiff's Lynx, which also bears the tail number XZ721; the latter will not change, but the former is altered when the helicopter is transferred to another ship

Nose landing wheel
This high energy absorption landing gear has twin wheels which can be controlled to allow the helicopter to be positioned on deck for take-off into wind, and to allow for taxiing at shore bases

ML Universal Carrier
To allow the Lynx HAS.Mk 2/3 to carry a range of naval weapons, the helicopter is fitted with a universal stores carrier manufactured by ML Aviation. Besides Sea Skua, the helicopter can carry Mk 44/46 anti-submarine torpedoes, Mk 11 depth charges and auxiliary fuel tanks

Sea Skua missile
Used operationally in the Falklands conflict, the British Aerospace Sea Skua missile is designed for anti-shipping operations. Four can be carried by the Lynx and the system is integrated with the nose-mounted Sea Spray radar. Sea Skua's range allows it to be launched outside most warship self-defence missile engagement zones

Naval Lynx in service:
units and example aircraft

Royal Navy

Only two RN squadrons operate the Lynx, both sharing RNAS Portland as their shore base. Ninety-one aircraft are on order, and they will be deployed on the ships' flights of some 40 vessels, replacing Wasps and Wessex. RN Lynx are equipped with Ferranti Seaspray radar, MIR-2 ESM, and ASQ-81 MAD. They can be armed with Sea Skua missiles or Marconi Stingray torpedoes.

A Westland Lynx HAS.Mk 3 of No. 815 Squadron, whose shore base is RNAS Portland.

702 Squadron
Formed: 3 January 1978
Base: RNAS Portland
Task: Lynx HQ Squadron
Aircraft: Lynx HAS.Mk 2 XZ243 '640/PO', XZ262 '644/PO', XZ232 '647/PO'; Lynx HAS.Mk 3 ZD250 '630/PO', ZD251 '631/PO'

815 Squadron
Formed: 1 January 1981
Base: RNAS Portland
Task: Shipboard ASW/ASV
Aircraft: Lynx HAS.Mk 2 (XZ- serials) and Lynx HAS.Mk 3 (ZD- serials) allocated as below:
HQ Flight: XZ699 '300', ZD252 '301', XZ237 '302', ZD253 '304', XZ727 '305', XZ726 '306', XZ731 '307'
Gibraltar Flt: ZD258 'GIB'
Trials Flt: ZD255 '479'
and to the following destroyers and frigates:
HMS *Alacrity* XZ254 '327/AL'
HMS *Amazon* XZ725 '320/AZ'
HMS *Ambuscade* '323/AB'
HMS *Andromeda* XZ244 '472/AM'

HMS *Argonaut* XZ695 '466/AT'
HMS *Arrow* XZ730 '326/AW'
HMS *Avenger* XZ697 '341/AG'
HMS *Battleaxe* XZ256 '430/BX'
HMS *Beaver* ZD268 '375/VB'
HMS *Birmingham* ZD259 '333/BM'
HMS *Boxer* XZ239 '376/XB'
HMS *Brave*
HMS *Brazen* XZ690 '330/BZ'
HMS *Brilliant* XZ691 '342/BT'
HMS *Broadsword* ZD257 '346/BW'
HMS *Cardiff* XZ234 '335/CF'
HMS *Charybdis* XZ734 '431/CY'
HMS *Danae* XZ726 '464/DN'
HMS *Edinburgh* XZ729 '377'
HMS *Exeter* XZ733 '420/EX'
HMS *Fife* XZ248 '404/FF'
HMS *Glamorgan* '400/GL'
HMS *Glasgow* XZ694 '344/GW'
HMS *Gloucester* XZ722 '410/GC'
HMS *Hermione* XZ720 '475/HM'
HMS *Jupiter* XZ719 '443/JP'
HMS *Liverpool* XZ728 '332/LP'
HMS *Manchester* XZ736 '360/MC'
HMS *Minerva* XZ698 '424/MV'
HMS *Newcastle* ZD265 '345/NC'
HMS *Nottingham* XZ241 '417/NM'
HMS *Penelope* XZ723 '454/PE'
HMS *Phoebe* XZ724 '471/PB'
HMS *Scylla* ZD256 '432/SC'
HMS *Sirius* XZ255 '450/SS'
HMS *Southampton* XZ233 '334/SN'
HMS *York* XZ689 '407/YK'

This Lynx HAS.Mk 2 wears the all-grey colour scheme, with toned-down codes and legends, applied to RN helicopters after the Falklands war.

Argentine naval aviation (Commando de Aviacion Naval Argentina)

Only two Lynx have been delivered to the Argentine navy, and one of these was destroyed during the Falklands war. A further batch of eight aircraft was never delivered. The Lynx Mk 23 is essentially similar to the British HAS.Mk 2. It is possible, but not likely, that Argentina's surviving Lynx is still airworthy.

1ª Escuadrilla Aeronaval de Helicopteros/3ª Escuadra Aeronaval
Equipped: September 1978
Base: Puerto Belgrano
Task: ASW
Aircraft: Lynx Mk 23 0734 '3-H-141' in storage (0735 '3-H-142' destroyed)

The exact status of Argentina's Lynx helicopter is uncertain, but post-war embargoes have probably grounded the surviving aircraft.

Brazilian naval aviation (Forca Aeronaval de Marinha do Brazil)

The Brazilian navy received nine Lynx Mk 21s for use from its British-designed frigates; they are basically similar to the early Mk 2s delivered to the Royal Navy. Brazil had previously operated British-built Westland Whirlwind helicopters, and had forged close links with the manufacturer and the Royal Navy.

1° Esquadrao de Helicópteros Anti-Submarinos
Equipped: March 1978
Base: Sã Pedro de Aldeia
Task: ASW
Aircraft: Lynx Mk 21 N3020, N3022, N3023, N3026, N3028

This Lynx is one of those operated by 1 Esquadrao de Helicópteros Anti Submarinos of the Brazilian navy.

Danish naval aviation (Danske Sovaernets Flyvetaeneste)

Denmark's Lynx Mk 80s are owned and flown by the navy, but are maintained and supported by the army. They can fly from 'Hvidbjornen' class fishery protection vessels and are similarly equipped to the RN HAS.Mk 2.

Eskadrille 722
Equipped: May 1980
Base: Vaerløse
Task: Fishery protection/SAR
Aircraft: Lynx Mk 80 S-134, S-142, S-175, S-187, S-191

A Westland Lynx Mk 80 of the Danish navy.

from June 1982 onwards, are HAS.Mk 3s employing the uprated Gem 41-1. In 1987 HAS.Mk 3s are to be retrofitted with a Racal central tactical system which will process all sensor equipment and present mission information on a single multi-function screen. Similar engine improvements are to be found in the two versions of the Lynx delivered to France's naval air arm, the Aéronavale, designated HAS.Mk 2(FN) and HAS.Mk 4(FN).

Built at Yeovil between 1977 and 1983, the 40 French helicopters were little more than flying shells when delivered. Before issue to the service they were fitted out by Aérospatiale or a subcontractor with a French avionics suite, comprising Omera-Segid ORB-31-W radar and Alcatel DUAV-4 'dunking' sonar, plus local radios and other equipment. The ORB-31-W uses two transmitter/receivers (one for long distances and the other with greater sensitivity and clutter resistance) but French Lynx helicopters are armed only with up to four Aérospatiale AS.12 wire-guided missiles (range 6000 m/6,562 yards) and the associated SFIM APX M335 gyro-stabilized sight mounted in the roof above the port seat. Aéronavale Lynxes are operated from the aircraft-carriers *Clemenceau* and *Foch*, the helicopter carrier *Jeanne d'Arc*, and 'C70' and 'F67' class destroyers, although occasional use from platform-equipped (but hangarless) frigates is also possible. A hydraulically-operated rescue winch is an optional fitment on the starboard side, above the cabin door.

Exports to other countries have been achieved, notably the Netherlands, which operates two variants, mainly from 'Van Speijk' and 'Kortenaer' class frigates. These are the locally-designated SH-14B and SH-14C models, equipped respectively with French Alcatel DUAV-4 'dunking' sonar and ASQ-81 MAD. As with other Lynx models, Decca TANS is used for accurate navigation at sea, and an autohover mode on the Marconi AFCS provides vertical precision for dipping the sonar. West Germany's Bundesmarine introduced a further variation on the theme by equipping its Lynx Mk 88s with Bendix AQS-18 sonar, again deployed from a central well by means of a

hydraulic winch. They operate in pairs from the 'Type 122' or 'Bremen' class frigates which patrol the Baltic and, unusually, have non-folding tailbooms.

Farther afield, Lynx helicopters are employed for the ASW/ASV role in South America and Africa. Argentina received two in 1978 for her British-built 'Type 42' destroyers *Hercules* and *Santisima Trinidad*, but one was lost in an accident at sea during the 1982 Falklands war and the other placed in storage when spares supplies were stopped. The first of a repeat order for eight Argentine Lynxes made its first flight two days before Argentine forces invaded the Falklands, so it was embargoed and used as a company demonstrator. Also in 1978, Brazil received nine Lynx helicopters for its British-designed 'Niteroi' class frigates. Finally, the Nigerian navy's newly-formed air component received three Lynxes in 1984 after crew training by Westland, these helicopters differing from their Latin American brethren through fitment of RCA 500 Primus radar in place of Seaspray. Nigeria's only Lynx-equipped vessel is the frigate *Aradu*.

Completing the Lynx picture, three more marks of the aircraft operate in Europe in surveillance and utility roles, rather than with ASW/ASV as their primary task. Apart from the Netherlands' UH-14As, which are assigned to SAR and light transport support of the Marines, these helicopters have unusual lines of administration. Those operated

The Dutch navy designate their Lynx UH-14A, SH-14B and SH-14C. The SH-14s serve with No. 860 Squadron for ASW duties. This aircraft is a UH-14A of No. 7 Squadron, a shore-based support and search and rescue unit.

from 'Hvidbjornen' class fishery patrol vessels of the Danish navy belong to that service, yet are attached to No. 722 Squadron of the air force for maintenance and support. Norway's air arm flies Lynx helicopters in its No. 337 Squadron, the helicopters wearing the marking *Kystvakt* (Coast Guard) to indicate their operating agency and role of fishery protection, oil rig security and SAR. From the evidence of such a broad range of assignments, it can be seen that the Lynx combines many of the attributes of a large helicopter within a small package, and so can be judged an invaluable component of NATO's naval forces.

Glossary
AFCS Automatic Flight-Control System
ASV Anti-Surface Vessel
ASW Anti-Submarine Warfare
ESM Electronic Support Measures
MAD Magnetic Anomaly Detector
SAR Search-And-Rescue
TANS Tactical Air Navigation System

A trials Lynx HAS.Mk 2 of the MOD(PE) launches a Sea Skua anti-ship missile. The missile itself was hurried into service in time to be used operationally during the Falklands war. Lynx operating in the Falklands also received door guns.

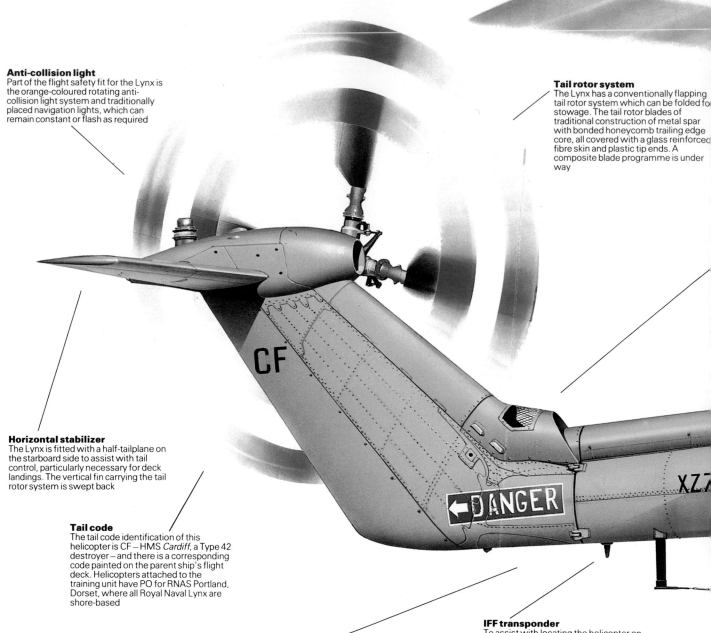

Anti-collision light
Part of the flight safety fit for the Lynx is the orange-coloured rotating anti-collision light system and traditionally placed navigation lights, which can remain constant or flash as required

Tail rotor system
The Lynx has a conventionally flapping tail rotor system which can be folded for stowage. The tail rotor blades of traditional construction of metal spar with bonded honeycomb trailing edge core, all covered with a glass reinforced fibre skin and plastic tip ends. A composite blade programme is under way

Horizontal stabilizer
The Lynx is fitted with a half-tailplane on the starboard side to assist with tail control, particularly necessary for deck landings. The vertical fin carrying the tail rotor system is swept back

Tail code
The tail code identification of this helicopter is CF – HMS *Cardiff*, a Type 42 destroyer – and there is a corresponding code painted on the parent ship's flight deck. Helicopters attached to the training unit have PO for RNAS Portland, Dorset, where all Royal Naval Lynx are shore-based

Tail rotor fold
To assist with the stowage of the helicopter in difficult hangar conditions, the Lynx is fitted with a fold/hinge system which allows the tail to be pivoted to port

IFF transponder
To assist with locating the helicopter on the parent ship's radar, an identification system has been fitted and below the tail is the lower IFF aerial. Details of the system are classified, but the system is thought to work in the X-band

Chelton UHF antenna
For longer-range radio communications, the Lynx is fitted with the Plessey PTR 377 UHF/VHF radio system and the Ultra D403 standby UHF radio. The radios have consoles in the cockpit and can be controlled by either the pilot or the observer

HF antenna system
The helicopter is fitted with a self-tuning high-frequency radio system, one of several sets available for tactical and flight safety communications. The aerial system is manufactured by British Aerospace

Westland Lynx HAS. Mk 2/3
815 Naval Air Squadron, Royal Navy
(HMS Cardiff Flight)

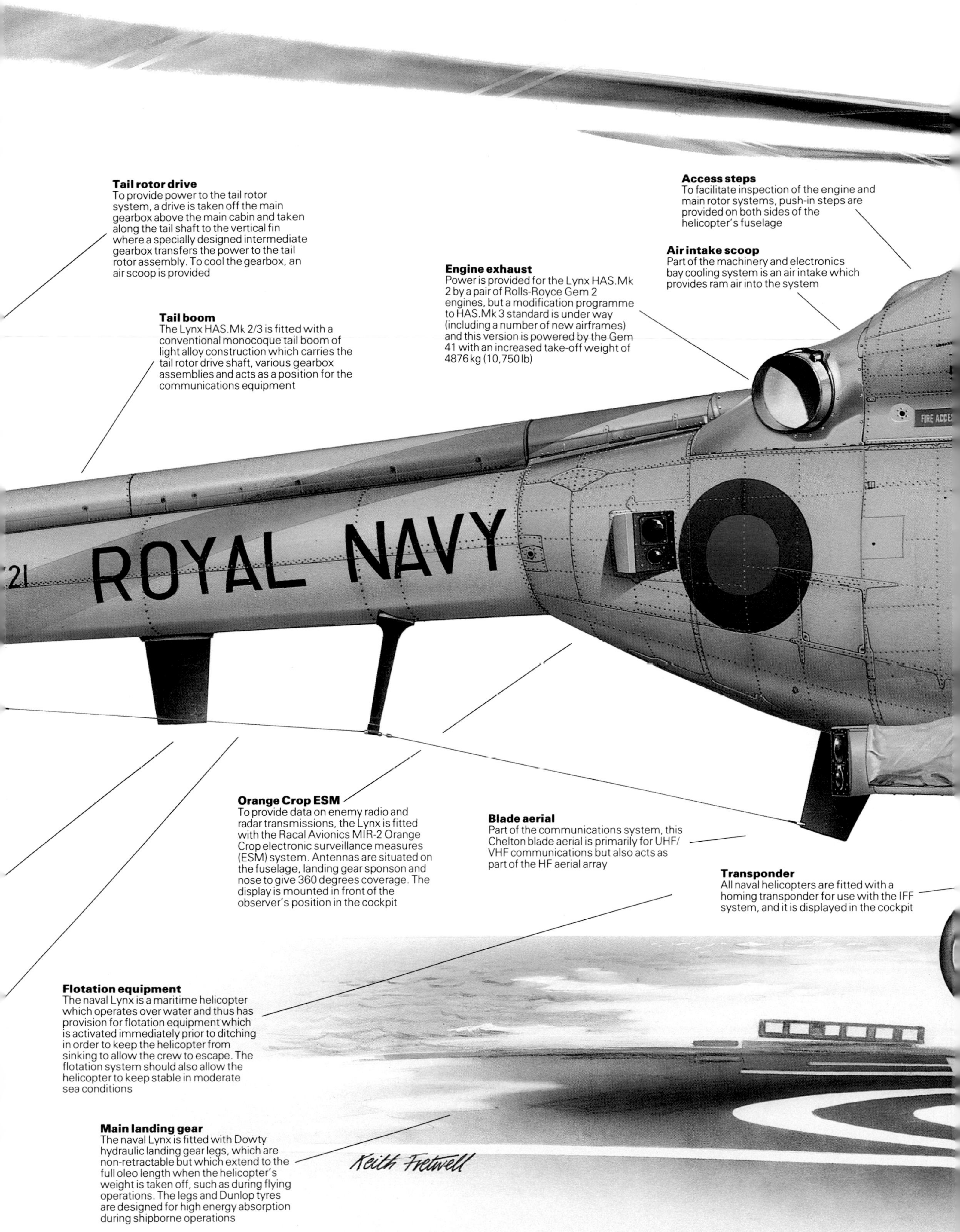

Tail rotor drive
To provide power to the tail rotor system, a drive is taken off the main gearbox above the main cabin and taken along the tail shaft to the vertical fin where a specially designed intermediate gearbox transfers the power to the tail rotor assembly. To cool the gearbox, an air scoop is provided

Tail boom
The Lynx HAS.Mk 2/3 is fitted with a conventional monocoque tail boom of light alloy construction which carries the tail rotor drive shaft, various gearbox assemblies and acts as a position for the communications equipment

Engine exhaust
Power is provided for the Lynx HAS.Mk 2 by a pair of Rolls-Royce Gem 2 engines, but a modification programme to HAS.Mk 3 standard is under way (including a number of new airframes) and this version is powered by the Gem 41 with an increased take-off weight of 4876 kg (10,750 lb)

Access steps
To facilitate inspection of the engine and main rotor systems, push-in steps are provided on both sides of the helicopter's fuselage

Air intake scoop
Part of the machinery and electronics bay cooling system is an air intake which provides ram air into the system

ROYAL NAVY

21

FIRE ACCES

Orange Crop ESM
To provide data on enemy radio and radar transmissions, the Lynx is fitted with the Racal Avionics MIR-2 Orange Crop electronic surveillance measures (ESM) system. Antennas are situated on the fuselage, landing gear sponson and nose to give 360 degrees coverage. The display is mounted in front of the observer's position in the cockpit

Blade aerial
Part of the communications system, this Chelton blade aerial is primarily for UHF/VHF communications but also acts as part of the HF aerial array

Transponder
All naval helicopters are fitted with a homing transponder for use with the IFF system, and it is displayed in the cockpit

Flotation equipment
The naval Lynx is a maritime helicopter which operates over water and thus has provision for flotation equipment which is activated immediately prior to ditching in order to keep the helicopter from sinking to allow the crew to escape. The flotation system should also allow the helicopter to keep stable in moderate sea conditions

Main landing gear
The naval Lynx is fitted with Dowty hydraulic landing gear legs, which are non-retractable but which extend to the full oleo length when the helicopter's weight is taken off, such as during flying operations. The legs and Dunlop tyres are designed for high energy absorption during shipborne operations

Keith Fretwell

type has a ratchet instead of pads, and so can only be set either fully on or fully off.

The prototype of what is occasionally still known as the 'Sea Lynx' flew on 25 May 1972, over a year after the first skid-equipped model (21 March 1971). Following the usual development programme, including landings on both British and French warships and service trials, the first Royal Navy operational Lynx detachment took up station aboard HMS *Birmingham* on 2 February 1978. After delivery of over 80 Lynx helicopters from 91 on order, RN deployment is now well on the way to completion on board some 40 vessels, replacing the Wasp on 'Leander' and 'Type 21' or 'Amazon' class frigates and the Westland Wessex on a couple of 'County' class destroyers, as well as equipping the newer 'Type 42' or 'Sheffield' class destroyers and 'Type 22' or 'Broadsword' class frigates still being delivered. The latter type of ship has hangarage for two Lynx helicopters, though the normal assignment remains one.

Extensive equipment

On the assumption that a warplane is only as good as its operational equipment, the Lynx must be reckoned a very capable helicopter. It benefits from several new, advanced systems, including Ferranti ARI 5979 Seaspray radar, which is able to detect and track the type of small, high-speed attack craft whose missiles pose an increasing menace to major warships. Operating in the I-band, Seaspray employs frequency agility for improved performance in high sea states and in the face of jamming, and may also be used for general maritime surveillance or the provision of over-the-horizon targeting facilities for the anti-ship missiles of allied vessels. The Seaspray scanner is located inside a completely removable radome which forms the Lynx's nose, and its findings are displayed on a bright TV screen tabulated with data including a readout of target range and bearing.

A prime function of Seaspray is target illumination for the BAe Sea Skua anti-ship missile. Being comparatively light, at 145 kg (320 lb) each, four of these weapons may be carried on outrigger

pylons on the lower side of the cabin (two missiles only if the Lynx is to patrol well away from its vessel), and each has a range of at least 15 km (9.3 miles). After release, the Sea Skua progressively descends to a level pre-set according to the wave height at the time, then homes in on reflected radar energy from the Seaspray until it strikes the target. The Lynx must slow to fire Sea Skua and then remain in the area to provide illumination, but is free to manoeuvre within reasonable bounds for its own safety. Premature service entry was achieved by the missile when development rounds were issued for operational use in the 1982 Falklands war. The score was four out of four.

Similarly, pre-production Marconi Sting Ray homing torpedoes were assigned to the Lynx in April 1982 as a replacement for the usual Aerojet Mk 46s. The torpedo is carried as an alternative to missiles or BAe Type 11 Mod 3 depth charges. A further hasty addition for the South Atlantic conflict concerned a general-purpose machine-gun, mounted in either of the cabin doorways on a 'home-made' pintle, which was first used in combat against small Argentine ships at night. Some Lynx helicopters were fitted with equipment which would decoy Argentine Exocet sea-skimming missiles away from their targets, an occupation not as dangerous as it might first appear as long as the helicopter remained above the maximum height permitted by the missile's autopilot (about 60 m/200 ft).

The Lynx HAS.Mk 3 is powered by uprated Gem-41 turboshaft engines, but otherwise differs little from late production and current mod-state HAS.Mk 2s. This example is seen at Portland but belongs to HMS Ambuscade, a Type 21 frigate.

Also boosted during 1982 were programmes of retrospective installation for ESM and MAD equipment. The former is a Racal MIR-2 'Orange Crop', the forward sensors for which are mounted prominently on the nose, to provide the bearing of enemy radar and radio transmissions. MIR-2 was the subject of an operational trial by the RN Lynx before widespread adoption, as was Texas Instruments ASQ-81 MAD. The towed 'bird' for the MAD equipment is installed in an attachment to the starboard main landing gear leg, first deployment having been made experimentally in August 1981.

In all, Lynx helicopters flew 1,728 sorties (generating 2,567 airborne hours and 3,796 deck landings) during the Falklands war, some of it at night with the aid of pilot's thermal imaging equipment.

French model

The first 60 RN Lynx helicopters were to HAS.Mk 2 standard with Gem 2 engines, whilst the balance, issued to units

The Lynx headquarters squadron is No. 702, based at RNAS Portland (or HMS Osprey, as the Navy call it). This squadron Lynx is armed with Sea Skua anti-shipping missiles, and is seen here over Lulworth Cove, Dorset.

Naval Lynx: Anglo-French feline

The Westland Lynx is fast, manoeuvrable and versatile. Comprehensively equipped with high technology navigation, detection and attack systems, the Lynx can also carry a range of potent weapons and can deliver a decisive blow against any enemy ship or submarine it finds, yet it is small and simple enough to operate from frigates and destroyers.

A West German Navy Lynx is directed in to make a landing on a 'Bremen'-class frigate. The Bundesmarine has six 'Bremen'-class vessels, all of which can handle the Lynx of MFG 3, whose shore base is Nordholz. The Lynx operate in pairs.

Although the operation of fixed-wing aircraft from aircraft-carriers is a phenomenally costly business which can be afforded only by the United States Navy, the helicopter has established itself firmly as an indispensible and cost-effective adjunct to maritime combat. Even the small vessels of navies which are, in reality, little more than coastal patrol forces now have landing platforms. Today's shipboard helicopter is a potent addition to its vessel's armoury, able to react with speed in both offensive and defensive situations.

Few better examples of the modern light maritime helicopter are availabe than that of the Westland Lynx. Illustrating the immense leap in military capability represented by this aircraft, it may be recalled that when Royal Navy frigates first began deploying their own helicopters, in 1963, the Westland Wasp was the type employed. Apart from the universal rotary-wing tasks of communications and SAR, the Wasp's sole duties were to carry a homing torpedo or depth charge to a suspected submarine contact plotted by the parent vessel's sonar, and to fire short-range, wire-guided missiles. At almost twice the maximum weight of its predecessor (yet still able to be stowed in some of the same minute deck hangars) the Lynx is additionally fitted with medium-range sea-skimming missiles for anti-ship attack; with radar for all-weather operation, search and targeting for other ships; with ESM equipment for

passive detection; and with optional 'dunking' sonar and MAD to provide an autonomous anti-submarine capability. Clearly, the Lynx is a weapon which no captain could afford to be without.

Naval Lynx

The naval Lynx, which is considered here, is the wheeled variant of a multi-role helicopter also serving the army on skids. Developed during the mid- and late-1960s, the Lynx is one of three rotary-wing machines covered by the 1967 Anglo-French helicopter agreement, under which Aérospatiale has a 30 per cent share in producing parts for the sole assembly line at Westland's Yeovil headquarters. In return, the British firm had a manufacturing stake in the Aérospatiale Puma and Gazelle. As part of the accord, a French requirement was established for over 200 Lynx helicopters of which only 40 were in fact procured.

Light alloy is used for primary structure in the semi-monocoque pod and boom of this helicopter, with glass fibre employed for such components as fairings and access doors. Two crew members sit side-by-side: pilot to starboard and navigator (with his radar display) to port. There is no bulkhead behind the crew, this feature giving easy access to the cabin. A semi-rigid main rotor was chosen for the Lynx, blades being constructed of glass reinforced plastics over a Nomex core. Manual rearward folding of the blades and forward folding of the fin facilitate

storage in confined spaces.

Naval requirements also specified a height restriction for the Lynx, with the result that the engines and gearbox are mounted neatly above the cabin and there is no visible rotor spindle. Westland produced a compact, reliable gearbox to reduce the engine speed of 6,150 rpm to 326 rpm for the main rotor, whilst Rolls-Royce exercised similar care in design of the Gem turboshaft. As first used in production Lynx, the Gem 2 had a continuous rating of 559 kW (750 shp) and a maximum contingency power of 671 kw (900 shp) for 2.5 minutes. This provided for a maximum aircraft weight of 4309 kg (9,500 lb), although progressive increases to 4763 kg (10,500 lb) have been made by uprating both engine and gearbox. Versions are now available with Gem 41s, or the even higher rated Gem 43-1, which has emergency power equivalent to 846 kW (1,135 shp).

Operating the Lynx from stern platforms requires special techniques. Projecting from the bottom of the cabin is a hydraulically-powered deck-lock, the jaws of which grasp a metal lattice set onto the deck. The single main (rear) wheels are splayed outwards and the twin nosewheel unit set at right-angles to the fuselage axis so that the helicopter can pivot into wind on its swivelling deck lock, without the parent vessel having to change course. With engines running at take-off power, the Lynx releases its lock and leaps into the air, so obviating the dangers of a more leisurely departure from a pitching and heaving deck.

Landing is undertaken with main-wheels splayed outwards at 27° and nosewheel set forward to prevent pivoting. Judging the appropriate moment, the pilot lands firmly on the deck, knowing that the landing gear can absorb descent rates of up to 2.3 m (7.5 ft) per second. By changing main rotor blade pitch, he can employ up to 1361 kg (3,000 lb) of reverse thrust to pin the Lynx to the deck until certain that the lock is firmly holding the grille. As a further safety measure, the helicopter is fitted with sprag brakes: the

This Portland-based Lynx HAS.Mk 2 is from HQ Flight No. 815 Squadron, and is equipped with a towed bird for its Texas Instruments ASQ-81 magnetic anomaly detector.

The WESTLAND AEROSPATIALE NAVAL LYNX

Performance:

Maximum cruising speed at sea level	140 kts	259 km/h (161 mph)
Most economical cruising speed at sea level	70 kts	130 km/h (81 mph)
Hovering ceiling out of ground effect	10,600 ft	(3230 m)
Maximum range	630 km	(392 miles)
Initial rate of climb	2,480 ft	(756 m) per minute

Maximum weapon load

Mil Mi-24 'Hind-E' 1500 kg
Agusta A 129 Mangusta 1000 kg
Bell AH-1S HueyCobra 750 kg E
Westland Lynx AH.Mk 1 550 kg E
Agusta A 109A Mk II 344 kg
Messerschmitt-Bölkow-Blohm BO 105 P (PAH-1) 250 kg E
Mil Mi-2 'Hoplite' 200 kg E
McDonnell Douglas 500MD/TOW Defender 150 kg E

Anti-tank missiles carried

Agusta A 109A Mk II 8 Hughes TOW
Agusta A 129 Mangusta 8 Hughes TOW
Bell AH-1S HueyCobra 8 Hughes TOW
Westland Lynx AH.Mk 1 8 Hughes TOW
MBB BO 105 P (PAH-1) 6 Euromissile Hot
Mil Mi-24 'Hind-E' 4 AT-6 'Spiral'
McDonnell Douglas Defender 500MD/TOW Defender 4 Hughes TOW
Mil Mi-2 'Hoplite' 4 AT-3 'Sagger'

Maximum speed at sea level

Mil Mi-24 'Hind-E' 173 kts E
Agusta A 109A Mk II 147 kts
Agusta A 129 Mangusta 140 kts E
Westland Lynx AH.Mk 1 140 kts
Bell AH-1S HueyCobra 123 kts
McDonnell Douglas 500MD/TOW Defender 119 kts
M B B BO 105 P (PAH-1) 119 kts
Mil Mi-2 'Hoplite' 108 kts

Combat radius

Mil Mi-24 'Hind-E' 160 km
Westland Lynx AH.Mk 1 100 km E
Agusta A 129 Mangusta 100 km E
MBB BO 105 P (PAH-1) 95 km E
Agusta A 109A Mk II 90 km E
Bell AH-1S HueyCobra 85 km E
Mil Mi-2 'Hoplite' 75 km E
McDonnell Douglas 500MD/TOW Defender 65 km E

Troops carried

Westland Lynx AH.Mk 1 10
Mil Mi-24 'Hind-E' 8
Mil Mi-2 'Hoplite' 7
Agusta A 109A Mk II 7
McDonnell Douglas 500MD/TOW Defender 6
Agusta A 129 Mangusta None
Bell AH-1S HueyCobra None
Messerschmitt-Bölkow-Blohm BO 105 P (PAH-1) None

---

53 Lightweight detachable troop seats, nine-fully armed troops
54 Side window panel
55 Port aft sliding cabin door
56 Sliding door latch
57 Door jettison handle
58 Forward underfloor fuel tank, total fuel capacity 733 kg (1616 lb)
59 Lower sliding door rail
60 Floor beam construction
61 Lower fuselage access panels
62 Fuselage keel web member

63 Fuel collector tanks (two)
64 Forged gearbox mounting main frame
65 Forward gearbox mounting
66 Lateral control autostabilized servo-actuator
67 Hydraulic reservoir, dual system
68 Hydraulic equipment module, port and starboard

69 Alternators (two)
70 Alternator cooling air duct

71 Collective pitch servo-actuator
72 Longitudinal pitch control autostabilized servo-actuator
73 Forward sliding equipment cowling

74 Hingeless main rotor hub, titanium
75 Blade pitch control horns
76 Pitch bearings
77 Flexible blade arm
78 Blade root attachment joints

79 Four-bladed main rotor
80 Drag hinge dampers

81 Blade pitch control rods
82 Main rotor mast
83 Main gearbox
84 Gearbox mounting deck
85 Sliding cabin door top rail fairing
86 Main cabin frame and stringer construction
87 Fuel tank access panel
88 Main fuel tanks, port and starboard
89 Fuel filler cap
90 Inlet debris guard

91 Gearbox aft mounting
92 Engine/gearbox transmission shaft
93 Rotor brake
94 Engine compressor inlet
95 Starter/generator intake/exhaust fairing
96 Starboard engine cowling
97 Engine bay dividing fireproof bulkhead, titanium
98 Starter/generator
99 Engine accessory equipment gearbox

100 Main engine mounting
101 Fireproof engine mounting deck, titanium

102 Rolls-Royce Gem 2 turboshaft engine
103 Engine bay rear fireproof bulkhead
104 Starboard engine exhaust nozzle
105 Ventilating air exit duct
106 Port engine exhaust nozzle
107 Tail rotor transmission shaft
108 Shaft bearings
109 Dorsal spine fairings/access panels
110 Bevel drive intermediate gearbox
111 Tail pylon bracing struts
112 Tail rotor angled drive shaft
113 Gearbox cooling air intake
114 Fixed horizontal stabilizer
115 Stabilizer tubular spar
116 Final drive right-angled gearbox
117 Articulated tail rotor hub
118 Tail rotor power control unit
119 Blade pitch control spider
120 Anti-collision light
121 Tail navigation light
122 Four-bladed tail rotor
123 Glass-fibre pylon tail fairing/access panel
124 Tail rotor control linkage
125 Tail pylon construction

126 Tailboom ring frame construction
127 Access panels
128 Tail rotor control cables
129 UHF/IFF aerial
130 Main rotor blade tip balance weights

131 VHF aerial
132 Tailboom attachment joint frame
133 TRACOR ALE-39 chaff/flare dispenser
134 Fuselage lower longeron
135 Rear fuselage frame construction
136 Top longeron
137 Aft fuselage equipment bay
138 Electrical system equipment racks
139 Cooling air scoop
140 HF homing aerial rail, port and starboard
141 Ventral access hatch
142 TOW missile carrier/launch tubes
143 Landing skid rear strut
144 External cargo hook, 1361-kg (3000-lb) capacity
145 Port landing skid
146 Landing skid front strut
147 Missile folding fins
148 Hughes TOW air-to-surface anti-armour missile (eight)
149 Skid boarding step
150 Oerlikon KAD 20-mm cannon (25-mm alternative)
151 FN ETNA gun pack, 2×7.62-mm machine-guns
152 Rockwell Hellfire laser-guided anti-armour missiles (eight)
153 Missile carrier/launch rail
154 69.8-mm (2.75-in) folding fin aircraft rockets (FFAR)
155 19×69.8-mm rocket launcher
156 SURA 80-mm air-to-surface unguided rockets
157 Ammunition magazine
158 Emmerson Flexible Turret System (FTS) gun mounting
159 M134 Minigun, 7.62-mm (0.3-in) six-barrel rotary machine-gun

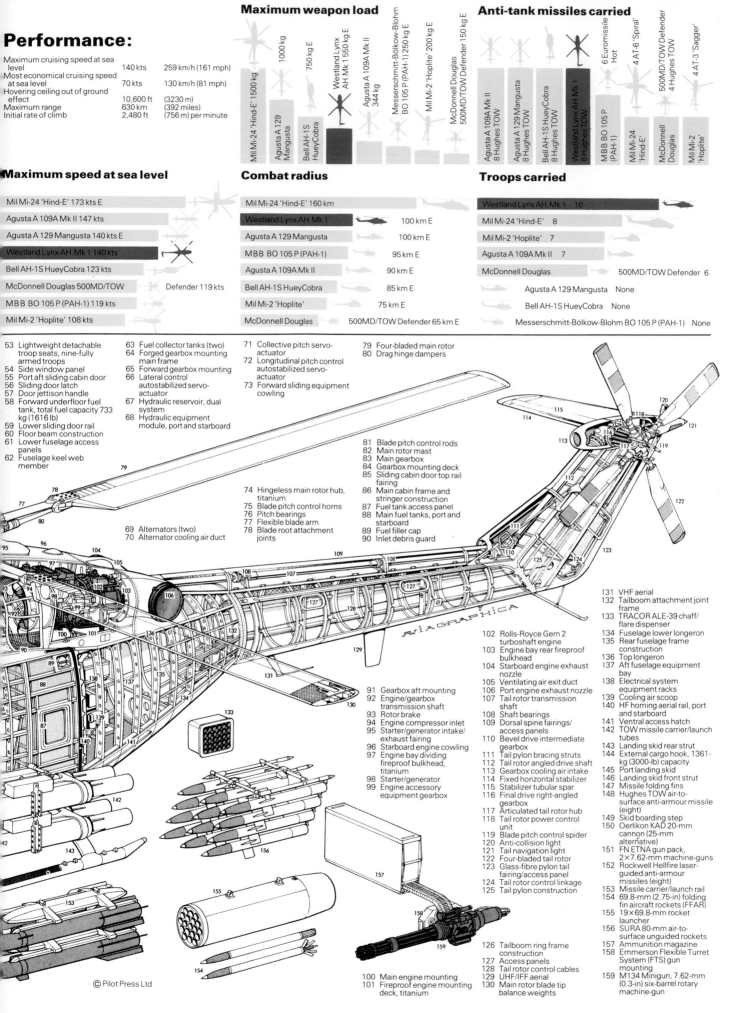

AVIAGRAPHICA

© Pilot Press Ltd

Specification: Westland WG.13 Lynx AH.Mk 7

Rotors
Main rotor diameter	12.80 m	(42 ft 0 in)
Tail rotor diameter	2.21 m	(7 ft 3 in)
Main rotor disc area	128.7 m²	(1,385.4 sq ft)

Fuselage and tail unit
Accommodation	pilot, observer and up to 10 fully-armed troops	
Length overall, both rotors turning	15.16 m	(49 ft 9 in)
Height overall, both rotors turning	3.66 m	(12 ft 0 in)
Tailplane half-span	1.78 m	(5 ft 10 in)

Landing gear
Non-retractable tubular twin skids		
Skid track	2.03 m	(6 ft 8 in)

Weights
Empty	2578 kg	(5,683 lb)
Maximum take-off	4876 kg	(10,750 lb)
Maximum external load	1360 kg	(3,000 lb)
Internal fuel load	733 kg	(1,616 lb)

Powerplant
Two Rolls-Royce Gem Mk 41-1 turboshafts		
Rating, each	835 kW	(1,120 shp)

A Lynx AH.Mk 1 on loan to Westland blasts off a salvo of unguided SURA rockets. The Lynx has flown with a wide variety of weapons loads, but the British Army uses only the ubiquitous TOW missile.

Army Lynx variants

WG.13: five prototype and eight pre-production aircraft, including two in army utility configuration, although early prototypes also equipped with skids

Westland 606: proposed civil model, announced 1974, powered by Pratt & Whitney Canada PT6A-34 turboshafts of 671 kW (900 shp), and with 30.5-cm (12-in) fuselage stretch for accommodation of 12 passengers; PT6-powered testbed flew 17 July 1976; project abandoned

Lynx AH.Mk 1: initial British army model with 671-kW (900-shp) Gem Mk 2 turboshafts and 4354-kg (9,600-lb) maximum weight; TOW sight retrofitted to early aircraft with no change of designation; 113 built between February 1977 and January 1984 (XZ170-199, XZ203-222, XZ605-617, XZ640-655, XZ661-681, ZD272-284)

Lynx AH.Mk 1/5: single helicopter (ZD285), first flown 21 November 1984 with uprated transmission (three-pinion gearbox) but Gem Mk 2 engines; assigned to RAE Bedford for trials
Lynx Mk 5X: single trials aircraft (ZD559) first flown 11 February 1985, for RAE Bedford; Gem Mk 41-1 turboshafts of 835 kW (1,120 shp), uprated transmission and 4536-kg (10,000-lb) maximum weight
Lynx AH.Mk 5: nine ordered; initial example (ZE375) flown 23 February 1985. Engine trials by Rolls-Royce, Bristol; remainder transferred to AH.Mk 7 contract, although ZE376 initially flew as Mk 5 on 23 April 1986
Lynx AH. Mk 6: proposed variant of Mk 5 for Royal Marines with unique wheeled landing gear; project abandoned
Lynx AH. Mk 7: variant of AH.Mk 5 with reversed-direction tail rotor and improved systems; maximum weight 4876 kg (10,750 lb); eight transferred from AH.Mk 5 contract (ZE376-383), plus five new orders; first flown (ZE376) 7 November 1985

Lynx Mk 22: proposed production by Arab Organization for Industrialization (AOI) in Egypt for Egyptian army; cancelled
Lynx Mk 24: planned AOI production for export to Iraqi army in utility configuration; cancelled
Lynx Mk 26: planned AOI production for export to Iraqi army in armed configuration; cancelled
Lynx Mk 28: three utility helicopters (QP31-33) delivered to the Qatar Police Air Wing, June 1978, in blue and white colour scheme with air intake and sand filters; British-built, with Gem Mk 41-1 engines
Lynx Mk 82: proposed AOI manufacture for export; none built
Lynx Mk 83: proposed AOI manufacture for Saudi Arabian army; cancelled
Lynx Mk 84: planned production for Qatar army by AOI; cancelled
Lynx Mk 85: AOI production for United Arab Emirates army; cancelled
(NB: Mks 2, 3, 4, 8, 21, 23, 25, 27, 80, 81, 86, 87, 88 and 89 are Naval Lynx versions.)

Westland Lynx AH.Mk 1 cutaway drawing key

1 Nose cone
2 Circuit breaker panel
3 Electrical system relays
4 Nose avionics equipment bay
5 Gyro platform
6 UHF aerials
7 Ventilating air intake
8 Flight control computer
9 Avionics bay access door, port and starboard
10 Battery
11 Cockpit front bulkhead
12 Pitot head
13 Underfloor control linkages
14 Yaw control rudder pedals
15 Cyclic pitch control column
16 Downward vision window
17 Instrument panel
18 Instrument panel shroud
19 Windscreen wipers
20 Curved windscreen panels
21 Outside air temperature probe
22 Main rotor blade two-section D-shaped stainless steel spar box
23 Honeycomb core trailing edge
24 Glass-fibre skin panelling
25 Leading edge erosion sheath, stainless steel
26 Rescue hoist/winch, 272-kg (600-lb) capacity
27 Hoist pintle mounting, starboard cabin doorway
28 Cockpit roof glazing
29 Engine power and condition levers
30 Overhead switch panel
31 Safety harness
32 Pilot's seat
33 Centre control pedestal
34 Chart case
35 Boarding step
36 Port navigation light
37 Collective pitch control lever
38 Jettisonable cockpit door
39 Control rod linkages
40 Forward fuselage arch double main frame
41 Direct vision sliding side window panel
42 Co-pilot/observer's seat
43 TOW missile sight periscope
44 Swivelling turret mounting
45 Hughes (British Aerospace licence-built) TOW sighting unit
46 Optical sighting aperture
47 Miniaturized thermal imaging system scanners
48 Control system ducting
49 Sliding cowling rail
50 Starboard aft sliding main cabin door
51 Cabin wall trim/soundproofing panelling
52 Glass-fibre/honeycomb cabin roof construction

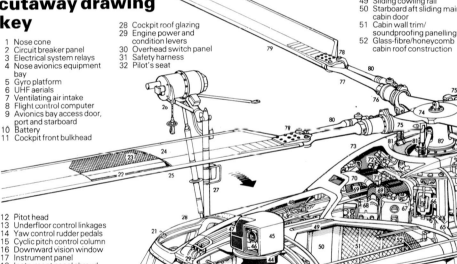

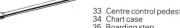
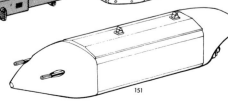

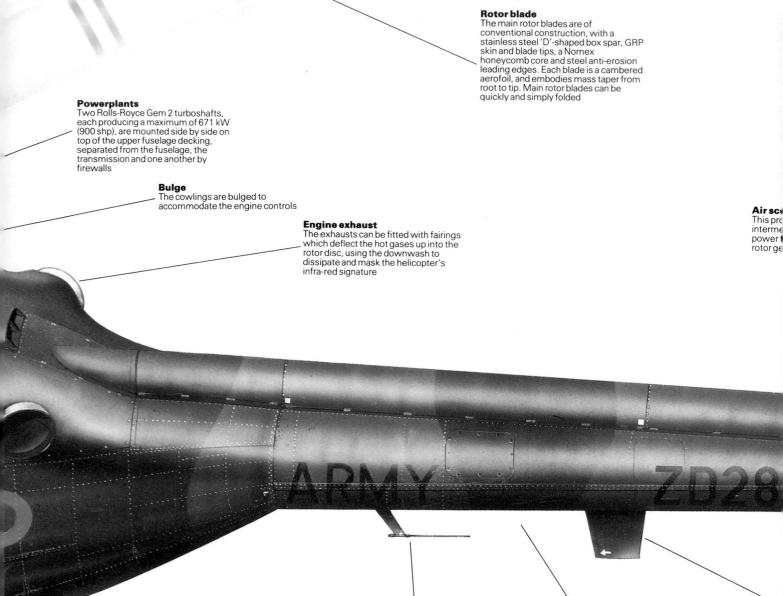

Rotor blade
The main rotor blades are of conventional construction, with a stainless steel 'D'-shaped box spar, GRP skin and blade tips, a Nomex honeycomb core and steel anti-erosion leading edges. Each blade is a cambered aerofoil, and embodies mass taper from root to tip. Main rotor blades can be quickly and simply folded

Powerplants
Two Rolls-Royce Gem 2 turboshafts, each producing a maximum of 671 kW (900 shp), are mounted side by side on top of the upper fuselage decking, separated from the fuselage, the transmission and one another by firewalls

Bulge
The cowlings are bulged to accommodate the engine controls

Engine exhaust
The exhausts can be fitted with fairings which deflect the hot gases up into the rotor disc, using the downwash to dissipate and mask the helicopter's infra-red signature

Air sc
This pro
interme
power
rotor ge

Antenna
This flush aerial serves the ARC 340 VHF/FM homing set

Access doors
These spring-loaded doors can be pushed inwards to insert a fire extinguisher if an engine fire should occur on the ground

VHF/FM aerial
This aerial allows air-to-ground communication and is compatible with ground forces radios and frequencies

Access panel
This panel gives access to the tailboom for inspection and servicing. The tailboom is of light alloy monocoque structure, and the tail rotor driveshaft runs along the top under a fairing

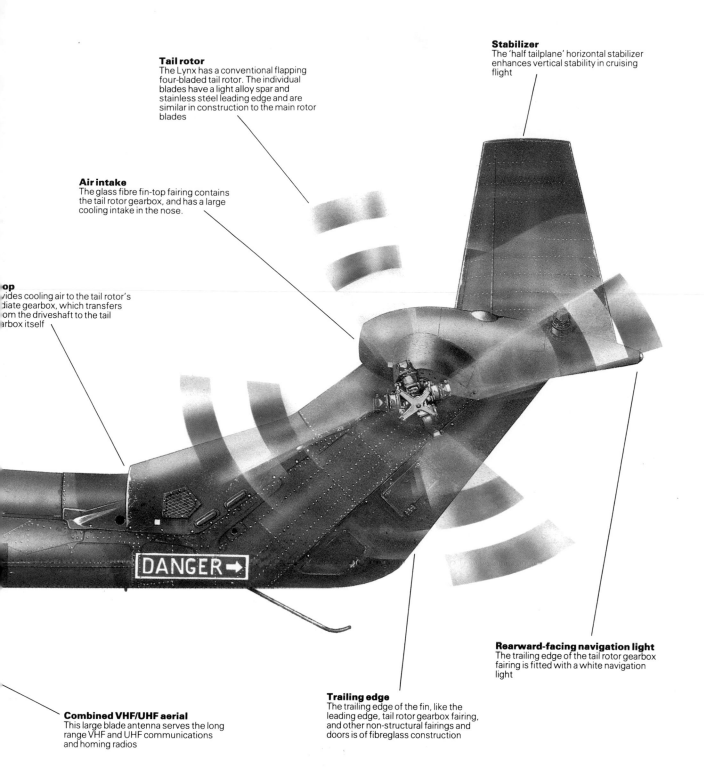

Stabilizer
The 'half tailplane' horizontal stabilizer enhances vertical stability in cruising flight

Tail rotor
The Lynx has a conventional flapping four-bladed tail rotor. The individual blades have a light alloy spar and stainless steel leading edge and are similar in construction to the main rotor blades

Air intake
The glass fibre fin-top fairing contains the tail rotor gearbox, and has a large cooling intake in the nose.

op
vides cooling air to the tail rotor's
diate gearbox, which transfers
om the driveshaft to the tail
arbox itself

DANGER ➡

Rearward-facing navigation light
The trailing edge of the tail rotor gearbox fairing is fitted with a white navigation light

Combined VHF/UHF aerial
This large blade antenna serves the long range VHF and UHF communications and homing radios

Trailing edge
The trailing edge of the fin, like the leading edge, tail rotor gearbox fairing, and other non-structural fairings and doors is of fibreglass construction

Westland Lynx AH Mk 1
No. 656 Squadron, Army Air Corps
Netheravon

Army Lynx warload

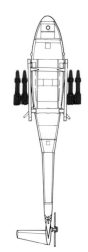
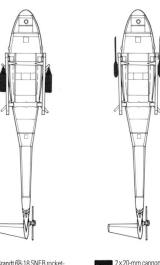

8 x Hughes BGM-71A TOW missiles

8 x Rockwell AGM-114A Hellfire missiles

2 x Brandt 68-18 SNEB rocket-launchers

2 x 20-mm cannon

The aircrewman/gunner fires the missile using a trigger in his right hand and steers it by keeping the crosshairs of the sight centred on the target, using a small joystick in his right hand.

British army anti-tank

Standard armament of the Lynx in British army service is eight TOW anti-tank missiles in externally-mounted launch tubes, plus eight reloads in the cabin. Missile aiming is via a BAe-built Hughes sight (above the cabin's port seat) which must track the target until the weapon hits.

Alternative anti-tank mode

Flown for trials purposes, but not adopted by any operator, the Hellfire/Lynx combination offers 'fire-and-forget' anti-tank capability to reduce vulnerability. A helicopter sight is not essential, as Hellfire homes onto target-generated reflections of laser energy produced by a ground illuminator or other aircraft.

Close support option

Although the Lynx is not sufficiently armoured for close attacks on well-defended ground positions, easier targets may be struck with the ubiquitous rocket. A Brandt Type 68-18 pod, containing 18 missiles of 68-mm (2.68-in) calibre, is one such option.

Armed escort

Apart from a machine-gun or light cannon in the cabin door, the Lynx can be fitted with 20- or 25-mm weapons on external mountings. The helicopter would be most unlikely to roam the battlefield looking for targets, but might be used in this configuration to deploy three-man teams armed with ground-launched anti-tank missiles.

Army Lynx in service

Army Air Corps

The British Army fields 11 front-line Lynx squadrons, seven of them permanently based in West Germany. Two more are based in Northern Ireland, with the last two being based at Netheravon and Oakington in the UK in reserve. Lynx also serve with the Army Air Corps Centre at Middle Wallop.

This Westland Lynx AH.Mk 1 is wearing the new grey/green colour scheme of the Army Air Corps.

1 Wing (BAOR)

1 Regiment, Hildesheim
651 Squadron*
652 Squadron*
(XZ173, XZ177, XZ192, XZ671, XZ678)

3 Regiment, Soest
653 Squadron*
662 Squadron*
663 Squadron*
(XZ185, XZ193, XZ212, XZ643, XZ669)

4 Regiment, Detmold
654 Squadron*
659 Squadron*
(XZ178, XZ184, XZ213, XZ650, XZ654)

2 Wing (UK)

5 Regiment, Northern Ireland
655 Squadron Balykelly
(XZ187, XZ188, XZ664, XZ665, XZ666)
665 Squadron, Aldergrove
(XZ195 'X', XZ218 'Y', XZ197 only)

Direct-reporting units:
656 Squadron, Netheravon (XZ210, XZ676, ZD272, ZD273, ZD281)
657 Squadron, Oakington (XZ206, XZ221, XZ613, XZ644, ZD275)

(All the above are mixed Gazelle/Lynx units: squadrons marked * normally nine Lynxes, remainder normally six.)

AAC Centre, Middle Wallop

Rotary-Wing Conversion Squadron
(Lynx Conversion Flight: XZ172 'K', XZ175 'C', XZ640 'L', XZ680 'F', ZD283 'M')

Development & Trials Squadron
(XZ222 only)

Royal Marines

No. 3 Commando Brigade Air Squadron is based at Yeovilton and provides the Royal Marines with their own anti-tank helicopter capability, frequently deploying to Norway.

3rd Commando Brigade Air Squadron,

Yeovilton
'B' Flight
(XZ182, '23B', XZ605 '23A', XZ614 '23D', ZD282 '24A', ZD284 '23B')

An Army Air Corps pilot makes a pre-flight check of this No. 656 Squadron Lynx AH.Mk 1 at Netheravon.

Qatar

The Qatar Emiri police force has a small air support unit using a pair of Westland-built Gazelles and three Lynx HC.Mk 28s. The Lynx are jointly operated with the air force.

The Qatar Police are the only foreign operator of the Lynx AH.Mk 1. Their aircraft wear a blue and white scheme.

Probe
This probe is fitted directly to the outside air temperature gauge fitted in the cabin roof of the Lynx

Cabin
The Lynx cabin can seat up to nine soldiers in normal kit, on lightweight bench seats, or six troops in full fighting order, with their equipment. The Lynx is frequently used to transport Milan anti-tank missile teams. The seats can be quickly and simply removed in the field, to permit the carriage of up to 907 kg (2,000 lb) of freight. Tie-down rings are provided on the cabin floor. Underslung loads of up to 1360 kg (3,000 lb) would be an alternative, albeit with a severe drag penalty

Roof-mounted sight
The sight fitted to the Lynx is designed by Hughes, but built under licence by British Aerospace. It is fitted with heating and demisting equipment, and has provision for laser rangefinding and designation. The sight can be used for observation and missile guidance at ranges of up to 3750 m (12,300 ft)

Windscreen
The windscreen is formed from glass and Perspex laminate and embodies electrical de-icing elements. Large windscreen wipers are also fitted

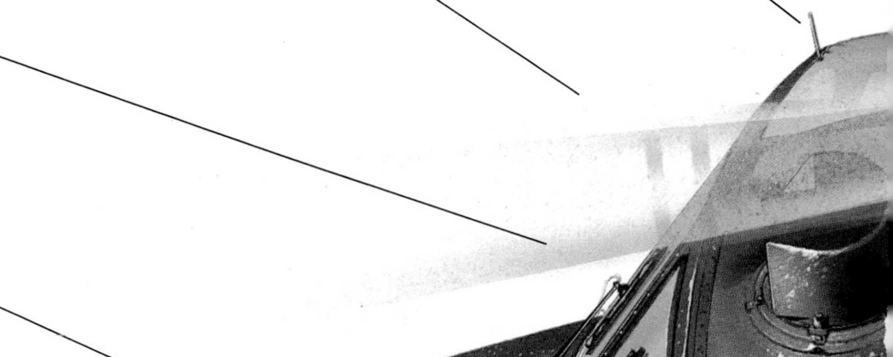

Aerials
These two small blade antennas are for the twin UHF/VHF homing radios operating on standard NATO frequencies. They are located well forward to avoid masking by the large cabin

Captain
The occupant of the right-hand seat acts as pilot in command and aircraft commander, and is responsible for flight safety and mission conduct. New plans call for the right-hand seater to become a pure 'driver-airframe' and for the occupant of the left-hand seat to become the tactical commander

Aircrewman
The left-hand seat is occupied by the aircrewman, who acts as gunner and is responsible for missile control and guidance and for navigation, using the Lynx's highly-accurate Decca TANS (Tactical Air Navigation System)

Warhead
TOW employs a shaped-charge HEAT (High Explosive Anti-Tank) warhead, weighing 3.9 kg

Hughes TOW missile
TOW is an acronym for 'Tube-launched, Optically-tracked, Wire-guided' missile. The solid-propellant 'launch' rocket motor fires first and the missile accelerates rapidly to a speed in excess of Mach 1 within one second of leaving its launcher. The missile coasts for a short period before a second solid-propellant 'booster' rocket fires. The missile then glides to its target, anything up to 3750 metres away

Control fins
Low-aspect ratio fins and tailfins flick open as the TOW leaves the tube. The operator guides the missile by keeping the target centred in the sight. Movement of the sight generates electrical signals which are passed down the wires to actuate the control surfaces

Guidance wires
The BGM-71 TOW missile relies on twin guidance wires to transmit corrections to its flight path via the SACLOS (Semi-Automatic Command to Line Of Sight) system

Navigation light
A small footstep under the cockpit door also acts as a convenient mounting point for navigation lights, red to port and green to starboard

Germany-based 654 Squadron received the first TOW Lynxes, and by the end of that year all five missile-equipped anti-tank units (then designated 661, 662, 663, 664 and 669 Squadrons) had replaced their Scouts with similarly armed Lynxes from a total of 60 initially fitted with the roof sight. Eventually over 130 units were built to enable the entire AAC Lynx force to be equipped.

TOW is a heavy anti-tank missile with a range of up to 3750 m (4,100 yards) which reaches a speed of at least 1000 km/h (621 mph) in flight. As applied to the Lynx, the TOW system is mounted in groups of four launch boxes on pylons projecting from the cabin sides behind the main door. A complete set of eight reload missiles is carried in the cabin so that the Lynx can put down in a quiet area of the battle zone for manual replenishment by its crew.

Finding the target

Acquisition of the target and direction of the missile after launch is the responsibility of the observer, sitting in the Lynx's left-hand seat. The sight is located in his position with its lens protruding from the cabin roof. System reliability in service has been a creditable 95+ per cent, leading the army to authorize an update programme early in 1986. The aim is to increase operational capabilities at night or in poor daylight by installing a Rank-Pullen thermal imaging sub-system in the sight. With the augmented equipment the observer is presented with a clearly-defined picture, in what would otherwise be marginal or 'no go' conditions, for the launching of TOW missiles in the usual way.

Expanded capability

With the advent of the Lynx (even with its original sight), the AAC was provided with a fourfold increase in operational capability compared with the Scout/SS.11 combination. Apart from a 90 per cent hit probability with TOW, the Lynx is able to stay on station for 2 hours rather than the Scout's 30 minutes. In certain tactical situations, units are now able to maintain a 'cab rank' of TOW-armed helicopters which can attack enemy armour within 2 minutes of demand. They still have to take care not to fall victim to ground fire or the increasing numbers of gunship helicopters being fielded by the Warsaw Pact, so 'nap of the earth' flying (making full use of every hill, tree and bush for concealment) is still very much the order of the day.

Studies have shown that it is the helicopter or tank on the move which is the most vulnerable, and so instead of patrolling on the look-out for opposing armour, the Lynx lies in wait. Following a re-organization of January 1984, seven of the nine AAC squadrons in West Germany are assigned to anti-tank roles with a complement of some seven TOW-Lynxes, two utility Lynxes and three smaller and more agile Aérospatiale Gazelles. The last-mentioned are being outfitted with magnifying sights to act as scouting helicopters, and it is they who are tasked with finding targets and directing the Lynxes to them.

Similar roles are assigned to the six Lynxes which entered service with the 3rd Commando Brigade Air Squadron of the Royal Marines in November 1982. These helicopters were intended for deployment by ship, so the Royal Marines requested an Army Lynx with wheeled landing gear. Simple addition of a set of naval wheels would not have been possible, as the rear pair obstruct the TOW launch tubes, but as the expense of special development could not be justified for a mere handful of helicopters, the requirement was abandoned. It is possible, however, that the Royal Marines will obtain the latest Lynx AH.Mk 7 variant, with its increased performance by way of compensation.

Qatar export

Because the only export order for the Army Lynx has been for three from the Qatar Police Air Wing, the full range of weapon options has never been applied, except for trial and demonstration purposes. One machine has been tested with eight Rockwell AGM-114A Hellfire missiles, whilst the addition of eight Euromissile HOT or six older SS.11s is easily accomplished. The external mounting will also hold a 20-mm or 25-mm cannon; or a 7.62-mm (0.3-in) Minigun; or a pod of 18 68-mm (2.68-in) SNEB, 12 80-mm (3.15-in) SURA or 19 2.75-in (69.85-mm) rockets. These and more might have been installed had not plans to build up to 200 Lynx in Egypt fallen victim of Arab politics in 1979, just as the first of 20 complete helicopters were taking shape on Westland's Yeovil assembly line.

Hopes for the future were then pinned on the Lynx 3, a considerably updated helicopter with all-weather capability. Flown for the first time on 14 June 1984, the Lynx 3 is 27 per cent heavier than its forebear, at 5897-kg (13,000-lb) maximum weight, better protected against enemy fire, and equipped with self-defence air-launched General Dynamics Stinger or Short Javelin missiles as well as HOT, TOW or Hellfire anti-tank weapons. Wheeled landing gear and fatter tail boom identify the Lynx 3, while the main internal advantage is greater cabin space derived from a fuselage length increase of 30 cm (11.75 in). Advanced avionics include the Martin-Marietta TADS and PNVS, allied to an alternative position for the sight in a mast above the rotor.

The future of the Lynx 3 is by no means assured, but after a gloomy period during which it seemed likely that the Italian Agusta A129 Mangusta would be ordered as a Lynx replacement, its prospects now look a little brighter. A mid-1985 review of the helicopter requirements of all three armed forces led to a report containing two purchasing options from the MoD's Concept Studies branch. The first recommended an immediate buy of 20 Boeing Vertol Chinooks and 60 Lynx 3s followed by 30 EH-101s. The second option was to order 60 Lynx 3s immediately, with 60 EH-101s following.

Glossary

AAC Army Air Corps
AFCS Automatic Flight Control System
BAOR British Army of the Rhine
PVNS Pilot's Night Vision System
TADS Target Acquisition and Designation System
TANS Tactical Air Navigation System
TOW Tube-launched, Optically-tracked, Wire-guided

Lynx 3 will pack a mighty punch, as this photo of the prototype clearly shows. Eight Rockwell Hellfire guided anti-tank missiles are carried, as are two Stinger tube-launched air-to-air missiles and a 20-mm cannon pod.

Rotor head
The semi-rigid titanium rotor head and flexible arms are cast as a single monobloc forging. This uniquely strong yet flexible system allows unparalleled manoeuvrability. Main rotor blades are attached by titanium root attachment plates

Window
This small glass 'porthole' allows visual inspection of hydraulic fluid levels before flight

Air intakes
These intakes provide cooling air for the engines, generator and oil cooler

Engine intakes
A particle separator is provided for each engine intake, with fine mesh providing FOD ingestion. The intakes are electrically de-iced

Non-slip areas
Small portions of the cabin roof are strengthened and coated to give groundcrew a surer footing

Landing gear
The army Lynx has a simple non-retractable tubular skid-type landing gear. There is provision for a pair of ground handling wheels, and flotation gear can also be fitted. Many believe that a simple, rugged, fixed-wheeled undercarriage would be more useful, giving a rolling take-off capability

External pylon
This fuselage pylon and standard NATO flange can carry a bewildering array of stores including 20-mm or 25-mm Oerlikon cannon, Minigun pods, ECM pods, flare or mine dispensers, Matra Magic air-to-air missiles, rocket launchers containing 18×68-mm SNEB,

12×80-mm SURA or 19×2.75-in rockets, six Aérospatiale AS.11 or eight Euromissile HOT, or Rockwell Hellfire anti-tank guided missiles. Eight Hughes TOW launch tubes are the standard anti-tank fit for British Army Lynx, and these are shown here

Footsteps
Kick-in steps/handholds are provided one each side of the fuselage to allow groundcrew access to the engine, gearbox and rotor head

is a ski landing gear. Made of tough tubular metal, this replaces the tricycle wheel arrangement of naval models and is more suited to the army's method of tactical landings, which to the uninitiated observer resembles a controlled crash.

Army Lynxes do not require the nose-mounted search radar of their naval companions, although they are fitted as standard with the same accurate navigation equipment in the form of a Decca TANS and associated Decca 71 Doppler and Sperry GM9 Gyrosyn compass unit. The pilot, seated on the right, is assisted in flying the helicopter by GEC Avionics duplex three-axis automatic stability equipment. As an optional extra the same firm's AFCS may be added, together with extra radios and navigation aids. With these the Lynx possesses a limited all-weather capability, which is now being matched by its weapons suite.

Revolutionary rotor

Bearing the Lynx aloft is a four-blade main rotor of cambered aerofoil section. The interchangeable blades are constructed on a stainless steel main spar from GRP with Nomex plastic filling and a stainless steel protective leading edge.

On 11 August 1986, the Lynx demonstrator, G-LYNX, equipped with BERP (British Experimental Rotor Programme) rotor blades and a water methanol injection system with tuned jetpipes and Westland 30 tail unit, took the world absolute helicopter speed record. G-LYNX managed a speed of 216.45 knots, compared with the 198.9 knots achieved by a modified Mil-Mi A-10 on 28 September 1978.

Manual folding is available for stowage in confined areas. Below the rotor head, made with extensive use of high-strength titanium, is the main gearbox. Engine speeds of 6,150 rpm are reduced to 326 rpm for the main rotor in two stages, comprising a conventional spiral bevel gear and then a conformal gear designed by Westland to give superior load-transmitting properties. Each engine is fitted with an independent control system which governs rotor speed, so that the pilot only selects the required revolu-

tions in different phases of the sortie and does not have constantly to juggle with the throttles.

In the event of an engine failure, the other unit automatically increases to its maximum emergency rating. The two small, light and powerful Gems are mounted side-by-side above the equipment bay in the rear of the nacelle, fed with fuel from five crashproof bag tanks. From its original rating in Gem Mk 2 form, the engine was increased in power to 835 kW (1,120 shp) as the Gem Mk 41. In this guise it has a modified compressor (to raise mass flow by some 10 per cent) and a small increase in operating temperature. From 1983 the option was available of the Gem Mk 43 of 846 kW (1,135 shp), featuring detail improvements such as an electronic fuel system.

Consequently, maximum weights have been raised since the Lynx AH.Mk 1 entered the field at 4309 kg (9,500 lb), subsequently raised to 4354 kg (9,600 lb). For the Lynx AH.Mk 5, with Gem Mk 41-1s and three-pinion gearbox, the limit is 4536-kg (10,000-lb), whilst the Lynx AH.Mk 7, announced in 1985 to meet specification GSOR 3947, is red-lined at 4876 kg (10,750 lb). Of note is the fact that the Mk 7 has a tail rotor turning in the opposite direction (clockwise when viewed from the aircraft's port side) to that of earlier Lynx. Advantages to this revised arrangement are reduced noise and an ability to hover for extended periods at high weights, both attributes that are very useful in the anti-tank role.

In terms of construction, all Lynx helicopters are similar. The conventional semi-monocoque pod and boom design relies mostly upon light alloy, but with glassfibre employed for access panels, door and fairings (including the leading edge of the tail fin and covering for the tail rotor gearbox). Inside the cabin, seats are available for 10 fully-armed troops and tie-down rings for up to 907 kg (2,000 lb) of freight. Access to the 5.21 m^3 (184 cu ft) of space to the rear of the pilot's seat is via a large sliding door on each side of the fuselage. If required, a load of 1361 kg (3,000 lb) can be slung below the Lynx on a freight hook.

The Westland Lynx 3 is a dedicated anti-armour helicopter with uprated engines, BERP rotor blades, and advanced avionics for night and adverse weather target-detection and tracking.

BAOR squadrons

When the Lynx began deploying to BAOR in Germany during August 1978 its function was as a utility helicopter. Though issued to squadrons of the AAC equipped with Westland Scout AH.Mk 1s carrying Aérospatiale SS.11 anti-tank missiles, it supported rather than replaced these machines. The UK had caused some disappointment to its friends on the continent in mid-1977 when the Euromissile HOT was declined in favour of the Hughes BGM-71A TOW as main armament for the Lynx in the anti-tank role. Delivery of TOW began in 1980, allowing the first 'all British' firing of the missile to take place on Salisbury Plain on 20 February that year.

As part of the agreement with the USA, a BAe-led consortium acquired a licence to produce a roof-mounted version of the Hughes sight used in the American M65 system. This has no specific British designation, as Hughes rejected the name proposed by BAe. In April 1981 West

No. 2 Commando Brigade Air Squadron, Royal Marines, operates a mix of Gazelles and TOW-armed Lynxes, and in wartime would operate in the anti-tank role in support of the Royal Marines in Norway.

Westland Sea King Mk 41
Marinefliegergeschwader 5
West German Navy (Kriegsmarine)

Tail rotor
The tail rotor is a six-bladed unit of 3.14 m (10 ft 4 in) diameter and is fitted with flapping hinges

Tail rotor gearbox
The tail rotor driveshaft terminates in a right-angled gearbox

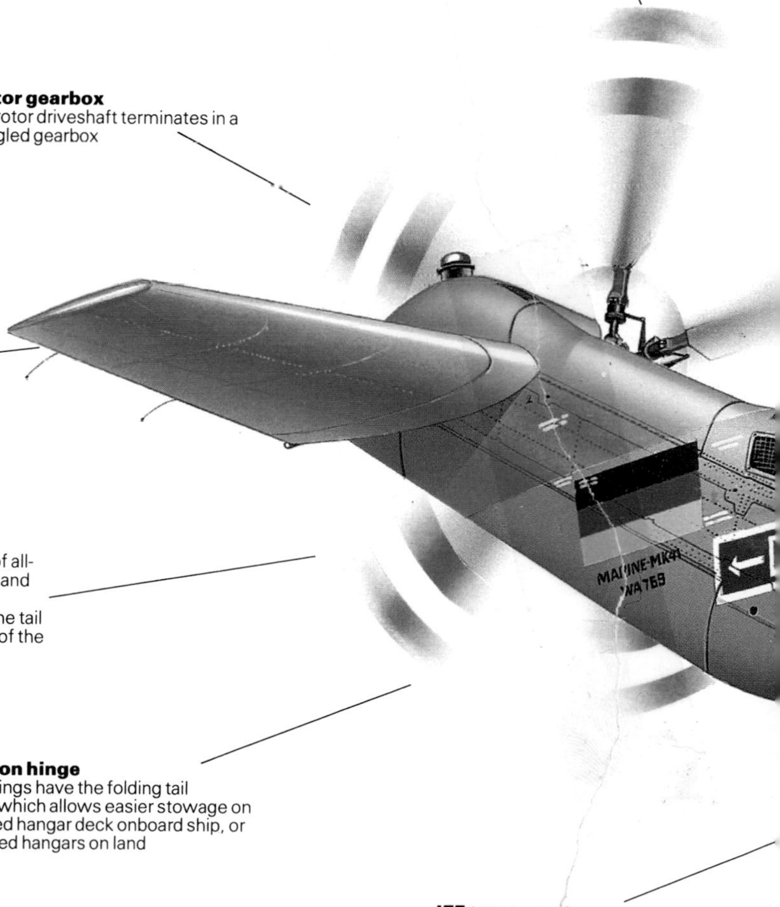

Fixed stabilizer
A fixed stabilizer is fitted to the starboard side of the vertical tail section, which also contains various tail rotor gearbox and drive assemblies

Tailboom
The tailboom, like the fuselage, is of all-metal semi-monocoque structure, and supports the tail rotor to port and a horizontal stabilizer to starboard. The tail rotor drive shaft runs along the top of the boom, encased in a fairing

Tail pylon hinge
All Sea Kings have the folding tail section, which allows easier stowage on a crowded hangar deck onboard ship, or in cramped hangars on land

IFF transponder
This is the I-band identification friend or foe (IFF) transponder aerial position; the display is in the front cockpit

and retrospective fitment to earlier RN Sea Kings. The first Advanced Sea King is the Indian Navy's Mk 42B, flown in May 1985, equipped with MEL Super Searcher radar. India is also the first customer to purchase the helicopter-launched version of the Sea Eagle.

Most distinctive of the Sea King family is the AEW model produced at great speed to meet the urgent requirement for an airborne early warning platform during the Falklands War. In just 11 weeks, two HAS.Mk 2s were fitted with a Thorn-EMI Searchwater radar (as in the Nimrod MR.Mk 2) in a kettledrum-shaped housing mounted on the starboard side, plus a Cossor Jubilee Guardsman IFF interrogator, a Ferranti FIN 1110 INS and MIR-2 ESM. The radome, which is inflated by warm air, is swung backwards through 90° for landing, but gives complete 360° coverage when deployed. From an operational height of 10,000 ft (3050 m) the Sea King AEW.Mk 2 can detect targets over 160 km distant and remain on station for up to four hours if refuelled at the hover, perhaps from a friendly ship which lacks landing space.

Completed just too late to see combat use, the AEW.Mk 2s have been joined by eight more conversions to provide early warning cover for the BAe Sea Harrier-equipped vessels HMS *Invincible, Illustrious* and *Ark Royal*. When at sea, these ships additionally carry a squadron of Sea King HAS. Mk 5s, the type also deploying on occasion to platform-equipped support vessels of the Royal Fleet Auxiliary. Shore-based units patrol the approaches to naval harbours from the Sea King HQ at Culdrose, Cornwall, and a single squadron at Prestwick watches over the Clyde and its submarine bases. Versions of the ASW Sea King have been exported to Australia, Egypt, India and Pakistan, those of the last-mentioned having the ability to launch Aérospatiale AM.39 Exocet anti-ship missiles.

Two further basic types of Sea King have been produced, for SAR and assault roles. RAF requirements for a long-range rescue helicopter were met by the Sea King HAR.Mk 3, which has all ASW equipment removed, uprated Gnome 1400-1 engines, a further 514 litres (113 Imp gal) of fuel (for a total of 3714 litres/817 Imp gal), MEL ARI 5955 search radar and a winch above the cabin door. The 19 Sea King HAR.Mk 3s supplied from 1977 onwards have participated in numerous headline-making rescues requiring extraordinary courage from their crews. A flight maintained in the Falkland Islands from 1982 onwards has aircraft which are painted light grey, instead of yellow, and equipped with an RWR and a chaff/flare dispenser. Belgium, Norway and the West German navy have received SAR Sea Kings, but the 20 remaining in German service are now being operated to combat standard with the addition of MBB Kormoran 2 anti-ship missiles, Ferranti Seaspray radar, RWR and chaff/flare equipment.

By removing the outboard floats, tail and rotor folding mechanisms, (as well as radar and ASW avionics) from the Sea King, Westland produced a tactical transport helicopter capable of lifting 3628 kg (8,000 lb) on an external hook, or 2722 kg (6,000 lb) internally. The first aircraft,

delivered to Egypt in 1974, were minimum-change versions of the West German navy Sea King model, retaining floats and known as the Commando Mk 1. Further production for Egypt and Qatar was to Commando Mk 2 standard, parallel to the Sea King HAS.Mk 2 with its uprated engines and transmission, and with room for 28 troops instead of the Mk 1's 21. Four of this model, designated Commando Mk 2E, serve the Egyptian armed forces in the stand-off jamming role with Selenia IHS-6 equipment in a reinstated spine radome and a large dish aerial on each side of the rear fuselage.

The UK ordered 37 versions of the Commando for support of the Royal Marines, deliveries beginning in 1979. Intended to operate from ships, they retain the folding tailboom and rotors and are designated Sea King HC.Mk 4. Equipment includes Decca TANS and Decca 71 Doppler navigation, plus the option to mount a 7.62-mm (0.3-in) machine-gun in the cabin doorway. Sea King HC.Mk 4s of No. 846 Squadron flew 1,818 sorties (2904.5 hours and 3,343 deck landings) during the Falklands war, ferrying supplies to troops ashore as well as inserting SAS/SBS observation and sabotage parties behind enemy lines.

Taking the basic theme further, Westland produced the Commando Mk 3, which brings back a spine radome, the outboard floats (and retractable landing gear) as mountings for 12.7-mm (0.5-in) machine-gun pods, a pair of Brandt rocket pods or 16 Sura rockets. The strengthened cabin floor will take pintle-mounted guns up to 20 mm in calibre, whilst a pair of Exocet missiles can be hung on fuselage side attachments. Commando Mk 3s supplied to Qatar will also be armed with an undisclosed type of anti-tank missile. Attacks upon armoured vehicles were perhaps not the first consideration of those who originally redesigned the Sea King for British use, but there can be no doubting the fact that this versatile Anglo-American performer has evolved in exemplary style to meet the demands of the age.

Belgian Sea King Mk 48s are operated by the 40e Escadrille/Smaldeel of the Force Navale Belge/Belgische Zeemacht, and are based at Koksijde. The large Dayglo patches on nose and tailboom betray the aircraft's SAR role.

Glossary
AEW Airborne Early Warning
ASW Anti-Submarine Warfare
ECM Electronic Countermeasures
ESM Electronic Support Measures
FAA Fleet Air Arm
IFF Identification Friend or Foe
INS Inertial Navigation System
LAPADS Lightweight Acoustic Processing And Display System
MAD Magnetic Anomaly Detector
RWR Radar-Warning Receiver
SAR Search-and-Rescue
TANS Tactical Air Navigation System

No. 202 Squadron is headquartered at Finningley, and its four flights are based at Boulmer, Brawdy, Lossiemouth and Culdrose. It also supplies aircrew and aircraft for No. 78 Squadron in the Falklands on a rotational basis.

Westland Sea King in service

Royal Navy

The Royal Navy has five ASW squadrons equipped with the HAS.Mk 5, one of them a training unit. One squadron uses the AEW.Mk 2, and one Commando assault squadron uses the HC.Mk 4. The ASW training squadron operates the HAS.Mk 2 and HAS.Mk 5, and the assault training squadron uses HC.Mk 4s.

706 Squadron
Equipped: January 1970
Base: RNAS Culdrose
Task: Crew conversion
Aircraft: Sea King HAS.Mk 2A XV657 '589', XV666 '598'; Sea King HAS.Mk 5 XV648 '587', XV668 '586', ZD631 '590'

707 Squadron
Re-equipped: October 1983
Base: RNAS Yeovilton
Task: Crew conversion
Aircraft: Sea King HC.Mk 4 ZA312 'ZB', ZD476 'ZA', ZD479, 'ZE', ZD626 'ZG', ZD627 'ZH'

810 Squadron
Formed: 15 February 1983
Base: RNAS Culdrose
Task: Operational training
Aircraft: Sea King HAS.Mk 5 XV653 '509', XV665 '508', XZ574 '506', ZA127 '511', ZA170 '504'

814 Squadron
Formed: 30 March 1973
Base: RNAS Culdrose and HMS Illustrious
Task: ASW
Aircraft: Sea King HAS.Mk 5 XV675 '274/L', XV676 '266/L', XV703 '271/L', XV712 '270/L', ZA167 '273/L'

819 Squadron
Formed: 9 February 1971
Base: RNAS Prestwick
Task: ASW
Aircraft: Sea King HAS.Mk 5 XV663 '703', XV677 '705', XV701 '706', ZD634 '702', ZD637 '704'

820 Squadron
Re-equipped: December 1972
Base: RNAS Culdrose and HMS Invincible
Task: ASW
Aircraft: Sea King HAS.Mk 5 XZ918 '020/N', ZA126 '012/N', ZA128 '014/N', ZA166 '010/N', ZA169 '015/N'

824 Squadron
Formed: 24 February 1970
Base: RNAS Culdrose
Task: ASW
Aircraft: Sea King HAS.Mk 5 ZA130 '353', ZA133 '352' only

826 Squadron
Formed: 2 June 1970
Base: RNAS Culdrose
Task: ASW
Aircraft: Sea King HAS.Mk 5 XV651 '131', XZ577 '138', ZA131 '133', XZ916 '130', ZA137 '137'

846 Squadron
Re-equipped: December 1979
Base: RNAS Yeovilton
Task: Assault transport
Aircraft: Sea King HC.Mk 4 ZA292 'VH', ZA293 'VK', ZA296 'VF', ZA312 'VS', ZD478 'VE'

849 Squadron
Formed: 1 November 1984
Base: RNAS Culdrose
Task: Shipboard AEW
Aircraft: Sea King AEW.Mk 2 XV650 '364', XV656 '186', XV671 '365', XV672 '367', XV714 '185'

One of No. 849 Squadron's Westland Sea King AEW.Mk 2s. These aircraft could have made an enormous contribution had they been available during the Falklands war.

Royal Air Force

The Royal Air Force has two Sea King search and rescue squadrons. One, No. 78, operates a mixture of Sea Kings and Boeing Vertol Chinooks in support of the British garrison on the Falkland Islands. A total of 16 HAR.Mk 3s are in use, with three more on order. The majority are finished in the overall SAR yellow colour scheme, though examples serving in the Falklands are finished in an overall dark grey colour with two-letter codes on the fuselage in black starting with the letter 'S'.

No. 202 Squadron
Formed: May 1978
Base: RAF Finningley (HQ); RAF Boulmer ('A' Flight); RAF Brawdy ('B' Flight); RAF Coltishall ('C' Flight); RAF Lossiemouth ('D' Flight)
Task: SAR
Aircraft: Sea King HAR.Mk 3 XZ589, XZ593, XZ598, XZ599, ZE368

No. 78 Squadron
Formed: April 1986 (from Nos 1564 and 1310 Flights)
Base: RAF Mount Pleasant, Falkland Islands
Task: SAR and garrison support
Aircraft: Sea King HAR.Mk 3 frequently rotated from UK, and Boeing Vertol Chinnook

Royal Australian Navy

Australian Sea King Mk 50s are derivatives of the HAS.Mk 1, and were delivered from late 1974. No. 817 Squadron formed during February 1976. Ten are in service. Some 30 per cent of component manufacture of the RAN Sea Kings was undertaken by Australian companies. Today, the remaining examples in service carry out a wide range of tasks, these including SAR, ASW, VertRep (Vertical Replenishment) and the newer role of mine countermeasures. This last role will see the Sea King in front-line use until at least the mid-1990s and possibly longer, depending on fatigue life.

817 Squadron
Re-equipped: February 1976
Base: Nowra, NSW
Task: ASW
Aircraft: Sea King Mk 50 N16-100 '902', N16-118 '907', N16-124 '909'; Sea King Mk 50A N16-235 '921', N16-238 '920'

This Westland Sea King Mk 50 of No. 817 Squadron, Royal Australian Navy, is based at Nowra, New South Wales, and is used for ASW duties.

Belgium (Force Aérienne Belge/ Belgische Luchtmacht)

The five Sea King Mk 48s that equip 40 Smaldeel (Squadron) come under the operational control of Tactical Air Force Command and are jointly operated by the Air Force and Navy. Four of the Sea Kings are equipped for SAR tasks, but the fifth has a VIP configuration for use by the Belgian royal family and Government ministers. All are finished in the sand/green camouflage with Dayglo trim and are serialled 'RS01' to 'RS05'. Their home base is, not surprisingly, the most westerly operating location for Belgian military units, though obviously the Sea Kings can deploy to points along the coastline in support of specific SAR operations.

40 Squadron
Re-equipped: 1976
Base: Coxyde/Koksijde
Task: SAR
Aircraft: Sea King Mk 48 RS01, RS03, RS04, RS05 only

The Sea King Mk 48s of the Koksijde-based No. 40 Squadron are used primarily for search and rescue duties.

Egyptian air force (Al Quwwat al Jawwiya il Misriya)

Egypt is the largest foreign user of the Westland-built Sea King. Five Commando Mk 1s and 19 Commando Mk 2s are in service in the assault role, although at least two of the Mk 2s are in VIP configuration. Four Mk 2Es have been delivered for electronic warfare duties.

? Squadron
Formed: 1976
Base: Alexandria
Task: ASW
Aircraft: Sea King Mk 47 e.g. 712, 716, 776

? Squadron
Formed: 1974
Base: not known
Task: Assault transport
Aircraft: Commando Mk 1 264; Commando Mk 2 732; Commando Mk 2B 725/SU-ARR, 726; Commando Mk 2E SU-BBJ

This is one of the 28 Commandos delivered to the Egyptian air force. Most are used in the commando assault role.

Pitot tube
This is used to provide air data for the helicopter's pressure responsive instruments; there is one head on each side of the FOD guard, both being electrically de-iced

e Gnome H.1400
es are mounted side by
abin. Each has a
gency rating of
shp)

FOD guard
The engine intake guard provides protection against the ingestion of foreign objects such as birds, ice and excess water during operations close to the water. It is known to the crews as the 'barn door'

Pilots
The helicopter carries two pilots for all flight operations, with one acting as first pilot and other as co-pilot. To assist in flying the helicopter there is the Louis Newmark Mk 31 automatic flight control system

Cockpit canopies
The cockpit of the Sea King is extensively glazed, giving an excellent all-round view. Main windscreens in front of the pilots' positions are electrically de-iced by fine wires running through the Perspex. Windscreen wipers are also provided

Pilot's side hatch
This can be jettisoned for emergency egress, and incorporates sliding windows. A similar hatch is located on the port side. Essential instructions are painted in English and German

First pilot's searchlight
Situated in the nose of the helicopter immediately above the boat hull is the searchlight, controlled by the first pilot in the right-hand seat

Co-pilot's searchlight
The pilot flying from the left-hand seat has the facility to use the searchlight mounted in the boat hull of the helicopter, which is stowed flush with the fuselage when not in use

RadAlt aerials
The Honeywell AN/APN 171 radio altimeter has twin aerials each side of the boat hull centreline, and this instrument is used to provide data for accurate height-finding, especially over water

Hover floodlights
During hovering operations, the ground immediately below the helicopter is illuminated with floodlights; this can be particularly useful during rescue operations

ILS aerial
The glide slope aerial for the instrument landing system is mounted on the helicopter's nose, and this is used for precise approaches to airfields so equipped in bad weather

Boat hull
The Sea King's boat-shaped single-step hull and pop-out floats allow amphibious operation in emergency

Anti-collision light
For flight safety reasons the helicopter is fitted with orange anti-collision lights under the nose and above the tail

Doppler aerial
Beneath the fuselage is the aerial for the Decca Doppler system, which provides navigation and position information

gear
main landing gear
rearwards into the
tyres are either
R Dunlop

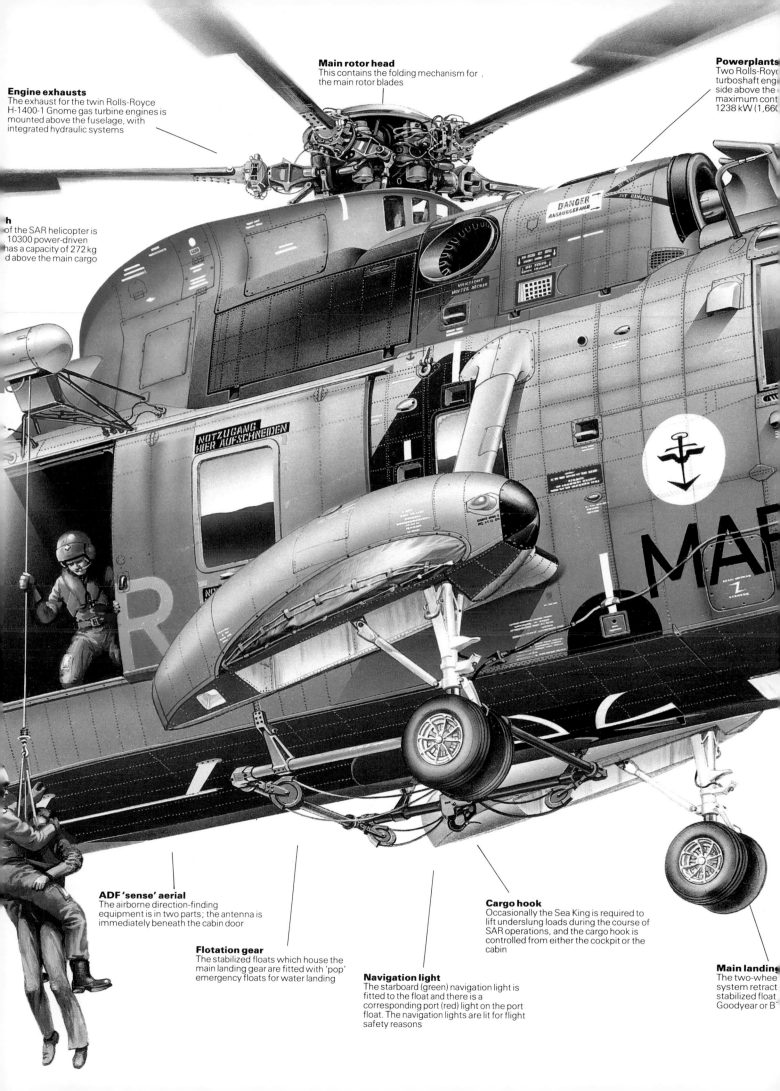

Engine exhausts
The exhaust for the twin Rolls-Royce H-1400-1 Gnome gas turbine engines is mounted above the fuselage, with integrated hydraulic systems

Main rotor head
This contains the folding mechanism for the main rotor blades

Powerplants
Two Rolls-Royce turboshaft eng side above the maximum cont 1238 kW (1,660

...h
of the SAR helicopter is 10300 power-driven has a capacity of 272 kg d above the main cargo

ADF 'sense' aerial
The airborne direction-finding equipment is in two parts; the antenna is immediately beneath the cabin door

Flotation gear
The stabilized floats which house the main landing gear are fitted with 'pop' emergency floats for water landing

Navigation light
The starboard (green) navigation light is fitted to the float and there is a corresponding port (red) light on the port float. The navigation lights are lit for flight safety reasons

Cargo hook
Occasionally the Sea King is required to lift underslung loads during the course of SAR operations, and the cargo hook is controlled from either the cockpit or the cabin

Main landing
The two-whee system retract stabilized float Goodyear or B

German Navy (Marineflieger)

German Navy Sea Kings are currently being modified to serve in a more active role, with Ferranti Sea Spray radar, RWR, ECM and Kormoran anti-ship missiles. Though they are home-based at Kiel-Holtenau, the Marineflieger Sea Kings regularly detach to Sylt, Borkum and Heligoland for regional SAR tasks. These detachments usually include at least two helicopters. The original order for 22 examples led to a serial allocation from '8950' to '8971' inclusive, though two have been written off over the years.

2.Staffel/ Marinefliegergeschwader 5

Re-equipped: 1974
Base: Kiel-Holtenau
Task: SAR

Aircraft: Sea King Mk 41
8950, 8955, 8959, 8966, 8970

Marineflieger Sea Kings currently wear a colourful grey and Dayglo paint scheme. The Dayglo patches will presumably be removed when the aircraft adopt a more aggressive role.

Indian Navy

Two Indian Navy squadrons operate 14 Sea King Mk 42/42As from Cochin and from INS *Vikrant*. When INS *Virat* (formerly HMS *Hermes*) is commissioned it will presumably embark some of these aircraft.

INAS 330

Formed: March 1971
Base: Cochin and INS *Vikrant*
Task: ASW
Aircraft: Sea King Mk 42
IN501, IN504, IN507; Sea King
Mk 42A IN551, IN553

INAS 336

Formed: 1975
Base: Cochin
Task: ASW
Aircraft: pooled with INAS 330

Indian Navy Sea Kings are shore-based at Cochin, but can be carried on board either of the service's two aircraft-carriers.

Norwegian Air Force (Kongelige Norske Luftforsvaret)

The 11 Sea King Mk 43s of Skv 330 are detached at airfields along Norway's long coastline, and operate in conjunction with the Lynx of Skv 337.

Skvadron 337

Re-equipped: November 1972
Base: Bodo (HQ and 'A' Flight); Banak ('B' Flight); Orland ('C' Flight); Sola ('D' Flight)

Task: SAR
Aircraft: Sea King Mk 43
060, 066, 068, 074, 189

The Sea King Mk 43s of Skvadron 337 wear an overall white colour scheme with Dayglo patches.

Pakistan Navy

Six Sea King Mk 45s are the only front-line aircraft owned by the Pakistan navy, although this modest air arm has operated a handful of loaned Dassault-Breguet Atlantics.

? Squadron

Formed: 1974
Base: Sharea Faisal
Task: ASW/ASV

Aircraft: Sea King Mk 45
4510, 4511, 4512, 4514, 4515

The Pakistan navy operates six Sea King Mk 45s in the ASW/ASV role.

Qatar Air Force (Al Quwwat al Jawwiya al Qatar)

This small but oil-rich state in the Gulf region operates a dozen Westland Commando 2A/2C/3s for general transport and VIP duties. It is possible that four Commando 3s will be fitted with Exocet missiles.

Formed: 1975
Base: Doha
Task: Assault support/ASV
Aircraft: Commando Mk 2A QA-20, QA-22; Commando Mk 2C QA-21; Commando Mk 3 QA-30, QA-37

Westland Sea King HAS.Mk 5 cutaway drawing key

1 Fixed tailplane construction
2 Static dischargers
3 Tail navigation light
4 Anti-collision light
5 Tail rotor gearbox
6 Six-bladed tail rotor
7 Blade pitch change mechanism
8 Tail rotor drive shaft
9 Tail pylon construction
10 Glassfibre trailing edge panel
11 Intermediate shaft gearbox
12 Shaft coupling
13 Folding tail pylon hinges
14 Transponder aerial
15 Rotor blade cross section
16 Blade tracking weight
17 Blade balance weights
18 D-section aluminium spar
19 Tail rotor control gear

20 Tailcone frame and stringer construction
21 Tail rotor transmisison shaft
22 Dorsal spine fairing
23 UHF aerial
24 Shaft bearings
25 Tie-down ring
26 Fuselage/tailcone production joint
27 Maintenance walkway
28 Fuel jettison pipe
29 Non-retracting tailwheel
30 Tailwheel levered suspension leg strut
31 Tailwheel castoring leg fixing
32 Mk 46 Torpedo
33 Torpedo propellers
34 Parachute launch pack
35 Mk 11 Depth charge
36 Weapon pylon shackles
37 Weapon release unit (4)
38 Cabin flooring
39 Smoke marker container
40 Door latch
41 Cabin rear bulkhead
42 Radar scanner support mounting
43 MEL Sea Searcher radar scanner
44 HF aerial cable
45 Cabin wall soundproofing panels
46 Rescue hoist/winch
47 Winch floodlight
48 Transponder transmitter/ receiver
49 Radar transmitter/receiver
50 Data processing station (Marconi LAPADS)
51 Crew emergency exit window
52 Sonobuoy launch tube
53 Swivelling seat mounting
54 Pressure refuelling connection
55 Plessey Type 195 dipping sonar
56 Emergency flotation bag (shown inflated)
57 Flotation bag inflation bottles
58 Bilge pump access covers
59 Underfloor fuel tanks, total fuel capacity 3200 litres (704 Imp gal) in five cells
60 Fuselage main longeron
61 Sonobuoy stowage racks
62 Winch operating control lever
63 Sliding freight door
64 Freight door rail
65 Data display panels
66 Sonar operator's seat
67 Portside radar observer's seat

68 Sonar/radar instrumentation racks
69 Gearbox mounting support structure
70 Hydraulic system connectors
71 Oil cooler

72 Oil cooler air outlet
73 Rotor head tail fairing
74 Engine fire extinguisher bottles
75 Handhold
76 Oil cooler fan
77 Gearbox driven accessory units

78 Rotor head hydraulic control jack (3)
79 Main gearbox
80 Swash plate mechanism
81 Blade pitch control rods
82 Blade attachment joints
83 Master (non-folding) rotor blade
84 Nos 2-5 rotor blades folded position
85 Rotor head fairing
86 Hydraulic oil reservoir
87 Blade folding hinge joints
88 Rotor head mechanism
89 Cooling air louvres
90 Engine exhaust duct
91 Cabin roof construction
92 Folding step/handhold
93 Tie-down ring
94 Main undercarriage strut mounting
95 Kick-in steps
96 Undercarriage energy absorbing side strut
97 Main undercarriage housing sponson
98 Starboard navigation light
99 Main undercarriage leg strut
100 Retraction strut
101 Twin mainwheels
102 Stub wing/walkway
103 Folding step
104 Forward underfloor fuel tanks
105 Cabin air ducting
106 Dipping sonar housing

107 Sonar winch cable drum
108 Winch 'pit-head' gear
109 Tape recorder
110 Engine mounting deck
111 Rolls-Royce Gnome H.1400-1 turboshaft engine

112 Engine bay firewall
113 Port engine nacelle
114 Engine oil tank
115 Port engine air intake
116 Engine starter housing
117 Starboard engine air inta
118 Engine mounting strut
119 Intake foreign object deflector
120 Pitot tube

121 Control rod linkages
122 Heating/ventilation sys air intake
123 Fuel control computers
124 Cabin heater/blower
125 Boat hull chine longeror
126 Electrical equipment ba
127 Cockpit floor level
128 Fire extinguisher
129 Sliding side window par
130 Pilot's seat
131 Cockpit bulkhead
132 Radio rack
133 Port entry doorway
134 Rotor brake lever

Sea King HAS.Mk 1: Sikorsky SH-3D equivalent; Ekco AW 391 radar, Plessey 195 sonar, Marconi AW.96 Doppler, 1119-kW (1,500-shp) Gnome H.1400 engines, 9299-kg (20,500-lb) maximum weight; four imported and 56 Westland-built

Sea King HC.Mk 4: Royal Marines tactical transport, based on Commando Mk 2, but with folding tailboom and rotors, plus additional fuel and external cargo hook; 37 ordered, further two **Sea King Mk 4X** delivered to Royal Aircraft Establishment for development work

Sea King Mk 42: Indian Navy ASW equivalent of Mk 1; 12 built; followed by three **Sea King Mk 42A** models of Mk 2, with DAF haul-down equipment; delivery under way of 20 **Advanced Sea King Mk 42B** with Super Searcher radar, AQS-902 LAPADS and Mk 6 improvements, plus Sea Eagle missiles
Sea King Mk 43: Norwegian SAR, similar to Mk 41; 10 built, plus single **Sea King Mk 43A** with H.1400-1 engines
Sea King Mk 45: Pakistani ASW, based on Mk 1, plus Exocet provision; six built
Sea King Mk 47: Egyptian navy ASW version of Mk 2; six built
Sea King Mk 48: Belgian SAR model, based on Mk 41; five built
Sea King Mk 50: Royal Australian Navy ASW version of Mk 1, except for H.1400-1 engines and AQS-13B 'dunking' sonar; 10 built, followed by two **Sea King Mk 50A** with repositioned cabin rear bulkhead
Commando Mk 1: Egyptian air force, based on Sea King Mk 41; five built
Commando Mk 2: H.1400-1 engines, uprated transmission, no sponsons; 17 for Egypt; **Commando Mk 2A** three for Qatar; **Commando Mk 2B** two VIP versions for Egypt; **Commando Mk 2C** one VIP version for Qatar; **Commando Mk 2E** four ECM aircraft for Egypt with IHS-6 jamming equipment

Sea King HAS.Mk 2: Gnome H.1400-1 engines, uprated transmission and six-blade tail rotor; 21 new-built; conversions from Mk 1 designated **Sea King HAS.Mk 2A**
Sea King AEW.Mk 2: Searchwater radar in external radome; 10 conversions from HAS.Mk 2, plus one aerodynamic testbed
Sea King HAR.Mk 3: RAF SAR version based on Mk 2; ARI 5955 radar, plus TANS and additional fuel; 19 built

Sea King HAS.Mk 5: Mk 2 re-equipped with ARI 5991 Sea Searcher radar in squared-off radome, AQS-902 LAPADS processing equipment, TANS, etc; MIR-2 ESM, composite main rotor blades and optional AQS-81 MAD later introduced; 30 new-built aircraft, plus conversions from HAS.Mk 2

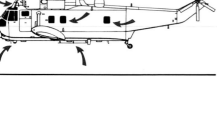

Sea King HAS.Mk 6: As Mk 5, with improved avionics and sensors, uprated transmission and 9752-kg (21,500-lb) maximum weight; no contracts yet placed for new and/or converted aircraft
Sea King Mk 41: West German navy SAR version based on HAS.Mk 1 but without sonar; 23 built (including one lost before delivery); currently receiving Sea Spray radar and four Kormoran 2 anti-ship missiles

Commando Mk 3: armed multi-role version; sponsons restored; eight built for Qatar

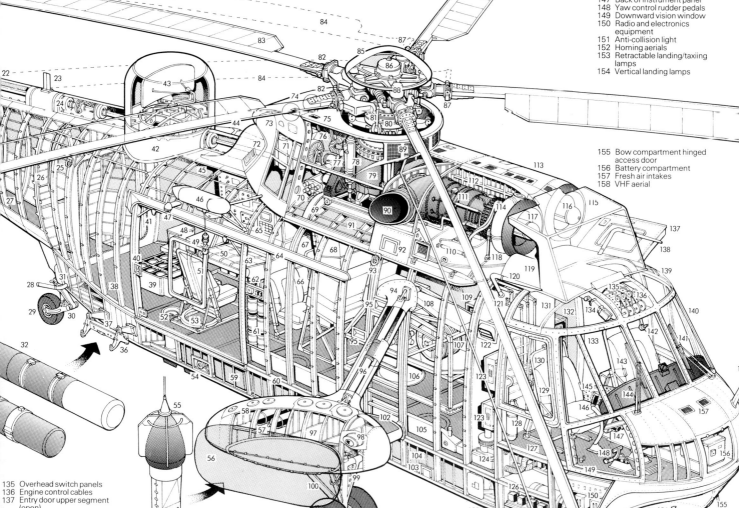

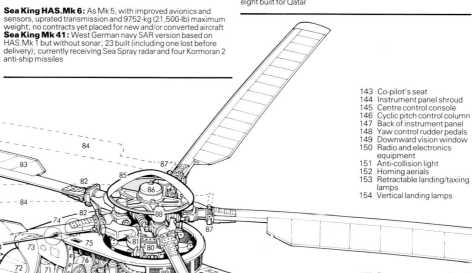

143 Co-pilot's seat
144 Instrument panel shroud
145 Centre control console
146 Cyclic pitch control column
147 Back of instrument panel
148 Yaw control rudder pedals
149 Downward vision window
150 Radio and electronics equipment
151 Anti-collision light
152 Homing aerials
153 Retractable landing/taxiing lamps
154 Vertical landing lamps

155 Bow compartment hinged access door
156 Battery compartment
157 Fresh air intakes
158 VHF aerial

135 Overhead switch panels
136 Engine control cables
137 Entry door upper segment (open)
138 Pitot tube
139 Cockpit eyebrow windows
140 Windscreen panels
141 Windscreen wipers
142 Air temperature probe

© Pilot Press Ltd

Westland Sea King/Commando warload

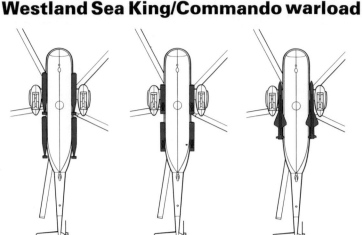
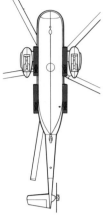
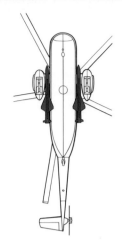
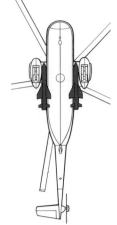

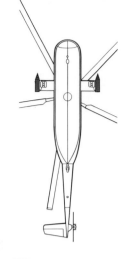

■ 4×Marconi Sting Ray homing torpedos

■ 4×BAe Mk 11 Mod 3 depth charges

■ 2×Aérospatiale AM.39 Exocet anti-ship missiles

■ 2×BAe Sea Eagle anti-ship missiles

■ 16×SURA missiles

■ 2×Brandt 68-18 rocket pods

Royal Navy ASW
Replacement of the Aerojet Mk 46 homing torpedo began in September 1983 with formal hand-over to the RN of its first Sting Rays. With a speed of at least 45 kts and maximum depth of 750 m (2,460 ft), it is effective against the latest generation of strong submarine hulls.

Royal Navy ASW
As an alternative to (or in combination with) homing torpedoes, the Sea King can be equipped with depth charges. Used against submarines in shallow water, the Mod 3 version is designed specifically for air dropping and weighs 145 kg (320 lb) including 80 kg (176 lb) of high explosive.

Pakistan navy ASV
Sea Kings of the Pakistan navy were the first of the type to be cleared to fire a large anti-ship missile, following qualification trials in 1976. Helicopter launched from 100 m (330 ft), the Exocet has a range of 52 km (32 miles).

Indian Navy ASV
First models of the Advanced Sea King to be produced were the Mk 42Bs of the Indian Navy. In addition to a full ASW armoury, they have an ASV option with a pair of BAe Sea Eagle anti-ship missiles. Two booster rockets have been added to the Sea Eagle for helicopter launches. The missile increases the Sea King's attack radius by some 110 km (68 miles).

Commando attack
In addition to carrying some 28 troops, the Commando can be armed with a broad variety of weaponry, including a machine-gun or 20-mm cannon in the cabin door. Outrigger pylons will accommodate a total of 16 Oerlikon 81-mm (3.2-in) SURA-D 3-kg (6.6-lb) rockets in two banks of four on each side.

Commando attack
Commando outrigger pylons will each carry a Brandt 68-18 launcher pod for 18 rocket projectiles of 68-mm (2.68-in) calibre, each installation weighing between 166 and 188 kg (366 and 414 lb) when loaded.

Specification: Westland Sea King HAS.Mk 5

Rotors
Main rotor diameter	18.90 m	(62 ft 0 in)
Main rotor disc area	280.59 m²	(3,020.30 sq ft)
Tail rotor diameter	3.16 m	(10 ft 4 in)

Fuselage and tail unit
Accommodation	two pilots and two systems operators	
Length overall, rotors turning	22.15 m	(72 ft 8 in)
Length, fuselage	17.01 m	(55 ft 9.75 in)
Length, tail and rotors folded	14.40 m	(47 ft 3 in)
Height overall, rotors stopped	4.85 m	(15 ft 11 in)

Landing gear
Reverse tricycle with retractable twin mainwheels
Wheel track	3.96 m	(13 ft 0 in)

Weights
Empty, equipped	6201 kg	(13,672 lb)
Maximum take-off	9525 kg	(21,000 lb)
Maximum external load	2948 kg	(6,500 lb)
Internal fuel load	2585 kg	(5,700 lb)

Powerplant
Two Rolls-Royce Gnome H.1400-1 turboshafts
Rating, each	1238 kW	(1,660 shp)

Sea King recognition features

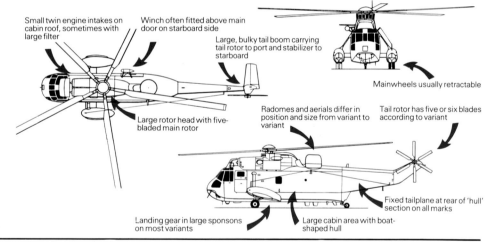

Small twin engine intakes on cabin roof, sometimes with large filter

Winch often fitted above main door on starboard side

Large, bulky tail boom carrying tail rotor to port and stabilizer to starboard

Mainwheels usually retractable

Large rotor head with five-bladed main rotor

Radomes and aerials differ in position and size from variant to variant

Tail rotor has five or six blades according to variant

Landing gear in large sponsons on most variants

Large cabin area with boat-shaped hull

Fixed tailplane at rear of 'hull' section on all marks

Performance:

Maximum cruising speed at sea level	112 kts	208 km/h (129 mph)
Hovering ceiling out of ground effect	3,200 ft	(975 m)
Hovering ceiling in ground effect	5,000 ft	(1525 m)
Maximum range with standard fuel load	1230 km	(764 miles)
Initial rate of climb	2,020 ft	(616 m) per minute

Weapon load
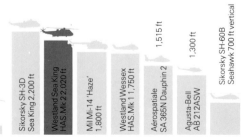

- Mil Mi-14 'Haze' 4000 kg E
- Westland Sea King HAS.Mk 2 2948 kg
- Westland Wessex HAS.Mk 1 1814 kg
- Aérospatiale SA 365N Dauphin 2 1600 kg
- Sikorsky SH-60B Seahawk 500 kg E
- Agusta-Bell AB 212ASW 490 kg
- Sikorsky SH-3D Sea King 381 kg

Maximum rate of climb per minute
- Sikorsky SH-3D Sea King 2,200 ft
- Westland Sea King HAS.Mk 2 2,020 ft
- Mil Mi-14 'Haze' 1,800 ft
- Westland Wessex HAS.Mk 1 1,750 ft
- Aérospatiale SA 365N Dauphin 2 1,515 ft
- Agusta-Bell AB 212ASW 1,300 ft
- Sikorsky SH-60B Seahawk 700 ft vertical

Speed at low altitude

Aérospatiale SA 365N Dauphin 2	151 kts
Sikorsky SH-3D Sea King	144 kts
Westland Sea King HAS.Mk 2	140 kts
Sikorsky SH-60B Seahawk	126 kts
Mil Mi-14 'Haze'	124 kts
Westland Wessex HAS.Mk 1	117 kts
Agusta-Bell AB 212ASW	106 kts

Range
Westland Sea King HAS.Mk 2	1230 km
Sikorsky SH-3D Sea King	1005 km
Aérospatiale SA 365N Dauphin 2	880 km
Mil Mi-14 'Haze'	800 km
Agusta-Bell AB 212ASW	667 km
Westland Wessex	HAS.Mk 1 628 km
Sikorsky SH-60B	Seahawk 600 km E

Service ceiling
- Aérospatiale SA 365N Dauphin 2 15,000 ft
- Sikorsky SH-60B Seahawk 15,000 ft E
- Sikorsky SH-3D Sea King 14,700 ft
- Westland Wessex HAS.Mk 1 14,100 ft
- Agusta-Bell AB 212ASW 14,000 ft E
- Mil Mi-14 'Haze' 14,000 ft E
- Westland Sea King HAS.Mk 2 14,000 ft

The WESTLAND WESSEX

Wessex and S-58: willing workhorses

The Sikorsky S-58 and Westland Wessex have seen extensive service worldwide since their introduction in the late 1950s. Numbers in service are now dwindling, but the Wessex remains an important part of the RAF's support helicopter force, and is still in the front line in the shooting war in Northern Ireland.

This Wessex HU.Mk 5 belongs to No. 771 Squadron, a Royal Navy SAR unit based at RNAS Culdrose in Cornwall. Until quite recently the rescue units operated Wessex HAS.Mk 1s, but have now re-equipped with HU.Mk 5s.

The rotary-wing technology developed by Igor Sikorsky in the USA has been responsible in no small measure for the worldwide acceptance of the helicopter in a broad variety of roles. Such was the commanding lead of the US in this field at the end of World War II that several firms wishing to enter the helicopter business purchased Sikorsky manufacturing rights rather than risk the failure of their own attempts to design a viable machine. Although it is the dynamic components of a helicopter (the moving parts, especially the rotor head) which are the most crucial components, licensees generally opted for manufacture of complete copies of Sikorsky products.

One such associate was Westland, which is now the sole major helicopter manufacturer in the UK. The Yeovil-based firm acquired the additional right to modify and update the helicopter designs it bought from Sikorsky, particularly with regard to installing British avionics and engines. As a follow-on to manufacture of the S-51 (Dragonfly/Widgeon) and S-55 (Whirlwind), in 1956 Westland obtained a licence for the S-58. It was intended that the helicopter should be converted to turbine power and become the first Royal Navy rotary-wing machine designed from the outset for ASW operations in all weathers. Appropriately, the WS-58 was named after the

The Wessex HC.Mk 2s of No. 72 Squadron operate in support of British forces in Northern Ireland, being based at RAF Aldergrove. For some tasks they carry door- and cabin-mounted machine-guns to provide suppressive fire.

Anglo-Saxon kingdom in which Yeovil once stood: Wessex.

Sikorsky forebear

The Westland Wessex's career has included episodes as varied as combat in the Falklands war and heroic rescue operations in atrocious weather conditions around Britain's coasts. First, however, it is appropriate to look briefly at the Sikorsky S-58, a small number of which remain in service overseas. The story begins in June 1952 with the placing of a contract by the US Navy for three XHSS-1 prototypes, powered by a 1137-kW (1,525-hp) Wright Cyclone R-1820 piston engine. After the first of these had flown on 8 March 1954, large-scale production ensued under the designation HSS-1 Seabat (and HSS-1N with improved avionics and autostabilizer for night operation), primarily for anti-submarine operations, although 16 passengers or eight stretchers could be carried as alternatives.

At the same time as the HSS-1 was preparing for shipborne deployment, the US Marine Corps was placing contracts which eventually covered over 500 of the HUS-1 Seahorse model, seating 12 assault troops in addition to the two crew located above and forward of the cabin. Sub-versions of the HUS-1 were supplied to the US Coast Guard or fitted with pontoons to acquire amphibious capability. The US Army also appreciated the S-58's value as a transport and bought over 350 as the H-34 Choctaw, seating up to 18 men. Not to be outdone, the USAF Reserve took delivery of a small number converted for

SAR. In 1962, with the adoption of tri-service nomenclature, navalized models were redesignated in the H-34 series.

In all, Sikorsky built 1,821 of the S-58 family, including civil models (passenger S-58C and passenger/freight S-58B and S-58D), while Sud-Aviation in France produced another 135. The French army and navy were principal operators, as were those two services in West Germany. Belgium, Brazil, Canada, Italy, Japan and Uruguay operated the type mainly in naval guise, whilst air forces and armies in Chile, Haiti, Laos, Nicaragua, Taiwan and South Vietnam flew the transport models. Those supplied to Europe have been retired, many finding a new lease of life on the civil market.

The main factor in the S-58's life-extension has been installation of turbine power, more specifically a pair of Pratt & Whitney Canada PT6s coupled in Twin-Pac configuration. Their output is restricted to a combined 1122 kW (1,505 shp) for take-off and 935 kW (1,254 shp) for continuous running because of limitations in the existing transmission, but the extra reliability and use of more readily available kerosene makes the conversion from piston power worthwhile. Air arms convinced of this include those of Argentina, Thailand and Indonesia. Sikorsky produced 146 conversion kits for what is known as the S-58T before transferring rights to California Helicopter Parts Inc. in 1981. Refurbished S-58s with either an R-1820 or PT6Ts are also available in several specialized models from Orlando Helicopter Airways.

British licensee

In the UK Westland purchased a USN HSS-1 as a pattern for the Wessex. After initial trials, begun on 11 August 1956 with the R-1820 powerplant, the helicopter took to the air on the power of an 820-kW (1,100-shp) Napier Gazelle NGa.11 on 17 May 1957, original plans to fit a turboshaft adaptation of the Rolls-Royce Dart having been abandoned. Soon progressing to the 1081 kW (1,450 shp) of a Gazelle Mk 161, the helicopter was accepted by the Royal Navy to meet Naval Requirement NR/AN/43 (Specification HAS 170) for a shipboard anti-submarine patrol machine. Production followed under the designation Wessex HAS.Mk 1,

this becoming the world's first quantity-built helicopter with a free gas turbine.

Particular advantages for the Fleet Air Arm were that the Wessex could carry both dipping sonar and offensive weapons such as homing torpedoes; be off the deck in 45 seconds from a cold start; and carry 16 troops or 1814 kg (4,000 lb) of cargo, internally or underslung, as an alternative to ASW equipment. Furthermore, it freed operating ships of the disliked and dangerous requirement to carry petrol in bulk.

Crewed by a pilot, co-pilot, observer and sonar operator, the Wessex HAS.Mk 1 began service trials in April 1960 and within a few years was operating from the stern platforms of 'County' class destroyers (so making more space aboard carriers for fixed-wing aircraft). Fitted with Ryan APN-97A Doppler radar and Lewis Newmark Mk 19 autostabilizer, the Wessex could transition to hover and remain above a predetermined spot in all weathers, either dunking its sonar or operating the self-contained winch unit which was an optional fitment above the cabin door (starboard side). Operated by a hydraulic motor with epicyclic gearing, clutch and a freewheel mode, the winch featured a 32.3-m (106-ft) cable having a maximum load of 272 kg (600 lb).

A significant shortcoming of the Wessex HAS.Mk 1 was the lack of automatic tracking equipment for accurate position-keeping out of sight of ships or the shoreline. That was rectified in the Wessex HAS.Mk 3, the first of whose three prototypes flew on 3 November 1964. In addition to what was then an all-British avionics fit, the Mk 3 possessed an uprated Gazelle NGa.22 Mk 165 of 1193 kW (1,600 shp) and search and secondary radar in a prominent spine dome, prompting immediate adoption of the nickname 'Camel'. Forty 'production' Mk 3s were acquired through conversion of Mk 1 airframes, these being the first RN helicopters capable of performing virtually all aspects of their ASW mission, from take-off to positioning for landing, entirely under automatic control. Sup-

The Queen's Flight operates a pair of Wessex HCC.Mk 4s to supplement its fixed-wing British Aerospace 146s and Andovers. They are comprehensively equipped and specially furnished for their Royal duties.

planted by Westland Sea King and Westland Lynx helicopters, the last Mk 3s were withdrawn from service in January 1984.

The 'Junglie'

Additionally charged with transporting Royal Marine Commandos to their beach-head assaults and sustaining them with supplies after landing, the FAA ordered 101 transport models of the helicopter, designated Wessex HU.Mk 5. The prototype, first flown on 31 May 1963, was based on the RAF's Mk 2 (see below) and thus reflected the change of powerplant to a coupled pair of Rolls-Royce/Bristol Gnomes. Service trials began in December 1963, and the type replaced the stripped-out Mk 1s previously used for support in such operations as the Borneo anti-guerrilla campaign. (It should be borne in mind that even mark numbers were reserved for the RAF, and thus progressed independently of the navy's sequence.)

In the transport role the Wessex equipped four front-line squadrons (845 to 848) at their peak, plus training unit, 707 Squadron. They flew from ordinary carriers, helicopter carriers and purpose-designed assault ships, accompanying the fleet wherever and whenever Commandos were required. Wessex HU.Mk 5s have now been largely replaced by Sea King HC.Mk 4s, which inherited their nickname of 'Junglies' (in an allusion to the dark green camouflage scheme introduced in 1969-70). The survivors remain in training and transport roles, additionally having replaced the aged Mk 1s on SAR tasking.

The yellow-painted Wessex HC.Mk 2s of No. 22 Squadron have a primary role of providing military SAR cover, but most 'customers' are civilian holidaymakers, mountaineers, sailors and seamen.

Apart from a homing torpedo (Mk 44 or Mk 46) on each side of the fuselage, all naval Wessex helicopters have possessed the ability to undertake air-to-surface missions with machine-guns (externally mounted and/or in the cabin doorway), 2-in (50.8-mm) rocket pods or up to four Aérospatiale (Nord) AS.11 wire-guided missiles. These were put to good use when the Wessex went to war in 1982.

No less than 54 transport Mk 5s and just two Mk 3s were deployed during hostilities with Argentina in the Falklands war, six of the former being lost when their transport ship, the *Atlantic Conveyor*, was sunk by an Exocet missile. Two more crashed on South Georgia in a snowstorm attempting to extricate an SAS party under indescribably hazardous conditions, but a radar-equipped 737 Squadron HAS.Mk 3 was able to rescue all the stranded personnel in a remarkable feat of airmanship and navigation.

The same aircraft used its radar on another occasion to detect an Argentine submarine on the surface, where it was crippled by Mk 11 depth charges before Westland Wasps armed with AS.12 missiles caused further damage, leading directly to the boat's capture. 845 Squadron, flying Mk 5s, launched two AS.12s at an Argentine HQ in Port Stanley town hall, narrowly missing it but damaging an intelligence centre in the requisitioned police station next door. Other 'Junglies'

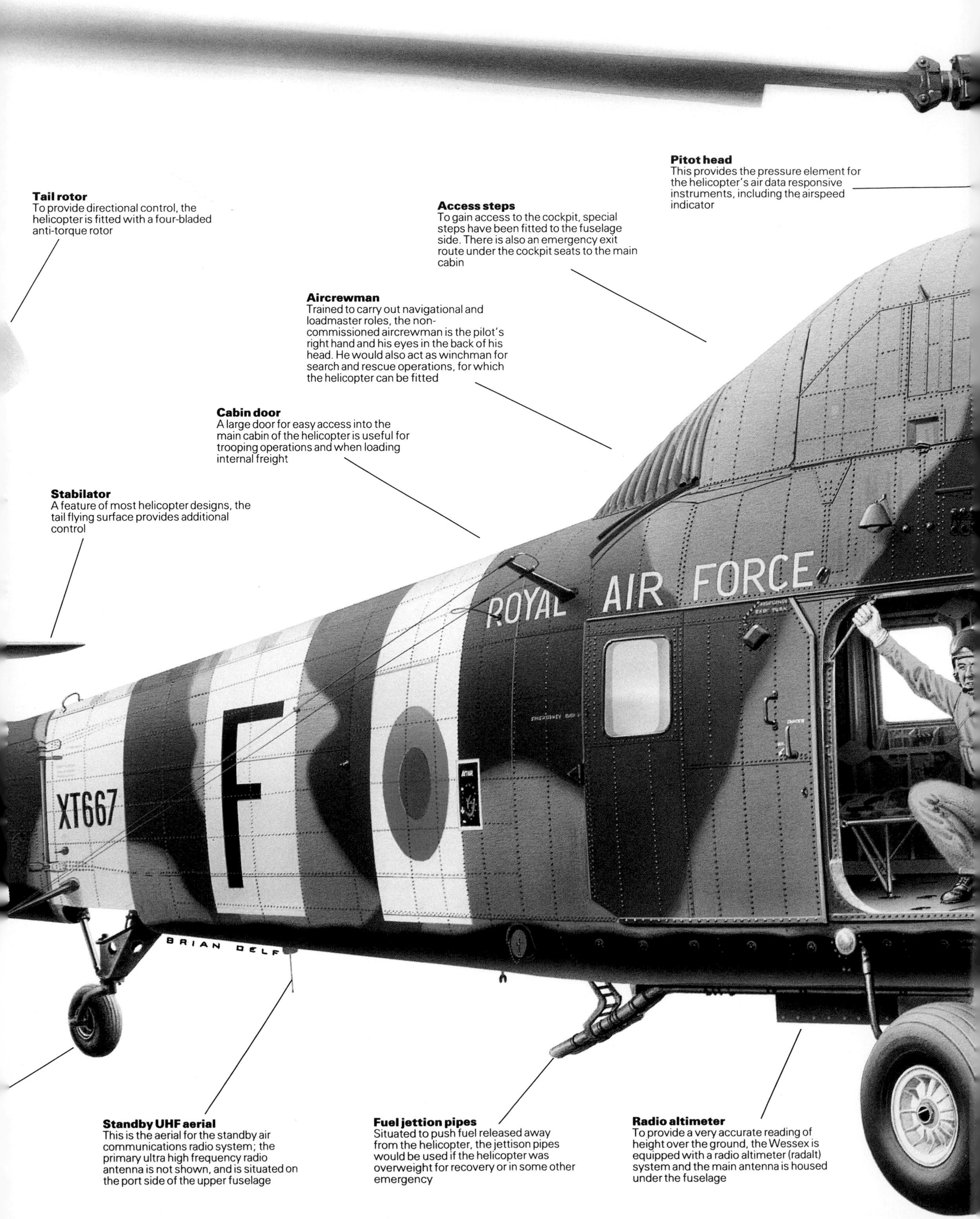

Tail rotor
To provide directional control, the helicopter is fitted with a four-bladed anti-torque rotor

Pitot head
This provides the pressure element for the helicopter's air data responsive instruments, including the airspeed indicator

Access steps
To gain access to the cockpit, special steps have been fitted to the fuselage side. There is also an emergency exit route under the cockpit seats to the main cabin

Aircrewman
Trained to carry out navigational and loadmaster roles, the non-commissioned aircrewman is the pilot's right hand and his eyes in the back of his head. He would also act as winchman for search and rescue operations, for which the helicopter can be fitted

Cabin door
A large door for easy access into the main cabin of the helicopter is useful for trooping operations and when loading internal freight

Stabilator
A feature of most helicopter designs, the tail flying surface provides additional control

ROYAL AIR FORCE

F

XT667

BRIAN DELF

Standby UHF aerial
This is the aerial for the standby air communications radio system; the primary ultra high frequency radio antenna is not shown, and is situated on the port side of the upper fuselage

Fuel jettion pipes
Situated to push fuel released away from the helicopter, the jettison pipes would be used if the helicopter was overweight for recovery or in some other emergency

Radio altimeter
To provide a very accurate reading of height over the ground, the Wessex is equipped with a radio altimeter (radalt) system and the main antenna is housed under the fuselage

Westland Wessex HC.Mk 2
No. 28 Squadron
Royal Air Force

Anti-collision light
To enable the helicopter to stand out against any landscape, it is fitted with orange anti-collision lights which are generally illuminated when the engines are running

No. 28 Squadron badge
The Pegasus and fasces (Italian symbol of authority) are representative of the unit's previous existences; it became a helicopter unit in March 1968

IFF housing
In certain locations, the helicopter is fitted with IFF (Identification Friend or Foe)

HF radio antenna
Stretching across the rear of the starboard fuselage is the high-frequency (HF) radio antenna; the system is used for long-range air-to-ground non-secure communications

Identification panels
To increase the rapid recognition of the Hong Kong-based Wessex against the local background in this non-tactical area, white-painted recognition panels have been adopted

Tailwheel
The traditional rugged rear landing gear of the tactical transport helicopter can absorb the shock of relatively heavy landings

←DANGER

flew observation flights and proved a vital element in the unceasing battle to provide forward troops with sufficient supplies to sustain their advance. Two squadrons, 847 and 848, were temporarily re-formed from training and reserve aircraft for this role.

RAF model

Of all the Wessex helicopters remaining in service, the best known and most highly regarded are the yellow-painted Wessex HC.Mk 2s of the RAF's SAR flights. A central aspect of the RAF Wessex is the additional safety margin obtained by the use of a pair of Gnome Mk 110/111 turboshaft engines. Though limited to a joint output at the rotor head of 1156kW (1,550shp), each engine is capable of delivering 1007kW (1,350shp) alone if its companion fails. The prototype HC.Mk 2 (converted from an HAS.Mk 1) first flew on 18 January 1962, the model entering service in the army support role in February 1964 in satisfaction of Army Operational Requirement 325.

RAF Wessex helicopters functioned in the UK and West Germany, additionally equipping a squadron in the Arabian Gulf area until 1971. Today their operational 'beat' has extended to Hong Kong for general support duties. In Cyprus, No. 84 Squadron provides SAR cover for the UK armament practice base at Akrotiri and patrols the UN-controlled frontier between Greek and Turkish areas of the island. Since 1985, No. 84 has been issued with an RAF adaptation of surplus FAA aircraft, designated Wessex HU.Mk 5C.

Wessex helicopters also play a significant role in security operations in Northern Ireland, where No. 72 Squadron has been based since November 1981 with over 20 helicopters. Having a far greater capacity than army helicopters, Wessex helicopters are used to airlift troops for no-notice searches and spot-checks. They have come under fire from the IRA on more than one occasion, notably when airlifting army casualties from a bomb explosion and ambush at Ronan Point.

British-based SAR operations began in September 1974 when 'D' Flight of No. 72 Squadron formed at Manston with a pair of Wessex helicopters adorned in yellow, rather than the dull green and grey camouflage. No. 22 Squadron assumed responsibility for all RAF Wessex SAR, receiving its first aircraft in May 1976 as Whirlwind HAR.Mk 10 replacements. Currently some 18 are in service with No. 22 Squadron's five detachments around the coast, partnered by the Sea Kings of No. 202 Squadron and to a lesser extent by the naval models of both types. Their winches have a 91.4m (300ft) cable with a maximum load limit of 272kg (600lb).

The Wessex has the advantage of being easier to manoeuvre in confined spaces than the Sea King, but it has only one-third the radius of action: 185km (115 miles) on its 1409 litres (310 Imp gal) of standard internal tankage, although a 1000-litre (220-Imp gal) tank can be quickly installed in the cabin for longer flights with a smaller payload. Each SAR detachment maintains one aircraft at 15-minute readiness and a second at 60-minute readiness during the day, but only

one on 45-minute stand-by at night. Space limitations prevent full justice being given to the exploits of the Wessex SAR helicopters and their crews, and it must suffice to say only that the many awards for bravery by helicopter crews are an indication of the hazardous conditions under which they are often called to operate.

In the training role, 10 Wessex HC.Mk 2s serve No. 2 FTS at RAF Shawbury, where helicopter pilots receive instruction. The course lasts 26 weeks, during which 75 hours are flown on Aérospatiale Gazelles and 50 more on Wessexes. Specific training in rescue techniques is provided at RAF Valley by the SAR Training Squadron, which converted from Whirlwinds in January 1981.

The RAF is also responsible for a pair of VVIP Wessex HCC.Mk 4s delivered in June 1969 and basically similar to the Mk 2, except that they are operated from RAF Benson by The Queen's Flight. In fact, HM Queen Elizabeth seldom flies by helicopter, although most other members of the royal family regularly use the Wessex and several of the princes (father and sons) are qualified rotary-wing pilots.

From the 378 Wessexes of all types built (including 16 civil Series 60 aircraft which undertook pioneering work in developing the oil support organization in the North Sea) 44 were direct exports. Of these, only 14 of the 27 Wessex

No. 28 Squadron is based in the Crown Colony of Hong Kong, and is tasked with supporting the British garrison and Hong Kong Police for anti-illegal immigrant duties, firefighting, air/sea recue and medevac tasks.

Australian Wessex HAS.Mk 31Bs of No. 816 Squadron are seen on board HMAS Tobruk. They are now used for utility duties, having been replaced in the anti-submarine role by Westland Sea Kings during 1976.

HAS.Mk 31s delivered to Australia from August 1962 onwards remain with their original owner. Based on the Mk 1, but powered by an uprated Gazelle, these have been converted to Mk 31B standard with improved ASW systems, a plan to install twin Gnomes having fallen victim to financial constraints. Following receipt of Sea Kings in 1976 for basing aboard the now-retired carrier HMAS *Melbourne*, the Royal Australian Navy Wessexes were reassigned to SAR and training with 817 Squadron. In February 1984 their tasks were expanded when the survivors transferred to newly-formed 816 Squadron, adding army support to their former duties.

Retirement for the RAN helicopters is not far distant; those nearer home have a longer career stretching ahead, plans for their replacement having yet to be decided. An American now regarded as a naturalized British citizen, the Wessex has lost its anti-submarine task, but remains highly active in the transport and rescue role. Royalty, soldiery, casualty – the Wessex carries them all.

Glossary

ASW Anti-Submarine Warfare
FAA Fleet Air Arm
FTS Flying Training School
SAR Search and Rescue
SAS Special Air Service

S-58 and Wessex in service

Wessex

United Kingdom

The Wessex is used in large numbers by the Royal Air Force, for training and SAR in this country and as a front-line support helicopter in Northern Ireland, Hong Kong and Cyprus. Most Royal Navy Wessex are now used for SAR, communications and training, and only one squadron remains operational in the commando assault support role. Small numbers are in use with various test establishments, operated by the MoD (Procurement Executive).

Royal Air Force

No. 22 Squadron
Re-equipped: May 1976
Bases: RAF Finningley (HQ), RAF Chivenor ('A' Flight), RAF Leuchars ('B' Flight), RAF Valley ('C' Flight), RAF Leconfield ('D' Flight) and RAF Manston ('E' Flight)
Task: SAR
Equipment: Wessex HC.Mk 2 XR497, XR504, XS675, XT604, XV730

No. 28 Squadron
Re-equipped: January 1972
Base: RAF Sek Kong, Hong Kong
Task: SAR and support
Equipment: Wessex HC.Mk 2 XR508 'D', XR528 'A', XT667 'F', XT673 'G', XT678 'H'

No. 72 Squadron
Re-equipped: August 1964 (at Odiham)
Base: RAF Aldergrove (from 12 November 1981)
Task: army support
Equipment: Wessex HC.Mk 2 XR511 'L', XR517 'N', XT607 'P', XV719 'B', XV725 'C'

No. 84 Squadron
Re-equipped: 1 March 1982 (Mk 2)
Base: RAF Akrotiri, Cyprus
Task: SAR ('A' Flight), United

Nations support ('B' Flight)
Equipment: Wessex HU.Mk 5C (since September 1984) XS485, XS498, XS518, XT463 (only)

No. 2 Flying Training School
Re-equipped: September 1977 (Mk 3)
Base: RAF Shawbury
Task: Pilot training
Equipment: Wessex HC.Mk 2 (from December 1980) XR505 'WA', XR519 'WC', XS677 'WK', XT672 'WE', XV722 'WH'

SAR Training Squadron
Re-equipped: January 1981
Base: RAF Valley
Task: SAR aircrew training
Equipment: Wessex HC.Mk 2 (pooled with No. 22 Squadron)

The Queen's Flight
Re-equipped: 25 June 1969
Base: RAF Benson
Task: VVIP transport
Equipment: Wessex HCC.Mk 4 XV732, XV733 (only, plus BAe 146 and Andover)

No. 28 Squadron's Wessex helicopters wear broad white recognition stripes on nose and tail boom for conspicuity in poor weather conditions. These aircraft provide mobility for British forces and the Hong Kong Police.

The two Wessex HCC.Mk 4s of The Queen's Flight wear a smart red and blue colour scheme, derived from the colours worn by King's Flight aircraft before the war. Tradition goes hand in hand with flight safety, since the colours give high conspicuity.

Royal Navy

707 Squadron
Formed: 9 December 1964
Base: RNAS Yeovilton
Task: assault transport training
Equipment: Wessex HU.Mk 5 XS507 'RN' (only, plus eight Sea King HC.Mk 4s)

771 Squadron
Formed: 23 June 1967 (at Portland)
Base: RNAS Culdrose (from 4 September 1974)
Task: SAR
Equipment: Wessex HU.Mk 5 XS484 '821/CU', XS523 '824/CU', XT471 '826/CU', XT474 '820/CU', XT769 '823/CU'

772 Squadron
Formed: 6 September 1974
Base: RNAS Portland (Detachment: Lee-on-Solent from 14 February 1983)
Task: SAR
Equipment: Wessex HU.Mk 5 XS492 '623/PO', XS510 '626/PO', XT458 '622/PO', XT468 '628/PO', XT485 '621/PO'

845 Squadron
Re-equipped: January 1966
Base: RNAS Yeovilton
Task: Commando assault support
Equipment: Wessex HU.Mk 5 XS513 'YE', XS516 'YQ', XT453 'YA', XT484 'YH', XT765 'YJ'

Australia

The Wessex HAS.Mk 31A was originally purchased for the Royal Australian Navy in the early 1960s, a number being converted to the HAS.Mk 31B standard by de Havilland Australia. The helicopters served with 817 Squadron until 1976, when they were replaced by Sea King HAS.Mk 50s. Following the demise of Australian carrier aviation, 14 form a utility support squadron (HC-723) at RANAS Nowra, one helicopter being lost at an air display in 1985.

Royal Australian Navy

816 Squadron (HU-816)
Formed: 9 February 1984
Base: HMAS *Albatross*, Nowra, NSW
Task: SAR, training and army support

Equipment: Wessex HAS.Mk 31B N7-200 '810', N7-205 '815', N7-216 '826', N7-218 '828', N7-224 '834'

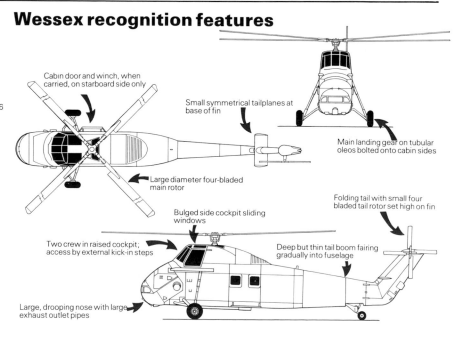

Australian Wessex are maritime aircraft and wear a naval colour scheme. They are now used solely for SAR, training and support duties, but retain their ASW radar hump. They serve with No. 816 Squadron, based at HMAS Albatross, Nowra.

Specification: Wessex HC.Mk 2

Rotors
Main rotor diameter	17.07 m	(56 ft 0 in)
Tail rotor diameter	2.90 m	(9 ft 6 in)
Main rotor disc area	228.81 m²	(2,463.0 sq ft)

Fuselage and tail unit
Accommodation	pilot and aircrewman; eight stretchers, or 12 paratroops, or 16 troops	
Length of fuselage	14.74 m	(48 ft 4.5 in)
Height overall	4.93 m	(16 ft 2 in)

Landing gear
Fixed tailwheel type
Wheel track	3.66 m	(12 ft 0 in)

Weights
Basic operating	3767 kg	(8,304 lb)
Maximum take-off	6123 kg	(13,500 lb)
Maximum external load	1814 kg	(4,000 lb)
Payload (with maximum fuel)	1117 kg	(2,462 lb)
Internal fuel load	1100 kg	(2,425 lb)

Powerplant
One each Rolls-Royce/Bristol Gnome Mk 110 and Mk 111 turboshaft engines
Normal rating, coupled	1156 kW	(1,550 shp)
Maximum single-engine rating	1007 kW	(1,350 shp)

Wessex recognition features

Cabin door and winch, when carried, on starboard side only

Small symmetrical tailplanes at base of fin

Main landing gear on tubular oleos bolted onto cabin sides

Large diameter four-bladed main rotor

Folding tail with small four bladed tail rotor set high on fin

Bulged side cockpit sliding windows

Two crew in raised cockpit; access by external kick-in steps

Deep but thin tail boom fairing gradually into fuselage

Large, drooping nose with large exhaust outlet pipes

Main rotor system
The Wessex HC.Mk 2 is fitted with a
conventional metal-bladed main rotor

letter
on the white
nels are individual
ters used to distinguish
specially in radio
, rather than using the
erial)

ngine exhaust
he two coupled Gnome engines of the
rbine-powered Wessex exhaust
rough the large duct on the starboard
de of the forward fuselage

IFF aerial
Part of the helicopter's friend or foe
identification system is carried in this
aerial housing

Engine compartment
Characterized by the large intake grille,
mounted in the hinged engine
compartment door, the helicopter is
powered by two Rolls-Royce Gnome
turboshaft engines situated in the nose

NO PUSH

Landing lamp housing
For non-tactical and general flight
operations, a retractable landing lamp is
carried in the helicopter's nose; control
is from the cockpit

atches
entially dangerous fire
art procedures, the
with special fire
ase of the engine
allow for rapid use of

Cockpit
Although fitted for two pilots, the standard operating procedure for the RAF Wessex (except in Northern Ireland) is one pilot (right-hand seat). Entry is through the sliding door

Cockpit windshield
Although not toughened against enemy action, the windshield is heated and has windscreen wipers. The position of the pilots' seats allows for a reasonable field of vision

Identificatio
Superimposed
identification p
identification le
the helicopter e
communication
tail number (or

E
T
t
t
s

Main landing wheel
The original design for the helicopter was for shipborne operations, and the main landing wheels have been stressed for such operations. This feature has also proved ideal for the tactical transport role

External lift gear
To assist in the carriage of unusual loads, especially during re-supply operations, the Wessex is fitted with a cargo hook on the fuselage bottom

Doppler system
Under the forward fuselage is the housing for the helicopter's Doppler navigational system

Firefighting
To prevent a po
during engine s
Wessex is fitte
hatches at the
compartment t
extinguishers

Sikorsky S-58

Argentine Air Force (Fuerza Aérea Argentina)

Although the navy's sole HSS-1 (0407) was lost in 1961, the air force possesses two ex-West German helicopters converted by Carson to S-58T standard. Serialled H-01 and -02, they are assigned to the president and operated by the Departmento de Aviones Presidencialles, I Brigada Aérea, at El Palomar, Buenos Aires.

Costa Rica

One of two S-58T helicopters remains with the Guardia Civil, a paramilitary force which formed an air wing in 1964. The helicopter bears the civilian registration TI-SPJ, but is used for border patrols. The two helicopters were delivered from surplus US stocks.

Haiti

Following the removal of the Duvalier dictatorship in 1986, the exact status of the Haitian air force has been impossible to check, but until the coup two S-58Ts were being operated for VIP transport, whilst three older S-58/H-34Js were used for troop transport.

Indonesian Armed Forces — Air Force (Tentara Nasional Indonesia – Angkatan Udara)

Indonesia acquired a number of UH-34Ds during the 1970s, serials beginning at H-3401. Twelve of these have been converted by California Helicopter to S-58T standard.

Iraq

Although the conflict between Iraq and Iran has meant that accurate aircraft inventories have not been forthcoming, there are reports that some six of the original nine or 12 Wessex Mk 52 helicopters remain in service. Original serials were between 558 to 595. No reliable details are available.

Nicaraguan Air Force (Fuerza Aérea Sandinista)

Following the 1979 revolution, only one of the original 12 CH-34As and S-58Ts, bearing the serial 51, has been reported in service with the re-formed air arm.

Republic of China Air Force (Chung-Kuo Kung Chuan)

Approximately seven CH-34 Choctaws are believed to remain in service in Taiwan as survivors of MDAP deliveries from the US

This elderly Sikorsky H-34J of Haiti was in use for troop transport duties at least until the fall of the Duvalier regime, but its current status is uncertain.

This US-surplus S-58 serves with the Gardia Civil, Costa Rica's paramilitary police force. The aircraft is used for border patrol duties but wears a civil registration.

Royal Thai Air Force

In September 1977, Thai-Am Inc. began conversion of 18 CH-34Cs to S-58T standard for the RTAF. These currently serve No. 201 Squadron of the 2nd Wing at Lop Buri, supporting counter-insurgency operations. Serial numbers include 20133 and 20153

Uruguayan Naval Aviation (Aviacion Naval Uruguaya)

Deliveries to Uruguay through MDAP comprised two SH-34Gs and four SH-34Js, including one for spares. Two (A-063 and A-064) remain in use at Base Aéronaval 2 'Capitan Curbelo', Laguna la Sauce

Westland Wessex HAS.M cutaway drawing key

1. Tail navigation lights
2. Anti-collision light
3. Cooling air grilles
4. Tail rotor gearbox fairing
5. Final drive right-angle gearbox

6. Tail rotor hub mechanism
7. Blade pitch angle control linkage
8. Four-bladed tail rotor
9. Handgrip

10. Tail rotor drive shaft
11. Tail pylon construction
12. Fixed horizontal tailplane construction
13. Ground handling grips
14. Cooling air grilles
15. Bevel drive gearbox
16. Port tailplane
17. Folding tail pylon hinge joint
18. Tail pylon latching mechanism
19. Tailwheel shock absorber strut
20. Castoring tailwheel
21. Hinged axle beam
22. Mooring ring
23. Aerial mast
24. HF aerial cable
25. Rotor blade trailing edge rib construction
26. Tip fairing
27. Blade tracking weight
28. Blade balance weights
29. D-section aluminium blade spar
30. Transponder aerial
31. Tailcone frame and stringer construction
32. Tail rotor control cables
33. Tail rotor transmission shaft
34. Upper IFF aerial
35. UHF aerial
36. Tailcone/fuselage joint frame
37. Equipment bay bulkhead
38. Dorsal radome
39. Search radar scanner
40. Radome mounting structure
41. Port side cabin heater
42. Electrical system equipment
43. Fuel delivery piping
44. Rear fuel tank group filler cap
45. Pressure refuelling connection
46. Mk 46 torpedo
47. External fuel tank, capacity 454 litres (100 Imp gal)
48. External cable ducting
49. Aft crashproof fuel cells; total fuel capacity 1209 litres (266 Imp gal)
50. Cabin window/escape hatch
51. Cabin rear bulkhead
52. Curtained aperture to equipment bay
53. Vent piping
54. Oil cooler air exit louvres
55. Rotor head rear aerodynamic fairing
56. Oil cooler
57. Rear fairing access panels
58. Cabin heating ducting
59. Smoke marker stowage
60. Marker launch tube cover
61. Cabin floor panelling
62. External stores carrier
63. Stores pylon fixing
64. Dipping sonar
65. Floor beam construction

Sikorsky S-58/Westland Wessex variants

Sikorsky CH-34A: originally designated **H-34A** and powered by one 1137-kW (1,525-hp) Wright Cyclone R-1820-84; 359 to US Army (plus 21 ex-USN HUS-1s); disposals included 12 to Nicaragua (serialled 517-527 and 519 No. 2) of which five became S-58T
Sikorsky VH-34A: VIP conversion of CH-34A
Sikorsky CH-34B: (ex **H-34B**) minor modifications to CH-34A
Sikorsky CH-34C: (ex **H-34C**) minor modifications to CH-34A, including 21 remanufactured for transfer to South Vietnam (some further transferring to Laos); others to Taiwan; new production of 75 (originally ordered as HSS-1N) for West German army (150733-807), of which 24 (150756-759, 150778-797) were diverted to Israel
Sikorsky HH-34D: SAR conversion of HUS-1 for USAF Reserve
Sikorsky LH-34D: (ex **HUS-1L**) winterized conversion of HUS-1; four only
Sikorsky UH-34D: (ex **HUS-1**) 606 for US Marines including 23 later exported via USAF (e.g. Indonesian air force H-251 and Netherlands navy 134)
Sikorsky VH-34D: (ex **HUS-1Z**) seven VIP conversions of HUS-1
Sikorsky UH-34E: (ex **HUS-1A**) 40 conversions of HUS-1 with pontoons
Sikorsky HH-34F: (ex **HUS-1G**) six conversions of HUS-1 for USCG
Sikorsky SH-34G: (ex **HSS-1**) three prototypes and 215 production helicopters for USN and export, including one to UK (XL722), six to Brazil (8050-8055), six to Italy (MM80163-164, MM80237, 143899, 143940 and 143949), two to West Germany (152188 and 155290) and two to Uruguay (A-061 and A-062)
Sikorsky VH-34G: (ex **HSS-1Z**) VIP conversions of HSS-1
Sikorsky SH-34H: (ex **HSS-1F**) single trial conversion with two General Electric YT58 turboshaft engines
Sikorsky HH-34J: 14 ex-USN SG-34Js transferred to USAF for SAR
Sikorsky SH-34J: (ex **HSS-1N**) all-weather HSS-1; prototype converted from HSS-1; 122 built for USN (including four later to Uruguay as A-063 to -066), plus 45 for export (comprising Chile 51-53; Italy 149082-087, 150821-822 and 153617-622; Netherlands 135-145; and West Germany 150808-819, 151729-731 and 152380-381)
Sikorsky S-58: direct purchases made by French army, navy and air force totalling 135 H-34As and HSS-1s (including 50 in kit form for assembly by Sud-Est Aviation) c/ns used as serials between 58-248 and 58-1376; by Canadian air force of six CH-34As (9630-9635); and by Japan of eight HSS-1s (8551-8558) and nine HSS-1Ns (8561-8569); seven ex-SABENA S-58Cs went to the Belgian air force as B9-B15
Sud-Est/Sikorsky S-58: licensed manufacture of 135 H-34A/HSS-1s serialled SA51-SA185, and including 39 (SA119-150, 181-185) to SH-34G standard of which SA145-146 and 183-185 went to the Belgian air force as UH-34Gs B4-B8 (B8 was the last European military S-58, withdrawn on 19 July 1986); two experimentally re-engined with two Turboméca Bi-Bastan turboshafts, each of 1000 kW (1,341 shp), the first being flown on 5 October 1962 in SA76
Sikorsky S-58T: H-34 re-engined with 1122-kW (1,505-shp) Pratt & Whitney Canada PT6T turboshafts and first flown August 1970; conversions by California, Carson and Orlando (no known military contracts for Orlando Airliner and Orlando Flying Armoured Personnel Carrier); users include Argentina, Costa Rica Public Securiy Force (TI-SPI/SPJ now withdrawn), Indonesia, Nicaragua and Thailand

Orlando S-58: refurbished H-34 retaining Wright Cyclone power, also offered in Agricultural, Heavy Lift and Heli-Camper models; six CH-34Cs supplied to Haiti, including H-1 to -4 and H-8, of which two (including H-4) are to S-58T standard
Westland Wessex: one Sikorsky prototype, XL722 (ex HSS-1 141602) and three UK-built development aircraft, XL727-729; powered by Napier Gazelle turboshaft
Westland Wessex HAS.Mk 1: production of 137 for FAA with 1081-kW (1,450-shp) Gazelle Mk 161; XM299-301, XM326-331, XM832-845, XM868-876, XM915-931, XP103-118, XP137-160, XS115-128, XS149-154 and XS862-889 for 700H, 706, 737, 814, 815, 819, 820, 826, 829 and 845 Squadrons, base and carrier SAR flights
Westland Wessex HC.Mk 2: converted prototype (XM299) and production of 72 for RAF with 1156-kW (1,550-shp) Rolls-Royce/Bristol-Siddeley Gnome Mk 110/110 turboshaft combination; XR588, XR498-511, XR515-529, XS674-679, XT601-607, XT667-681 and XV719-731 for Nos 18, 22, 28, 72, 78, and 84 Squadrons, plus No. 2 FTS, No. 240 OCU, HOCF, IFTU, SARTS and WTF; (XR525 and XT675 loaned to Oman air force 1974-5)
Westland Wessex HAS.Mk 3: updated Mk 1 with 1193-kW (1,600-shp) Gazelle Mk 165 and avionics changes, including spine radar; three new-build pre-series aircraft (XT255-257), two pre-series conversions (XM836 and XM871) and 40 'production' conversions (XM834, XS153, XS121, XS119, XM870, XM918, XM919, XP105, XP110, XM872, XM916, XP137, XM837, XM844, XM927, XP139, XM838, XM833, XP150, XP147, XS127, XM328, XP143, XM327, XS122, XM331, XM923, XP118, XS862, XS126, XM920, XP138, XP116, XP156, XP153, XP103, XP104, XS149, XP142 and XP140, in order) for 706, 737, 814, 819, 820 and 826 Squadrons
Westland Wessex HCC.Mk 4: two VIP aircraft (XV732-733) based on Mk 2 for The Queen's Flight
Westland Wessex HU.Mk 5: naval assault/transport based on Mk 2 (Gnome engines); 101 built as XS241, XS479-500, XS506-523, XT448-487 and XT755-774 for 700V, 707, 772, 781, 845, 846, 847 and 848 Squadrons as well as ships' and base flights; XT452 and XT478 transferred to Bangladesh as WA274 and WA300
Westland Wessex Mk 6: projected Mk 2/5 replacement to Naval Staff Target 365 of 1965; extended nose and cabin, upswept tail boom, stub wings and sponsons (holding additional fuel); rebuild (£45,000) and new-built (£208,000) options considered before abandonment
Westland Wessex HAS.Mk 31: 27 helicopters for Royal Australian Navy, based on Mk 1 but with 1148-kW (1,540-shp) Gazelle Mk 162; serialled WA200-226, later N7-200 to -226; avionics updated to **Wessex HAS.Mk 31B** standard; projected twin-Gnome conversion not implemented
Westland Wessex Mk 51: projected export version; not built
Westland Wessex Mk 52: 12 for Iraq, based on Mk 2; delivered April 1964 to February 1965; serialled 588-599
Westland Wessex Mk 53: three for Ghana, based on Mk 2; serialled G630-G632
Westland Wessex Mk 54: two for Brunei, based on Mk 2; serialled 106 and 101
Westland Wessex Srs 60: civil utility version, 16 sold, plus conversions from Brunei and Ghana military aircraft

Performance:

Maximum speed at 6123 kg (13,500 lb)	115 kts	(212 km/h; 132 mph)
Maximum cruising speed at 6123 kg (13,500 lb)	105 kts	(195 km/h; 121 mph)
Service ceiling	10,000 ft	(3050 m)
Hovering ceiling (OGE)	4,000 ft	(1220 m)
Range with standard fuel	538 km	(334 miles)
Range with standard fuel and maximum auxiliary fuel and 10 per cent reserves	770 km	(478 miles)
Initial climb rate, inclined	1,650 ft	(503 m) per minute
vertical	630 ft	(192 m) per minute

External load

- Aérospatiale SA 330L Puma 3000 kg
- Bell UH-1H Iroquois 2000 kg E
- Mil Mi-4 'Hound' 2000 kg E
- Westland Wessex HU.Mk 5 1814 kg
- Sikorsky Choctaw 1500 kg E
- PZL
- Swidnik (Mil) Mi-2 800 kg
- Westland Whirlwind HAR.Mk 10 800 kg E

Initial rate of climb, feet per minute

- Westland Wessex HU.Mk 5 1,650 ft
- Bell UH-1H Iroquois 1,600 ft
- Aérospatiale SA 330L Puma 1,200 ft
- Westland Whirlwind HAR.Mk 10 1,200 ft
- Sikorsky S-58/CH-43A Choctaw 1,100 ft
- PZL Swidnik (Mil) Mi-2 885 ft
- Mil Mi-4 'Hound' not quoted

Maximum cruising speed at optimum altitude

- Aérospatiale SA 330L Puma 139 kts
- Westland Wessex HU.Mk 5 115 kts
- Mil Mi-4 'Hound' 113 kts
- Bell UH-1H Iroquois 110 kts
- PZL Swidnik (Mil) Mi-2 108 kts
- Sikorsky S-58/CH-43A Choctaw 106 kts
- Westland Whirlwind HAR.Mk 10 106 kts

Range with maximum payload

- Westland Wessex HU.Mk 5 628 km
- Aérospatiale SA 330L Puma 550 km
- Bell UH-1H Iroquois 511 km
- Westland Whirlwind HAR.Mk 10 480 km
- Sikorsky S-58/CH-43A Choctaw 400 km
- Mil Mi-4 'Hound' 200 km E
- PZL Swidnik (Mil) Mi-2 170 km (5% reserves)

Number of troops carried

- Aérospatiale SA 330L Puma 20
- Sikorsky S-58/CH-43A Choctaw 18
- Westland Wessex HU.Mk 5 16
- Bell UH-1H Iroquois 14
- Mil Mi-4 'Hound' 14
- Westland Whirlwind HAR.Mk 10 10
- PZL Swidnik (Mil) Mi-2 8

---

66 Cabin door
67 Seat mounting rails
68 Tactical navigator and sonar operator seats
69 Instrument consoles
70 Rescue hoist/winch
71 Gearbox mounting deck
72 Gearbox support struts
73 Rotor brake
74 Oil cooler fan
75 Gearbox deck access panels

76 Rotor head servo control units
77 Blade pitch control linkage
78 Torque scissor links
79 Blade drag damper
80 Hydraulic oil reservoir
81 Rotor head mechanism
82 Four-blade main rotor
83 Blade root attachment joints

92 Main landing gear leg strut attachment
93 Cabin door jettison lever
94 Sliding cabin door
95 Door latch
96 Shock absorber leg strut
97 Boarding step
98 Flotation bag inflation bottle
99 Starboard mainwheel
100 Flotation bag stowage
101 Mooring ring
102 Pivoted main axle beam
103 Step
104 Hydraulic brake pipe
105 Forward group of fuel cells
106 Fuel filler cap
107 Dipping sonar winch mechanism
108 Cockpit access steps

109 Bifurcated engine exhaust pipes, port and starboard
110 Cockpit floor level
111 External cable ducting
112 Handgrip
113 Rudder pedals
114 Instrument panel
115 Cyclic pitch control column
116 Collective pitch lever
117 Co-pilot's seat
118 Rotor brake control lever
119 Temperature gauge
120 Windscreen panels
121 Windscreen wipers
122 Instrument panel shroud

123 Windscreen de-icing fluid spray nozzle
124 Sloping cockpit front bulkhead
125 Engine/gearbox transmission shaft
126 Electrical equipment bay, radio and electronics bay on port side
127 Nose equipment bay access hatches
128 Cooling air scoop
129 Batteries (two)
130 Engine oil tank
131 Engine turbine section
132 Exhaust compartment firewalls

133 Ground power socket
134 Ventilating air intake
135 Starboard navigation light
136 Main axle beam mounting
137 Nose compartment framing
138 Engine bay access door
139 Throttle control linkage
140 Engine withdrawal rail
141 Engine mounting struts
142 Rolls-Royce (Napier) Gazelle 22 turboshaft engine
143 Engine bay ventilating air intake
144 Starter cartridge magazine

145 Hydraulic pump
146 Fire extinguisher bottles
147 Engine air inlet
148 Hinged nose cone access panel
149 Engine accessory equipment gearbox
150 Generator
151 Intake plenum
152 Retractable landing lamp
153 Lower IFF aerial

34 Cooling air grilles
35 Cockpit roof glazing
36 Overhead switch panel
37 Chart case
38 Servo motor switching control panel
39 Cockpit rear bulkhead
40 Pilot's seat
41 Sliding side window/entry hatch

© Pilot Press Ltd

53

The McDONNELL DOUGLAS AH-64 APACHE

Apache: Wild West Warrior

The ever-advancing science of military technology has ensured that the contemporary battlefield is no place for the vulnerable or weak-willed. Enter the Apache, tank-buster extraordinaire and a key element in the United States Army's modern-day fighting force. Like the tribe of Indian warriors, the Apache is ever-alert, always one step ahead in the fight, and ready at a moment's notice to bring its formidable firepower down on its hapless victims.

Destined to become an ever more familiar sight as the US Army's principle tank-busting helicopter, the AH-64A Apache is the final result of a long and tortuous search to find a dedicated attack helicopter to support the ground forces.

Ever since NATO was formed in 1949, the greatest disparity between its own forces and those of the Warsaw Pact has been in armour. There are too many differing estimates to quote any meaningfully, but there is no doubt that, for every NATO main battle tank, there are many on 'the other side'. Tank killing from the sky has thus become vitally important, but it has led to controversial aircraft. Can a helicopter, no matter how well protected, survive against armies with thousands of SAMs? For that matter, can a low-flying jet such as the Fairchild A-10A?

The American answer is obviously in the affirmative, because both types are very important in NATO's front line. In a brand-new plant at Mesa, Arizona, McDonnell Douglas Helicopter Company is turning out 12 AH-64A Apaches each month, and is fast approaching the half-way point in a production run of 675, all for the US Army. Clearly, this customer (and the Apache crews themselves) have no doubts about the ability of this very special helicopter to survive and kill tanks. Indeed, one cannot overlook the fact that the USSR's latest attack helicopter, the Mil Mi-28 'Havoc', appears to be almost a direct copy of the Apache!

The US Army began trying to procure a helicopter in this class over 20 years ago but the result, the Lockheed AH-56A Cheyenne, was eventually cancelled. In the Vietnam War the only dedicated attack helicopter was the Bell AH-1G Cobra, deployed in large numbers, but this lacked the vital ability to operate at night or in bad weather. Over the years various improved Cobras rectified some shortcomings, but the Army never lost sight of the fact that it really wanted a total capability that it did not possess. It wanted a helicopter that could survive in the face of at least some of the enemy's defences, and could detect, aim at and destroy every kind of battlefield target (fixed or moving, soft-skinned or heavily armoured) no matter what the time of day or weather.

Enter the Apache

This inevitably demands a rather large, powerful and expensive helicopter, and this time the Army determined to get it right. It picked not one finalist but two, issuing contracts on 22 June 1973 to Bell Helicopter Textron and to Hughes Helicopters. Bell's YAH-63 featured tricycle landing gear and put the gunner in the back seat and the pilot in the front. The Hughes YAH-64 had tailwheel landing gear and put the pilot in the back, considerably higher up than the co-pilot/gunner in the front seat. Hughes also put the sight sensors in the nose and the trainable gun farther back underneath, again the reverse of Bell's choice. The engines, General Electric T700s, were identical in both helicopters, but Hughes put them outside the fuselage in left and right pods driving via inclined shafts at the front.

The first YAH-64 flying prototype, called Air Vehicle 02, beat the deadline by one day to get into the air on 30 September 1975. By this time the design had changed in many respects, the most striking being the use of a T-tail (originally the all-moving tailplane had been low down on the slim tailboom). Over the next eight years (much longer than planned) the Apache was to change a lot more, but at last the first production helicopter emerged from the Mesa factory on 30 September 1983.

Visually the production Apache differs most notably from the first Apache in having the tailplane (horizontal stabilizer) back in the low position, though as the entire tail end has been twice redesigned it is not in its original location. The angle of the tailplane varies according to helicopter speed and pilot demand, the latter being passed through a powerful hydraulic boost system with back-up electric (fly-by-wire) signalling. Despite its size and weight, the Apache has had to meet severe demands for agility as well as all-round flight performance, a particu-

Though it is an awesome fighting machine, the Apache is designed to operate in the most hostile of battlefield scenarios. With this in mind, the helicopter has an excellent degree of manoeuvrability, with a roll rate of 100° per second.

larly stringent set of demands stipulating the vertical rate of climb with various weapons loads, even at high altitudes or on a hot day. Suffice to say none of today's Apache crews is complaining about lack of manoeuvrability.

Many of the Apache's design features are rather surprising. The most remarkable is the location of the sighting system and sensors which, as explained below, are grouped low down in the nose. Another is that the main rotor is not of the simple rigid type but fully articulated, with each blade attached via flapping (vertical) and drag (horizontal) hinges. At least the massive hub and hinges need little maintenance and no lubrication. More unusual is the design of each main-rotor blade, which has no fewer than five spars, made of stainless steel, lined and separated by glassfibre interleaving tubes. The rear of each blade is a honeycomb-filled composite. The wrap-around skins are of thin stainless steel, the number of laminations increasing rapidly towards the root. The result is a blade which has stayed intact even after taking hits from a Soviet 23-mm cannon, which no other helicopter blade has ever done.

The same kind of fail-safe 'survivable' structure is found everywhere that it matters, and in addition many vital areas are armoured. Both crew seats, for example, are surrounded at rear and sides by Kevlar plate, and critical parts of the transmission are surrounded by collars of ESR steel, which are proof against gunfire of up to 12.7-mm (0.5-in) calibre. Even the gearboxes are intended to 'survive battle damage', and all lubricated parts are designed to keep running for an hour after loss of lubricating oil.

Lumps and bumps

One of the most striking features of the Apache is the giant blister on each side of the fuselage under the cockpit windows. These house the numerous boxes containing the avionics, immediately accessible for checking or replacement simply by opening a large door on each side. Electric power for checking all items on the ground, and for starting the main engines, can be generated by a gas-turbine APU mounted immediately aft of the main rotor. Of course as far as possible all operating systems are at least duplicated,

with pipes and cables as widely separated as possible so that no single battle damage should knock out more than one.

From the start of design it was taken for granted that the winning AAH would carry rockets and missiles under stub wings and have a pivoted gun aimed by the CPG. One of the reasons for selection of the Hughes machine was that the company developed a special gun for this helicopter, and this gun has since demonstrated many good qualities including outstanding reliability. Known as the M230 Chain Gun, it has a unique rotating bolt which is externally powered and driven via a chain. This makes possible a simplified operating cycle, one feature of which is that each round is under complete positive control in space and time from the moment it reaches the gun. With a calibre of 30 mm, and able to fire Aden and DEFA ammunition as well as the US M789/799 type, the Chain Gun is fed from a giant box under the main rotor gearbox housing 1,200 rounds. It can fire from single shots up to 625 rounds per minute, and is aimed by the CPG via a Lear Siegler electronic control system. It can fire 100° to left or right and at any angle from 11° nose-up (the normal rest position) to 60° nose-down, and with extremely high accuracy.

The gun is known as the AWS. Though primarily used to knock out lightly armoured ground targets, and main-threat air defences, it can also serve in a self-protection role to destroy other aircraft, especially hostile helicopters. Until

The most ardent fan of the Apache would have to admit that it is never going to win an aviation beauty contest, but all the lumps and bumps have a purpose. Note the deflected tailplane, the angle of which influences the helicopter's speed.

the appearance of the Soviet 'Havoc' no other helicopter had so powerful a gun, and certainly not one with such precise control in all weathers. A feature of the electronic control is that it automatically re-aims the gun 10 times per second according to the CPG demand and the pointing angle of the sensor systems.

Missile muscle

The main offensive weapon against armour was originally to be the TOW missile, but long before the Apache entered service this was replaced by the bigger and more powerful AGM-114A Hellfire. Weighing 45.8 kg (101 lb), Hellfire can knock out any tank with one hit, and its pinpoint accuracy is virtually assured through its advanced laser guidance. As in semi-active radar homing guidance, the Hellfire automatically detects and flies towards any suitable laser light which it sees ahead. Such a light source, which to prevent confusion must be

This brute of a machine fairly bristles with ordnance, always ready to ruin an enemy tank crew's day. This awesome array includes up to 16 Hellfire anti-tank missiles, their use being slaved to the TADS/PNVS sensor package.

Air data probes
An air data sensor head is mounted on the mast (which is normally in less-disturbed airflow, giving an accurate dynamic pressure reading)

Side windows
Cockpit side windows are set in upward-hinged doors

Armoured seats
Crash-resistant Kevlar armoured seats are provided for both crew

UHF antenna

VHF antenna

Armoured windscreen
Two armoured glass windscreen panels are incorporated in the Teledyne Ryan canopy

Rockwell Hellfire
This AH-64 carries four precision-guided Hellfire anti-armour missiles, although up to 16 can be carried

McDonnell Douglas AH-64A Apache
6th Air Cavalry Combat Brigade
United States Army
Fort Hood Army Air Field, Texas

Front cockpit
The front cockpit is occupied by the CPG, or co-pilot/gunner, with the handling pilot sitting behind in the stepped rear seat. The two cockpits are separated by a transparent acrylic blast barrier and protected by lightweight boron armour shields

Night vision system
The PNVS (pilot's night vision system), consists of a stabilized FLIR (forward-looking infra-red) receiver for safe low flying at night

Forward-looking IR
The TADS (target acquisition designation sight) has a FLIR, forming the right-hand half of unit for night vision

Optical and TV trackers
The left hand half of the TADS consists of the TADS DTV (day television) and DVO (direct-view optics i.e. telescope), with a laser rangefinder and tracker, which share common optics

Rocket projectile
The folding-fin 2.75-in high velocity aircraft rocket can be fitted with high explosive or target marking warheads.

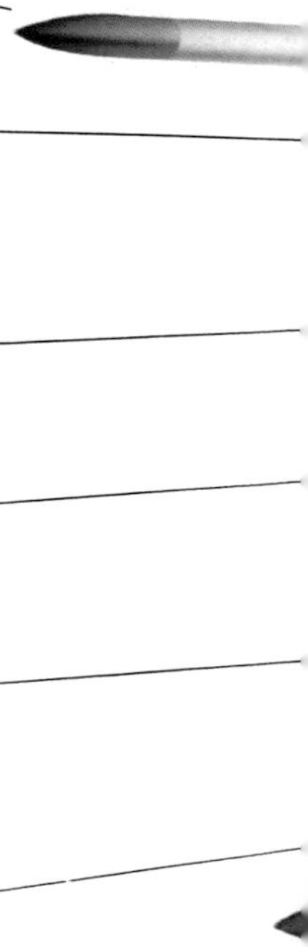

RWR
The Loral APR-39 (v) radar warning receiver antenna, warns whenever the helicopter is 'painted' by enemy radar. The pilot receives a warning on a CRT and in his headset

Avionics pods
Avionics pods give immediate access to all main avionics equipment bays (both sides)

Crashworthy gun mount
The gun mount is designed to collapse in a crash without injuring the crew

Cannon
The 30-mm calibre M230A-1 Chain Gun, with powered elevation and traverse, is slaved to sight systems. Normal rate of fire is 625 rounds per minute

Main undercarriage
Long-stroke main landing gears have low-pressure tyres and integral boarding steps

Magazine
The cannon magazine contains 1,200 rounds

coded to match the seeker in the missile, is provided by using a laser to designate each target. The designating laser can be that in the Apache itself, in which case the missile is said to be used in the autonomous mode. Alternatively the laser can be carried in the mast-mounted ball of an accompanying Bell OH-58D scout helicopter, or it can be aimed by a friendly soldier on the ground. In either case the Apache's missile can be fired from behind cover in the general direction of the target. As soon as the missile has risen within sight of the target it detects the reflected laser light and homes on to it. Hellfire flies at an exceptional Mach 1.17, so it strikes home very quickly. No current tank can dodge, or resist the formidable 7.7-kg (17-lb) warhead.

For the future new forms of Hellfire missile are under development. Thanks to the missile's modular design it will be possible to remove one type of seeker head and attach one of a different kind. The three new forms of seeker currently being perfected are IIR, combined RF and IIR, and MM. The MM would make the missile virtually autonomous (self-contained), carrying its own miniature radar along with it. The IIR seeker would offer great advantages at night or in conditions where targets were obscured by dust or smoke which would prevent the human agents from knowing where to aim the designating lasers. Of course, by about the year 2020 it may be possible in a Hellfire-size missile to fit all the alternative forms of guidance, so that there would always be one method that would not be defeated by the conditions or by enemy defensive countermeasures.

The main alternative load to Hellfire is the familiar FFAR of 2.75-in (69.85-mm) calibre, which is stabilized in flight by spinning but otherwise has no guidance. The normal maximum load is 76 rockets, fired from four 19-tube launchers. The rockets are aimed by aiming the whole helicopter in azimuth (direction), the exact range being adjusted by slightly pivoting the four underwing pylons according to the range input from the sensors. Since 1984 Hughes Helicopters has been part of McDonnell Douglas, but early in the development of the Apache a sister to Hughes Helicopters, the Missile Systems Group of Hughes Aircraft, developed a new rocket launcher which saved weight and bulk by incorporating its own self-contained fuzing, stores management and fire-control subsystem. With four 19-tube launchers the weight saved is 120 kg (265 lb).

Target tracking

So far little has been said about the vital sensors and sight system. It might have been thought that these items should have been mounted high above the helicopter on a mast, but in fact they are at the end of the downsloping nose which forces the helicopter to expose itself completely in order to see the enemy. The sighting sensors are grouped in a giant

Fleet of foot and with many eyes, the Apache is a 'super insect', always on the lookout, always ready to pounce. Clearly visible in this shot are the nose-mounted TADS/PNVS 'turret' and the large avionics-packed 'cheeks'.

turret and comprise two quite separate groups, the TADS and PNVS. The TADS is the more complex group, consisting of direct-view optics, a telescope with x3.5 or x16 magnification, a laser rangefinder/designator, a laser spot tracker for finding targets designated by any wavelength of friendly laser, a day TV camera which looks through the magnifying optical system but 'sees' much better through dust and smoke because it operates at a near-IR wavelength, and a FLIR, which has a huge aperture and can see brilliantly on the darkest night. The PNVS is a simpler infra-red sensor to give the pilot a night-vision capability. The outputs from the sensors can be fed to various cockpit displays, one advantage being that with PNVS imagery the CPG could fly the helicopter at night should the pilot be incapacitated.

Pilot input

A particularly advanced feature is that both men wear an IHADSS built into their helmets. By merely looking at a target they can automatically cue (aim) the main sensors as well as informing the Hellfire missiles of the target direction. Of course all the pictures displayed on the various screens also contain comprehensive numerical information about helicopter airspeed, height, target direction and range and possibly other variables.

Further devices are needed to help the helicopter to survive in a hostile environment. The most obvious is the ALQ-144 IRCM turret, which looks like a small lighthouse just behind the main rotor. This pumps out intense IR radiation in a coded sequence. When the heat rays are being emitted they strongly attract any

heat-seeking missile that may be fired at the helicopter. When the radiation suddenly ceases the missile becomes confused and breaks its lock. The repeated pulsing causes heat-seeking missiles to lose interest, whereas without the ALQ-144 they might home on the heat emitted by the T700 engines, despite the addition of giant cooling and shrouding systems to the two jetpipes. On each side of the tail boom, near the tail, is a box which can dispense chaff or flares to left or right, either on command of the crew or automatically when warned by a sensor. Firing the standardized cartridges either sends out brilliant heat sources to decoy a heat-homing missile away from the helicopter or else blankets it in a cloud of radar-reflective slivers of aluminium-coated plastic, so that hostile radars cannot see the helicopter. Probably in the course of its long active career the AH-64A will be protected by additional countermeasures operating at different wavelengths.

Glossary

AAH Advanced Attack Helicopter
APU Auxiliary Power Unit
AWS Area Weapon System
CPG Co-Pilot/Gunner
ESR Electro-Slag Remelt
FFAR Folding-Fin Aircraft Rocket
FLIR Forward-Looking Infra-Red
IHADSS Integrated Helmet And Display Sighting System
IIR Imaging Infra-Red
IR Infra-Red
IRCM Infra-Red CounterMeasures
MM MilliMetre-wavelength radar
PNVS Pilot's Night Vision Sensor
RF Radio Frequency
SAM Surface-to-Air Missile
TADS Target Acquisition and Designation Sight
TOW Tube-launched, Optically-tracked, Wire-guided

AH-64 Apache in service

US Army

For the US Army, acquisition of the AH-64 Apache represents a quantum leap in its attack helicopter force capability, and the Army's faith in the type is reflected in the masssive orders stretching through to Fiscal Year 88.

The number on order now stands at 593, this including a recent cut back of 82 machines due to economy measures and other financial commitments.

Original plans in the early 1980s called for 536 machines, the first of which would enter service by mid-1983, and the FY 82 finances provided $537.5 million for procurement of the first 11 production AH-64As.

Increases in the production total to 675 called for an initial output of four per month for Lot One machines, rising to 12 per month for FY 85-87 totals. The full production breakdown was as follows:

Fiscal Year	Quantity
1982	11
1983	48
1984	112
1985	144
1986	144
1987	144
1988	72

In reality, the goal of the first Apache's entering service during 1983 was to prove over-optimistic, and production problems with such a complex piece of machinery have taken their toll. The final output for 1985 was 135, a highly credible performance from McDonnell Douglas, and the US Army has now received well over half of its total order.

But economies have taken their toll. The FY 87 financing has only allowed for 120 machines as against 144 planned. It remains to be seen whether the Army's desire for a force of over 1,000 Apaches by the early 1990s will ever become a reality.

Training programme

The core of the US Army's Apache training programme is split between four bases, all of which come under the auspices of Training and Doctrine Command (TRADOC). A basic break down of their responsibilities is as follows:

This production-standard McDonnell Douglas AH-64A illustrates the typical US Army colour scheme of overall olive drab with lettering and serial applied in black. Any unit markings are carried in very small format, such as the crest immediately below the forward cockpit.

Fort Eustis, Virginia, houses the Army Aviation Logistics School and School of Transportation, and is responsible for the maintenance crew training programme. The majority of Apache's based here are airworthy, though their role is basically one of ground instruction. A small number are also assigned to the Maintenance Test Pilot programme.

Fort Gordon, Georgia, is responsible for avionics and automated test equipment training. No actual AH-64As are assigned, the programme using a pair of simulated airframes fitted out with communications and navigational systems.

Fort Rucker, Alabama, is the Aircrew Training Center, conducting a three-month course for Apache crews. Some 32 Apaches are assigned for this task, along with a handful of Bell AH-1s fitted with the PNVS suite. There is also an Aircraft Development Test Activity unit which operates one Apache as a 'Lead the Fleet' machine, it having higher hours than any other Apache.

Plans call for 34 Air Cavalry and Army National Guard Squadrons and Battalions to be Apache-equipped, each having 18 examples, though one or both of these figures will have to change given the recent cutback in the total on order. The majority of units will trade in their Bell AH-1Ss, but some will be completely new.

All units will work up on the Apache at Fort Hood, Texas, the first to do so being the 7th Squadron/17th Cavalry of the 6th Air Combat Cavalry Brigade, which started work-up during April 1986. This is one of five units to train at Fort Hood during 1986 which will be permanently based there to support the future training programme, which is expected to run through to 1992.

Fourteen of the battalions will deploy overseas to West Germany, while the Stateside units will include Army National Guard units such as the North Carolina ANG's 28th Aviation Battalion, this being the first ANG unit to convert during 1986/87.

A quartet of early-production Apaches sit on the apron at Hanchey Army Heliport (a satellite base for helicopter training operations from Fort Rucker) prior to another day's flying. Fort Rucker houses the Aircrew Training Center, and operates some 32 Apaches in support of the AH-64A training programme. All 34 US Army and Army National Guard units due to convert to the Apache will do so here.

Flying low over the Arizona desert, these Apaches undergo their final flight testing from the manufacturing plant at Mesa, before being ferried to Fort Rucker and assignment to another Army unit.

Performance (at 6552 kg/14,445 lb AUW)

Maximum level speed	160 kts 296 km/h	(184 mph)
Initial vertical rate of climb 2,500 ft (762 m) per minute		
Service ceiling	21,000 ft	(6400 m)
Maximum range, internal fuel	482 km	(300 miles)
Ferry range, maximum internal and external fuel	1701 km	(1,057 miles)

Service ceiling

AH-64A Apache 20,000ft
UH-60A Blackhawk 19,000ft
AS.332 Super Puma 15,090ft
Mi-8 'Hip' 14,760ft
Mi-24 'Hind-D' 14,750ft
Bell AH-1S 12,200ft
Agusta A.129 10,800ft
Westland Lynx 10,600ft
Bell AH-1T 7,400ft

Max rate of climb at sea level

UH-60A Blackhawk 2770 ft/min
AH-64A Apache 2500 ft/min
Westland Lynx 2480 ft/min
Mi-24 'Hind-D' 2460 ft/min
Agusta A.129 2090 ft/min
Bell AH-1T 1785 ft/min
AS.332 Super Puma 1732 ft/min
Bell AH-1S 1620 ft/min

Speed at sea level

Mi-24 'Hind-D' 173kt
AH-64A Apache 162kt
UH-60A Blackhawk 160kt
AS.332 Super Puma 151kt
Bell AH-1T 149kt
Agusta A.129 149kt
Westland Lynx 140kt
Mi-8 'Hip' 140kt
Bell AH-1S 123kt

Combat radius

AS.332 Super Puma 300km
UH-60A Blackhawk 250km
Agusta A.129 250km
AH-64A Apache 230km E
Westland Lynx 212km
Mi-8 'Hip' 200km E
Bell AH-1T 200km
Bell AH-1S 200km
Mi-24 'Hind-D' 160km

Weapons load

Mi-8 'Hip' 6,000-lb E
AH-64A 4,000-lb E
Mi-24 3,000-lb E
Bell AH-1T 3,300-lb E
Bell AH-1S 2,523-lb
Westland Lynx 2,500-lb E
Agusta A.129 2,205-lb
UH-60A Blackhawk nil
AS.332 Super Puma nil

Rotor blades
The tail rotor blades are set at 55°/125° spacing to reduce rotor noise. All blades are manufactured by Tool Research and Engineering Corporation

Engine cowls
Cowl panels hinge down to serve as maintenance platforms

IR suppressor
The IR suppressors consist of giant boxes in which engine jet exhaust is mixed with cold air to prevent IR homing missiles 'seeing' anything hot enough for them to home on

Colour scheme
The colour scheme worn by the Apache consists of an overall olive drab finish with low visibility black stencilling

Tailplane
The power driven variable-incidence tailplane (horizontal stabilizer) provides stability in the pitching plane

Chaff/flare dispensers
Large boxes on each side of the fuselage dispense chaff and flares to protect against enemy radar and heat-seeking missiles, and to 'jam' hostile fire control radars

RWR
This antenna serves the ventral APR-39 (v) radar warning antenna giving rear hemisphere coverage

Rotor head
The main rotor blades have five stainless-steel spars and glass-fibre spacers giving fail-safe strength after bullet strikes. They are of high camber aerfoil section and broad chord, with sweptback tips, and are de-iced by Sierracin Corporation heater blankets

Anti-flutter weights
Anti-vibration masses are attached to the front and rear of each blade root

Main rotor driveshaft
The main rotor shaft is a strong tubular shaft providing a double load path

Gearbox
The main transmission and engine nose gearbox are made by Litton, but the grease-lubricated intermediate and tail rotor gearboxes are made by Aircraft Gear Corporation. Driveshafts and couplings are by Bendix

IR jammer
An ALQ-144 pulsed heat radiator IRCM (infra-red countermeasures) is provided to protect against homing missiles

Powerplant
The Apache is powered by two General Electric T700-GE-701 turboshafts, each rated at 1,265 kW

Rocket pod
A standard US rocket launcher, containing 19x2.75-in rocket projectiles is frequently carried by the AH-64

Stub wings
The Apache's wings carry navigation and strobe lights, and pairs of pylons which can be pivoted to achieve correct rocket range

Antenna
ADF (auto direction finder) blister and UHF blade antenna

Keith Fretwell

Specification: AH-64A Apache

Rotors

Main rotor diameter	14.63 m	(48 ft 0 in)
Main rotor disc area	168.11 m²	(1,809.5 sq ft)
Tail rotor diameter	2.79 m	(9 ft 2 in)
Tail rotor disc area	6.13 m²	(66.0 sq ft)

Fuselage and tail unit

Accommodation	two flight crew in tandem seating	
Length overall, both rotors turning	17.76 m	(58 ft 3.2 in)
Height over tail rotor	4.30 m	(14 ft 1.25 in)
Height to top of air data sensor	4.66 m	(15 ft 3.5 in)

Wings and tailplane

Wing span	5.23 m	(17 ft 2 in)
Tailplane span	3.40 m	(11 ft 2 in)

Landing gear

Two non-retractable rearward-folding mainwheels and a lockable tailwheel

Wheel track	2.03 m	(6 ft 8 in)
Wheelbase	10.59 m	(34 ft 9 in)

Powerplant

Two General Electric T700-GE-701 turboshafts

Rating, each	1265 kW	(1,696 shp)
One engine out rating	1285 kW	(1,723 shp)

AH-64A Apache recognition features

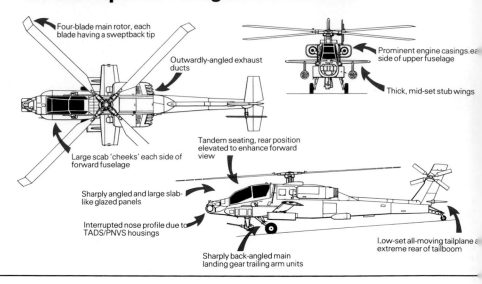

Four-blade main rotor, each blade having a sweptback tip

Outwardly-angled exhaust ducts

Prominent engine casings, each side of upper fuselage

Thick, mid-set stub wings

Large scab 'cheeks' each side of forward fuselage

Tandem seating, rear position elevated to enhance forward view

Sharply angled and large slab-like glazed panels

Interrupted nose profile due to TADS/PNVS housings

Sharply back-angled main landing gear trailing arm units

Low-set all-moving tailplane at extreme rear of tailboom

AH-64A Apache variants

YAH-64: development of Hughes Model 77 in response to US Army's Advanced Attack Helicopter competition; six prototypes, including one ground test vehicle; five flying prototypes known as Air Vehicles 02 to 06 (AV02 to AV06); first flight by AV02 on 30 September 1975, powered by two General Electric T700-GE-700 turboshafts; the prototypes originally had a T-tail configuration and pointed nose, but the former was eventually repositioned much lower down; as the Phase I and II programmes progressed, several major modifications were introduced to the various prototypes, these being incorporated in the final production model

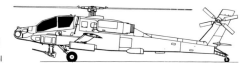

AH-64A Apache: production standard model, first flew on 9 January 1984: the first two were assigned to non-operational tasks as dedicated test vehicles; powered by T700-GE-701 turboshafts derated to provide reserve power for combat emergencies; the tailplane has been relocated to the base of the fin, single-curvature glazing has replaced the flat panels originally fitted, longer forward fuselage fairings cover expanded avionics bays, the tail rotor has been moved up some 7.6 cm (30 in) and the rotor diameter increased, the nose profile has been significantly altered by the addition of the TADS/PNVS turrets; a total of 593 are currently on order for the US Army

AH-64A ADFCS: a single AH-64A Apache is currently being used as an Advanced Digital Flight Control System demonstrator in support of McDonnell Douglas' answer to the Army's LHX requirement; the front cockpit has been modified to reflect the single-pilot LHX configuration, this including advanced rotorcraft technology integration; first flew on 12 October 1985
Sea Apache: a company-initiated programme to tailor the AH-64A Apache to US Navy and Marine Corps requirements; the USMC version would retain the TADS/PNVS equipment, but the Chain Gun would be deleted; would be capable of firing TOW missiles, Zuni unguided rockets and wingtip-mounted AIM-9L Sidewinders; the Navy model would also retain the TADS/PNVS equipment, but also get surface-search radar housed in a mast mount or ventral radome in place of the Chain Gun; would be capable of carrying up to four Harpoon or Penguin missiles, and six AIM-9L Sidewinders; the tail section would be folding and the tailwheel moved forward. Common features would include upgraded brakes, Doppler INS, additional tie-down points and a new rotor hub to permit a 45° movement of the rotor blades to facilitate deck storage; no orders to date.

AH-64B/G Apache: company proposal for co-development and co-production with West Germany of an advanced variant to meet the German's PAH-2 requirement; features would include advanced crew station avionics and flight controls to reduce overall workload, improvements in gun and ammunition performance, and better air-to-air missile aiming; a small TV camera would be fitted to the extreme rear of the tailfin to enhance crew rearward vision; state-of-the-art data transfer system and pre-programmed mission cassettes would be used to reduce pre-flight tasks time; computer capacity would be tripled to a 192,000 word memory; overall, 75 per cent commonality with the AH-64A Apache; no orders to date.

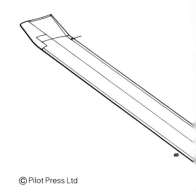

© Pilot Press Ltd

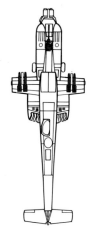

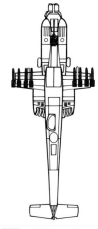

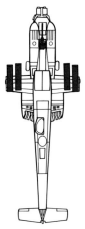

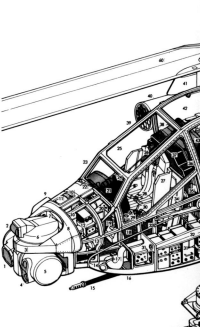

■ 1×M230 Chain Gun 30-mm automatic cannon with 320 rounds of ammunition
8×AGM-114A Hellfire anti-armour missiles

Basic anti-armour (primary mission)

In action the Apache would be extremely unlikely to carry its maximum permissable external weapon load of 16 Hellfire missiles as this would considerably degrade overall performance. Each Hellfire missile can be independently targeted and has a maximum effective range of 8km (5 miles)

■ 1×M230 Chain Gun 30-mm automatic cannon with 320 rounds of ammunition
16×AGM-114A Hellfire anti-armour missiles

Anti-armour (Middle East operations)

Operating in hot-and-high conditions of 4,000 ft (1220 m) and 35°C (95°F), the Apache could just manage a full load of 16 Hellfire missiles. Maximum speed would be cut to 147 kts (272 km/h; 169 mph) with a mission endurance time of just under 2 hours. The vertical rate of climb is 450 ft (137 m) per minute.

■ 1×M230 Chain Gun 30-mm automatic cannon with 1,200 rounds of ammunition
38×2.75-in (69.85-mm) FFARs in two 19-round pods
8×AGM-114A Hellfire anti-armour missiles

Air cavalry (Northern Europe)

In the cooler conditions of Northern Europe the Apache has a more sprightly performance, carrying this diverse load at 150 kts (278 km/h; 173 mph) with a vertical rate of climb of 860 ft (262 m) per minute.

■ 1×M230 Chain Gun 30-mm automatic cannon with 1,200 rounds of ammunition
76×2.75-in (69.85-mm) FFARs in four 19-round pods

Airmobile escort (Northern Europe)

The inner weapons pylons have had their usual complement of Hellfire missiles replaced by an additional pair of FFAR pods, this being the maximum permissible load for this mission profile at a maximum combat height of 2,000 ft (610 m). Mission endurance is about 2.5 hours.

Clearly illustrating the higher seating position afforded to the pilot, this view of the crew area also shows the chunky but lightweight boron armour shields either side of the seats, their position helping to protect each crew member's torso. Shielding is also applied to the floor, sides and between the crew stations.

The front cockpit houses the co-pilot/gunner (CPG), with an uncluttered layout in front and to the sides. The central unit is the multi-purpose sight system, including an optical relay tube linked to the TADS nose turret. The left-hand section of the forward console contains the integrated weapons controls, while the right-hand section contains basic flying instruments. The latter, in conjunction with a central control column, allow the CPG to fly the helicopter if necessary.

The pilot is seated in the rear cockpit, some 48 cm (19 in) above the CPG to enhance forward view. State-of-the-art technology results in a very neat layout of the forward console. The vertical strip instruments in the left-hand area cover engine and rotor information, while the central square is a Video Display Unit which covers items such as attitude, speed, altitude and hover. The VDU can also display information relating to the TADS and PNVS operations.

McDonnell Douglas AH-64 Apache cutaway drawing key

1 Night systems sensor scanner
2 Pilot's Night Vision Sensor (PNVS) infra-red scanner
3 Electro-optical target designation and night sensor systems turret
4 Target acquisition and designation sight daylight scanner (TADS)
5 Azimuth motor housing
6 TADS/PNVS swivelling turret
7 Turret drive motor housing
8 Sensor turret mounting
9 Rear view mirror
10 Nose compartment access hatches
11 Remote terminal unit
12 Signal data converter
13 Co-pilot/gunner's yaw control rudder pedals
14 Forward radar warning antenna
15 M230A1 Chain Gun barrel
16 Fuselage sponson fairing
17 Avionics cooling air ducting
18 Boron armoured cockpit flooring
19 Co-pilot/gunner's 'fold-down' control column
20 Weapons control panel
21 Instrument panel shroud
22 Windscreen wiper
23 Co-pilot/gunner's armoured windscreen
24 Head-down sighting system viewfinder

25 Pilot's armoured windscreen panel
26 Windscreen wiper
27 Co-pilot/gunner's Kevlar armoured seat
28 Safety harness
29 Side console panel
30 Engine power levers
31 Avionics equipment bays, port and starboard
32 Avionics bay access door
33 Collective pitch control lever
34 Adjustable crash-resistant seat mountings
35 Pilot's rudder pedals
36 Cockpit side window panel

37 Pilot's instrument console
38 Inter-cockpit acrylic blast shield
39 Starboard side window entry hatches
40 Rocket launcher pack
41 Starboard wing stores pylons
42 Cockpit roof glazing
43 Instrument panel shroud

44 Pilot's Kevlar armoured seat
45 Collective pitch control lever
46 Side console panel
47 Engine power levers
48 Rear cockpit floor level
49 Main landing gear shock absorber mounting
50 Linkless ammunition feed chute
51 Forward fuel tank; total fuel capacity 1419 litres (375 US gal)
52 Control rod linkages
53 Cockpit ventilating air louvres

54 Display adjustment panel
55 Grab handles/maintenance steps
56 Control system hydraulic actuators (three)
57 Ventilating air intake
58 UHF aerial
59 Starboard stub wing
60 Main rotor blades
61 Laminated blade-root attachment joints
62 Vibration absorbers
63 Blade pitch bearing housing
64 Air data sensor mast
65 Rotor hub unit
66 Offset flapping hinges
67 Elastomeric lead/lag dampers
68 Blade pitch control rod
69 Pitch control swashplate
70 Main rotor mast
71 Air turbine starter/auxiliary powered unit (APU) input shaft
72 Rotor head control mixing linkages
73 Gearbox mounting plate
74 Transmission oil coolers, port and starboard
75 Rotor brake

76 Main gearbox
77 Gearbox mounting struts
78 Generator
79 Input shaft from port engine
80 Gearbox mounting deck
81 Tail rotor control rod linkage
82 Ammunition magazine, 1,200 rounds
83 Stub wing attachment joints
84 Engine transmission gearbox
85 Air intake
86 Engine integral oil tank
87 General Electric T700-GE-701 turboshaft
88 Intake particle separator
89 Engine accessory equipment gearbox
90 Oil cooler plenum
91 Gas turbine starter/auxiliary power unit
92 Starboard engine cowling panels/fold-down maintenance platform
93 Starboard engine exhaust ducts
94 APU exhaust
95 Pneumatic system and environmental control equipment
96 Cooling air exhaust louvres

97 Particle separator exhaust duct/mixer
98 'Black Hole' infra-red suppression engine exhaust ducts
99 Hydraulic reservoir
100 Gearbox/engine bay tail fairings
101 Internal maintenance platform
102 Tail rotor control rod
103 Spine shaft housing
104 Tail rotor transmission shaft
105 Shaft bearings and couplings
106 Bevel drive intermediate gearbox
107 Fin/rotor pylon construction
108 Tail rotor drive shafts
109 All moving tailplane
110 Tail rotor gearbox housing
111 Right-angle final drive gearbox
112 Fin tip aerial fairing
113 Rear radar warning antennae
114 Tail navigation light
115 Cambered trailing edge section (directional stability)
116 Tail rotor pitch actuator
117 Tail rotor hub mechanism
118 Asymmetric (noise attenuation) tail rotor blades

119 Tailplane construction
120 Tailplane pivot bearing
121 Castoring tailwheel
122 Tailwheel shock absorber
123 Tailwheel yoke attachment
124 Handgrips/maintenance steps
125 Tailplane control hydraulic jack
126 Fin/rotor pylon attachment joint
127 Chaff and flare dispenser
128 Tailboom ring frames
129 Ventral radar warning aerial
130 Tailcone frame and stringer construction
131 UHF aerial
132 ADF loop aerial
133 ADF sense aerial
134 Access hatch
135 Handgrips/maintenance steps
136 Radio and electronics equipment bay
137 Rear fuel tank
138 Reticulated foam fire suppressant tank bay linings

139 VHF aerial
140 Main rotor blade stainless steel spars (five)
141 Glassfibre spar linings
142 Honeycomb trailing edge panel
143 Glassfibre blade skins
144 Trailing edge fixed tab
145 Swept blade tip fairing
146 Static discharger
147 Stub wing trailing-edge flap
148 Stub wing rib construction
149 Twin spar booms
150 Port navigation and strobe lights
151 Port wing stores pylons
152 Rocket pack: 19 7-cm (2.75-in) FFAR rockets
153 Rockwell Hellfire AGM-114A anti-tank missiles
154 Missile launch rails
155 Fuselage sponson aft fairing
156 Boarding step
157 Port mainwheel
158 Main landing gear leg strut
159 Shock absorber strut
160 Boarding steps
161 Main landing gear leg pivot fixing
162 Ammunition feed and cartridge case return chutes
163 Gun swivelling mounting
164 Azimuth control mounting frame
165 Hughes M230A-1 Chain Gun 30-mm automatic cannon
166 Blast suppression cannon muzzle

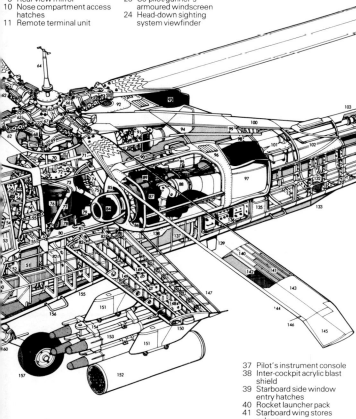

The BELL
UH-I 'HUEY'

Bell UH-1 to 412: Huey hierarchy

Faintly at first but growing louder by the second, the familiar clatter of a UH-1 'Huey' signals the arrival of another batch of troops ready for battle. This is the UH-1 in its most familiar role, but no one can deny the operational versatility of this champion among champions in the helicopter world.

Between 1950 and 1953 the Korean War gave the US Army its first major opportunity to evaluate the helicopter under operational conditions, initially with the Bell H-13 Sioux in the observation and casualty evacuation roles. The advent of the larger Sikorsky H-19, with a capacious cabin able to accommodate up to 10 fully-armed troops or an equivalent load of food or ammunition, opened the road to logistic resupply and the tactical deployment of men and equipment in both attack and reinforcement operations.

These two widely used helicopter types, and the Sikorsky HO4S used so successfully for planeguard and rescue duties by US Navy Squadron HU-1, were each powered by a piston engine. But at the Stratford, Connecticut headquarters of engine manufacturer Lycoming, a team of engineers led by Dr Anselm Franz was developing a light and very compact gas turbine engine under US government contract. The XT-53 turboshaft, initially rated at 522 kW (700 shp), was selected to power the Army's new utility helicopter, the Bell Model 204, whose XH-40 prototype was eventually declared winner of

the 1955 Support System 443L competition.

Detailed design work began in June 1955 and less than 16 months later, on 22 October 1956, Bell test pilot Floyd Carlson flew the first of three XH-40 prototypes. Six pre-production YH-40s were built, with a 30.5-cm (12-in) increase in cabin length to make possible the accommodation of four stretchers: one prototype was evaluated by the US Air Force at Edwards AFB, one was type-tested at Eglin AFB and three were delivered to the US Army at Fort Rucker for a comprehensive test and evaluation programme which was completed in June 1957.

Production begins

Bell received an initial production order on 13 March 1959 and in June the company began to deliver the first HU-1As, the designation giving rise to the 'Huey' nickname which was universally preferred to the official Iroquois. Compared with the prototype's 2563 kg (5,650 lb) the HU-1A was cleared to operate at a gross weight of 3266 kg (7,200 lb) and was powered by the T53-L-

A familiar sight for nearly three decades as Hueys sit with rotors turning, ready to take ground troops on board and ferry them into or out of the battle area. A basically simple design, the UH-1 family will serve with many nations for years to come.

1 engine, rated at 574 kW (770 shp). Fourteen TH-1A dual-control trainers were manufactured for the Army Aviation School, and many more HU-1As were used for training in support of a significant aircrew expansion programme.

As the position of government forces in South Vietnam began to deteriorate during the early 1960s, and as President Kennedy recognized the need for US support in the form of technical advisers and equipment, the first HU-1As began to arrive in South East Asia. The casevac helicopters of the 57th Medical Detach-

Forever synonymous with the US involvement in Vietnam, the UH-1 continues to serve in massive numbers with the US Army as the backbone of the helicopter transport force. This trio of UH-1Hs is seen about to land during 'Bright Star' operations in Egypt.

ment (Helicopter Ambulance) were deployed in April 1962, at the beginning of what was to be an 11-year tour of duty, and September saw the arrival of the HU-1As of the Utility Tactical Transport Company. These helicopters were armed, usually with a 7.62-mm (0.3-in) machine-gun attached to the forward portion of the skids on each side and, farther to the rear, launching tubes for up to eight 2.75-in (69.85-mm) rockets.

The unit's initial task was to provide fire support for Piasecki CH-21 Shawnee and other transport helicopters operating in the assault role. As a result of the lessons that were all too quickly learned, it became clear that heavier armament was required. The development of the UH-1B (redesignated in accordance with the tri-service system introduced on 18 September 1962), with the uprated 716-kW (960-shp) T53-L-11 engine and gross weight increased to 3856 kg (8,500 lb), made this possible. Not only could quadruple 7.62-mm M60 machine-guns and rocket projectile launchers be carried externally, but cabin-mounted weapons could also be installed for operation by a door gunner.

Nevertheless, it was the UH-1C which was the first version to be built primarily as a gunship, with increased fuel capacity and performance improvements which enabled it to be used more effectively in the 'shotgun' role for the troop-carrying Hueys in operations against the Viet Cong. The T53-L-11 engine drove the new Bell 540 'door-hinge' rotor system, with a single-piece flex-beam rotor head and blades increased in chord from 45.7 to 68.6 cm (18 to 27 in) as a means of providing improved manoeuvrability and more lift.

Beefed-up 'Delta'

The UH-1B in troop-carrier configuration could carry seven armed soldiers in addition to its crew of two, but Bell took advantage of the extra power of the T53-L-11 to produce an improved UH-1B as the UH-1D: the latter's enlarged cabin could accommodate the pilot and 12 troops, or a medical attendant and six stretcher cases, or 1814 kg (4,000 lb) of stores and equip-

ment. This version, designated Model 205 by Bell, also introduced a new 14.63-m (48-ft) diameter rotor. The first YUH-1D development machine flew on 16 August 1961 and deliveries to Army units began in August 1963.

Continued development of the T53 resulted in its further uprating to 1044 kW (1,400 shp) in the T53-L-13 version, exactly twice the power available to the XH-40. This was fitted in the UH-1D airframe to produce the UH-1H (civil Model 205A), delivered from September 1967. The US Army alone received 3,573 UH-1Hs and plans to keep some 2,700 of them in service into the 21st century.

Upgrading the UH-1H

The Army has, therefore, introduced an upgrade programme for its Huey fleet. Items in the schedule are improved avionics and equipment, including UHF radio and DME, Doppler navigation system, radar altimeter and radar-warning receiver, infra-red jammer and hot metal/exhaust plume suppressor. Other major improvements include closed-circuit refuelling, fuel tank vent and a crashworthy auxiliary fuel system, a night vision compatible cockpit, and improvements to the main input drive shaft, rotor stabilizer bar and tail rotor hub. New composite blades are also being fitted, following the 1982 award of a $19 million development contract to a joint Bell/Boeing Vertol proposal tendered in response to an Army request for proposals issued on 16 November 1981. The

Natural disasters around the world always seem to bring out the best in helicopters, and the Hueys are no exception. Here the main cabin of a Colombian UH-1H Iroquois is packed to the gills with urgent supplies for victims of a mudslide in a remote area.

first flight of the new blades on a UH-1H took place early in 1985, and the anticipated orders for production up to 1989 are for 6,000 units. The two participating companies have an equal manufacturing qualification and capability.

The development of the far more powerful Lycoming T55 engine, initially rated at 1976 kW (2,650 shp), resulted in the experimental Model 214 Huey Tug. This was first flown in October 1970 on the power of a 1417-kW (1,900-shp) T53-L-702. The basic UH-1H airframe had to be redesigned, together with the dynamic train, to accommodate the T55. The tail boom and tail rotor were enlarged and strengthened, the rotor diameter was increased to 15.24 m (50 ft) and a stability control and augmentation system replaced the rotor stabilizer bar of previous models.

The sheer operational versatility of the Huey family has been a key factor in their long-running success story. While many act as aggressors with a variety of armament, many others, such as this US Army example, operate as medevac air ambulances.

Main rotor
Unlike many naval helicopters, the AB
212ASW has a main rotor which cannot
be folded to save valuable space aboard
ship. Of 14.69 m (48 ft 2.25 in) diameter,
the rotor is of semi-rigid, all-metal
construction with interchangeable
blades

Air inlet
One located port and starboard for the
two PT6 engines

VHF aerial
Used for VHF (Very High Frequency)
radio communications

Upper anti-collision light
This red rotating beacon is
complemented by a similar fitment
below the flight-deck for all-round
coverage

Engine exhaust outlet

Air inlet
Admits cooling air to the engine bay

Hatch
For access to the tailboom equipment
stowage area

Weapons pylon
Several types of offensive equipment
are available for carriage on the AS
212ASW's pylons. For anti-submarine
operations these can be the Mk 44, Mk
46 or the Italian Motorfides 244AS
homing torpedoes. Anti-ship weapons
include Aérospatiale AS-12 wire-guided
missiles or (in export helicopters with
Ferranti Sea Spray radar fitted) BAe Sea
Skua

Refuelling point
The AB 212ASW's standard tanks –
totalling 814 litres (179 Imp gal) – are
filled via a single pressure refuelling
point. A long-range tank can be fitted in
the cabin and two auxiliary tanks added
externally for increased endurance

Deck lashing point
Compared with the army and civil AB
212, the naval model has local fuselage
strengthening for tie-down rings

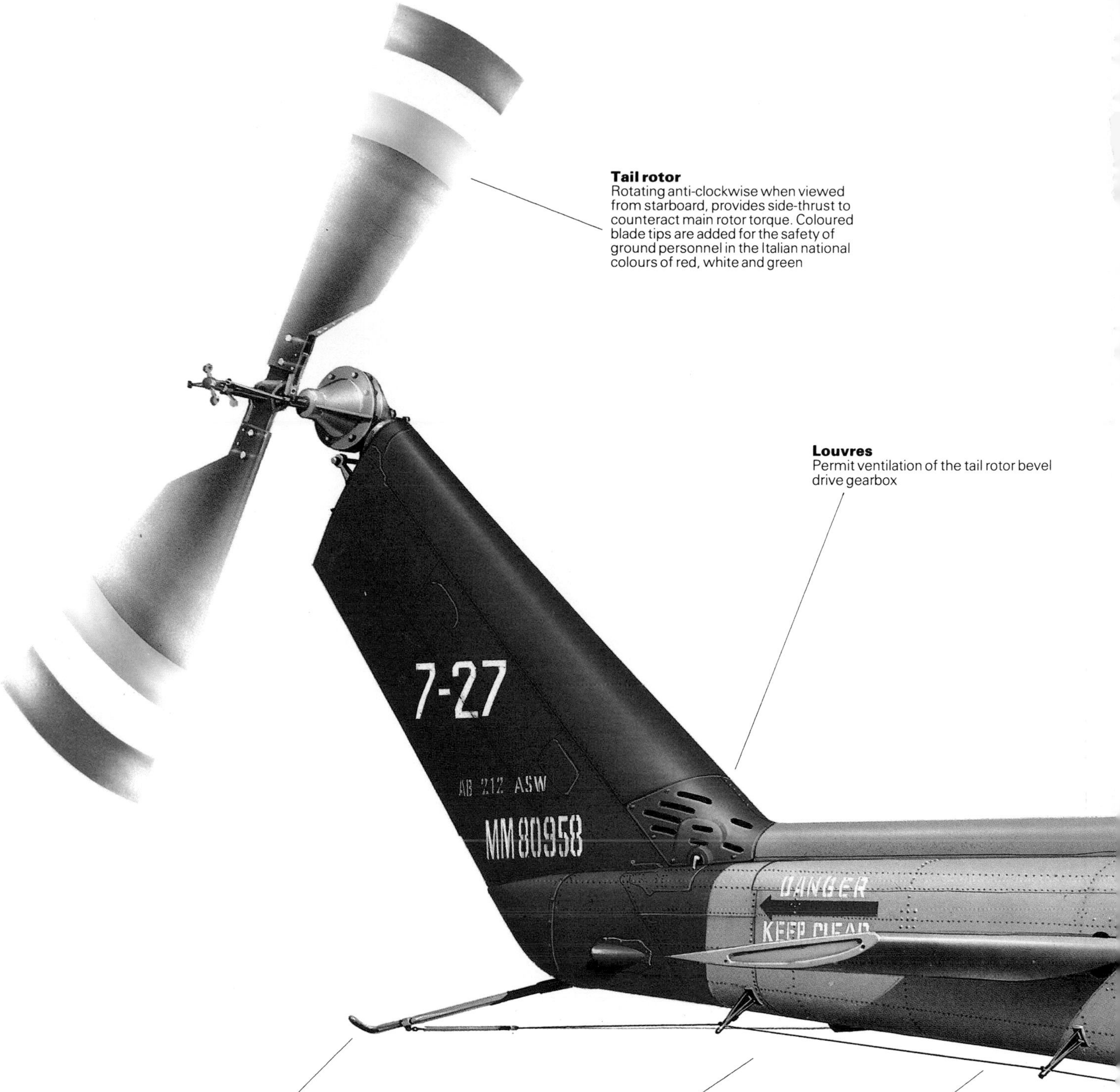

Tail rotor
Rotating anti-clockwise when viewed from starboard, provides side-thrust to counteract main rotor torque. Coloured blade tips are added for the safety of ground personnel in the Italian national colours of red, white and green

Louvres
Permit ventilation of the tail rotor bevel drive gearbox

7-27

AB 212 ASW

MM 80958

DANGER
KEEP CLEAR

Tail skid
Prevents damage to the tailboom when the helicopter makes a nose-high landing

Stabiliser
Stabilisers are present on both sides of the tailboom

HF radio aerial
For high frequency radio communications

Sistel Marte Mk 2 ASM
Based on the surface-launched Sea Killer missile, Marte carries a 70 kg (154 lb) warhead over 20 km (12.4 miles) at Mach 0.74, skimming the wavetops to complicate detection. Mk 1 required a command guidance system, but the Mk 2 is a fire-and-forget weapon with an active radar seeker. Because of weight considerations, only one Marte is carried by the AB 212ASW

UH-1 in service

Argentina
The Argentine air force, army and coast guard operate modest numbers of Bell UH-1D/Hs for transport and assault tasks. All three also operate the Bell 212 for VIP communications and search and rescue.

Australia
The Royal Australian Air Force operates UH-1D/Hs in support of the Army, examples being distributed between Nos 5, 9 and 35 Squadrons. It is likely that this responsibility will be transferred to the Army in due course to improve operational effectiveness. Helicopters have also been used to support United Nations operations in Lebanon. The Royal Australian Navy operates a small number of UH-1B/Cs, these being assigned to HC-723 at Nowra, though they can also operate from RAN frigates. Tasks include liaison and SAR.

Austria
Twenty-six AB.204Bs and 25 AB.212s were supplied to the Austrian air force for utility tasks. A small number of the former remain in use with I Helicopter Squadron, while the latter are assigned to II and III Helicopter Squadrons. A maintenance unit operates examples of both.

Bahrain
Helicopters in this Gulf state are primarily operated by the Public Security Force. One Bell 205A-1 (BPS-7) and two Bell 412s (BPS-03 and -04) are in use.

Bangladesh
The Bangladesh Defence Force Air Wing acquired 11 Bell 212s, 10 of which remain in use. Examples include BH-772 and -806. A pair of AB.205s are reputedly in use with the Bangladesh Army.

Bolivia
Extensive use of US-supplied equipment includes up to 10 UH-1Hs, six of which were delivered in late 1986. A pair of Bell 212s are in use for VIP tasks, these bearing the serials 101 and 102.

Brazil
A sizeable UH-1D/SH-1D/UH-1H force is in use with the Air Force's Tactical Air Command, Coastal Command and Helicopter Training Command. All are serialled in the 8500 and 8600 range. A small number are ex-Israeli machines.

Brunei
The Air Wing's No. 1 Squadron at Berakas Camp has 11 Bell 212s, one of which is used for VIP tasks. In addition, a Bell 214ST and Bell 412 are operated. Examples of the Bell 212s include AMDB-117 and -118.

Burma
Anti-guerrilla operations along the Laotian border and in the northern areas have occupied UH-1Hs in use with the Burmese Armed Forces Air. Eighteen have been supplied (UB-6201 to -6218), though up to six have been lost.

Canada
Nine of ten CH-118 Iroquois (UH-1H) and 41 of 50 CH-135 Twin Huey (CUH-1N) helicopters are in use with several Canadian Armed Forces-Air units. Primary duties are SAR and transport. Respective serial blocks were 118101 to 118110, and 135101 to 135105. Nine have seen service in the Middle East in support of the United Nations multi-national peacekeeping force.

Chile
The Chilean air force's Grupo de Transporte No. 10 operates nine UH-1Hs and one Bell 212 on SAR tasks from Los Cerillos, while the Army operates two UH-1Hs amongst a diverse helicopter fleet.

Colombia
Nine UH-1Bs were delivered in 1963, followed by 18 UH-1Hs in 1969 and in the early 1980s. These, along with a pair of Bell 412s and a quartet of Bell 212s equip a Helicopter Group with detachments at several air force bases.

Dominican Republic
Search and rescue and border patrol are the primary tasks occupying 11 Bell 205A-1s/UH-1Hs operated by the air force. Serials include 3018 and 3019.

Ecuador
The Ecuadorian air force has one Bell 212 and two 214Bs for VIP/utility tasks, and four UH-1Hs for SAR. The army has two Bell 214Bs and a single UH-1D for transport tasks.

El Salvador
Fourteen UH-1Hs were supplied by the United States in early 1981, though six of these were lost in a guerrilla raid on Ilopango air base less than a year later. Since then at least 56 more have been supplied under US assistance, but losses have been high.

Ethiopia
Though mostly armed with Soviet equipment, a handful of AB.204Bs and UH-1Hs are reputedly still in use with the air force and army aviation respectively.

One of a handful of AB.204Bs serving with the Austrian air force.

A Brunei Air Wing Bell 212 configured for VIP transport duties.

At least 80 Bell UH-1Hs have been supplied to El Salvador.

An AB.412 Griffon of the Lesotho Police Mobile Unit Air Wing.

Forty-eight AB.205As have been delivered to Morocco over the years.

Three Norwegian squadrons operate a mix of Bell UH-1B/C transports.

Ghana
Two Bell 212s (G650 and G651) are based at Accra for VIP duties

Greece
The Hellenic air force, army and navy all operate Hueys. The former has received 14 AB.205As and three Bell 212s for transport, SAR and VIP duties; the army operates almost 100 AB.205A/UH-1Hs as transports, and the navy has 18 AB.212ASWs.

Guatemala
Three UH-1Ds, six UH-1Hs, three Bell 212s and six Bell 412s have been acquired for use by the air force. All can be armed for COIN tasks.

Guyana
The Guyana Defence Force Air Command is a policing force which operates a single Bell 412 and two Bell 212s for liaison and utility tasks. The Bell 212s are registered 8R-GEO and -GEP, while the Bell 412 is 8R-GFP.

Honduras
US aid to the air force to counter guerrilla operations from Nicaragua has included 10 Bell 412SPs (deliveries starting during 1986) and a mix of UH-1B/Hs.

Indonesia
Locally-built Bell 412s (known as NB 412s) are to replace Bell 205A-1s currently in use with the army, 28 having been ordered to date, but with a potential requirement for up to 150. The air force currently operates a pair of Bell 204Bs on utility tasks.

Iran
Prior to the Islamic revolution, this oil-rich state ordered huge numbers of Hueys, most notably the Bell 214A 'Isfahan' for the army. Other equipment included AB.212s and Bell 214B/Cs for the air force; AB.205s and AB.212ASs for the navy; AB.205A-1s and AB.212s for the army. In post-revolution Iran, the armed forces have been decimated in both manpower and equipment, and it is likely that very few of the Hueys delivered remain in service.

Israel
Twenty-five Bell 212s and up to 35 AB.205s have been supplied to the Heyl Ha'Avir over the years, along with some ex-US Army UH-1Ds. Combat losses have been incurred, and some of the AB.205s were supplied to Rhodesia in 1978.

Italy
Not surprisingly, Agusta-built Hueys have been acquired by the air force, navy and army over the years. Principal operator is the army, with some 95 AB.205As and 19 AB.204Bs for transport and training respectively. There are also some 20 AB.212s, and an expanding fleet of AB.412s. Navy ASW operations are assigned to over 60 AB.212ASWs, with 20 AB.204ASs for support training. The air force is receiving over 30 AB.212s, these serving alongside a similar number of AB.204s for liaison and SAR tasks.

Jamaica
The Jamaica Defence Force Air Wing operates a trio of Bell 212s (JDFH-6, -7 and -8) from Up Park Camp, Kingston. They were all delivered during 1975.

Japan
Licence-built by Fuji, 90 UH-1Bs (41501 to 41590) were produced between 1963 and 1970, followed by production of the UH-1H from 1973 onwards. Some 130 of the latter are eventually planned, all for use (like the UH-1B) by the Japan Ground Self-Defence Force.

Laos
Remnants of US equipment supplied to the then Royal Laotian air force in the 1970s includes about a dozen UH-1D/Hs which reputedly equip two helicopter transport squadrons.

Lebanon
Twelve AB.212s (L-551 to -562) were delivered to the Lebanese air force, nine of which remain in service.

Lesotho
The Police Mobile Unit Air Wing includes a pair of AB.412s in its inventory.

Libya
A pair of AB.212s serve as VIP transports within the army aviation element.

Malta
The Helicopter Flight of the Armed Forces of Malta has been loaned a pair of Italian air force AB.204Bs for coastal patrol and SAR duties.

Mexico
Bell 205As and 212s are operated by the Mexican air force, primarily with Escuadron Aéreo 209 and the Presidential Air Transport Squadron at Santa Lucia and Mexico City International Airport respectively. The Mexican navy has a pair of UH-1Hs for transport and SAR.

Morocco
Forty-eight AB.205As (CN-AJA to -AJZ, CN-AKA to -AKV) and five AB.212s (CN-APA to -APE) have been supplied to the Royal Moroccan air force. At least three of the former have been lost over the years.

New Zealand
No. 3 Squadron, Royal New Zealand Air Force operates a handful of UH-1B/Ds from Wigram on Army support and SAR missions. UH-1Ds delivered were NZ3801 to 3805, while the UH-1Hs were NZ3806 to 3815. There is also a support unit for the New Zealand Force South East Asia at Tengah, Singapore which operates a handful of Hueys. Two UH-1Hs have also been used in the Sinai as part of the United Nations Aviation Support Group.

North Yemen
The Yemen Arab Republic Air Force operates six AB.212s on utility/VIP tasks, along with a pair of AB.204Bs.

Norway
Thirty-three UH-1Bs and four UH-1Cs have been operated by Nos 339, 719 and 720 Squadrons, but the surviving examples are now beginning to be replaced by Bell 412s, 18 of which are currently on order. The latter are being assembled by Helikopter A/S at Stavanger, with more orders likely to follow.

A Peruvian air force UH-1H, one of three Huey models in service.

A Singaporean Bell 212 with nose radar, operated by No. 120 Squadron.

Taiwan has licence-built the UH-1H for use by its army and air force.

Oman
The Sultan of Oman's Air Force has made good use of 20 AB.205A-1s, four AB.214Bs and two AB.212s (the latter for VIP tasks). There are also six Bell 214STs (A40-CJ to -CO) operated by the Police Air Wing.

Pakistan
The Pakistan Army Aviation Corps has received 10 Bell 205s and five UH-1Hs, these being operated by No. 6 (Disaster Relief) Squadron. This unit comes under direct civilian control.

Panama
A dozen UH-1Bs were delivered in 1976/77, followed by 10 UH-1Hs and six UH-1Ns. The survivors form the core of the air force's helicopter force.

Peru
Both the air force and navy operate Hueys, the former a mixture of Bell 212s, 214STs and UH-1Hs, the latter six AB.212ASWs and six UH-1Ds.

Philippines
Amongst the strong US representation in Philippine military equipment are a sole Bell 212 and two Bell 214s for VIP tasks, and a combined force of 80+ Bell 205A-1s/UH-1Hs.

Saudi Arabia
Nos 12 and 14 Squadrons, Royal Saudi Air Force, operate some 20 AB.205As and 29 AB.212s from the Taif air base. These undertake utility transport, SAR and VIP tasks around the country.

Singapore
A diverse Huey force includes Bell 212s for SAR and UH-1B/Hs and AB.205A/A-1s for general transport. No. 120 Squadron operates the Bell 212s, AB.205s and the UH-1Hs, while No. 123 Squadron operates the UH-1Bs. All are serialled in the 200 range, e.g. the Bell 212s are 210 to 212. Both units are based at Sembawang.

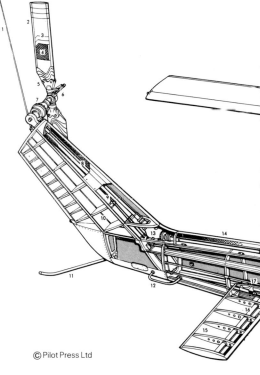

© Pilot Press Ltd

The Republic of Korea air force operates five UH-1Ds in the SAR role, this example being seen during a training exercise.

The United States has passed small numbers of Hueys to Pakistan over the years, most being on long-term loan for disaster relief.

Agusta Bell 212ASW
5° Gruppo Elicotteri/6° Reparto Elicotteri Aviazione per la Marina Militare Italiana (Italian Naval Aviation)

Search radar
Apart from the first 12 such helicopters (fitted with MEL ARI-5955 in a domed cupola), Italian navy AB 212ASWs are equipped with an SMA MM/APS-705 or -706 search and navigation radar. Operating on two frequencies in the I-band for improved clutter-rejection and reliability, the APS-705 system includes a 1.20 m (3 ft 11.25 in) antenna rotating at 20 or 40 rpm (according to selection) and a 23-cm (9-in) diameter plan-position readout screen for the operator. Eight range display options are available between 0.5 and 80 nautical miles (0.9 and 148 km). The similar APS-706 is associated with carriage of Sea Killer missiles and features enhancements including two antennas (back-to-back), frequency-agility and ECCM

Windscreen wipers
Low-level flying over the sea soon produces a build-up of salt on the windscreen, making wipers essential for a naval helicopter

Flight deck
Pilot and co-pilot (who are protected by anti-flash masks) have a comprehensive range of instrumentation available for all-weather oversea operation. ADF (Automatic Direction Finding), TACAN (Tactical Air Navigation), homing UHF, a radar altimeter, Doppler radar and a General Electric SR-3 gyro platform are amongst the main navigation aids, and are complemented by a Sperry four-axis autopilot which includes an 'automatic approach to hover' mode

Avionics bay
Electrical equipment, including the battery, is fitted in the nose. Access is gained via side-panels (marked with the yellow, internationally-recognized 'sine wave' symbol to indicate electrical components), or through a larger hatch which opens like a car's bonnet

Pitot tube
The pitot senses air pressure generated from forward movement, converting the reading to forward air speed after making allowance for ambient atmospheric pressure

Downwards-vision window
The helicopter's ability to execute vertical landings makes direct downwards vision for the pilot a most useful provision

Missile guidance equipment
Mid-course directions can be signalled to an anti-ship missile after launch by a TG-2 real-time data link which updates information on the target's position

Flight deck doors
Both members of the flight crew have an access door, hinged to open forward

Compressed air cylinder
Containing an air supply for the emergency floats

Landing skids
Although many naval helicopters operating from ships' platforms have a wheel undercarriage, the AB 212ASW is fitted with skids, so that a 'harpoon' or 'beartrap' type of deck anchor is not required. Moving the helicopter on the deck is accomplished by fitment of auxiliary wheels

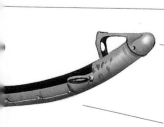

Emergency floats
Floats are valuable in saving a naval helicopter which is forced down with mechanical problems, but cause excessive drag. The solution is to install deflated floats of rubberised material which expand and burst out of their covers when an attached compressed air bottle is activated in an emergency

Stabilizing bar
Mounted at right-angles to the main blades and with counterweights at the tips, the bar has a balancing effect on the lifting rotor

Cabin
According to internal equipment fit and operational duty, up to two crew members can be carried in addition to the pilots, operating the radar and (optionally) 'dunking' sonar. Alternatively, the cabin will hold seven passengers or four stretchers

Winch
A standard fitment for secondary SAR roles is a rescue winch on the starboard side. A maximum load of 270 kg (595 lb) is possible – generously above the weight of two men

tor control rods
sponding to pilot's inputs, rods ange both the angle of the blades and lination of the rotor disc to the rizontal, so permitting movement on e vertical and lateral axes

vicing steps
external access to the cabin top, two k-in' steps and an external hand-hold provided on the starboard side

Cabin door
A sliding door is installed on both sides of the cabin

Doppler
Doppler radar bounces a signal off the surface (water or land) and measures the frequency shift produced by the relative movement of source and reflector. The shift is directly proportional to surface speed, and so can be used in computation of the helicopter's position

Navigation light
Conforming to international convention, all aircraft (and ships) show a green light to starboard and a red to port

Somalia

The Somalia Aeronautical Corps has received four AB.212s (MM60218 to MM60221) and a single AB.204. Two of the former have been converted to VIP configuration.

South Korea

The UH-1H is to be locally built by Samsung Industries, with up to 50 being required, some of which will go to the Army aviation element. Currently the air force operates three Bell 412s (VIP duties), seven Bell 212s/UH-1Hs (VIP and SAR duties) and five UH-1Ds (SAR duties). The army has received 15 UH-1Bs and 47 UH-1Hs for general transport and troop support tasks.

Spain

Hueys serve with the Spanish air force, army, navy and air rescue service, these comprising a mix of Bell and Agusta-Bell machines. The major user is the army, with 60 UH-1Hs (HU.10B) and six each of UH-1B/Cs (HU.8) and AB.212s (HU.18B) having been delivered since 1966. The navy has AB.204Bs and AB.212ASs, while the ARS has received AB.205s and UH-1Hs. A handful of UH-1Hs have been delivered to the air force.

Sri Lanka

No. 4 Squadron is responsible for Air Force rotary operations, and has received nine Bell 212s and four Bell 214s since 1985. Examples of the former include CH538, 539 and 542. The war against Tamil guerrillas has resulted in these helicopters being armed with side-mounted guns.

The majority of UH-1s in service with the Canadian Armed Forces are CH-135 Twin Hueys, but there is also a small force of CH-118 Iroquois. This example of the latter model serves with No. 403 Squadron.

Sudan

The Sudanese air force has received 11 AB.212s for use alongside Soviet Mil Mi-8s and Romanian-built Pumas.

Sweden

Both the air force and army operate aged AB.204Bs (local designation: Hkp 3B). The former received six examples (03421 to 03427), while the army air corps received a dozen examples (03301 to 03312).

Taiwan

Large numbers of UH-1Hs have been supplied to the Chinese Nationalist air force and army, these being locally produced by AIDC. Over 120 are in service between the two forces.

Tanzania

Four AB.205As are in service with the Tanzanian People's Defence Force – Air Wing. These form the communications element of the TPDF-AW.

Bell UH-1B Iroquois
cutaway drawing key

1 FM communications aerial
2 Two-blade tail rotor
3 Laminated glassfibre blade skins
4 Honeycomb blade core
5 Blade root attachment joint
6 Pitch control linkage
7 Final drive right-angle gearbox
8 Tail rotor drive shaft
9 Tail rotor control cables
10 Tail pylon construction
11 Rotor protecting tailskid
12 VHF navigation aerial
13 42-deg bevel drive gearbox
14 Dorsal spine fairing
15 Starboard all-moving tailplane construction
16 Tailplane torque shaft
17 Radio compass transmitter
18 Port all-moving tailplane
19 Main rotor blade
20 Fixed tab
21 Glassfibre blade skins
22 Honeycomb core construction
23 Extruded aluminium blade spar
24 Leading edge anti-erosion strip, stainless steel
25 Tail rotor transmission shaft
26 Shaft bearings
27 Tailboom upper longeron
28 Tailboom frame and stringer construction
29 Lower longeron
30 Tailplane control linkage
31 Engine exhaust fairing
32 Exhaust nozzle
33 Jet pipe
34 Cooling air louvres
35 Anti-collision light
36 UHF aerial

37 Detachable engine cowling panels
38 Avco Lycoming T53-L-11A turboshaft engine
39 Ignition control box
40 Accessory equipment gearbox
41 Engine bearer struts
42 Main engine mounting
43 Engine/gearbox mounting deck
44 Maintenance access step
45 Baggage compartment
46 Baggage restraint net
47 Armament system electronics
48 XM-21 sub-system external stores pylon
49 Gun mounting adaptor
50 Swivelling gun mounting
51 M-134 Minigun, 0.30-in (7.62-mm) rotary machine-gun
52 Gun drive motor
53 7-cm (2.75-in) rocket launcher

54 Ammunition feed chute
55 Two 7.62-mm (0.30-in) machine-guns
56 Gun swivelling mounting
57 Ammunition feed chutes
58 Detachable ground handling wheels
59 Wheel hydraulic jack
60 Landing skid rear strut
61 Maintenance access steps
62 Cabin combustion heater
63 Main fuel tank, port and starboard; total capacity 625 litres (165 US gal)
64 Fuel filler cap
65 Sliding cabin door rail
66 Hydraulic oil reservoir
67 Maintenance step
68 Oil tank
69 Oil filler cap
70 Engine bay fireproof bulkhead
71 Gearbox oil sump
72 Main gearbox mounting
73 Rotor head control jacks
74 Main gearbox
75 Engine/gearbox shaft coupling

76 Engine inlet guard
77 Annular air inlet
78 Rotor head swashplate mechanism
79 Blade pitch control rods
80 Main rotor mast
81 Semi-rigid rotor head
82 Blade counterweights
83 Rotor stabilizing bar
84 Blade root attachment joints
85 Laminated joint stiffeners
86 Two-blade main rotor
87 Rotor head fairing
88 Cooling air intake
89 Cabin rear bulkhead
90 Bulkhead soundproof trim panelling
91 Starboard sliding door panel
92 Ammunition feed chutes
93 External stores pylon
94 Pylon mounting struts
95 Landing skid
96 External cargo hook
97 Landing skid front strut
98 Starboard lower navigation light†

99 Cabin side pillar construction
100 Cabin floor panelling
101 Floor beam construction
102 Cargo lashing points
103 Ventral retractable landing lamp
104 Ammunition magazine
105 Starboard upper navigation light
106 Troop seating; seven seats, not fitted with armament installations
107 Anti-downwash cabin roof strake
108 DF loop aerial
109 Cabin ventilating air intake
110 Port upper navigation light
111 Cabin skin panelling
112 Cockpit eyebrow windows
113 Cockpit fresh air intakes
114 VHF aerial
115 Overhead switch panel
116 Port side sliding cabin door
117 Aft-facing troop seats
118 Pilot's seat
119 Safety harness
120 Jettisonable crew door
121 Door latches
122 Seat mounting rails

123 Control system access panel
124 Cockpit step
125 Door jettison mechanism
126 Cyclic pitch control column
127 Collective pitch control lever
128 Centre control pedestal
129 Pilot's retractable reflex sight
130 Co-pilot/gunner's seat
131 Cyclic pitch control handgrip
132 Retractable XM-60 reflex sight
133 Port jettisonable crew door
134 Windscreen wipers
135 Windscreen panels
136 Instrument panel shroud
137 Instrument console
138 Stand-by compass
139 Footboards
140 Yaw control rudder pedals
141 Downward vision window
142 XM-5 40-mm grenade launcher
143 Detachable nose turret
144 Ammunition feed chute
145 FM homing aerials
146 Radio and avionics equipment bay
147 Nose compartment framing
148 Avionics compartment access panel
149 Pitot head

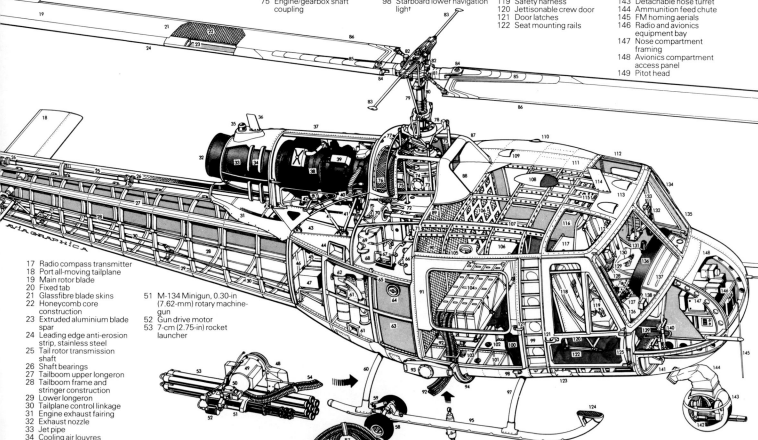

Thailand

No. 203 Squadron, Royal Thai Air Force operates 29 UH-1Hs; No. 4 Squadron, Royal Thai Navy has small numbers of UH-1Hs and Bell 212s; the Army operates a handful of Bell 214B/STs and six Bell 212s, alongside 75+ Bell UH-1B/Ds. Plans to acquire Bell 214STs for the Navy have run into financial and political problems. Additionally, the Border Police have received two Bell 214s, 14 Bell 205s and 11 Bell 212s. A Royal Flight operated by the Air Force is equipped with two AB.412s, though they are due for replacement.

Tunisia

The Republic of Tunisia air force has received 18 AB.205As and six UH-1Hs over the years. The survivors are in service with No. 31 Squadron. The AB.205As are serialled L81701 to L81718.

Turkey

High levels of US equipment have included some 50 UH-1Hs for the air force, these equipping the 224th Squadron and various base flights. Duties include SAR, VIP transport and refresher training. The Navy conducts ASW operations from its frigates with six AB.212ASWs and AB.204ASs. The Turkish army has some 40 UH-1Hs and 130+ AB.205As, 20 AB.204Bs and three AB.212s, all for transportation and liaison duties. The paramilitary Gendarmerie has a mixture of AB.204B/205A/212s for utility and VIP tasks.

Uganda

The Uganda Army Air Force operates three AB.205s and two AB.412s, while the Police Air Wing has received three Bell 412s. The UAAF examples have apparently been modified to carry 'missiles' (most likely unguided rocket packs). The PAW aircraft are serialled AW-1 and -2.

United Arab Emirates

Air elements of this seven-state military force are split between Western Command (Abu Dhabi) and Central Command (Dubai). The latter operates the transport force, this including four each of the Bell 212 and 214B and six Bell 205As, all of which are based at Mindhat AB.

United States (Air Force)

The principal users are Military Airlift Command and Tactical Air Command. The former operates UH-1Fs for missile site support and HH/UH-1Ns for base crash rescue duties. Three Air Force Reserve squadrons operate HH/UH-1Hs, while the USAF in Europe has a small number of UH-1Hs for VIP transport.

United States (Army)

The first Hueys were delivered to the US Army during 1959 (HU-1As), and the variants still in use should easily see front-line service into the 21st century. The world's biggest helicopter operator, the US Army has well over 3,500 UH-1s in use, these supporting ground operations worldwide. The majority are UH-1Hs, but several other variants serve in respectable numbers.

United States (Marine Corps)

An important asset for US Marine Corps operations, the UH-1E/N serves with no less than 14 squadrons, these comprising a mix of Attack, Light, Medium, Heavy and Training units, while the VH-1H equips HMX-1 for VIP transport tasks. The UH-1N would also form part of a notional composite squadron for deployment aboard Marine or Navy vessels.

VIP transport duties are the responsibility of HMX-1's VH-1H fleet.

A Bell UH-1H of Headquarters 1st Tactical Air Force, Turkish Air Force during 1985.

A Bell UH-1N of the 67th ARRS, US Air Force based in Europe for VIP transport duties.

A pair of Bell 412s have been supplied to the Venezuelan Air Force.

United States (Navy)

Two Light Attack Helicopter Squadrons are equipped with HH-1Ks, both being part of the Reserve forces. The Hueys have now been replaced in the training role by Bell TH-47 Sea Rangers, but small numbers still equip some base flights, VXE-6 for support of Arctic operations (UH-1Ns), and Helicopter Combat Support Squadron 16 (HC-16) with UH-1Ns.

Uruguay

Six Bell UH-1Bs (60 to 65), three UH-1Hs (50 to 52) and a pair of Bell 212s (one of which is 071) have been supplied to Grupo Aéreo 5 of Tactical Flying Command, Uruguayan air force.

Venezuela

The air force has received two Bell 412s, two Bell 214STs, two UH-1Hs and 15 UH-1Ds. Naval ship and shore ASW operations are conducted by 12 AB.212ASWs, these being assigned to Esc.03. The army performs utility transport tasks with eight UH-1Hs and three Bell 205A-1s, and the national guard has two Bell 214STs.

Vietnam

The Vietnam People's Army Air Force retains up to 40 UH-1B/D/Hs which were left behind by the US forces at the end of the war in 1975. Their operational status is open to question.

West Germany

Both the air force (Luftwaffe) and army aviation corps (Heeresflieger) have received substantial numbers of UH-1Ds, the vast majority of which were built by Dornier under licence. A total of 142 were supplied to the Luftwaffe, these bearing the serials 7001, 7002 and 7041 to 7180. The Heeresflieger received 204 examples serialled 7181 to 7384. Most remaining Luftwaffe examples serve with Lufttransportgeschwader 61 at Landsberg. The army machines are split between Leichtes Heeresflieger Transportregiments 10, 20 and 30, along with a sizeable number assigned to the army flying school and Heeresfliegerregiment 6. A small number serve with Est 61 for testing purposes. The Federal German border police also operate the UH-1D, though their examples are civil-registered.

Zambia

A mixed helicopter force within the Zambian Air Force and Air Defence Command includes 13 AB.205As and two AB.212s for communications tasks.

Zimbabwe

When still known as Rhodesia, 11 AB.205A Cheetahs were received from Israeli stocks. The current Air Force of Zimbabwe still operates at least six of these, with two more acting as spares ships. Also in use are 12 AB.412s. No. 8 Squadron at New Sarum operates the helicopter force.

Minimal bracing enhances the already excellent forward visibility for both Huey flight crew. Note the retracted XM-60 reflex sight in use by the co-pilot.

Suppressive firepower from the Huey has more often than not taken the form of door-mounted 7.62 mm machine guns on flexible mounts, as effective today in Sri Lanka as it was in Vietnam.

Bell UH-1 variants

XH-40: Bell Model 204, three prototypes powered by 522-kW (700-shp) Lycoming XT53-L-1 turboshafts
YH-40: six evaluation and development machines with minor changes and 574-kW (770-shp) T53-L-1 engines
UH-1A: nine pre-production **HU-1** helicopters were followed by 173 **HU-1A** helicopters delivered between June 1959 and March 1961; gross weight increased to 3266 kg (7,200 lb), and the type was fitted initially with the 574-kW (770-shp) T53-L-1A; later upgraded with 716-kW (960-shp) T53-L-5
TH-1A: 14 fitted with dual controls and instrument flying training equipment for US Army Aviation School, Fort Rucker
XH-1A: modified for initial armament trials with rocket and grenade launchers, and machine-guns
UH-1B: four **YUH-1B** helicopters initially with 716-kW (960-shp) T53-L-5 and later with 821-kW (1,100-shp) L-9 or L-11 engines; new rotor blades of honeycomb construction with chord increased from 35.6 to 53.3 cm (14 to 21 in), rotor mast 33 cm (13 in) taller than that of the UH-1A; gross weight increased to 3856 kg (8,500 lb), and cabin stretched

UH-1C: increased fuel capacity, from 625 to 916 litres (165 to 242 US gal); Bell 540 68.6-cm (27-in) chord rotor system and inverted aerofoil section elevators; pitot tube and FM radio aerial relocated from nose to cabin roof; 767 built
UH-1D: seven **YUH-1D** helicopters for service trials, 2,001 production machines manufactured by Bell for US forces, with 14.63-m (48-ft) main rotor driven by 820-kW (1,100-shp) T53-L-11; fuel cells relocated to increase cabin capacity to 6.23 m³ (220 cu ft) and able to carry pilot and 12 troops; first operational unit was 11th Air Assault Division based at Fort Benning; also for export and 360 built by Dornier in Germany
HH-1D: UH-1D conversions for rescue duties
UH-1E: US Marine Corps version of UH-1B with aluminium structure for shipboard use and fitted with rotor brake; electrical system changed from DC to AC; roof-mounted hoist and initially armed with TAT-101 chin turret mounting two 7.62-mm M60 machine-guns, later replaced by laterally-mounted weapons and

racks for 2.75-in rocket pods; first delivery to Marine Squadron VMO-1 on 24 February 1964
TH-1E: 20 dual-control trainers for US Marine Corps
UH-1F: 120 built for US Air Force and re-engined with 949-kW (1,272-shp) General Electric T58-3 engine driving the Bell 540 rotor; gross weight 4082 kg (9,000 lb) and a cargo compartment was provided at front of boom; first flown 20 February 1964, used to support SAC Minuteman and Titan sites
TH-1F: 26 instrument trainers for the US Air Force
UH-1H: UH-1D airframe with 1044-kW (1,400-shp) Lycoming T53-L-13 engine; 5,435 built for US Army and 118 in Taiwan for Nationalist Chinese army; also widely exported

CUH-1H: 10 built for Canadian Armed Forces Mobile Command, later redesignated **CH-118**
EH-1H: ECM/Elint version for US Army, developed under Army Security Agency's Project 'Quick Fix'
JUH-1H: four UH-1Hs modified to carry a ventral radar pod in trials connected with the Stand-Off Target Acquisition System (SOTAS) for EH-60B Black Hawk
HH-1K: 27 machines, similar to US Marines' UH-1E and powered by T53-L-13 engine; improved avionics installed and helicopters were used by US Navy for SAR duties
UH-1L: eight utility helicopters for the US Navy with T53-L-13
TH-1L: US Navy advanced rotary-wing trainer; 90 built to equip navy training wings
UH-1M: US Army UH-1Cs with INFANT (Iroquois Night Fighter And Night Tracker) equipment, essentially a low-light-level TV tracking system for night attack operations
UH-1N: twin-engined development of UH-1H with Pratt & Whitney Canada PT6T-3 Turbo Twin Pac; gross weight 5080 kg (11,200 lb) including maximum underslung load of 1814 kg (4,000 lb); 300 for US armed forces plus exports
CUH-1N: 50 for Canadian Armed Forces, later redesignated **CH-135**
HH-1N: 22 manufactured for US Air Force for base rescue duties, mainly with Air Force Reserve units and for the anti-terrorist and counter-insurgency Special Operations Force at Hurlburt Field, Florida
VH-1N: VIP transport version for US Air Force and US Marines (six

plus conversions of UH-1Ns)
UH-1P: 20 converted from UH-1F airframes for psychological warfare duties, primarily with the 1st Special Operations Wing at Hurlburt Field, Florida
UH-1V: approximately 220 UH-1Hs converted by US Army Electronics Command at Lakehurst, New Jersey, with improved avionics which include radio altimeter, ARN-124 DME and glideslope; used for medevac duties and also fitted with a rescue hoist; first deliveries to 397th Aeromedical Detachment, New Hampshire ANG
Model 204: civil utility model equivalent of UH-1B
Model 205: improved civil production model equivalent to UH-1D
Model 205A: civil version of UH-1H
Model 212: civil version of UH-1N, available and certificated for commercial IFR operations; in June 1977 became first helicopter to be type-certificated by FAA for single-pilot IFR operation

Model 214: enlarged development of UH-1H for 'hot and high' conditions with Lycoming T55 engine; 287 Model 214As for Imperial Iranian army and 39 Model 214Cs for Imperial Iranian air force; **Model 214B BigLifter** is civil version
Model 214ST: civil development of Model 214A with two General Electric CT7-2A engines, for crew of two and up to 18 passengers

Model 412: improved Model 212 with four-blade rotor of advanced design, type-approved in January 1981 and February 1981 for VFR and IFR operations respectively; gross weight 5262 kg (11,600 lb); built in Italy as **AB 412 Grifone**

Specification: UH-1H Iroquois

Rotors
Main rotor diameter	14.63 m	(48 ft 0 in)
Tail rotor diameter	2.59 m	(8 ft 6 in)
Main rotor disc area	168.11 m²	(1,809.56 sq ft)

Fuselage and tail unit
Accommodation one or two pilots, and up to 14 fully equipped troops in main cabin
Length, rotors turning	17.62 m	(57 ft 9.6 in)
Fuselage length	12.77 m	(41 ft 10.75 in)
Height overall	4.41 m	(14 ft 5.5 in)

Landing gear
Tubular skids with lock-on ground handling wheels and flotation bags
Width over skids	2.91 m	(9 ft 6.5 in)

Weights
Empty equipped	2363 kg	(5,210 lb)
Maximum take-off	4309 kg	(9,500 lb)
Mission weight	4100 kg	(9,039 lb)

Powerplant
One Avco Lycoming T53-L-13 turboshaft engine
Rating	1044 kW	(1,400 shp)

UH-1H Iroquois recognition features

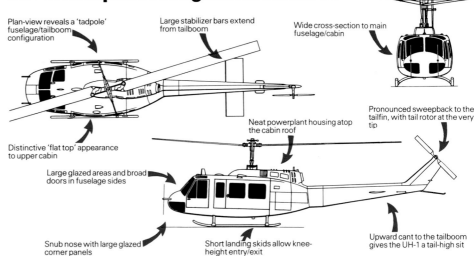

Plan-view reveals a 'tadpole' fuselage/tailboom configuration

Large stabilizer bars extend from tailboom

Wide cross-section to main fuselage/cabin

Pronounced sweepback to the tailfin, with tail rotor at the very tip

Neat powerplant housing atop the cabin roof

Distinctive 'flat top' appearance to upper cabin

Large glazed areas and broad doors in fuselage sides

Snub nose with large glazed corner panels

Short landing skids allow knee-height entry/exit

Upward cant to the tailboom gives the UH-1 a tail-high sit

Performance
Maximum speed	110 kts; 204 km/h	(127 mph)
Initial rate of climb	1,600 ft	(488 m) per minute
Service ceiling	12,600 ft	(3840 m)
Hovering ceiling, in ground effect	13,600 ft	(4145 m)
Range at sea level with maximum fuel	512 km	(318 miles)

External load
- Boeing Vertol CH-46D Sea Knight 453b kg
- Aérospatiale AS 332M Super Puma 4500 kg
- Sikorsky UH-60A Black Hawk 3630 kg
- Westland Commando Mk 2 3628 kg
- Mil Mi-8 'Hip' 3000 kg
- Aérospatiale (Westland) Puma HC.Mk 1 2500 kg
- 2000 kg E
- Bell UH-1H Iroquois
- Westland Wessex HU.Mk 5 1814 kg

Initial rate of climb, in feet per minute
- Westland Commando Mk 2 2,020 ft
- Sikorsky UH-60A Black Hawk 2,000 ft E
- Mil Mi-8 'Hip' 1,800 ft E
- Aérospatiale AS 332M Super Puma 1,730 ft
- Boeing Vertol CH-46D Sea Knight 1,660 ft
- Westland Wessex HU.Mk 5 1,650 ft
- Bell UH-1H Iroquois 1,600 ft
- Aérospatiale (Westland) Puma HC.Mk 1 1,400 ft

Maximum cruising speed at optimum altitude
- Sikorsky UH-60A Black Hawk 160 kts
- Aérospatiale AS 332M Super Puma 151 kts
- Aérospatiale (Westland) Puma HC.Mk 1 143 kts
- Boeing Vertol CH-46D Sea Knight 140 kts
- Mil Mi-8 'Hip' 124 kts
- Westland Wessex HU.Mk 5 115 kts
- Westland Commando Mk 2 112 kts
- Bell UH-1H Iroquois 110 kts

Range with internal fuel
- Aérospatiale AS 332M Super Puma 635 km
- Aérospatiale (Westland) Puma HC.Mk 1 630 km
- Westland Wessex HU.Mk 5 628 km
- Sikorsky UH-60A Black Hawk 600 km — 30 minutes reserves
- Bell UH-1H Iroquois 511 km
- Mil Mi-8 'Hip' 500 km — 20 minutes reserves
- Westland Commando Mk 2 445 km — 30 minutes reserves
- Boeing Vertol CH-46D Sea Knight 383 km — 10% reserves

Number of troops carried
- Westland Commando Mk 2 28
- Mil Mi-8 'Hip' 28
- Boeing Vertol CH-46D Sea Knight 25
- Aérospatiale AS 332M Super Puma 25
- Westland Wessex HU.Mk 5 16
- Aérospatiale (Westland) Puma HC.Mk 1 16
- Bell UH-1H Iroquois 14
- Sikorsky UH-60A Black Hawk 11

The BELL AH-1 COBRA

HueyCobra: the biter from Bell

If ever an aircraft or helicopter could strike fear into the heart of an enemy just by its menacing appearance, it has to be the Bell AH-1 HueyCobra. But this is a true fighter, armed to the teeth with a variety of armour-piercing weaponry suitable for various mission profiles.

The extremely narrow and compact fuselage of the AH-1 make it an incredibly difficult helicopter to sight. That's just as well as it is tasked with highly dangerous nap-of-the-earth missions against enemy armour.

Although the idea of arming helicopters had been around for a few years (and, indeed, had been successfully implemented in South Vietnam where Bell's remarkably versatile UH-1 Iroquois, or 'Huey' as it was probably far better known, had compiled a fairly impressive combat record) such machines were invariably modifications of existing types which in many cases were by no means ideally suited for the very different demands inherent in battle.

This is not to say that such machines were incapable of effective operation in a combat role, but rather that this class of helicopter essentially represented a compromise: they were generally based on utility types which although able to carry a respectable ordnance load (including air-to-surface rockets and machine-guns) were generally regarded as deficient in performance. What was clearly needed was a dedicated attack helicopter which married high performance with the ability to operate with a worthwhile payload, and which was rather less vulnerable than interim types to ground fire, a constant hazard in Vietnam.

Bell was only one of a number of companies engaged in research of this nature, and much of the company's pioneering work was employed to advantage on the Model 209 which was the result of a privately-funded crash project intended to meet the US Army's AAFSS requirement. Originally the Lockheed AH-56 Cheyenne was earmarked to satisfy this need, but this was ultimately abandoned on the grounds of high cost although the Army was still anxious to obtain a dedicated attack helicopter for use in Vietnam and elsewhere in the world.

Design similarities

In terms of physical appearance, the Model 209 was very different from the UH-1. However, in this instance, appearances were most definitely deceptive for it was, in fact, closely allied to the Iroquois in that it incorporated many of the design features employed by that type. For example, the rotor assembly was virtually identical, whilst the Model 209 also inherited the transmission system employed by the UH-1C as well as the Avco Lycoming T53-L-13 turboshaft engine. These items were married to an entirely new fuselage of much narrower frontal section with small stub wings to provide a measure of lift as well as somewhere to hang weapons, it being intended from the outset that the new helicopter would be heavily armed in comparison with existing types.

Some idea of the urgency attached to this project can be gleaned from the fact that although development was initiated only in March 1965, a Model 209 prototype was fabricated and assembled during the summer of that year and flew for the first time on 7 September 1965. Subsequently, following a fairly brief company flight test programme, it was transferred to Edwards AFB, California for a somewhat more exhaustive series of service trials which quickly convinced Army personnel that the Model 209 was a most promising newcomer and one that was worthy of consideration to meet the still-vacant AAFSS requirement. By early March 1966, the Army had decided in principle to purchase Bell's gunship, subsequently placing an order for a couple of pre-production prototypes on 4 April and following up just nine days later with a contract for an initial batch of 112 production AH-1G helicopters, stipulating that these should be made available at the earliest possible moment in order to permit rapid deployment to Vietnam, where the US commitment was reaching record levels almost daily. Eventually, this proved to be the forerunner of a series of contracts, procurement for the Army passing the 1000 mark in Fiscal Year 1972, whilst the US Marine Corps received 38 on loan pending availability of that service's custom-built AH-1J SeaCobra derivative. Modest quantities were also supplied to Israel and Spain.

Battle debut

The initial production version of the HueyCobra was the AH-1G, delivery of which began in June 1967. It soon became clear that haste was still very much the order of the day, for the first HueyCobras arrived in South Vietnam on 1 September 1967. An organization known as Cobra-NETT was entrusted with the responsibility of introducing the type to combat, and this began in-country training sorties on 18 September, firstly undertaking pilot

A dramatic view of an AH-1 as it looses off the first of 38 unguided rockets from two underwing pods. Primary control of weapons firing is assigned to the co-pilot/gunner in the front seat of the cockpit.

transition in concert with instruction in maintenance and support procedures.

Subsequently, as the number of AH-1Gs increased, the HueyCobra began to range far and wide, operating mainly in the en route escort reconnaissance and direct fire support roles, for which it quickly proved well suited. Armament configurations varied according to mission requirements, early production machines being fitted with an Emerson TAT-102A turret unit consisting of a single 7.62-mm (0.3-in) Gatling-type machine-gun complete with 8,000 rounds of ammunition. Almost inevitably, though, armament capability was greatly enhanced as the HueyCobra matured, later examples of the AH-1G featuring the M28 tactical armament turret system which could mount a pair of 7.62-mm guns each with 4,000 rounds, or a pair of M129 40-mm grenade-launchers each with 300 grenades, or, alternatively, one gun and one grenade-launcher. In addition, four external stores stations were fitted to the stub wings, permitting the AH-1G to carry as many as 76 pod-mounted 2.75-in (70-mm) rockets or additional gun armament in the shape of M18E1 Minigun pods.

Close air support

At about the same time as the AH-1G entered service, the Marine Corps began to take a long hard look at the possibility of employing the HueyCobra (or a variant thereof) in the close air support role. Once again, this service very quickly reached the conclusion that Bell's Model 209 would indeed be able to fill a gap in the existing inventory. Like the Army, the Marines had also begun to hang armament on existing helicopters (most notably the Sikorsky UH-34D Seahorse) and had determined that a dedicated attack helicopter would greatly enhance the chances of success in the assault role with which this service is traditionally linked. However, since USMC operations fre-

quently entail extended flight over sea it was felt that the Marine requirement should stipulate a twin-engined machine.

Undeterred by this, Bell came up with a variation on the Model 209 theme based on the Pratt & Whitney Aircraft of Canada T400-CP-400 turboshaft engine, which was satisfactory since this was built up around two PT6 power sections. Fitted with this powerplant, the USMC model was ordered into production as the AH-1J SeaCobra. Adoption of a different engine in turn necessitated further redesign in other areas and the opportunity was also taken to change to the three-barrelled General Electric XM197 20-mm rotary cannon.

As already noted, the USMC received a modest number of standard AH-1G HueyCobras from 1969, using these mainly for training tasks whilst awaiting delivery of the definitive AH-1J, a process which began in mid-1970. Eventually, some 84 examples of the AH-1J were acquired between 1970 and 1977, a couple of these being modified to serve as prototypes for the more advanced AH-1T. Some 202 AH-1Js were purchased by the Imperial Iranian army during the early 1970s; it is doubtful if many of these are still operational.

Scouting around at tree-top height, a Cobra can drop down to a few feet above ground level when the enemy is detected. The laser rangefinder in the nose has a detection range of up to 32,000 ft (9750 m).

Further improvement initiatives undertaken at a much later stage in the Model 209's service career have resulted in the appearance of several more variants, most of which are capable of operation with the Hughes TOW anti-tank missile and, in Army service at least, the AH-1 now appears to be viewed as primarily an anti-armour system although it does retain the ability to deliver other weaponry.

Missile armament

TOW capability first emerged in about the mid-1970s when about 100 AH-1Gs were modified to carry this weapon, and were redesignated AH-1Qs. Another derivative which resulted from modernization and modification was the AH-1R,

A firepower demonstration by a gaggle of US Army AH-1Ss is a fearsome sight as missiles and rockets head towards their targets. The undernose M197 three-barrel gun provides an extra punch for closer-range attack.

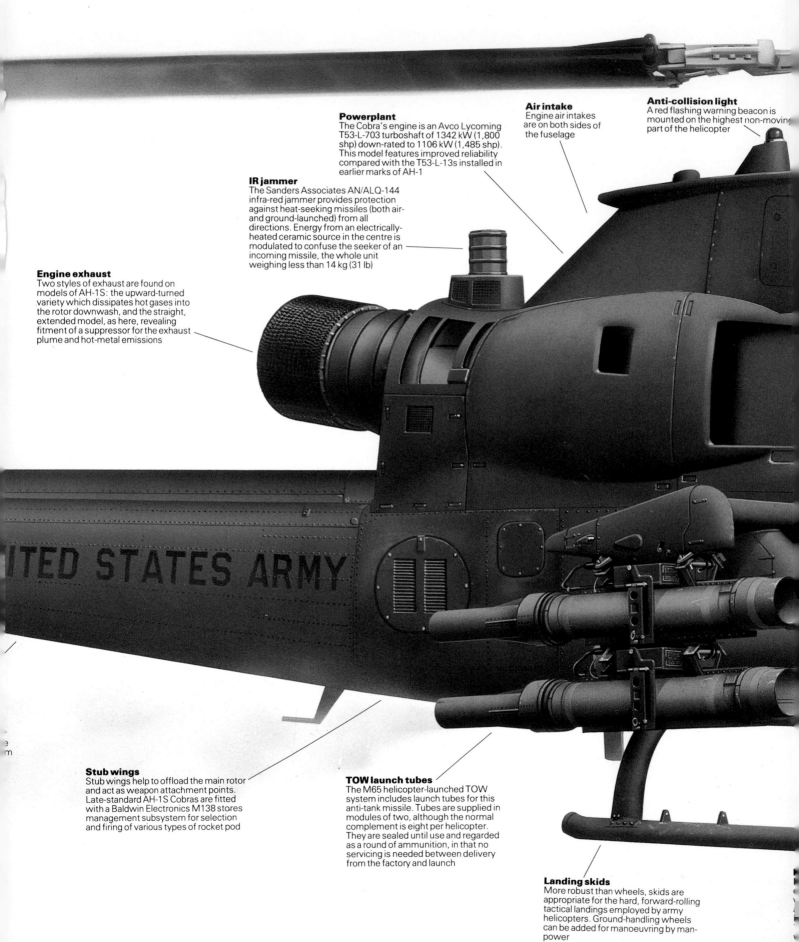

Rotor head
Devoid of c[...]
rotor head t[...]
rpm in a cloc[...]
from above

Powerplant
The Cobra's engine is an Avco Lycoming T53-L-703 turboshaft of 1342 kW (1,800 shp) down-rated to 1106 kW (1,485 shp). This model features improved reliability compared with the T53-L-13s installed in earlier marks of AH-1

Air intake
Engine air intakes are on both sides of the fuselage

Anti-collision light
A red flashing warning beacon is mounted on the highest non-moving part of the helicopter

IR jammer
The Sanders Associates AN/ALQ-144 infra-red jammer provides protection against heat-seeking missiles (both air- and ground-launched) from all directions. Energy from an electrically-heated ceramic source in the centre is modulated to confuse the seeker of an incoming missile, the whole unit weighing less than 14 kg (31 lb)

Engine exhaust
Two styles of exhaust are found on models of AH-1S: the upward-turned variety which dissipates hot gases into the rotor downwash, and the straight, extended model, as here, revealing fitment of a suppressor for the exhaust plume and hot-metal emissions

ITED STATES ARMY

Stub wings
Stub wings help to offload the main rotor and act as weapon attachment points. Late-standard AH-1S Cobras are fitted with a Baldwin Electronics M138 stores management subsystem for selection and firing of various types of rocket pod

TOW launch tubes
The M65 helicopter-launched TOW system includes launch tubes for this anti-tank missile. Tubes are supplied in modules of two, although the normal complement is eight per helicopter. They are sealed until use and regarded as a round of ammunition, in that no servicing is needed between delivery from the factory and launch

Landing skids
More robust than wheels, skids are appropriate for the hard, forward-rolling tactical landings employed by army helicopters. Ground-handling wheels can be added for manoeuvring by man-power

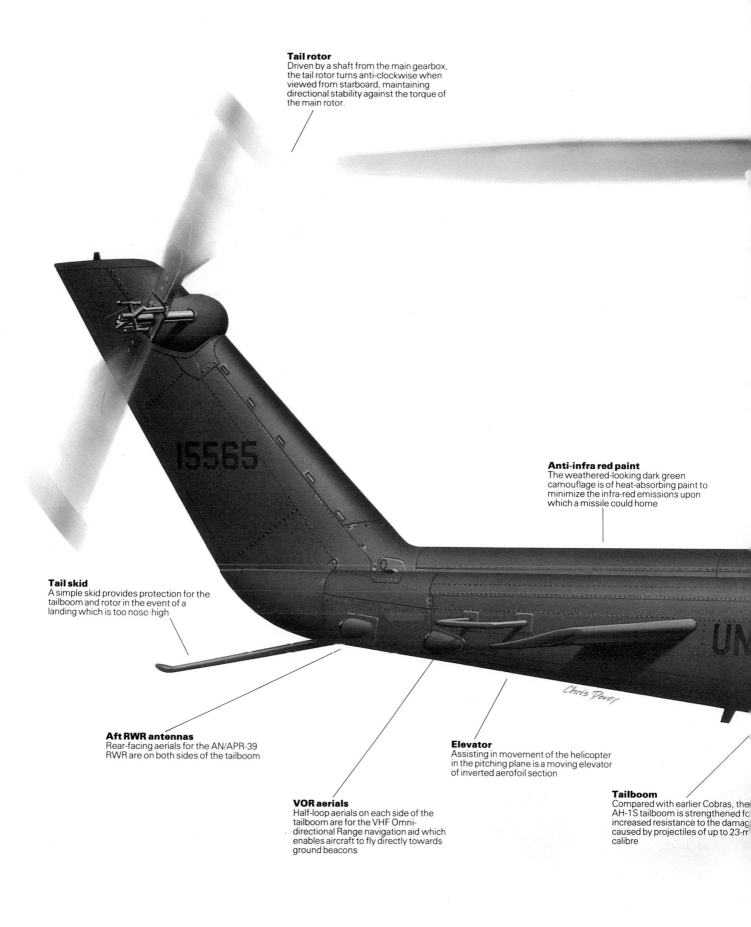

Tail rotor
Driven by a shaft from the main gearbox, the tail rotor turns anti-clockwise when viewed from starboard, maintaining directional stability against the torque of the main rotor.

Anti-infra red paint
The weathered-looking dark green camouflage is of heat-absorbing paint to minimize the infra-red emissions upon which a missile could home

Tail skid
A simple skid provides protection for the tailboom and rotor in the event of a landing which is too nose-high

Aft RWR antennas
Rear-facing aerials for the AN/APR-39 RWR are on both sides of the tailboom

VOR aerials
Half-loop aerials on each side of the tailboom are for the VHF Omni-directional Range navigation aid which enables aircraft to fly directly towards ground beacons

Elevator
Assisting in movement of the helicopter in the pitching plane is a moving elevator of inverted aerofoil section

Tailboom
Compared with earlier Cobras, the AH-1S tailboom is strengthened fo increased resistance to the damag caused by projectiles of up to 23-m calibre

which was fitted with an uprated T53-L-703 engine although this was not configured for TOW. Ultimately, all of the surviving AH-1Qs and many AH-1Gs and AH-1Rs were brought to AH-1S standard, this now being the definitive US Army HueyCobra model, although at least four different configurations are known to have seen service with the Army, these varying with regard to weapons fit, sensor systems and external appearance. Many feature the much in vogue flat-plate canopy and upturned infra-red suppressing exhaust efflux nozzle.

As well as procurement of the AH-1S by means of conversion, the Army has also contracted for a substantial number of new-build machines, and aircraft of this type have also been supplied to a number of friendly nations (including Pakistan, Israel and Jordan), with the result that the combined production and conversion total will eventually exceed 1,000. In addition, a licence agreement negotiated with Fuji has led to production in Japan, which is to acquire 54 examples of the AH-1S for the Japan Ground Self-Defence Force.

Not to be outdone, the Marine Corps has also undertaken delivery of an improved version of the SeaCobra, this being designated AH-1T. Although basically similar to the earlier AH-1J, the AH-1T model employed the dynamic system of the Bell 214, some of the features conceived and developed for the Bell 309 KingCobra and an upgraded powerplant/transmission, permitting it to tote rather more in the way of offensive payload.

Entering service during 1977-8, about 50 examples of the AH-1T were eventually built for the Marines, and most of the survivors have subsequently been reconfigured to carry the TOW missile. Further updating, undertaken in the early 1980s, has resulted in the appearance of the AH-1T+ SuperCobra first flying on 16 November 1983. This in turn has been accepted for USMC service as the AH-1W,

of which 44 are being built. Plans expect the AH-1Ts to be converted to W standard, the entire AH-1W fleet being assembled by 1989.

With regard to overall capability, the SuperCobra is undoubtedly the most potent member of the Cobra family, weapons payload and performance being much enhanced as a direct result of adoption of the rather more powerful General Electric T700-GE-401 turboshaft, which has a combined output of no less than 2423 kW (3,250 shp).

Continual updates

Possessing the ability to undertake such missions as anti-armour, escort, fire support and armed reconnaissance, the AH-1T+ has armament options that include 76 2.75-in or 16 5-in (127-mm) Zuni rockets, or two AIM-9L Sidewinder or Stinger air-to-air missiles, or up to eight TOW or Hellfire anti-armour air-to-surface missiles. In addition, integral gun armament is retained, the magazine for the 20-mm M197 cannon permitting a maximum of 750 rounds to be carried.

As far as combat experience is concerned, the original AH-1G racked up a most impressive record in South East Asia, but since then opportunities for battle have

Israel has utilized its mixed force of AH-1 models in anti-tank operations against its Arab neighbours on several occasions. This AH-1G has the smooth-contour canopy glazing and undernose Minigun/grenade launcher set.

been rather limited, at least as far as the US armed forces are concerned. Some US Marine Corps AH-1Ts are known to have taken part in the invasion of Grenada during the autumn of 1983, however. In recent years, therefore, the acquisition of further battle honours by Bell's potent Cobra family has been the sole responsibility of Israel, for it is almost inconceivable that this nation has failed to 'blood' its small fleet of AH-1s.

Glossary
AAFSS Advanced Aerial Fire-Support System
AFB Air Force Base
NETT New Equipment Training Team
TOW Tube-launched Optically-tracked Wire-guided

A pair of Japanese AH-1Ss out on patrol display the curious blend of smooth and severe airframe contours. The flat-plate canopy glazing is intended to reduce the chances of low-level detection and glint.

AH-1 in service

Greece
A total of eight Modernized AH-1Ss have been ordered for the Hellenic Army Aviation force along with stocks of TOW anti-armour missiles.

Iran
By far the largest number of Cobras exported went to pre-revolutionary Iran in the form of 202 AH-1J SeaCobras delivered in the mid-1970s. As with most military hardware in Iranian service, the actual numbers left in use are much reduced through a lack of spares, attrition and cannibalization. In the case of the AH-1Js the number could be as low as 10, all of which serve with the Islamic Republic of Iran Army for anti-tank and COIN operations.

Israel
The Israel Defence Force/Air Force initially received 12 AH-1Gs, 18 AH-1Qs and 16 AH-1Ss for anti-armour operations. They have seen action against Arab adversaries on several occasions and the surviving examples are to be fitted with an advanced night targetting system. They will be joined by 25 new-build Modernized AH-1Ss from the USA in exchange for IAI Kfirs.

Japan
The Japan Ground Self-Defence Force is in the process of receiving 40 Modernized AH-1Ss, the majority of which will be constructed by Fuji. The 1987 Fiscal Year appropriations have allowed for eight examples to be built.

Jordan
Twenty-four Modernized AH-1Ss have been supplied to the Royal Jordanian Air Force for use by Nos 10 and 12 Squadrons.

Pakistan
Supplied in two batches of 10 in 1984 and 1986, the Modernized AH-1S force is assigned to the Pakistan Army Aviation Corps. The HueyCobra squadron was declared operational during March 1985.

South Korea
Strong US military assistance under the Foreign Military Sales (FMS) programme has included eight AH-1J SeaCobras and 21 Modernized AH-1Ss for use by the Republic of Korea Army. Their AH-1Js were delivered during 1978 while the newer examples are on order with delivery imminent following the 1986 signing of a contract to supply.

Thailand
Four AH-1Ss (the exact sub-type is not known) are on order for the Royal Thai Army as part of a Foreign Military Sales contract. Delivery is scheduled for 1988 with further orders most likely.

Turkey
The sale of six Modernized AH-1Ss to the Turkish Army air arm was authorized as long ago as 1983, but delivery has yet to take place.

United States Army
The largest helicopter force in the Western world has some 1,200 AH-1 HueyCobras, all but a small number of which are TOW-equipped AH-1S sub-models. The AH-64A Apache is supplementing the HueyCobra force which is based worldwide in support of US Army operations.

United States Marine Corps
While the US Army has acquired the vast majority of AH-1s produced over the years, the Marine Corps has also proved a major user in the shape of the SeaCobra and now SuperCobra variants. A total of 13 squadrons operate the AH-1, this figure including Reserve forces, with home bases in California, Hawaii, Georgia and North Carolina.

United States Navy
A very small number of AH-1Js are used by VX-5 'Vampires' at the China Lake Naval Weapons Center for research and testing duties.

A suitably aggressive and flamboyant colour scheme adorned the AH-1T+, which was an AH-1T leased back by the manufacturer from the US Marine Corps for development and evaluation. The principal area of flight testing was the General Electric T700-GE-401 powerplant, with the first flight taking place on 16 November 1983. The full evaluation programme led in turn to development of the AH-1W SuperCobra.

The seemingly insatiable orders for American military hardware for Iran during the 1970s included 202 AH-1J SeaCobras, their main operating base being Isfahan. This is the first example delivered (c/n 26501) and wears the standard Middle East camouflage applied to Iranian AH-1s and UH-1s.

An Israeli Defence Force/Air Force AH-1S HueyCobra with the rare sight of a squadron marking visible on the tailfin. More examples are on order to bolster existing machines in the anti-armour role.

The latest Middle East customer to receive the HueyCobra is the Royal Jordanian Air Force, as evidenced by this trio of Modernised AH-1Ss.

This AH-1J wears the 'MP' tailcode of Marine Attack Helicopter Squadron 773.

Bell 'Mod' AH-1S Cobra 13th Attack Helicopter Battalion United States Army Giebelstadt, West Germany

Gunner/co-pilot
The gunner commands a fine view from the front cockpit, although his 'Mk 1 eyeball' is augmented by several electronic aids. The nose turret is normally the gunner's responsibility, but if his hands are not on the controls the turret automatically returns to the neutral (ahead) position and the pilot may fire the cannon, if so desired. The gunner also functions as co-pilot.

Armoured windscreen
New and converted AH-1S helicopters have revised cockpit glazing comprising seven flat transparencies of hardened glass, providing increased headroom for the pilot and a reduced risk of glinting which might attract the enemy's attention

Radar warning receiver
The E-Systems AN/APR-39(V) RWR includes four spiral, cavity-backed antennas, each responsible for one quadrant, mounted around the fuselage. APR-39 provides automatic warning of emitters in the E, F, G, H, I and J bands (plus relevant parts of C and D spectra), displaying bearing, identity and mode of operation of the signals on a cockpit indicator. Where appropriate, an audio alarm is generated in the crew's headsets

M65 sight
As part of the M65 airborne TOW sighting system, the gunner is provided with a magnifying thermal imaging system, made up of USAF common modules in a Hughes-designed turret, to enable targets to be located and attacked at night. Later Cobras have the LAAT (Laser-Augmented Airborne TOW) adaptation, in which a laser transmitter is fitted alongside the original equipment. The laser operates on a 10-second cycle – four pulses per second for five seconds, then five seconds off – to give accurate target range information to the Teledyne System's digital fire control computer. Wind and weapon ballistic data is added to the equation to produce a highly accurate sighting solution

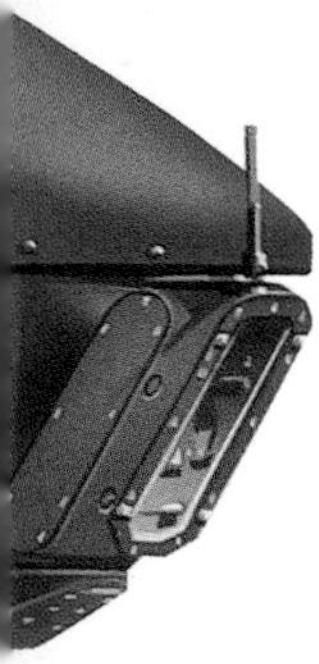

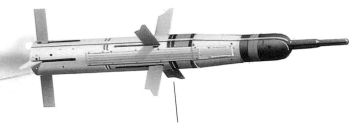

TOW missile
The title of the widely-used TOW anti-tank missile indicates Tube-launched, Optically-tracked, Wire-guided, and there are ground- as well as air-launched systems. With the characteristic spring-loaded 'pop-out' fins of all models, this BGM-71C Improved TOW has a new warhead featuring an extensible probe. The range is 3750 m (4,100 yards) and flight speed around 1000 km/h (621 mph)

M197 cannon
Beginning with the 'Up-Gun AH-1S' the original M28 turret with its twin 7.62-mm Minigun and/or M129 grenade launcher is replaced by a General Electric universal turret capable of mounting 20-mm or 30-mm cannon. The General Electric M197 three-barrel 20-mm cannon here fitted has a magazine of 750 rounds and a rate of fire variable up to 3,000 rounds per minute. Field of fire is 220° laterally, 50° down, and 20° 30' up, whilst aiming is via either both crew-members' helmet sights, or through the gunner's telescopic M65 unit

ockpit side panels are
rton Co 'Noroc'
tion against small-arms

the main
294 and 324
as viewed

Rotor blades
New blades, produced by Kaman, are
fitted to most 'S' versions of Cobra.
Identifiable by their tapered tips, they are
made of composite materials and
tolerant to damage by weapons of up to
23 mm calibre

Pitot head
Measurement of air pressure generated
in the pitot head by forward movement
compared with standard atmospheric
pressure provides a reading for indicated
air speed which is fed to the helicopter's
flight instruments

Wire cutter
Ultra-low level flying, as daily practised
by combat helicopters, carries the ever-
present risk of striking high-tension
wires. Cutting blades above and below
the cabin minimize the risk, although
they would be of little use in the event of
an unlucky contact in the region
between the cannon and sighting turret

Air data system probe
Positioned well away from disturbed
airflow close to the fuselage, an omni-
directional air data probe gathers the
atmospheric information required for
minute corrections to the weapon
aiming system

Explosive-jettison door
The unusual application to a helicopter
a warning triangle indicates that an
explosive jettison system is fitted to the
crew's doors to facilitate rapid exit in an
emergency. Entry and exit is normally
gained by raising these upward-hinged
side doors, the pilot's being on the
starboard side and the gunner's to port

Armour
Crew seats and
constructed of N
armour for protec
fire

Pilot
The pilot occupies the rear cockpit of the
Cobra, looking forwards through the
inclined glass panel above the gunner's
head. Cockpit instrumentation is
improved over earlier Cobra models and
blue lighting makes it compatible with
pilot's night vision goggles.

t of TOW tubes, the inner
chments on each stub
able for other stores, such
od, which contains 19
g-Fin Aircraft Rockets) of
n) calibre. Each loaded pod
(542 lb)

AH-1 variants

AH-1G HueyCobra: initial production model with two pre-production prototypes, powered by a single 1,044-kW (1,400-shp) Avco Lycoming T53-L-13 turboshaft engine derated to 820 kW (1,100 shp) for take off and maximum continuous rating; ordnance could be carried on four pylons below stub wings; an undernose turret could house a 7.62-mm (0.3-in) machine-gun, though later machines had this replaced by an M28 turret housing two of the machine-guns, two M129 grenade launchers, or an example of both; total of 1,127 built

AH-1G 'Snake': two HueyCobras operated by the Cobra Air Interception Team of the US Customs Service on anti-trafficking and night surveillance operations; the undernose armament has been replaced by a powerful Nitesun searchlight
Z.14: local military designation used by the Spanish navy for eight AH-1Gs acquired for anti-shipping operations; all now retired
TH-1G HueyCobra: designation applied to small number of AH-1Gs fitted with dual controls for training duties with the US Army
JAH-1G HueyCobra: single AH-1G used as an armament testbed
AH-1J SeaCobra: first model specifically for US Marine Corps; twin turboshaft configuration powered by a 1,342-kW (1,800-shp) Pratt & Whitney Canada T400-CP-400 coupled free-turbine turboshaft engine; configured to fire TOW anti-armour missiles; 69 examples to the Marine Corps and 202 supplied to Iran; two-stage update programme has led to the incorporation of a night vision system and the ability to fire Hellfire missiles; the undernose armament was revised to include an M179 turret with a three-barrel 20-mm cannon

Model 309 KingCobra: development of the AH-1J produced by Bell as a company-funded project in the early 1970s; two examples built, flying in 1971 and 1972 respectively; the first was powered by the Pratt & Whitney T400-CP-400 turboshaft, the second by an Avco Lycoming T55-L-7C turboshaft engine; both featured a modified nose which housed a stabilized multi-sensor sight and enlarged ammunition bay, larger span stub wings, a ventral fin for improved longitudinal stability and an extended tailboom to compensate for the larger, wide-chord main rotor unit

AH-1Q HueyCobra: conversion of 92 US Army AH-1Gs as interim examples before the introduction of the AH-1S models; anti-armour capabilities were enhanced by wiring for TOW missiles on the underwing pylons
AH-1R HueyCobra: essentially similar to the AH-1G but with a new powerplant in the form of a 1,342-kW (1,800-shp) T53-L-703 turboshaft engine
Mod AH-1S: designation applied to 290 AH-1Gs updated to include a TOW firing capability and new powerplant in the shape of a 1,342-kW (1,800-shp) Avco Lycoming T53-L-703; the conversion figure includes 93 AH-1Qs which were jointly modified by Bell and Dornier
Production AH-1S: 100 examples delivered to the US Army in the late 1970s; featuring a seven-element flat-plate canopy, uprated engine, much improved nap-of-the-earth instrument panel layout, enhanced communications equipment and a Continental United States (CONUS) navigation system; original rotor blades replaced by composite units from the 67th example.
Up-gun AH-1S: 98 examples produced, with all the improvements found in the Production AH-1S along with a universal 20-mm or 30-mm undernose gun turret; other features include automatic compensation for off-axis gun firing and better stores management for firing of 2.75-in unguided rocket packs
Modernized AH-1S: the fully upgraded AH-1S from the 199th example produced; a new fire control subsystem including a laser rangefinder and tracker and HUD for the pilot, air data system, plume infra-red suppressor and jammer are among the new features in addition to those detailed in the AH-1S entries above; a new Laser Augmented Airborne TOW (LAAT) sight package is fitted in the existing sight turret of over 100 Modernized AH-1Ss.

TH-1S: 10 examples fitted with the Pilot Night Vision Sensor (PNVS) system of the McDonnell Douglas AH-64A Apache attack helicopter to act as crew trainers; this (and associated equipmen was fitted under the 'Night Stalker' conversion programme
AH-1T Improved SeaCobra: enhanced and updated development of the AH-1J for the US Marine Corps; the last pair AH-1Js acted as prototypes and were followed by 57 production examples; payload and performance capabilities were significan increased and the powerplant changed to a 1,469-kW (1,970-shp T400-WV-402 turboshaft engine; the dynamic system developed the Bell 214 was incorporated in the design, as were features tes in the Model 309 KingCobra; 51 received TOW firing capability as retrofit; a sole example was flight tested with two General Electr T700-GE-700 turboshaft engines with a total power output exceeding 2,386 kW (3,200 shp); this test programme led in turn the AH-1W
AH-1T+: designation applied to an AH-1T flying testbed powere by a T700-GE-401 as a forerunner to full-scale production of the AH-1W
AH-1W SuperCobra: latest version of the AH-1 to enter servic with the US Marine Corps; 44 examples have been ordered with more likely to follow; surviving AH-1Ts will be brought up to this standard, the first being set to enter service during 1989; powere by General Electric T700-GE-401 turboshafts with a combined rat of 2,423 kW (3,250 shp); fuel system has been designed to withstand 23-mm shell damage. A wider variety of ordnance can now be carried, allowing the helicopter to undertake a greater ran of mission profiles
Model 249: a single Modernized AH-1S incorporating the advanced rotor system of the Bell 412; easily distinguished by the four main rotor blades as opposed to the standard two-blade configuration

Cobra 2000: a proposal by Bell for an attack helicopter for servi in the 21st century; based on the Modernized AH-1S, this could include the four-blade main rotor system of the Bell 412 linked to existing 1,342 kW (1,800 shp) T53-L-703 turboshaft engine, night vision equipment, 20-mm cannon and an airborne laser and tracke

Above: The large hinged panels either side of the Cobra's Avco Lycoming powerplant mean that access is easy when maintenance has to be carried out. This is particularly important as most AH-1 operations are flown from sites in the field.

Left: The gunner/co-pilot occupies the front cockpit in the AH-1 so that forward vision is unrestricted for selection of target and weapons firing. Instrument panel layout and cockpit lighting are compatible with the use of night vision goggles.

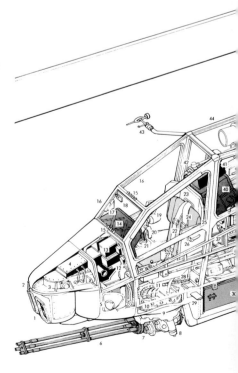

The stepped tandem seating configuration maximizes the crew's field of vision, this in turn being enhanced by the excellent visibility afforded by the large 'half shell' canopy glazing.

Bell 'Modernized' AH-1S HueyCobra cutaway drawing key

1. M65 Laser Augmented Airborne TOW (LAAT) sighting unit
2. Sight visual position indicator
3. Gimballed sight mounting
4. Laser electronics unit
5. Forward AN/APR-39 radar warning receiver, port and starboard
6. Cannon barrels
7. M197 20-mm three-barrel rotary cannon
8. Cannon elevation control gear
9. Swivelling gun turret mounting
10. Azimuth control gear ring
11. Ammunition feed chute
12. Co-pilot/gunner's instrument panel
13. AN/APX-100 lightweight IFF unit
14. Instrument panel shroud
15. Windscreen rain dispersal air ducts
16. Flat plate windscreen panels
17. Stand-by compass
18. Rear view mirror
19. Sighting system viewfinder
20. Sight control handle and trigger
21. Starboard side cyclic pitch control lever
22. Co-pilot/gunner's seat
23. Seat armour
24. Safety harness
25. Cockpit side window/entry hatch
26. Entry hatch handle
27. Port console mounted collective pitch control lever
28. Energy absorbing seat mountings
29. Boarding step
30. Ammunition magazine, 750 rounds
31. Ammunition bay access door, port and starboard
32. Automatic flight control system equipment (AFCS)
33. Lateral equipment ducting
34. Armoured cockpit sidewalling
35. Control linkages
36. Port side console panel
37. Anti-torque rudder pedals
38. Collective pitch control lever
39. Cyclic pitch control column
40. Pilot's instrument panel shroud
41. Head-up display
42. Co-pilot/gunner's helmet mounted sight attachment
43. Low speed omni-directional air data sensor system probe
44. Cockpit roof glazing
45. Starboard TOW missile launchers
46. Pilot's starboard side entry hatch
47. Starboard side console panel
48. Seat armour
49. Pilot's seat
50. HF aerial rail
51. DF loop aerial
52. Skin panelling coated with radar absorbent material
53. Upper fuselage equipment bay
54. Generator
55. Hydraulic system reservoir
56. Control linkage mixing unit
57. Position of refuelling connection on starboard side
58. Forward fuselage self-sealing fuel tank, total fuel capacity 980-litres (259 US gal)
59. Fuel tank access panel
60. Crash-resistant bag-type fuel tanks
61. Landing skid front strut
62. Ventral doppler antenna
63. Fuel system equipment bay
64. Port inboard stores pylon
65. Port stub wing construction
66. Stub wing attachment joints
67. Gearbox oil sump
68. Wing/fuselage/gearbox main frame
69. Anti-vibration gearbox mounting
70. Alternator
71. Engine air intake
72. Rotor head control jack (three)
73. Gearbox input shaft
74. Main gearbox
75. Swash plate mechanism
76. Rotor head torque link
77. Pitot head
78. Fresh air intake
79. Starboard wing tip stores pylon
80. Laser spot tracker housing
81. Rotor head fairing
82. Rotor blade root attachment joints
83. Drag links
84. Blade pitch control links
85. Teetering rotor head attachment
86. Blade pitch control rods
87. Main rotor mast
88. Anti-collision light
89. Oil tank vent
90. Main oil tank
91. Oil filler cap
92. Engine intake particle separation plenum
93. Fireproof bulkhead
94. Fuselage upper longeron
95. Rear self-sealing crashproof fuel tank
96. Fireproof engine mounting deck
97. Engine mounting struts
98. Engine fuel control equipment
99. Avco-Lycoming T53-L-703 turboshaft engine
100. Engine turbine section
101. Rotor head tail fairing
102. Exhaust air mixing intake grille
103. Infra-red jammer unit
104. All-composite main rotor blade
105. Laminated glass-fibre main spar
106. Honeycomb core construction
107. Laminated glass fibre skin panelling
108. Exhaust mixer air plug
109. Infra-red suppression exhaust nozzle
110. Tail rotor transmission shaft
111. Shaft bearings
112. Starboard all-moving tailplane
113. Dorsal spine fairing
114. Bevel drive gearbox
115. Tail rotor drive shaft
116. Final drive right-angle gearbox
117. Blade root attachment
118. Blade pitch control linkages
119. Feathering counterweights
120. Tail rotor blade construction
121. Tail navigation light
122. Cambered trailing edge panel
123. Tail rotor pylon construction
124. Rotor protection tail skid
125. Tail position light
126. Rotor pylon sloping frame
127. Aft AN/APR-39 radar warning antenna, port and starboard
128. VOR aerial, port and starboard
129. Port all-moving tailplane construction
130. Tailplane torque shaft
131. All-moving tailplane control linkage
132. Tailboom longerons
133. Avionics equipment bays
134. Avionics bay access doors
135. Tailboom attachment joint frame
136. UHF aerial
137. Radar altimeter aerial
138. Electrical equipment bay
139. Rear fuselage equipment bay
140. Ground power socket
141. Environmental control system air intake
142. Port navigation light
143. Port wing tip stores pylon
144. Four-round TOW missile carriage unit
145. Seven tube 7-cm (2.75-in) rocket launcher
146. 7-cm folding fin aircraft rockets (FFAR)
147. M18 Minigun pod, 7.62-mm six-barrel rotary minigun
148. Hughes TOW air to surface missile
149. Folding missile fins
150. Detachable TOW missile launcher/transportation tubes
151. 19-tube rocket launcher
152. 7-cm (2.75-in) FFAR
153. Wing skid strut fairing
154. Port landing skid
155. Skid tie-down point

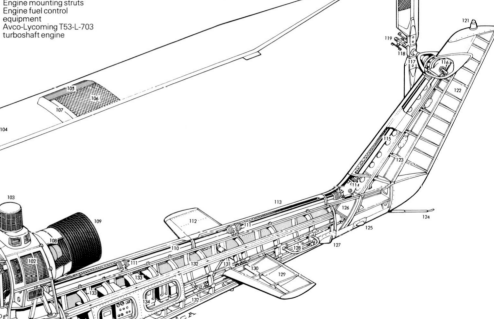

AH-1 HueyCobra warload

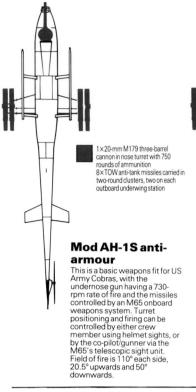

◼ 1×20-mm M179 three-barrel cannon in nose turret with 750 rounds of ammunition
8×TOW anti-tank missiles carried in two-round clusters, two on each outboard underwing station

Mod AH-1S anti-armour
This is a basic weapons fit for US Army Cobras, with the undernose gun having a 730-rpm rate of fire and the missiles controlled by an M65 onboard weapons system. Turret positioning and firing can be controlled by either crew member using helmet sights, or by the co-pilot/gunner via the M65's telescopic sight unit. Field of fire is 110° each side, 20.5° upwards and 50° downwards.

◼ 1×20-mm M179 three-barrel cannon in nose turret with 750 rounds of ammunition
8×TOW anti-tank missiles carried in two-round clusters, two on each outboard underwing station
38×2.75-in (70-mm) unguided rockets split between two 19-round M159 launchers carried on each inner underwing pylon

Up-gun AH-1S close air support
This upgraded Cobra model is fitted with an M38 wing stores management sub-system allowing the selection and firing of the underwing unguided rockets singly or in groups. The undernose turret is a General Electric universal model which can also house a 30-mm multi-barrel gun in place of the current M179 model. There is also auto-compensation for off-axis firing, though the gun must be centred before underwing stores are fired.

◼ 1×20-mm M179 three-barrel cannon in nose turret with 750 rounds of ammunition
2×GAU-13/A 30-mm four-barrel guns each with 353 rounds of ammunition carried on each inner underwing pylon
2×AIM-9L Sidewinder short-range air-to-air missiles divided between the outer underwing pylons

AH-1T helicopter escort
For the US Marine Corps effective escort of their large troop transport helicopters during landings is essential, hence the use of the highly manoeuvrable Cobras to neutralize air and ground threats. The ability to carry air-to-air missiles is a significant boost as these have an all-aspect engagement capability, improved optical tracking and fuse lethality. The multi-barrel gun packs have a fire rate of 2,400 rounds per minute.

◼ 1×20-mm M179 three-barrel cannon in nose turret with 750 rounds of ammunition
38×2.75-in (30-mm) unguided rockets split between two 19-round M159 launchers carried on the inner underwing pylons
2×GPU-2/A 20-mm gun pods, each with a three-barrel 20-mm gun and 300 rounds of ammunition, carried on the outer underwing pylons

AH-1W fire support
The latest Cobra model to enter service has a variety of operational applications and wide range of ordnance available. The lightweight, self-contained gun pods require only a trigger signal from the gunner for activation. Rates of fire available are 750 or 1,500 rounds per minute, with a barrel life of 15,000 rounds.

Specification and performance: Bell AH-1S HueyCobra

Rotors and wings
Main rotor diameter	13.41 m	(44 ft 0 in)
Tail rotor diameter	2.59 m	(8 ft 6 in)
Main rotor disc area	141.26 m²	(1,520.53 sq ft)
Stub wings, span	3.23 m	(10 ft 7 in)

Fuselage and tail unit
Accommodation	pilot and co-pilot/gunner	
Length overall, main rotor fore and aft	16.14 m	(52 ft 11.5 in)
Length, fuselage	13.59 m	(44 ft 7 in)
Height overall	4.12 m	(13 ft 6.25 in)
Tailplane span	2.11 m	(6 ft 11 in)

Landing gear
Fixed tubular skid type

Weights
Empty	2939 kg	(6,479 lb)
Maximum take-off	45369 kg	(10,000 lb)
Maximum internal fuel	764 kg	(1,684 lb)

Powerplant
One Avco Lycoming T53-L-703 turboshaft		
Rating	1342 kW	(1,800 shp)

AH-1S HueyCobra recognition features

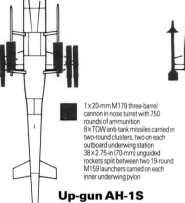

Broad twin main rotor blades with tapered outer sections

Distinctive outward arc on landing skids

Extensive flat-plate glazing covers tandem crew positions

Very compact powerplant housing does not disturb the narrow fuselage cross-section

Small mid-mounted stub wings carry armament packages

Pronounced sweepback to vertical tailfin

Extremely narrow profile and low silhouette fuselage

Petite 'snout', smoothly contoured on top, but sharply angled at front, sides and below

Noticeable tapering of upper and lower forward fuselage lines

---

Performance:

Maximum speed at sea level in TOW configuration	122 kts; 227 km/h	(141 mph)
Service ceiling at normal rated power	12,200 ft	(3720 m)
Hovering ceiling in ground effect	12,200 ft	(3720 m)
Maximum range at sea level with maximum fuel and 8 percent reserves	507 km	(315 miles)
Initial rate of climb at normal rated power	1,620 ft	(494 m) per minute

Troops carried/weapon load

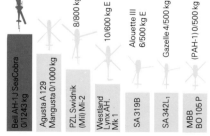

- Bell AH-1J SeaCobra 0/1243 kg
- Agusta A 129 Mangusta 0/1000 kg
- PZL Swidnik (Mil) Mi-2 8/800 kg
- Westland Lynx AH. Mk 1 10/600 kg E
- SA 319B Alouette III 6/500 kg E
- SA 342L₁ Gazelle 4/500 kg
- MBB BO 105 P (PAH-1) 0/500 kg E
- 500MD McDonnell Douglas Defender 6/425 kg E

Service ceiling
- McDonnell Douglas 500MD Defender 13,800 ft
- MBB BO 105 P (PAH-1) 13,780 ft
- Aérospatiale SA 342L₁ Gazelle 13,450 ft
- PZL Swidnik (Mil) Mi-2 13,125 ft
- Agusta A 129 Mangusta 12,000 ft E
- Westland Lynx AH. Mk 1 11,600 ft E
- Aérospatiale SA 319B Alouette III 11,000 ft E
- Bell AH-1J SeaCobra 10,550 ft

Maximum cruising speed at optimum altitude
- Bell AH-1J SeaCobra 180 kts
- Agusta A 129 Mangusta 140 kts
- Aérospatiale SA 342L₁ Gazelle 140 kts
- Westland Lynx AH.Mk 1 140 kts
- McDonnell Douglas 500MD Defender 119 kts
- MBB BO 105 P (PAH-1) 119 kts
- Aérospatiale SA 319B Alouette III 118 kts
- PZL Swidnik (Mil) Mi-2 108 kts

Range with maximum payload
- Agusta A 129 Mangusta 750 km E
- Aérospatiale SA 342L₁ Gazelle 710 km
- Aérospatiale SA 319B Alouette III 605 km
- Bell AH-1J SeaCobra 577 km
- MBB BO 105 P (PAH-1) 570 km E
- Westland Lynx AH.Mk 1 540 km
- McDonnell Douglas 500MD Defender 428 km
- PZL Swidnik (Mil) Mi-2 170 km (5% reserves)

Initial rate of climb, feet per minute
- Westland Lynx AH.Mk 1 2,480 ft
- Agusta A 129 Mangusta 2,090 ft E
- MBB BO 105 P (PAH-1) 1,770 ft.
- McDonnell Douglas 500MD Defender 1,650 ft
- Aérospatiale SA 342L₁ Gazelle 1,535 ft
- Bell AH-1J SeaCobra 1,090 ft
- Aérospatiale SA 319B Alouette III 885 ft
- PZL Swidnik (Mil) Mi-2 885 ft

The McDONNELL DOUGLAS MODEL 500

Osage, Cayuse and Defender

Rising into the skies like a strange-looking insect, the first flight of the Hughes Model 269 heralded the beginning of a family of helicopters that can accomplish many military tasks. From basic trainer through aerial scouting, to tank-busting and the sinking of submarines, each of these distinctively-contoured models has proved itself to be an excellent performer.

Essentially simple in design, the Model 269 has served military forces for many years as a primary helicopter trainer. This US Army TH-55A Osage illustrates the extensive forward and upper glazing, a feature that has remained with the Model 500 over the years.

Sausage and Egg: though complementary, these nicknames are hardly complimentary to the pair of light helicopters produced at Culver City, California, by what was originally the Aircraft Division of the Hughes Tool Company. However, it was inevitable that when the Model 269 was named for the Osage tribe of North American Indian, the prospective pilots of the US Army would find an alternative epithet for their training helicopter.

Its larger brother, the Model 369, was officially the Cayuse and otherwise the 'Loach' (from LOH – Light Observation Helicopter), yet its distinctive cabin shape was strongly suggestive of a chicken's egg.

By no means all Hughes helicopters have been for military customers. Design of the Model 269 was initiated as a private venture in September 1955, and when the prototype flew in October of the following year it was clearly an aircraft of utmost simplicity – like its most successful predecessor, the Bell 47. Initially available with one or two seats, the Model 269 was borne aloft on a fully-articulated three-blade metal rotor, powered by a 134-kW (180-hp) Lycoming HIO-360-A1A four-cylinder air-cooled engine. Transmission was a V-belt system which obviated the more complex rotor clutch. This basic approach was mirrored in the welded steel-tube fuselage, with its Plexiglas cabin and single-piece aluminium

tail boom. Two skids on Hughes oleo-pneumatic shock-absorbers comprised the landing gear, although at the weight penalty of 27 kg (60 lb) the Model 269 could be equipped with air-filled floats made of polyurethane-coated nylon fabric.

Military interest in the proposed production variant, the Model 269A, resulted in a US Army order for five, designated YHO-2. Tested in the command and observation roles at Fort Rucker, the Hughes helicopter acquitted itself well against the contemporary Brantly B-2 (YHO-3) and Sud-Aviation Djinn (YHO-1), but but no production order ensued.

First military orders

At last, in November 1964 the US Army placed contracts for the Model 269A, but for training rather than front-line duties. Designated TH-55A Osage, the helicopter soon became the standard basic trainer for future pilots, of whom large numbers were required for the escalating war in Vietnam. The cabin had two seats, each behind a full set of controls. With an all-up weight of 457 kg (1,008 lb), the TH-55A had an exceedingly modest maximum speed of 75 kts (138 km/h; 86 mph) and an endurance of 2 hours 35 minutes. By March 1969, all 792 on order had been delivered, around 400 remaining in the inventory today. At any one time, some 150 are to be found operating from the

Army Aviation Center at Fort Rucker.

Under a joint training scheme, many NATO helicopter pilots are trained on TH-55s at Fort Rucker. The number gaining an introduction to rotating wings via the diminutive helicopter has been further increased by foreign sales, notably to the Brazilian navy, Spain and Japan, the last employing the TH-55J variant built locally under licence by Kawasaki.

More widely used than its stablemate, the Hughes 500/OH-6 originated in a US Army competition of 1961, in which it was pitted against the Bell HO-4A (later to become the OH-58) and Hiller HO-5 (later FH-1100). The Army Aviation Test Board announced the Hughes submission (likewise originally designated HO-6) as winner in May 1965, orders following immediately for service in Vietnam. Having the factory designation Model 369, the helicopter was also offered on the civil market as the Hughes 500, and ultimately spawned a whole family of related

Low drag was a key factor in the development of the OH-6A Cayuse for the US Army, this being reflected in the smooth contours of the teardrop fuselage. A stalwart of the Vietnam war as a scout helicopter, the Cayuse still serves with US Army National Guard units.

military models for export. Only the entry doors and forward glazing hint at the relationship with the Model 300, for the OH-6A Cayuse differs greatly from its predecessor. Most obvious is the efficiently streamlined cabin of aluminium semi-monocoque structure, whilst within is an Allison T63 turboshaft engine, derated from 236 kW (317 shp) to 188 kW (252.5 shp) and linked to the rotor by a more normal system of a clutch and gears.

The main rotor is of interest in employing a laminated strap retention system for each of its four blades, together with folding pins for quick disconnection. The blades themselves are based on an extruded aluminium spar, which has a one-piece aluminium skin attached by hot-bonding. A two-blade tail rotor of glassfibre is mounted to starboard, in association with twin vertical fins and a steeply canted horizontal stabilizer. Twin skids form the landing gear in the usual military style, the civil model having the option of increased ground clearance. Seating is provided for two crew and two passengers in the rear compartment, though four troops can sit on the floor if the back seats are removed.

Enter the 'Loach'

First flown in prototype form on 27 February 1963, the OH-6A was ordered in vast quantities in the period 1965-9. Procurement fell short of the 4,000 of some optimistic estimates, yet an eventual total of 1,417 had been supplied by August 1970. During 1968, Hughes was turning out 70 OH-6s per month. Service in Vietnam began early in the same year, with issue to division, brigade and battalion or equivalent units. The 'Loach' rapidly established a reputation for manoeuvrability at low level. Despite its ability to absorb punishment, 635 were lost to small-arms fire during the conflict. Mechanical failures were comparatively few, and even accidents were often survivable. In addition to these attributes, the OH-6A proved to be one of the fastest helicopters in the world (a useful boost to civil sales) having broken 23 world records for speed, range and altitude during March and April 1966.

Prime armament of the OH-6A is a Hughes-developed XM27E1 subsystem, combining a 7.62-mm (0.3-in) six-barrel General Electric M134 Minigun with an XM70E1 reflector sight in the observer's port-side position. Complete with a container for 2,000 rounds in the rear cabin, the XM27 has its M134 weapon also on the left side, with a limited vertical movement of +10° to −24°. Hughes delivered 874 XM27s, which fired over 10 million rounds during the Vietnam war. Like their helicopter, they proved highly reliable, and have been supplied to other Model 500 customers under the designation HGS-5. The US Army also ordered development of the XM8 system, which on the OH-6A is interchangeable with XM27, but uses an M129 grenade-launcher of 40-mm calibre. Later models of Hughes 500 supplied to foreign governments have the option of the Hughes HGS-55, which uses a similar mounting and sighting system allied to the high-reliability 7.62-mm Hughes EX-34 Chain Gun.

Despite their illustrious record in Vietnam, remaining US Army OH-6As are now relegated to the National Guard, serving in Aviation Companies or jointly with Bell UH-1s in Aviation Battalions. By implication, none is stationed outside the USA. Elsewhere, members of the same family are important components of the front-line forces, and first of an expanding series of variants for the foreign market was the Model 500M. In this up-rated version of the OH-6, an Allison 250-

In contrast to the smooth lines of the basic OH-6/Model 500 family, the Model 500MD/ASW Defender sports various appendages in line with its anti-submarine warfare duties. Of particular note are the nose search radar fairing and starboard MAD sensor mounting.

C18A (i.e. a civil T56) is de-rated to 207 kW (278 shp) to provide power, whilst normal take-off weight is increased from 1089 kg (2,400 lb) to 1157 kg (2,550 lb). Maximum speed rises fractionally to 132 kts (244 km/h; 152 mph), but normal range is slightly down, at 589 km (366 miles) because of a reduction in fuel capacity from 232 litres (51 Imp gal) to 227 litres (50 Imp gal).

Defender diversity

The navalized Model 500M found favour with Spain, which bought 14 for anti-submarine operations as the Model 500M/ASW. Equipped with Spanish avionics and an ASQ-81 MAD 'bird' stowed prominently on the starboard side of the cabin, the Model 500M/ASW operates from the stern platforms of destroyers. For a small helicopter, it packs a large punch in the form of a Mk 44 or Mk 46 homing torpedo beneath the cabin: two such weapons are the theoretical

The enhanced role of the helicopter on the battlefield over the years has resulted in many highly effective variants of the basic Model 500. This is an Israeli Model 500MD/TOW Defender equipped with four missile launch tubes and a nose-mounted launch sight.

Rotor head fairing
This 'coolie hat' fairing helps smooth out rough airflow as it passes over the helicopter

Blade flap
A blade flap restraint system limits the upward flap of the short diameter main rotor to 18.7°

E 3110

陸上自衛隊

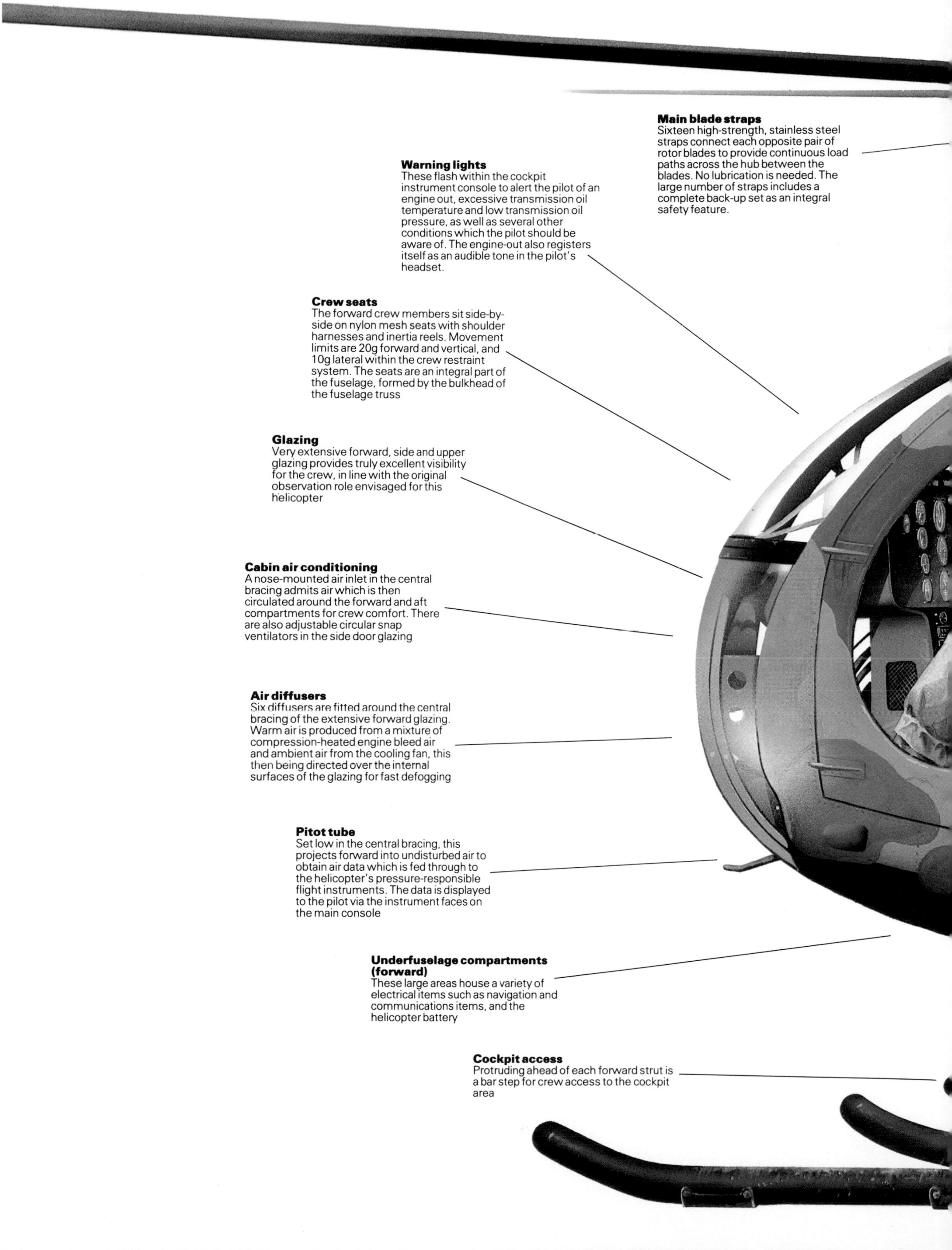

Main blade straps
Sixteen high-strength, stainless steel straps connect each opposite pair of rotor blades to provide continuous load paths across the hub between the blades. No lubrication is needed. The large number of straps includes a complete back-up set as an integral safety feature.

Warning lights
These flash within the cockpit instrument console to alert the pilot of an engine out, excessive transmission oil temperature and low transmission oil pressure, as well as several other conditions which the pilot should be aware of. The engine-out also registers itself as an audible tone in the pilot's headset.

Crew seats
The forward crew members sit side-by-side on nylon mesh seats with shoulder harnesses and inertia reels. Movement limits are 20g forward and vertical, and 10g lateral within the crew restraint system. The seats are an integral part of the fuselage, formed by the bulkhead of the fuselage truss

Glazing
Very extensive forward, side and upper glazing provides truly excellent visibility for the crew, in line with the original observation role envisaged for this helicopter

Cabin air conditioning
A nose-mounted air inlet in the central bracing admits air which is then circulated around the forward and aft compartments for crew comfort. There are also adjustable circular snap ventilators in the side door glazing

Air diffusers
Six diffusers are fitted around the central bracing of the extensive forward glazing. Warm air is produced from a mixture of compression-heated engine bleed air and ambient air from the cooling fan, this then being directed over the internal surfaces of the glazing for fast defogging

Pitot tube
Set low in the central bracing, this projects forward into undisturbed air to obtain air data which is fed through to the helicopter's pressure-responsible flight instruments. The data is displayed to the pilot via the instrument faces on the main console

Underfuselage compartments (forward)
These large areas house a variety of electrical items such as navigation and communications items, and the helicopter battery

Cockpit access
Protruding ahead of each forward strut is a bar step for crew access to the cockpit area

load, but one is more practical. Limited extra equipment for the ASW role includes an attitude indicator and radar altimeter plus, of course, control equipment and displays for MAD on the instrument panel and centre pedestal.

Taking further the principle of a quart in a pint pot, Hughes responded to international demand by producing a hard-hitting anti-tank helicopter from the next civil model, the Model 500D. Designed for those unable to afford a purpose-built Bell AH-1 HueyCobra or the even more up-market Hughes AH-64 Apache, the resultant Model 500MD Defender is easily recognizable as the result of external changes. The Model 500D prototype, flown in August 1974, features a 'T' tail for increased stability, and a five-blade main rotor. Available power is increased substantially by derating the Allison 250-C20 only to 280 kW (375 shp), thereby increasing maximum take-off weight to 1361 kg (3,000 lb). There are self-sealing fuel tanks and an engine inlet particle separator, plus the optional extras of armour, the Hughes 'Black Hole' engine efflux diffuser for reduced IR signature, and a variety of externally-carried weapons and sensors.

In fact, different designations have been raised to cover the armament variations available, starting with the basic Model 500MD Scout Defender which has provision for the previously-mentioned Minigun, Chain Gun and grenade-launcher, or 14 2.75-in (69.85-mm) rockets. The Republic of Korea (South Korea) is a major operator, its fleet including examples of licensed manufacture by Korean Air (a subsidiary of the local airline). Interestingly, South Korea's sworn enemy, North Korea, obtained 86 Model 500s illegally, so threatening a grave security problem if it ever chose to operate them over the South in false colours. In preparation for such an eventuality, South Korea practises snap groundings of its Model 500M fleet: any Hughes 500 still in the air is regarded as hostile and treated accordingly!

South Korea and Israel are among the operators of the Model 500MD/TOW Defender, equipped with a stabilized

telescopic sight on the port side of the nose and a pair of wire-guided Hughes TOW anti-tank missiles on each side of the cabin. A variant, the Model 500MD/MMS-TOW, features a mast-mounted sight to enable the helicopter to remain concealed behind natural features whilst seeking its prey. There is a naval model, the Model 500MD/ASW Defender, which improves on its Spanish predecessor by having provision for a thimble radome in the nose. Many other varieties of Model 500 originally produced for the civil market or law enforcement agencies have also found a place in the inventories of many air forces.

Future fighter

Latest to be announced is the 'MG' series of multi-role helicopters, comprising the Model 500MG and Model 530MG. Both have the sharply contoured nose introduced with the civil Model 500E, but the Model 530 additionally benefits from a boosting of power to 317 kW (425 shp) and a related increase of 30.5 cm (1 ft) in main rotor diameter. Truly a helicopter with a future, the 'MG' is equipped with an advanced crew station including multi-function displays replacing traditional dials and gauges, and has provision for a mast sight and FLIR in a chin turret. All the previous weapon options are available, together with the planned addition of up to four General Dynamics Stinger missiles uplifted from SAM to AAM use to give an anti-helicopter potential.

The third generation of light attack helicopters is epitomized by the all-new Model 530MG Defender. Features include a state-of-the-art integrated crew station, and an awesome range of weapons which can be changed in a matter of minutes for differing tasks.

One sad note is that this potent combat helicopter no longer bears the Hughes label. The parent firm was sold in January 1984, and it was perhaps inevitable that the new title, McDonnell Douglas Hughes, was too clumsy to last. The McDonnell Douglas Helicopter Company accordingly emerged in August 1985 to direct the Models MD500 and MD530 into the 1990s. Hughes may be gone, but the little helicopter with the big punch will ensure that it is not forgotten.

Glossary
AAM Air-to-Air Missile
AFB Air Force Base
ASW Anti-Submarine Warfare
FLIR Forward-Looking Infra-Red
IR Infra-Red
JGSDF Japan Ground Self-Defence Force
MAD Magnetic Anomaly Detector
SAM Surface-to-Air Missile

Sniffing out the enemy is not only done from above, as evidenced by this Model 500MD/MMS-TOW Defender. Small and nimble, the Defender makes excellent use of the terrain to mask its presence while scanning via the mast-mounted sight atop the rotor head fairing.

Model 300/500 in service

Major operators

Argentina

The Fuerza Aérea Argentina obtained 14 Hughes 500Ms in 1969, comprising two executive (Model 369HE) helicopters serialled H-20/21, and 12 armed (Model 369HM) helicopters serialled H-22/33. These are currently operated from Moró, Buenos Aires, by I Escuadron de Exploración y Ataque of VII Brigada Aérea. Four general transport Model 500Ms were supplied in 1985, serialled PGH-01/04, whilst the Prefectura Naval (coast guard) force has six 500Ms serialled PA-30/35.

Brazil

Naval Aviation, the Fôrça Aéronaval da Marinha do Brasil, received 16 Hughes 300s (Model 269As), serialled N-5005/5020, all of which have been withdrawn. Four OH-6As serve with the air force (Fôrça Aérea Brasileira) helicopter training school, the Centro de Instrução de Helicópteros, at Santos.

Colombia

The Grupo Aéreo de Helicópteros at Melgar has 10 Hughes 500Ms from 1977 deliveries, plus the survivors of 12 Model 500Ms (Model 369HMs) from 1969 deliveries (serials 241-252). Also in Fuerza Aérea Colombiana service are six TH-55s (and possibly eight Model 300Cs) with the Escuela de Helicópteros, also at Melgar. In 1985-6 Colombia received six MD500MGs and two MD500Es.

Iraq

Although covered by a US arms embargo because of the Gulf War, Iraq received authorization in 1983 to buy 30 Model 300Cs and 30 Model 500Ds for civilian duties such as crop-spraying. It is alleged, however, that they have been used to train military pilots. A further 24 MD500Fs were approved for delivery in 1985.

Israel

Delivery of 32 Model 500MD/TOWs to La Tsvah Hagana le Israel/Hey Ha'Avir was undertaken in 1979, and plans were announced in 1984 to buy a further six. 'Scrambled' serial numbers include 206, 214 and 254.

Italy

A long-awaited order was placed in 1986 for 50 Nardi-Hughes 500Ds for training duties with 72° Stormo (the Scuola Volo Elicotteri) at Frosinone. The para-military Guardia di Finanza customs agency flies 10 NH500Ms, 47 NH500MCs and 11 NH500MDs.

Japan

Kawasaki-built versions of Hughes helicopters serve both army and navy. TH-55J contracts in 1971-5 covered 38 helicopters (serials 31301-31338) for the Ground Self-Defence Force's training school, the Koki Gakko at Akeno. Larger orders for the Model 500 family comprise 117 OH-6Js (31001-31117) delivered from March 1969 onwards, and further batches of OH-6Ds (Model 500MD). Between 1978 and 1986 firm funding was allocated for 77 OH-6Ds (beginning 31121), while at least 52 more are planned. OH-6s serve the Koki Gakko and its detachments at Kasumigaura, Utsunomiya and Akino; plus Nos 1-13 Helicopter (Hikotai) at Tachikawa, Asahigawa, Yao, Metaburu, Obihiro, Jinmachi, Okadama, Takayubaru, Hachinoe, Akeno, Okadama, Utsunomiya and Hofu respectively. Others form part of the Northern, North Eastern, Eastern Central and Western Air Squadrons at Okadema, Kasuminome, Tachikawa, Yao and Takayubaru respectively; and Nos 1 and 2 Helicopter Units, both at Kisarazu. The navy obtained three OH-6Js (8761-8763) in 1973-4 and five OH-6Ds from 1982-4 purchases (8764-8768), all for No. 211 Squadron (Kokutai) at Kanoya in the training role.

Kenya

Deliveries under a 1979 Army Air Wing contract concerned two Model 500Ds for training (received November 1979), 15 500D Scouts with 7.62-mm Chain Gun or 2.75-in rockets and 15 500MD/TOWs, serials 501-532. Eight Model 500Es were supplied in 1985.

North Korea

Acting through a West German dealer to avoid an arms embargo, North Korea placed orders for 100 Hughes helicopters, of which 66 Model 500Es, 20 Model 500Ds and a single Model 300C were delivered by sea before the operation was uncovered by US investigators in January 1985. Most are reported to be in military service.

South Korea

Following delivery of 34 US-built Model 500MD/TOWs, the Hanjin Helicopter Plant of Korean Air began co-production of a further 89 Model 500MD Scouts in 1976, followed by orders for 50 500MD/TOWs and 25 500MD Scouts. Most serve the army, with serials including 78-0031, 78-0088, 78-0097, whilst a few are in naval use, e.g. FP802 and FP805. Late in 1986 a further 55 were funded, being Scout and TOW models in approximately equal proportions.

Spain

The Ejercito del Aire received 17 Model 300s (Model 269A-1s) from early 1979, for training squadron Escuadron 782 of Ala 78 at Granada; these have the local type designation HE.20 and serials HE20-1/17. Naval aviation (Arma Aérea de la Armada) retains 11 of the 14 Model 500M/ASWs supplied from April 1972 onwards. Serialled HS13-1/14 they serve Escuadrilla 006 at El Ferrol and aboard 'Gearing FRAM I' class destroyers.

Denmark's Army Air Service (Haerens Flyvetjaeneste) retains 13 Model 500Ms, all being home-based at Vandel.

Delivered in July 1983, the two Finnish Air Force (Ilmavoimat) Model 500Ds serve with the Helicopter Flight (Helikopterilentue).

The bright yellow colour scheme identifies this as a Breda Nardi NH-500MC of Italy's anti-smuggling/trafficking Guardia di Finanza.

Kenya's '82 Air Force operates a mix of Model 500D/M/MD and ME helicopters for anti-tank and counter-insurgency operations.

Bright colour schemes are synonymous with training aircraft and helicopters, as evidenced by this Fort Rucker-based TH-55A Osage.

Main rotor blades
This fully articulated unit features four blades, each of which has an aluminium spar hot-bonded to a one-piece wraparound aluminium skin. Each blade has an outboard trim tab, and all four can be folded via hinged lock pins

Tail rotor
A conventional shaft-driven unit at the end of the slender tailboom, this features two rotor blades, each with a steel tube spar and glassfibre skin covering

[Tailbo]om
slender, fail-safe, four-bolt unit
ally adopted to limit the
[wa]s lift force, which was far too
[powerfu]l when a previous, deeper
[s]ection tailboom had been fitted

Tail skid
Located at the very rear of the ventral tailfin, this small unit provides a degree of protection for the tail unit during landings

Kawasaki OH-6J
Eastern Army Aviation Squadron
Eastern Army Aviation Group
Tachikawa Air Base
Japan Ground Self-Defence Force

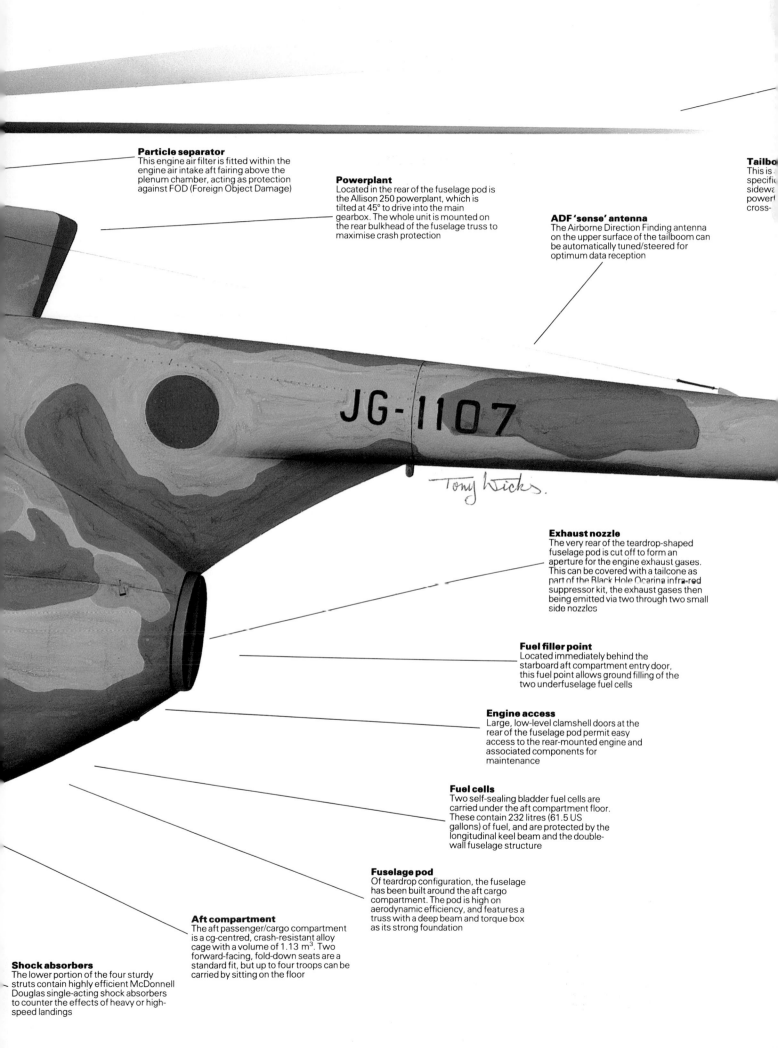

Particle separator
This engine air filter is fitted within the engine air intake aft fairing above the plenum chamber, acting as protection against FOD (Foreign Object Damage)

Powerplant
Located in the rear of the fuselage pod is the Allison 250 powerplant, which is tilted at 45° to drive into the main gearbox. The whole unit is mounted on the rear bulkhead of the fuselage truss to maximise crash protection

ADF 'sense' antenna
The Airborne Direction Finding antenna on the upper surface of the tailboom can be automatically tuned/steered for optimum data reception

Tailbo
This is
specifi
sidewa
powert
cross-

JG-1107

Tony Wicks.

Exhaust nozzle
The very rear of the teardrop-shaped fuselage pod is cut off to form an aperture for the engine exhaust gases. This can be covered with a tailcone as part of the Black Hole Ocarina infra-red suppressor kit, the exhaust gases then being emitted via two through two small side nozzles

Fuel filler point
Located immediately behind the starboard aft compartment entry door, this fuel point allows ground filling of the two underfuselage fuel cells

Engine access
Large, low-level clamshell doors at the rear of the fuselage pod permit easy access to the rear-mounted engine and associated components for maintenance

Fuel cells
Two self-sealing bladder fuel cells are carried under the aft compartment floor. These contain 232 litres (61.5 US gallons) of fuel, and are protected by the longitudinal keel beam and the double-wall fuselage structure

Fuselage pod
Of teardrop configuration, the fuselage has been built around the aft cargo compartment. The pod is high on aerodynamic efficiency, and features a truss with a deep beam and torque box as its strong foundation

Aft compartment
The aft passenger/cargo compartment is a cg-centred, crash-resistant alloy cage with a volume of 1.13 m³. Two forward-facing, fold-down seats are a standard fit, but up to four troops can be carried by sitting on the floor

Shock absorbers
The lower portion of the four sturdy struts contain highly efficient McDonnell Douglas single-acting shock absorbers to counter the effects of heavy or high-speed landings

Taiwan

Naval aviation received 12 radar- and MAD-equipped Hughes 500MD/ASWs in 1979, serialled 6901-12, these flying from the stern platforms of 'Gearing' and 'Sumner' class destroyers. Six OH-6As are in air force (Chung-Kuo Kung Chuan) service.

Thailand

The Thai army was assigned 23 TH-55As by the US Army in 1974. Survivors have been augmented in the training role by 24 Schweizer-built TH300Cs delivered between March and November 1986, serials including 1208, 1210 and 1212.

Turkey

Army aviation (Türk Kara Kuvvetleri) received 30 Schweizer-built Model TH300Cs between December 1982 and March 1983 for the training school at Güvercinlik.

USA

The US Army was the recipient of five YHO-2s (58-1324/1328); 792 TH-55As (64-18001/18020, 64-18025/19239, 65-18240/18263, 66-18264/18355, 67-15371/15445, 67-16686/17002 and 67-18356/18404); six YHO-6As (62-4212/4216 and 62-12624); 30 Schweizer-Hughes Model 300Cs (in 1986); 1,417 OH-6As (65-12916/13003, 66-7775/7942, 66-14376/14419, 66-17750/17833, 67-16000/16686, 68-17140/17369 and 69-15960/16075); and eight Model 500Es (in 1985). TH-55s serve the Army Aviation Center at Fort Rucker. OH-6A operators of the National Guard include 26 Aviation Battalion at Otis AFB, Massachusetts; 31 Av Bn at Birmingham and Donnelly Field, Alabama; 40 Av Bn at Buckley, Colorado; 42 Av Bn at Albany and Niagara Falls, New York; 149 Av Bn at Austin, Texas; 150 Av Bn at Philips AAF, Maryland; 76 Aviation Company at Byrd, Virginia; 198 Av Co at Wilmington, Delaware; 328 Av Co at Trenton, New Jersey; 155 Arm Brig at Tupelo, Mississippi; 1/104 Air Commando Sqdn at Muir AAF, Pennsylvania; 1/126 ACS at Quonsett Pt, Rhode Island; 163 ACR at Salt Lake City, Utah; and 278 ACR at Robinson AAF, Arkansas. About 350 OH-6s remain in active service. Model 500Es are assigned to Army Aviation Systems Command at St Louis.

Minor operators

Algeria: six Model 300s
Bahrain: two Model 500Ds (BPS-8/9) of Public Security Force
Bolivia: 12 Model 500Ms (reported but unconfirmed)
Denmark: 15 Model 500Ms (serialled H-201 etc)
Dominican Republic: seven OH-6As
Finland: two Model 500Ds (HH-4/5); three 500Cs withdrawn

Greece: two BredaNardi NH300Cs
Haiti: two Model 300Cs and two Model 500Cs (e.g. 1245)
Jordan: eight Model 500Ds (e.g. 507/508)
Nicaragua: five OH-6As (status uncertain)
Nigeria: 15 TH-55s
El Salvador: three Model 500s and four Model 500Ms (including 32 and 39)
Sweden: 16 Model 300Cs (05221-05236, local designation HKP 5B)

The Model 269/300 is still going strong with several air forces around the world, this example being a Model 300C (local designation: Hkp 5) serving with the Swedish Army Air Corps.

A typically drab US Army OH-6A Cayuse displays one of the armament options available, this being a side-mounted 7.62 mm six-barrel Minigun. Surviving machines now serve with Army National Guard units.

Almost old-fashioned in comparison to the ultra-modern crew station of the Model 530MG above, that of the Model 500MD/TOW Defender features a larger main instrument panel. To the left is the M-65 TOW missile sighting unit mounted on a tubular truss.

Undoubtedly the most advanced cockpit in a light helicopter is that of the Model 530MG. This fully integrated two-man crew station features an extraordinarily compact layout that enhances the already excellent visibility through the forward glazing. The primary flight instrument is the Multi Function Display unit at centre-top. This provides a continuous alphanumeric and symbolic flight data display which can be overlaid with the video images from the TOW Virtual Image Display unit immediately ahead of the co-pilot/gunner.

McDonnell Douglas Model 500MD/TOW Defender cutaway drawing key

1 Horizontal stabilizer construction
2 Tail navigation light
3 Stabilizer end plates
4 Honeycomb panels
5 Anti-collision beacon
6 Tailfin construction
7 Fin attachment bolts
8 Tail rotor gearbox
9 Ventral fin
10 Honeycomb core panel
11 Tailskid
12 Two-blade tail rotor
13 Tail rotor pitch control mechanism
14 Tubular tail boom
15 Tail rotor drive shaft
16 Tail rotor control rod
17 Tailboom joint ring
18 Antenna
19 Fuselage tailboom extension frame construction
20 Boat tail fairing construction
21 Fuselage tailcone (only if

BHO, item 23, is fitted)
22 Engine compartment access doors
23 Infra-red suppressor (Black Hole Ocarina) exhaust pipe
24 Engine bay construction
25 Sloping firewall
26 Allison 250-C20B turboshaft engine
27 Engine inlet
28 Cooling air fan
29 Air inlet plenum chamber
30 Inlet filter by-pass door
31 Communications aerial
32 Rotor head fibre-glass tail fairing
33 Inlet filtered air particle separator
34 Engine air inlet
35 Rotor brake
36 Engine drive shaft
37 Rotor gearbox
38 Rotor support mast
39 Flexible strap, blade retaining rotor head
40 Rotor head fairing

41 Blade attachments
42 Lead lag dampers
43 Aluminium spar rotor blades
44 Blade articulating links
45 Pitch control rods
46 Rotor head swash plate linkage
47 Control rods
48 Fuselage main frame
49 Control rod guard duct
50 Rotor brake control
51 Gunsight reticle image generator
52 Co-pilot's seat
53 Crew seat armour plating
54 Co-pilot's reflector gunsight, HGS-5 sub-system
55 Outside air temperature probe
56 Grab handle
57 Ammunition magazine, 2,000 rounds
58 HGS-5 gun system mounting
59 General Electric 7.62-mm M-134 Minigun
60 Electric gun drive
61 Cockpit canopy glazing
62 Co-pilot's weapon aiming viewfinder — XM65 (TOW) sight
63 Co-pilot's control column
64 Sight controller
65 Pilot's steering indicator
66 Instrument panel shroud

YHO-2: original designation for five Hughes Model 269As tested by the US Army in the late 1950s but not ordered; serials were 56-1324/1328

TH-55A Osage: based on the Model 269C (a development of the Model 269A) and ordered for the US Army as its primary training helicopter; powered by a 134-kW (180-hp) Lycoming HIO-360-B1A; side-by-side seating for two in the small fuselage body; three-blade main rotor and light alloy tubular tail boom; full dual controls for training tasks; a total of 792 was built, approximately half of which remain in service

TH-55J: designation applied to licence-built TH-55As powered by Kawasaki in Japan

Model 300C: development of the commercial Model 300 featuring a larger tail rotor and fin of greater area; the main rotor mast and tailboom were lengthened to compensate for the larger and heavier main rotor blades; new powerplant, the 142-kW (190-hp) flat-four Lycoming HIO-360-D1A, was fitted, allowing a 45 per cent increase in payload and 757-kg (1,670-lb) maximum take-off weight; three people could be carried; total of 550 produced

NH-300C: designation applied to licence-built Model 300Cs produced by BredaNardi of Italy

TH300C: designation applied to a dual-control variant of the Model 300C

Model 300QC: quiet version based on the Model 300C with 75 per cent decrease in audible sound emission levels; tailboom lengthened; main rotor diameter of 8.18 m (26 ft 10 in)

HKE.20: Spanish military designation applied to 17 Model 300s (Model 269A-1s) supplied for training tasks

HKP 5B: Swedish military designation applied to 16 Model 300Cs (Model 269Cs) supplied to the Swedish army for training and observation duties

YHO-6: original US Army designation applied to five Model 369s supplied by Hughes as prototypes for full evaluation in the LOH competition; military serials were 62-4212/4216

YOH-6A: redesignation of the five YHO-6 prototypes in line with the US tri-service unified designation system adopted in 1962; a sixth example (62-12624) was later added, while the first example was modified and supplied to the US Air Force for use in VTOL test programmes

OH-6A Cayuse (Model 369M): full production armed light observation model based on the YOH-6A winner of the LOH competition; powered by a 188-kW (252.5-shp) Allison T63-A-5A turboshaft; main fuselage much larger than that of the Model 269/300; engine fully enclosed in the lower rear portion of the fuselage; rotor transmission and gearbox housed in top fairing; four-blade main rotor; engine exhaust at rear of fuselage pod; tailboom and rotor pylon completely redesigned, the former including a large forward fairing which blends into the upper rear portions of the pod. Tubular main landing skids and strong support pylons added; two-man crew in cockpit, and various internal configurations in rear seating area; maximum normal take-off weight of 1089 kg (2,400 lb); armament carried on the port side of the fuselage; improvements added during the production run of 1,417 machines included the Light Observation Helicopter Avionics Package (LOHAP) and an air inlet filter

OH-6A 'The Quiet One': a single OH-6A Cayuse fitted with a muffler on its T63-A-5A and an acoustic blanket around the entire engine; main rotor blade span reduced (a fifth blade was added to compensate), and two- or four-blade tail rotor configuration available; tested during 1971 as part of a US Defense Advance Research Projects Agency programme; the perceived noise level reduction was claimed to be in the order of 90 per cent over a standard OH-6A Cayuse

OH-6C: US Army test example based on the experience gained with the above variant; powerplant was a 298-kW (400-shp) Allison 250-C20 which gave a demonstrated airspeed of 174 kts (322 km/h; 200 mph)

OH-6D: derivative of the OH-6C offered to the US Army for an Advanced Scout Helicopter (ASH) requirement

Model 500: commercial development of the OH-6A Cayuse but with military applications and orders; powered by a 207-kW (278-shp) Allison 250-C18A, increasing the maximum normal take-off weight to 1157 kg (2,550 lb); accommodation for up to seven people and a variety of internal configurations including ambulance/medevac with litter kits

Model 500C: hot-and-high variant of the Model 500; same powerplant as the OH-6C; main rotor diameter of 8.03 m (26 ft 4 in); licence-built by Kawasaki in Japan and RACA in Argentina

Model 500D: commercial derivative of the OH-6C with military customers; five-blade slow-turning main rotor of the OH-6C with the addition of a 'coolie hat' fairing over the rotor hub to smooth the airflow over the tail surfaces; powered by a 313-kW (420-shp) Allison 250-C20B; T-tail configuration; maximum normal take-off weight 1361 kg (3,000 lb) and main rotor diameter 8.05 m (26 ft 5 in)

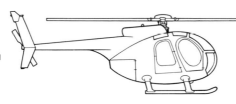

Model 500E: development of the Model 500D; first flight on 28 January 1982; revised forward fuselage profile based on sharply-angled, more streamlined nose glazing; increased legroom and headroom; four-blade tail rotor, with the 'Quiet Knight' model available; new endplate fins to the horizontal stabilizer

Model 500M Defender: uprated OH-6A Cayuse for foreign military customers; first examples delivered to Colombia in April 1968; powered by the Allison 250-C18A derated to 205 kW (275 shp) for take-off and 181 kW (243 shp) for maximum cruise speed

HS.13: Spanish military designation applied to 11 (of 14) Model 500Ms used by the Spanish navy for anti-submarine warfare tasks

NH500M: designation applied to licence-built Model 500Ms produced by BredaNardi of Italy

NH500MC: designation applied to licence-built Model 500Ms produced by BredaNardi of Italy with 'hot and high' features of the Model 500C

OH-6D: designation applied to licence-built Model 500Ds produced by Kawasaki of Japan for the JGSDF

OH-6J: designation applied to licence-built Model 500Ms produced by Kawasaki of Japan for the JGSDF

Model 500MD Defender: multi-role counterpart of the Model 500D, using a similar airframe and powerplant; new features include an engine inlet particle separator, armour protection for the crew, 'Black Hole Ocarina' infra-red suppressor, and the ability to carry a wide range of external ordnance

Model 500MD Scout Defender: basic military variant capable of carrying a variety of ordnance including rocket pods

Model 500MD/ASW Defender: offers enhanced capabilities over the HS.13 (Model 500M) in the ASW role; bulbous nose radome offset to port houses a search radar; the ASQ-81 towed MAD is again carried on the starboard fuselage; the landing skids have been heightened to increase ground clearance for the two underslung torpedoes

Model 500MD/TOW Defender: anti-tank variant; four TOW missile tubes are carried, two outboard each side on a tubular pylon mounting that passes through the fuselage and out each side to act as the weapons pods support pylon; stabilized telescopic sight fairing extends forward from the port side of the nose; a sight control and armrest are provided for the co-pilot/gunner

Model 500MD/MMS-TOW Defender: development of the Model 500MD/TOW Defender with a Hughes mast-mounted sight (MMS) on a 61-cm (2-ft) static mast above the main rotor; a 30-mm Chain Gun automatic cannon can also be carried

Model 500MD Defender II: multi-mission variant introduced in 1980; five-blade main rotor and optional four-blade tail rotor, the latter turning 25 per cent slower than the standard models; noise levels are some 47 per cent below normal for a Model 500MD Defender; mast-mounted sight is optional

Model 500MG Defender: multi-role variant with revised nose profile and advanced cockpit equipment and layout; powered by a 313-kW (420-shp) Allison 250-C20B turboshaft; incorporates the MD500E rotor system; six supplied to Colombia

Model 500S: utility variant of the Model 500 with a useful payload of 681 kg (1,501 lb)

Model 530F Lifter: derived from the Model 500D for hot-and-high operations; retains the fuselage configuration of the Model 500E; Allison 250-C30 is derated to 321 kW (430 shp) for take-off; cargo hook available which can lift loads up to 907 kg (2,000 lb)

Model 530MG: multi-role variant based on the airframe and powerplant of the Model 530F Lifter; advanced cockpit, avionics and instrumentation including multi-function display console; the compactness of the latter enhances the field of vision available to the crew; mast-mounted sight fitted above main rotor; mission equipment includes FLIR pod on forward underfuselage

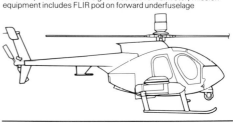

Nightfox: low-cost night surveillance platform available in both Model 500MG and Model 530MG versions; FLIR thermal imaging ability; introduced in January 1986

Paramilitary MG Defender: low-cost patrol/rescue platform available in both Model 500MG and Model 530MG versions

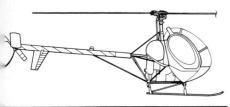

67 Instrument panel pedestal/ avionics housing
68 Cabin ventilating air intake
69 Sight stabilizing mechanism
70 XM65 telescopic sight (TOW installation only)
71 Sight support mounting
72 Landing lamp
73 Heated pitot tube
74 Port landing skid
75 Nose glazing
76 Rudder pedals
77 Centre instrument console
78 Cockpit floor support structure
79 Cockpit door
80 Pilot's collective pitch control column
81 Cyclic pitch control
82 Pilot's seat
83 Inertial reel safety harness
84 Cargo compartment door
85 TOW missile system power supply
86 Stabilization control amplifier
87 Missile control amplifier
88 Servo controller
89 Starboard navigation light
90 Fuel filler cap
91 Cargo compartment floor
92 Self-sealing fuel cells, capacity 233 litres (61.5 US gal)
93 Engine mounting struts
94 Missile launcher hardpoint
95 Support tube fairing
96 Quick-release, jettisonable launcher fixing
97 Twin TOW missile launcher

98 Landing skid rear strut
99 TOW anti-tank missile
100 Spring loaded folding fins
101 6.99-cm (2.75-in) rocket launcher
102 Landing skid front strut

103 Strut fairing mounting
104 Shock absorber
105 Cockpit step
106 Starboard landing skid

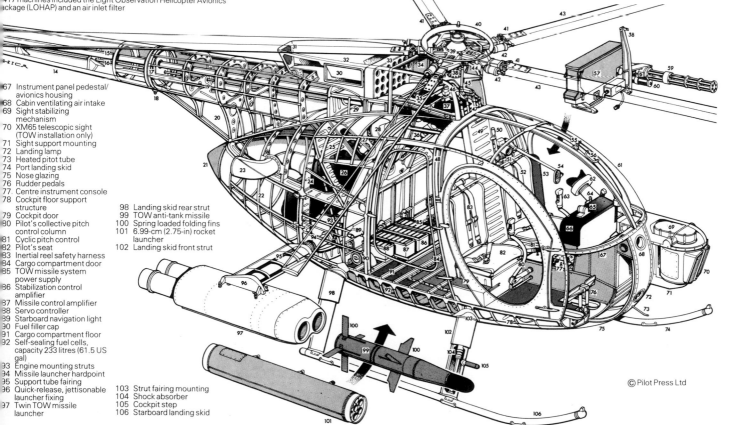

OH-6A Cayuse/Model 500 warload

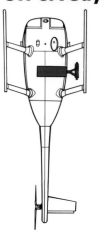 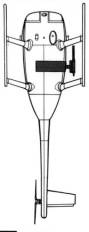  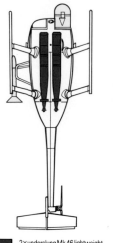 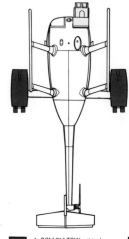

■ 1×XM8 armament subsystem with an M129 40-mm grenade-launcher and up to 150 rounds of belted M384 ammunition	■ 1×XM27E1 Armament subsystem with a General Electric M134 7.62-mm (0.3-in) Minigun and up to 2,000 rounds of belted 7.62-mm NATO ammunition	■ 1×underslung Mk 44 or Mk 46 lightweight homing torpedo □ 1×Texas Instruments ASQ-81(V)2 towed MAD	■ 2×underslung Mk 46 lightweight homing torpedoes □ 1×Texas Instruments ASQ-81(V)2 towed MAD 1×nose-mounted search radar offset to port	■ 4×BGM-71A TOW anti-tank missiles □ 1×electro-optical sight	■ 2×FN gun pods, each with two 7.62-mm (0.3-in) machine-guns □ 1×mast-mounted sight 1×undernose FLIR thermal imaging system

US Army air support 1
This is one of the two principal OH-6A Cayuse armament configurations. The M129 has a muzzle velocity of 241 m (790 ft) per second and a firing rate of 400 rounds per minute. The gun has flexible elevation and for fire control is slaved to an XM70E1 reflex sighting unit operated by the gunner in the port seat. The unit can be mounted or demounted in about 10 minutes.

US Army air support 2
Carried in similar style and position to the M129 grenade-launcher, the M134 has a 'two-step trigger' firing rate of either 2,000 or 4,000 rounds per minute. The gunner operates an XM70E1 reflex sighting unit for fire-control purposes. Export Model 500s are available with a similar system designated HJGS-5 or, alternatively, the HGS-55 mounting an EX-34 7.62-mm Chain Gun. The latter has a firing rate of 570 rounds per minute.

Spanish navy ASW
The Model 500/ASW is capable of short-range attack upon a submarine whose approximate position has been established by the helicopter's parent destroyer. Magnetic anomaly detection provides pinpoint location by detecting variations in total magnetic field intensity produced by submarines. The Mk 44 or Mk 46 homing torpedo can then be released, and can dive to about 305 m (1,000 ft)

Taiwan navy ASW
An enhanced ASW capability as featured on the Taiwanese Model 500MD/ASW helicopter fleet. These operate from stern platforms aboard destroyers, the nose-mounted radar giving a degree of operational autonomy. Targets can be located up to 275 km (172 miles) from the parent vessel in the course of a 2-hour patrol. Maximum depth of the Mk 46 is classified.

Israeli anti-tank
Equipped with a turret-mounted sight, the Israeli Model 500MD/TOW helicopters can engage armoured vehicles out to a range of 3750 m (4,100 yards). The TOW missiles are carried individually in two pods on each side of the fuselage. Reloads can be carried in the main cabin and inserted during the mission. The gunner's sight is of high magnification with very accurate moving target tracking capabilities.

Model 530MG fire-support
A variety of armament options are available for this advanced multi-role combat helicopter, allowing it to operate in roles such as point attack, anti-armour and day-night surveillance. NATO 356-mm (14-in) racks are provided for external stores. Both of the cyclic sticks in the integrated crew station have triggers for gun/missile firing, while the co-pilot/gunner has a pair of handgrips on the visual image display for TOW/FLIR operation.

Specification: Model 500MD/TOW

Rotors
Main rotor diameter	8.03 m	(26 ft 4 in)
Main rotor disc area	50.89 m²	(547.81 sq ft)
Tail rotor diameter	1.40 m	(4 ft 7 in)
Tail rotor disc area	1.53 m²	(16.50 sq ft)

Fuselage and tail unit
Accommodation	pilot and gunner, plus options such as four troops, or two stretchers and attendant	
Length overall, rotors turning	9.40 m	(30 ft 10 in)
Length excluding main rotor	7.29 m	(23 ft 11 in)
Height overall, to top of rotor mast	2.64 m	(8 ft 8 in)
Width over skids	1.95 m	(6 ft 4.75 in)
Width over TOW pods	3.23 m	(10 ft 7.25 in)

Powerplant
Two Allison 250-C20B turboshafts		
Rating, take-off	280 kW	(375 shp)
Rating, maximum continuous	261 kW	(350 shp)

Model 500MD/TOW Defender recognition features

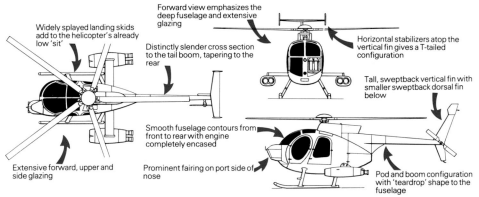

Forward view emphasizes the deep fuselage and extensive glazing

Widely splayed landing skids add to the helicopter's already low 'sit'

Distinctly slender cross section to the tail boom, tapering to the rear

Horizontal stabilizers atop the vertical fin gives a T-tailed configuration

Tall, sweptback vertical fin with smaller sweptback dorsal fin below

Smooth fuselage contours from front to rear with engine completely encased

Extensive forward, upper and side glazing

Prominent fairing on port side of nose

Pod and boom configuration with 'teardrop' shape to the fuselage

---

Performance

Maximum cruising speed, at sea level	119 kts; 221 km/h	(137 mph)
Maximum cruising speed at 5,000 ft (1525 m)	115 kts; 213 km/h	(132 mph)
Service ceiling	13,800 ft	(4205 m)
Maximum range at sea level (without reserves)	389 km	(242 miles)
Endurance at sea level (standard fuel, no reserves)	2 hours 34 minutes	
Endurance at 5,000 ft (1525 m)	2 hours 47 minutes	
Maximum rate of climb at sea level	1,650 ft	(503 m) per minute

Maximum external load
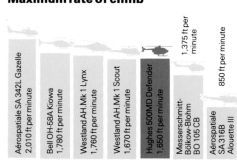

- Westland AH.Mk 1 Lynx 1,360 kg
- Aérospatiale SA 316B Alouette III 750 kg
- Aérospatiale SA 342L Gazelle 700 kg
- Westland AH.Mk 1 Scout 680 kg
- Hughes 500MD Defender 550 kg
- Messerschmitt-Bölkow-Blohm BO 105 CB 500 kg
- Bell OH-58A Kiowa 400 kg E

Maximum rate of climb
- Aérospatiale SA 342L Gazelle 2,010 ft per minute
- Bell OH-58A Kiowa 1,780 ft per minute
- Westland AH.Mk 1 Lynx 1,760 ft per minute
- Westland AH.Mk 1 Scout 1,670 ft per minute
- Hughes 500MD Defender 1,650 ft per minute
- Messerschmitt-Bölkow-Blohm BO 105 CB 1,375 ft per minute
- Aérospatiale SA 316B Alouette III 850 ft per minute

Speed at high altitude
- Aérospatiale SA 342L Gazelle 142 kts
- Westland AH.Mk 1 Lynx 140 kts
- Messerschmitt-Bölkow-Blohm BO 105 CB 130 kts
- Bell OH-58A Kiowa 120 kts
- Hughes 500MD Defender 119 kts
- Westland AH.Mk 1 Scout 114 kts
- Aérospatiale SA 316B Alouette III 113 kts

Range at optimum altitude
- Messerschmitt-Bölkow-Blohm BO 105 CB 657 km
- Westland AH.Mk 1 Lynx 630 km
- Westland AH.Mk 1 Scout 510 km
- Bell OH-58A Kiowa 481 km
- Aérospatiale SA 316B Alouette III 480 km
- Hughes 500MD Defender 428 km
- Aérospatiale SA 342L Gazelle 360 km

Maximum number of passengers
- Westland AH.Mk 1 Lynx 10
- Hughes 500MD Defender 6
- Aérospatiale SA 316B Alouette III 6
- Aérospatiale SA 342L Gazelle 4
- Westland AH.Mk 1 Scout 4
- Messerschmitt-Bölkow-Blohm BO 105 CB 4
- Bell OH-58A Kiowa 3

The BOEING-VERTOL CH-47 CHINOOK

CH-47 Chinook: Western Workhorse

The Boeing Vertol Chinook has been in production since 1961, but the basic aircraft has been radically improved since then, with uprated engines, transmission and rotors giving a dramatically improved performance and with new avionics and systems to enhance its versatility. An impressive combat record in Vietnam and the Falklands war has ensured the Chinook a place in the history books.

A pair of No. 7 Squadron Chinook HC.Mk 1s wait for an early morning sortie from their base at RAF Odiham, Hants. RAF Chinooks are virtually CH-47Ds, although only a small number have NVG compatible cockpits.

Since the earliest times of the cinema, the US Cavalry has established a tradition of arriving in the nick of time to save a potentially disastrous situation. Today, the horse is no longer combat issue, but the principle of rapid movement of troops and their equipment remains as valid as it was in the era of the Wild West. In defence, mobility allows an area to be defended by a smaller number of soldiers than would be the case with a static army; in offence, elements can be employed with imagination to exploit any weakness which becomes apparent in the enemy's line.

Medium lift

Quite clearly, whole armies cannot be whisked around the continents at a moment's notice, but a fleet of large helicopters provides a means of moving significant tactical forces with efficiency. The helicopter tends to be more expensive than the truck, so it is only the two superpowers which have been able to lavish large-scale rotary-wing transport upon their ground forces. Other nations have had to satisfy themselves with far smaller numbers of such helicopters and carefully restrict their use.

Giant helicopters like the Mil Mi-26 'Halo', with a hold the size of that in the Lockheed Hercules tactical transport, are regarded as cumbersome in or near the battlefield. Thus it is the medium-lift helicopter (MLH) which is established as the workhorse of the modern army. For NATO and other allies of the USA, the logical choice of MLH has been the Boeing Vertol Chinook.

Development

As producer of the H-21 'Flying Banana', Vertol (merged with Boeing in 1960) was well placed to offer a twin-rotor design to meet a US Army requirement (Weapon System SS471L) issued in 1956. An offshoot of this was the smaller naval CH-46 Sea Knight, whereas the Army wanted a bigger machine with a 185-km (115-mile) mission radius and the ability to hover out of ground effect at 6,000 ft (1830 m) in a temperature of 35°C (95°F). The design office designation was V-114, and the Army called it the YHC-1B (the YHC-1A was the Sea Knight) until the more lasting designation CH-47 was bestowed in 1962. In line with the policy of naming Army helicopters for indigenous North American tribes, the popular name given was Chinook.

The CH-47's principal features are readily apparent. From the Army's viewpoint, they include an unobstructed main cabin 9.20 m (30 ft 2 in) long, with a height of 1.98 m (6ft 6in) and average width of 2.29 m (7ft 6in). This accommodates, according to internal fittings, 33-44 troops (in peacetime, but many more in an emergency), or 24 stretchers or up to seven tons of cargo. To be accurate, freight load varies considerably according to atmospheric conditions and distance to be transported. In the initial production CH-47A, 6078 kg (13,400 lb) could be moved over a 37-km (23-mile) radius of action, but only 2790 kg (6,150 lb) across 185 km (115 miles), and slightly less in a hot-and-high environment. Easy loading of cargo and small vehicles is assured by a rear ramp which can be left open in flight for carriage of extra-long items. The floor has 83 tie-down points stressed to 2268 kg (5,000 lb) and a further eight to twice that figure. Below, a single cargo hook allowed early models to lift a 9072-kg (20,000-lb) slung load over short distances.

Technicalities not of immediate concern to the soldiers include twin rotors which turn in opposite directions to cancel out torque and so obviate the requirement for a traditional helicopter tail rotor. Viewed from above the front rotor turns counter-clockwise. Power is provided by a pair of Avco Lycoming T55 turboshaft engines mounted externally on each side

The Boeing Vertol CH-47Cs delivered to the Royal Australian Air Force currently equip No. 12 Squadron at Amberley, but will be transferred to the Australian Army during the next two years.

of the rear fuselage and geared so that either can drive both rotors if its companion fails. The three-blade rotors intermesh, requiring a synchronization unit to ensure their separation, although in two serious accidents (one to a civilian variant) this unit has allegedly suffered a mechanical failure.

Panniers on each side of the fuselage contain fuel, whilst the whole of the underside is waterproofed for an emergency water landing. Crew and passengers enter via a door in the starboard side, immediately behind the cockpit. Dual controls are provided as standard and there is a jump-seat in the central entrance to the cockpit for a crew-chief or loadmaster.

The Vietnam War

Soon after entering service the Chinook began to establish its formidable reputation for versatility and reliability. The YHC-1B first took to the air on 21 September 1961, and on 16 August 1962 deliveries began to the US Army of CH-47As, initially to the 1st Cavalry Division (Air Mobile). Large production contracts were placed as a result of the Chinook's performance in the combat conditions of Vietnam, its achievements including airlifting 100 downed aircraft in the first year. By late 1972, as the US withdrawal from South East Asia was beginning, no less than 550 of the 684 Chinooks then built had been deployed to the area and the number of rescued aircraft had increased to over 11,500. Chinooks had also ferried troops and equipment far and wide over the troubled countryside, accumulating over 750,000 flying hours in theatre from the 1 million hours flown by the type up to 1972. About 170 fell victim to the conflict, and others were transferred to the South Vietnamese air force from 1971 onwards, including a few which were absorbed by the victorious North Vietnamese in 1975.

Far from all the Chinooks in Vietnam were of the CH-47A model. After 354 (including prototypes) had been built, manufacture turned to the CH-47B, of which 108 were delivered from 10 May

1967 onwards. Increased power was matched by new rotor blades, which extended disc diameter from 18.02 m (59 ft 1.25 in) to 18.29 m (60 ft 0 in) and had a cambered leading edge, a strengthened steel spar and honeycomb-filled trailing-edge boxes (in place of aluminium ribs and glassfibre).

Chinook improved

More sweeping were the changes introduced by the next model, the CH-47C first flown on 14 October 1967. Higher-rated T55 turboshafts permitted the third model of Chinook to meet a new US Army requirement for lifting a 6804-kg (15,000-lb) underslung load over 55.5 km (34.5 miles) at 4,000 ft (1220 m) and 35°C (95°F). Internal fuel capacity was boosted considerably, although a slight penalty was suffered by export customers who specified the optional 'crashworthy' fuel system as a safety measure. The CH-47C emerged as a great improvement over its predecessors, typically with a short-range (37-km/23-mile) payload capacity of 10528 kg (23,212 lb), which was 73 per cent better than that of the CH-47A under similar conditions. The last of 270 US Army CH-47Cs was delivered in mid-1980, though the greater proportion was produced in the early 1970s. Later batches were for attrition replacement and fortunately were small, for at 5.3 major accidents per 100,000 flying hours the

A total of 54 Chinooks, co-produced by Boeing Vertol and Japan's Kawasaki Heavy Industries, are being procured by the Japan Air and Ground Self Defence Forces, following the success of the earlier CH-46/ KV-107 Sea Knight in Japan.

Chinook's record was the best in the Army.

For export

Boeing Vertol activity during the 1970s was increasingly directed towards foreign customers' requirements, and the changes they specified resulted in a progressive upgrading of the Chinook, even above the Army CH-47C standard. As the four CH-47As for Thailand were ex-US Army, the first new export customer for BV-built Chinooks was Australia, which ordered 12 with the 'crashworthy' fuel system and a higher single-engine rating for hot-and-high operations in Papua New Guinea. The new fuel system was retrofitted to US aircraft from March 1973. Spain's Chinooks, of which a batch of six was delivered in 1973, pioneered a more advanced model of automatic flight-control system (a stability aid) and quick-change ferry fuel and VIP kits. They also

This colourful CH-47C is used by VII Brigade Aérea, Fuerza Aérea Argentina, for Antarctic support tasks. Argentine army and air force Chinooks played a minor role during the Falklands war, both Army machines being lost.

Emergency escape door
...alklands war, this aircraft, as
...mber' of No. 18 Squadron,
...door and was hastily fitted
...cement scavenged from a
...gentine Chinook

Rescue winch
A hydraulically powered rescue winch
can be fitted above the main door on the
starboard side of the fuselage. The
strong rotor downwash produced by the
Chinook gives a rather high minimum
hover height, and the lack of an internal
'wet fit' means that salt-water 'wet'
winching is not regularly practised. The
Chinook was used extensively in the
aftermath of the Air India tragedy,
recovering bodies and wreckage by
winching

**External emergency hatch
jettison handle**

GEC AD2770 Tacan aerial

Formation keeping li...

Blade antennas
Twin aerials serve the
UHF/AM homing
system

Flush aerials
Two flush antennas serve the GEC-
made radar altimeter

Doppler transmitter/receiver
The Decca Doppler Mk 71 radar and Mk
19 area navigation system use this
antenna

**Lower VHF/UHF communications
aerial**

AD380 ADF loop antenna
This serves the automatic direction-
finder equipment and the NDB (non
directional beacon) locator

Main landing gear
The Chinook is fitted with non-
retractable quadricycle type landing gear
with twin-wheel forward units. All units
have oleo-pneumatic shock absorbers,
and the forward units are fitted with
single-disc hydraulic brakes. There is
provision for detachable wheel skis.
Mainwheel tyres are inflated to 6.07 bar
(88 lb/sq in)

Decca Mk 19 aeria...

Forward hook
The forward hook has a maximu...
capacity of 9000 kg (19,841 lb)

Cockpit
The Chinook's cockpit is spacious and modern, with side-by-side seating for the captain (to starboard) and co-pilot (to port) and with a folding jump seat in the cockpit entrance. Like all RAF and Army Air Corps tactical helicopters, the Chinook HC.Mk 1 is fitted with Decca TANS, a useful precision navigation computer. Only a handful of RAF Chinooks have NVG compatible cockpits.

Windscreen
The laminated plastic windscreen panels are heated electrically through a transparent gold coating embedded between the layers

Pilot's em
During the
'Bravo Nov
lost its port
with a repla
captured A

Access panel
This small panel covers the self-tuning vibration absorber and various electrical components.

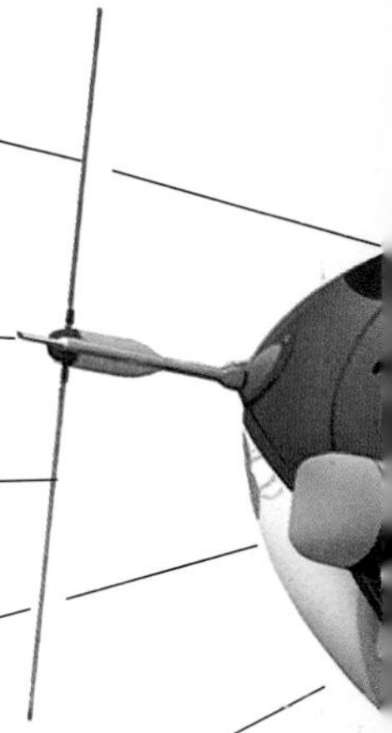

Starboard pitot probe
The starboard pitot provides static and dynamic pressure data for the captain's airspeed indicator and the No. 2 AFCS unit. VHF/FM homing whip antenna is mounted on the probe

VHF/AM homing aerial
This aerial serves the GEC Avionics ARC-340 communications and homing radio

Radar warning receiver
A small radome mounted under the nose provides the pilot with warnings of hostile radar emissions on a small cathode ray tube and aurally in his headset. Threats are classified by type, bearing and range.

Port pitot probe
The left-hand probe 'feeds' the co-pilot's ASI, the No. 1 AFCS unit and the true airspeed transducer. Both probes are electrically heated. The AFS is a redundant system with two identical control units and two sets of stabilizer actuators. Stability is maintained without constant control inputs by the pilot.

Bracket
This serves as the mounting point for a 'Nitesun' searchlight, when carried

Yaw and sideslip detectors
These small detectors supply data to AFCS and are electrically heated

Landing lights
These are fully articulated. One is operated by the captain and the other by the co-pilot

Boeing Vertol Chinook HC.Mk 1
No.7 Squadron
Royal Air Force
RAF Odiham
Hants

were equipped with the ISIS (Integral Spar Inspection System) for monitoring of blade fatigue,

For Canada, Boeing Vertol installed a central aisle of 11 seats to provide accommodation for a total of 44 troops, a cargo hook restressed to 12701 kg (28,000 lb), hydraulic power for the rear ramp, and uprated transmission, avionics and autopilot. After considerable delays (and two cancellations) the RAF at last began receiving Chinooks in 1980. Based on the Canadian model, British variants added zoned cockpit lighting for night operations (pilots wearing night-vision goggles), a 22680-kg (50,000-lb) gross weight, a triple-hook external carrying system rated at 12701 kg (28,000 lb), an automatic fuel fire-suppression system and a rotor brake. During deliveries, glassfibre rotor blades and a single-point pressure refuelling system were introduced (and retrofitted to earlier aircraft).

In RAF service

New Chinook capabilities available to the RAF include use of the forward and aft hooks to steady a large underslung load or carry two additional cargoes (for example three pairs of rubberized fuel cells to be dropped off at three dispersed BAe Harrier or helicopter operating locations). The centre hook can accept the full maximum external load, and the two other attachments are stressed to 9072 kg (20,000 lb), though not simultaneously! Pressure refuelling reduces the time that the Chinook is vulnerable on the ground at a tactical refuelling point in the battle zone, and glassfibre blades need overhaul only every 3,000 hours (compared with 1,200 hours for the engines and most other items in the power train), presenting a valuable economy. In addition, the new blades have a 'get-you-home' capability even after hits by 23-mm shells, and an increased chord of 81 cm (2ft 8 in), compared with 64.1 cm (2ft 1.25 in) on the CH-47B/C.

Refurbishment programme

Many of the above improvements have at last found their way into the US Army fleet through an extensive refurbishment programme currently under way at Ridley. In 1976, the Army commissioned BV to modify a single example of the CH-47A, B and C to Model 414/CH-47D standard, powered by a pair of T55-L-712s. This variant of the turboshaft has some internal changes, but delivers the same normal power as the earlier T55-L-11, except that it has an emergency rating of 3356 kW (4,500 shp) and can be run 'dry' for 30 minutes after battle damage. The first CH-47D conversion returned to the air on 11 May 1979, followed on 26 February 1982 by the initial aircraft from a larger conversion contract.

With the aid of some 300 sub-contractors and a complete strip-down and rebuild, 13 major improvements are made to each old airframe, fitting it for useful service until the 21st century. The cockpit and instruments are revised for decreased pilot workload and for the use of night vision goggles; electrical, hydraulic and survivability equipment is modernized and modified for ease of maintenance; pressure refuelling and triple cargo hooks are added; and some components are re-

placed by composite materials for weight-saving. In August 1985, an experimental inflight-refuelling probe 11.6m (38 ft 0 in) long was fitted to one CH-47D for successful trial hook-ups with a Lockheed KC-130 Hercules tanker.

In typical European conditions, a CH-47D provides a 100 per cent performance improvement over the CH-47A, and still-creditable 68 per cent improvement in hot-and-high environments. It is little wonder, therefore, that the Army has ordered upgrading of its entire fleet of 436 Chinooks to CH-47D standard, and additionally is looking to purchase a further 142 new examples from 1987 onwards. Service entry was achieved on 20 May 1982, and the CH-47D gained its initial operational capability with the 101st Airborne Division of Central Command (the Rapid Deployment Force) in February 1984. CH-47As and CH-47Bs are first to be transformed, whilst the CH-47C is making do with a glassfibre rotor blade refit programme until it can be recalled to Ridley for the full treatment.

The ultimate Chinook

Tasked with such duties as battlefield resupply, troop movement and artillery emplacement, the CH-47D will even lift the sizeable M198 155-mm (6.1-in) howitzer, its 11-man crew and 32 rounds in one 9979-kg (22,000-lb) load. (Similarly, the RAF model can transport a Rapier SAM fire unit, its crew, Land Rover, trailer and reload missiles.) The CH-47D is coming to Europe in 1987-8

This Elicotteri Meridionali-built, ski-equipped CH-47C Chinook serves with the 11th Gruppo Squadroni ETM 'Ercole', 1 Raggruppamento ALE 'Antares', of the Italian army, based at Viterbo.

when the Army plans to deploy 64 as replacements for CH-47Cs, although the model is already in service on the continent in the guise of the CH-47D International Chinook supplied to Spain in 1986. In other countries bordering the Mediterranean and in the Middle East, licensed production by Elicotteri Meridionali SpA of Frosinone, Italy, has expanded the CH-47C population by over 160 and holds the prospect of a European-built CH-47D variant if more orders can be obtained. More recently, Kawasaki of Japan delivered the first of a planned 54 CH-47J International Chinooks for the JASDF and JGSDF in 1986,

Dazzled by the potential of a fighter or bomber, it is easy for the observer to pass quickly over the MLH with the thought that 'a transport is a transport is a transport'. Nothing could be further from the truth. Over a long career which is still only half complete, the Chinook has subtly transformed itself in order to keep up with the changing requirements in army support helicopters.

This CH-47D underwent inflight-refuelling trials in support of the programme to produce a dedicated special forces Chinook-variant, the MH-47E. A single converted CH-47D will serve as a prototype, with 20 production aircraft.

Chinook in service:

Argentine Air Force (Fuerza Aérea Argentina)

From an original requirement for 35 Chinooks, only three CH-47Cs were delivered to the Argentine air force before the imposition of a US arms embargo. The three aircraft were originally serialled H-91/93 and delivered in 1980. H-92 was written off on 28 January 1982. During the Falklands war, Chinook AE-520 was abandoned at Port Stanley and later brought to the UK aboard the MV *Tor Caledonia*. It is now at RNAY Fleetlands where it is being used in the repair of RAF Chinook ZA676 which was badly damaged near Andover on 15 November 1984. One Argentine CH-47C remains in service.

Royal Australian Air Force

A force of 12 CH-47C Chinooks was ordered to form the main heavy-lift helicopter component of the RAAF, and is used mainly for logistical support of the Australian army. Eleven aircraft remain in service.

No. 12 Squadron
Base: RAAF Amberley
Aircraft: A15-001 to A15-012

Canadian Armed Forces

Nine CH-47C Chinooks (Canadian designation CH-147) were ordered for the CAF, with deliveries starting in September 1974. These aircraft, eight of which remain in service with Nos 447 and 450 Squadrons in Canada, have T55-L-11C engines, ISIS (Integrated Spar Inspection System), crashworthy fuel system, rescue hoist, an advanced flight-control system and a rear ramp with water dam. The cargo hook has a capacity of 12700 kg (28,000 lb).

Egyptian Air Force (Al Quwwat at Jawwiya il Misriya)

Egypt's requirement for 15 Italian-built CH-47Cs was quickly satisfied as the result of Iranian cancellations, permitting deliveries to begin to the base at Kom Amshim late in 1981.

Hellenic Air Force (Helliniki Aeroporia)

Greece began to take delivery of 10 Italian-built Chinooks, equally divided between the air force and the army, in 1981.

Iranian Army

The major customer for Italian-built CH-47Cs was pre-revolutionary Iran, which ordered batches of 16, 26 and 50. Two were destined for the air force and the remainder for the army. Only 67 of these had been delivered by April 1981, when the USA embargoed further supplies. The army Chinooks are home-based at Isfahan, but have been deployed to other locations for use in the Gulf War with Iraq.

Italian Army Light Aviation (Aviazione Leggera del Escercito)

The Chinook entered service with the ALE in the spring of 1973, when a specialist unit, 1° Reparto Elicotteri Medi, formed at Viterbo to evaluate the type's use. The Centro ALE also conducted trials and crew training, a Nucleo CH-47C being established. On 1 February 1976 the 1° REM was divided into two front-line *gruppi squadroni* (11° and 12°) and these continued to operate the CH-47C at Viterbo. Twenty-six aircraft (MM80822 to 80847) were delivered, but two have been written off, one by the ALE and the other in Abu Dhabi. A further two CH-47Cs (MM81168/9) have been delivered to replace earlier losses.

11° Gruppo Squadroni
Base: Viterbo
Example aircraft:
MM81169 'EI-827'

12° Gruppo Squadroni
Base: Viterbo
Example aircraft:
MM80840 'EI-818'

Japan Air Self-Defence Force (Nihon Koku Jietai)

In the spring of 1984, the Japan Defense Agency approved the purchase from Boeing Vertol of two CH-47s for the JGSDF and one for the JASDF. It is expected that subsequent licensed manufacture by Kawasaki will equip the JGSDF and JASDF with total of about 40 and 15 respectively.

Libyan Air Force (Al Quwwat al Jawwiya al Libiyya)

Libya was permitted to receive 20 Italian-built CH-47Cs despite strict US controls on trade with this regime. Delivered between July 1976 and early 1980, six aircraft went to the air force and the remainder to the army. Serials are LC-001 to 020.

Italian army Chinooks have been manufactured by Elicotteri Meridionali SpA (the airframe is produced under sub-contract by the SIAI-Marchetti company) since 1970. Duties other than transport include fire-fighting with a 5000-litre (1,100-Imp gal) tank of retardant fitted in the main cabin. A mobile hospital variant known as the EFSC (Emergency Surgery Flying Centre) entered service with the army during 1986.

Canadian Armed Forces CH-47s equip two Tactical Air Group units, these ski equipped examples being assigned to No. 447 Squadron at CFB Namao.

One of 15 Italian-built CH-47Cs supplied to the Egyptian air force.

This Hellenic air force CH-47C sports a prominent undernose searchlight.

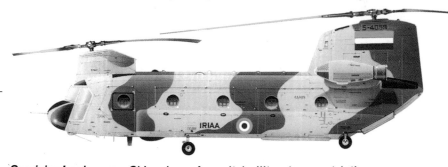

Surviving Iranian army Chinooks perform vital military transport duties.

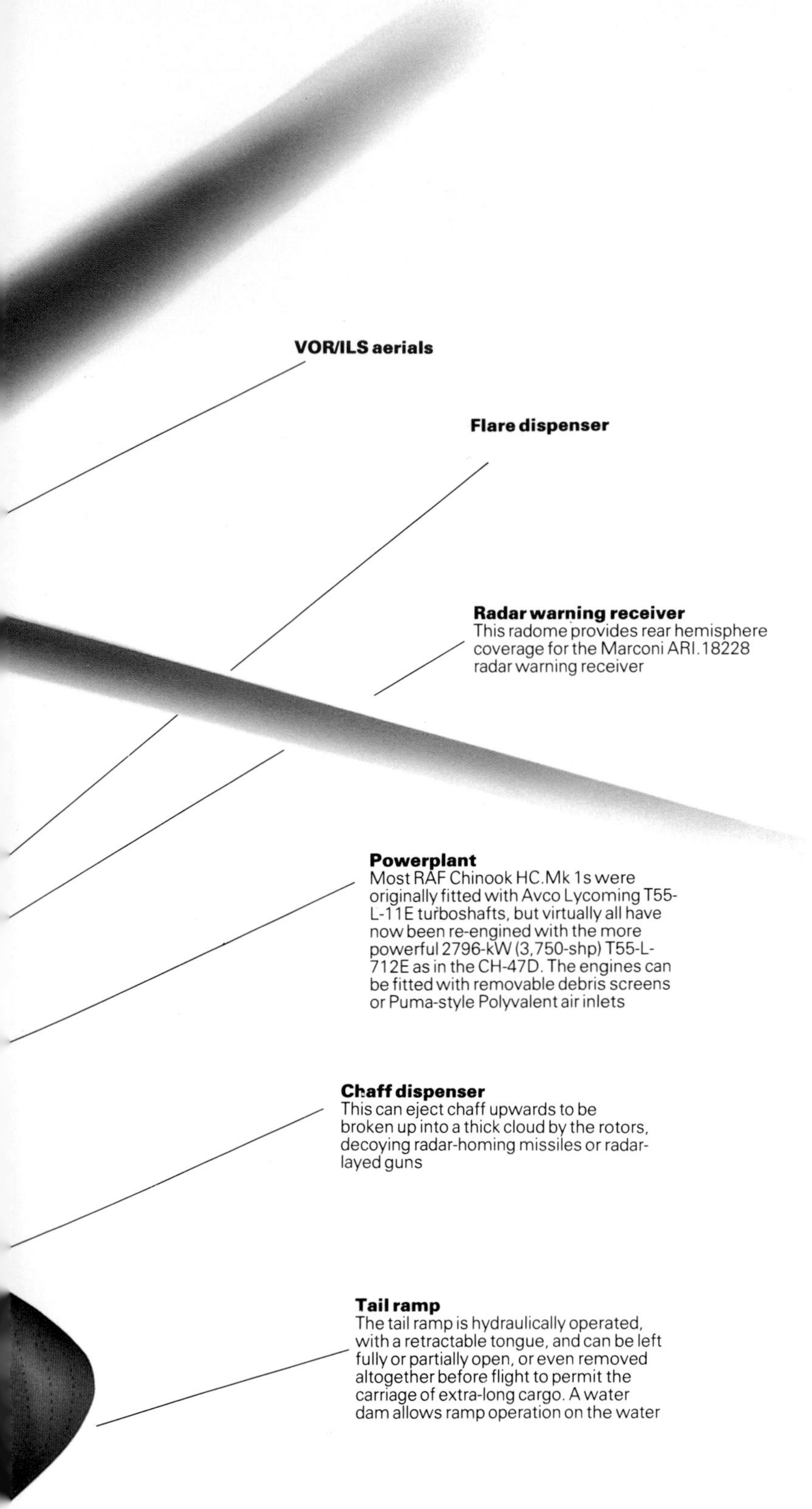

VOR/ILS aerials

Flare dispenser

Radar warning receiver
This radome provides rear hemisphere
coverage for the Marconi ARI.18228
radar warning receiver

Powerplant
Most RAF Chinook HC.Mk 1s were
originally fitted with Avco Lycoming T55-
L-11E turboshafts, but virtually all have
now been re-engined with the more
powerful 2796-kW (3,750-shp) T55-L-
712E as in the CH-47D. The engines can
be fitted with removable debris screens
or Puma-style Polyvalent air inlets

Chaff dispenser
This can eject chaff upwards to be
broken up into a thick cloud by the rotors,
decoying radar-homing missiles or radar-
layed guns

Tail ramp
The tail ramp is hydraulically operated,
with a retractable tongue, and can be left
fully or partially open, or even removed
altogether before flight to permit the
carriage of extra-long cargo. A water
dam allows ramp operation on the water

Steps
These steps provide groundcrew
access to the rotor pylons and
transmission tunnel

Directional stability fins
These shallow strakes minimize air flow
buffeting when the ramp is operated

ling gear
nding gear units consists of
castoring main wheels. The
unit can be steered from the

uelling points
vity refuelling points are located
g the top of the fuselage fairings,
are augmented by a single pressure
elling point on the starboard side.
 allows for the simultaneous
elling of all tanks, or the selective
elling of any combination of tanks.

Fuselage
The mainly metal semi-monocoque
fuselage is of constant section and can
accommodate up to 44 troops or 24
standard NATO stretchers. During the
Falklands war more than 80 troops were
carried in an RAF Chinook on occasion

Rotor blades
The glassfibre blades now being fitted to
all RAF Chinooks consist of a cambered
leading edge, a glassfibre D-section
spar, Nomex honeycomb core and a
crossply glassfibre laminated skin.
These tough blades can survive a direct
hit by a 20-mm cannon shell

**Upper VHF/UHF
communications
aerial**

Static vent
This feeds the vertical and air-speed
indicators, the true air speed transducer,
the altimeters, and the AFCS units

HF aerial

Centre hook
The centre hook is the main lifting hook
and carry up to 11300 kg (24,912 lb)
including loads such as the FH-70
howitzer

Rear hook
Like the front hook this has a capacity of
9000 kg (19,841 lb) and can be used for
lifting individual loads or in conjunction
with the front hook to take tandem slung
loads such as ISO containers or even
another Chinook. The triple hook system
gives tremendous flexibility and
adaptability

Rear lan
The rear la
single full
starboard
cockpit

Royal Air Force

Thirty-three Chinook HC.Mk 1 helicopters were ordered for the RAF in 1978. The first example (ZA670) made its initial flight on 23 March 1980 and was later allocated to No. 240 OCU. The first all-Chinook squadron, No. 18, was formed at RAF Odiham in August 1981 and in 1983 deployed to RAF Gutersloh in support of BAOR. During the Falklands war three of No. 18 Squadron's Chinooks were lost with the sinking of the *Atlantic Conveyor*. Eight more aircraft were ordered as replacements. A second Chinook Squadron, No. 7, was formed at Odiham in September 1982, and No. 1310 Flight in the Falkland Islands has become No. 78 Squadron based at Mount Pleasant.

No. 7 Squadron
Formed: 1 September 1982
Base: RAF Odiham, Hampshire
Task: Tactical support
Aircraft: (Chinook HC.Mk 1) ZA671 'EO', ZA678 'EZ', ZA713 'EN';, ZA718 'EQ'

No. 78 Squadron
Formed:
Base: RAF Mount Pleasant, Falkland Islands
Task: Tactical transport
Aircraft: (Chinook HC.Mk 1) ZA684 'F', ZA709 'A', ZA717 'B'

No. 18 Squadron
Formed: 4 August 1981
Base: RAF Gutersloh, West Germany
Task: Tactical support
Aircraft: (Chinook HC.Mk 1) ZA672 'BH', ZA675 'BB', ZA708 'BK', ZD984 'BE'

No. 240 OCU
Formed:
Base: RAF Odiham, Hampshire
Aircraft: (Chinook HC.Mk 1) ZD574 'FH', ZD575 'FF', ZD576 'FG', ZD980 'FJ'

Royal Moroccan Air Force

(Al Quwwat al Jawwiya al Malakiya Marakishaya)
Morocco's first six Italian-built CH-47Cs were received in 1979 and employed in the Western Sahara conflict against the Polisario guerrillas. Further deliveries began in June 1982. Serials began with CN-ALA.

Chinese Nationalist Air Force

Taiwan has taken delivery of three utility Model 234MLR Chinooks. Although basically a commercial version of the CH-47D, the type has entered operation with the Chinese Nationalist Air Force in the heavy-lift and trooping roles.

Tanzanian People's Defence Force Air Wing

Tanzania ordered two Italian-built CH-47Cs in 1981 for delivery the following year, but the contract appears to have lapsed.

Royal Thai Army

Four of the 354 CH-47As built for the US Army were diverted to the Royal Thai Army. Two are thought to remain in service, one being 13140.

Spanish Army Air Corps

(Fuerza Aero Moviles del Ejército de Tierra)
The Spanish army received 13 CH-47Cs. The first aircraft, Z.17-1, was delivered as air freight in April 1972 but was subsequently written off on 20 March 1973. The remaining aircraft are serialled HT.17-2 to HT.17-13 and equip BHELTRA V (Batallon de Helicopteros de Transporte V) at Los Remedios air base, Colmenar. The Army took delivery of its first pair of CH-47Ds at the end of July 1986, with two further pairs scheduled for delivery in October 1986 and April 1987.

Photographed during joint exercises in Spain are a Spanish Army HT.17, and a Chinook HC.Mk 1 of No. 18 Squadron, Royal Air Force.

US Army

The CH-47 Chinook has been the US Army's standard medium-lift transport helicopter since October 1963. Several hundred CH-47A, B and C models are in service, and a planned 436 aircraft are to be remanufactured to CH-47D standard, extending the service life of the army's Chinook fleet into the next century. Initial operational capability for the CH-47D was achieved on 28 February 1984, with the type first equipping the 101st Airborne Division followed by other units of the Central Command. The US Army has about 70 CH-47Cs and CH-47Ds in West Germany, where they equip three aviation companies.

180th Aviation Company
Base: Schwabisch Hall
Example aircraft:
68-15846, 69-17118, 70-15002, 74-22281

205th Aviation Company
Base: Mainz-Finthen
Example aircraft:
68-15847, 70-15028, 71-20946, 74-22285

295th Aviation Company
Base: Coleman Barracks
Example aircraft:
68-15849, 70-15012, 71-20954, 74-22283

Though in military use, Moroccan CH-47Cs wear quasi-civil registrations.

With rotors turning at full speed, a No. 78 Squadron, Royal Air Force Chinook HC.Mk 1 is readied for another transport mission in the Falkland Islands. Note the rescue hoist/winch unit protruding outwards above the forward starboard access door.

US Army Chinooks in Europe are assigned to three units, namely the 180th, 205th and 295th Aviation Companies in West Germany.

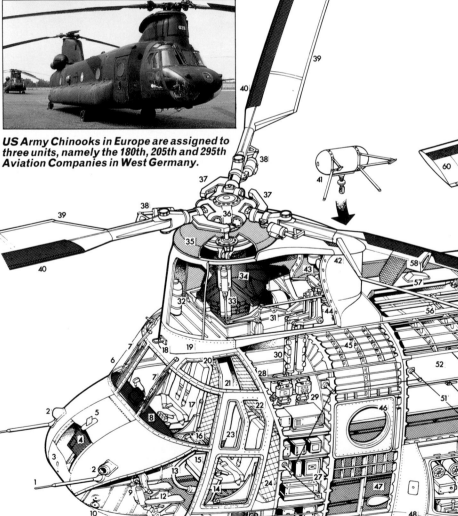

© Pilot Press Ltd

Boeing Vertol CH-47D cutaway drawing key

This view of a **CH-47C** Chinook graphically illustrates the tandem main rotor configuration with the two Avco Lycoming turboshaft engines pod-mounted on each side of the rear vertical pylon. The rotor units rotate in opposite directions, and each can be driven by either engine via interconnecting drive shafts. Note also the constant cross-section to the main cabin.

1 Pitot tubes
2 Forward lighting
3 Nose compartment access hatch
4 Vibration absorber
5 IFF aerial
6 Windscreen panels
7 Windscreen wipers
8 Instrument panel shroud
9 Rudder pedals
10 Yaw sensing ports
11 Downward vision window
12 Pilot's footboards
13 Collective pitch control
14 Cyclic pitch control column
15 Co-pilot's seat
16 Centre instrument console
17 Pilot's seat
18 Glideslope indicator
19 Forward transmission housing fairing
20 Cockpit overhead window
21 Doorway from main cabin
22 Cockpit emergency exit doors
23 Sliding side window panel
24 Cockpit bulkhead
25 Vibration absorber
26 Cockpit door release handle
27 Radio and electronics racks
28 Sloping bulkhead
29 Stick boost actuators
30 Stability augmentation system actuators
31 Forward transmission mounting structure
32 Windscreen washer bottle
33 Rotor control hydraulic jack
34 Forward transmission gearbox
35 Rotor head fairing
36 Forward rotor head mechanism
37 Pitch change control levers
38 Blade drag dampers
39 Glassfibre rotor blades
40 Titanium leading-edge capping with de-icing provision
41 Rescue hoist/winch
42 Forward transmission aft fairing
43 Hydraulic system modules
44 Control levers
45 Front fuselage frame and stringer construction
46 Emergency exit window, main entry door on starboard side
47 Forward end of cargo floor
48 Fuel tank fuselage side fairing
49 Battery
50 Electrical system equipment bay
51 Aerial cable
52 Stretcher rack (up to 24 stretchers)
53 Cabin window panel
54 Cabin heater duct outlet
55 Troop seats stowed against cabin wall
56 Cabin roof transmission and control run tunnel
57 Formation-keeping lights
58 Rotor blade cross section
59 Static dischargers
60 Blade balance and tracking weights pocket
61 Leading-edge anti-erosion strip
62 Fixed tab
63 Fuselage skin plating
64 Maintenance walkway
65 Transmission tunnel access doors
66 Troop seating, up to 44 troops
67 Cargo hook access hatch
68 VOR aerial
69 Cabin lining panels
70 Control runs
71 Main transmission shaft
72 Shaft couplings
73 Centre fuselage construction
74 Centre aisle seating (optional)
75 Main cargo floor, 40.78 m³ (1,440 cu ft) cargo volume
76 Ramp-down 'dam' for waterborne operations
77 Ramp hydraulic jack
78 Engine bevel drive gearbox
79 Transmission combining gearbox
80 Rotor brake
81 Transmission oil tank
82 Oil cooler
83 Engine drive shaft fairing
84 Engine screen
85 Starboard engine nacelle
86 Cooling air grilles
87 Tail rotor pylon construction
88 Hydraulic equipment
89 Access door
90 Maintenance step
91 Tail rotor drive shaft
92 Tail rotor bearing mounting
93 Rotor head fairing
94 Tail rotor head mechanism
95 Main rotor blades, glassfibre construction
96 Rotor control hydraulic jack
97 Vibration absorber
98 Pylon aft fairing construction
99 Rear lighting
100 Solar T62T-2B auxiliary power unit
101 APU-driven generators
102 Maintenance walkways
103 Engine exhaust duct
104 Avco Lycoming T55-L-712 turboshaft engine
105 Detachable engine cowlings
106 Aft fuselage frame and stringer construction
107 Rear cargo doorway
108 Ramp extensions
109 Cargo ramp, lowered
110 Ramp ventral strake
111 Fuselage side fairing aft extension
112 Ramp control lever
113 Ramp hydraulic jack
114 Rear landing gear shock absorber
115 Landing gear leg strut
116 Single rear wheels
117 Rear wheel optional ski fitting
118 Maintenance steps
119 Rear fuel tank
120 Fuel tank interconnections
121 Ventral strake
122 Main fuel tank; total system capacity 4137 litres (1,093 US gal)
123 Floor beam construction
124 Fuel tank attachment joint
125 Fuel system piping
126 Fire extinguishers
127 Forward fuel tank
128 Fuel filler caps
129 Fuel capacity transmitters
130 Front landing gear mounting
131 Twin forward wheels
132 Forward wheels optional ski fitting
133 Triple cargo hook system; forward and rear hooks, 9072 kg (20,000 lb) capacity
134 Main cargo hook, 12701 kg (28,000 lb) capacity

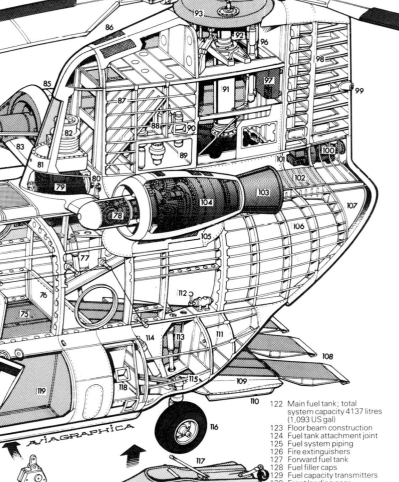

CH-47 Chinook variants

YCH-1B: pre-production aircraft; five built and redesignated **YCH-47A** in 1962, when the name Chinook was allocated
CH-47A: production aircraft with fuselage lengthened by 1.88 m (6 ft 2 in), increased-diameter rotors, 1641 kW (2,200-shp) Lycoming T55-L-5 engines (later 1976-kW/2,650-shp T55-L-7s); 354 built for the US Army, including four aircraft diverted to Thailand
ACH-47A: four CH-47As modified to gunships and armed with two 20-mm Vulcan cannon, 40-mm grenade-launchers, and 12.7-mm (0.5-in) machine guns; these Chinooks were nicknamed 'Go-Go Birds'
JCH-47A: CH-47A 60-3449 used for temporary flight testing
YCH-47B: prototypes for the production CH-47B; two built
CH-47B: introduced modified rotor blades, detail improvements and 2125-kW (2,850-shp) T55-7C turboshafts; 108 built
CH-47C: final production version for the US Army, with 2796-kW

(3,750-shp) T55-L-11A turboshafts, strengthened transmissions and increased internal fuel; 270 built for the US Army; under a 1978 contract Boeing Vertol uprated the transmissions of surviving CH-47A/Bs to CH-47C standard
CH-47D: one each of the three earlier CH-47 marks modified as CH-47D standard prototypes; in 1980 the first CH-47D 'production' modernization contract was awarded by the US Army; 88 aircraft were funded by annual contracts by 1984; in April 1985 Boeing Vertol was awarded a contract for an additional 240 CH-47Ds in Fiscal Years 1985-9; a planned total of 436 aircraft are to be remanufactured; there are 13 major improvements involved in the conversion, including the introduction of T55-L-712 turboshafts with standard and emergency ratings of 2796 kW (3,750 shp) and 3356 kW (4,500 shp) respectively
CH-147: designation of nine CH-47Cs delivered to Canada; these

aircraft have T55-L-11C engines, seating capacity increased to 44 by introducing 11 centre aisle trooping seats, and power drive fitted to the rear ramp, plus an inflatable water dam; avionics and the automatic flight-control system also updated
Chinook HC.Mk 1: 33 were ordered in 1978 for the RAF (ZA670-684 and ZA704-721); similar to CH-147, with T55-L-11E turboshafts, but with provision for glassfibre rotor blades and three external cargo hooks; extensive range of British avionics and equipment; eight more HC.Mk 1s (ZD574-576 and ZD980-984) with uprated T55-L-712 engines delivered as replacements for earlier losses; it is planned that all RAF Chinooks will be powered by the T55-L-712 engine
Model 414: international military version; six ordered for the Spanish army's 5th Helicopter Transport Battalion; the aircraft are fitted with nose-mounted weather radar

Though quite a size in itself, the Chinook can fit quite snuggly into many transport aircraft such as this C-5A Galaxy. Such an ability is vital to the US Army.

Should the need arise, the Chinook can land on water as the lower half of the fuselage is completely sealed during manufacture to form a watertight compartment.

Specification: CH-47D Chinook

Rotors
Rotor diameter, each	18.29 m	(60 ft 0 in)

Fuselage and tail unit
Length overall, rotors turning	30.18 m	(99 ft 0 in)
Fuselage length	15.54 m	(51 ft 0 in)
Height to top of rear rotor head	5.68 m	(18 ft 7.8 in)

Landing gear
Fixed quadricycle landing gear with two fixed twin-wheel nose units and two fully steerable single-wheel rear units
Wheelbase	6.86 m	(22 ft 6 in)

Weights
Empty	10475 kg	(23,093 lb)
Maximum take-off	22680 kg	(50,000 lb)
Internal payload over 185 km (115-mile) radius	6512 kg	(14,356 lb)
External payload over 55.5 km (34.5 mile radius	7192 kg	(15,856 lb)
Fuel load	3076 kg	(6,782 lb)

Powerplant
Two Avco Lycoming T55-L-712 turboshafts
Standard rating, each	2796 kW	(3,750 shp)
Maximum rating, each	3356 kW	(4,500 shp)

Performance
Maximum speed at 14968 kg (33,000 lb) AUW	157 kts; 291 km/h	(181 mph)
Cruising speed at maximum take-off weight	138 kts; 256 km/h	(159 mph)
Initial rate of climb	1,330 ft	(405 m) per minute
Ferry range	2020 km	(1,255 miles)
Service ceiling, one engine out, at maximum AUW	12,800 ft	(3900 m)

CH-47 recognition features

Contra-rotating main rotors that turn very slowly
Large, three-blade main rotors
Distinctive tandem rotor configuration
Engines externally mounted in pods attached to rear rotor mast
Long pannier fairings along lower sides of cabin
Retractable four-unit landing gear
Forward landing gear units have twin wheels
Large, evenly-spaced circular cabin windows
Large, frameless canopy
Large rear loading ramp
Heavily glazed cockpit with prominent 'nose'

Maximum cruising speed at optimum altitude

Aérospatiale AS 332M Super Puma	151 kts
Sikorsky CH-53E	150 kts
Boeing Vertol CH-46D Sea Knight	140 kts
Boeing Vertol Chinook HC.Mk 1	138 kts
Mil Mi-26 'Halo'	137 kts
Mil Mi-17 'Hip-H'	122 kts
Westland Commando	112 kts

Maximum external load

Mil Mi-26 'Halo'	20000 kg
Sikorsky CH-53E	16329 kg
Boeing Vertol Chinook HC.Mk 1	12700 kg
Boeing Vertol CH-46D Sea Knight	4535 kg
Aérospatiale AS 332M Super Puma	4500 kg
Westland Commando	3628 kg
Mil Mi-17 'Hip-H'	3000 kg

Range with standard fuel

Mil Mi-26 'Halo'	800 km
Aérospatiale AS 332M Super Puma	635 km
Mil Mi-17 'Hip-H'	500 km
Westland Commando	445 km
Boeing Vertol CH-46D Sea Knight	380 km
Boeing Vertol Chinook HC.Mk 1	370 km
Sikorsky CH-53E	not quoted

Initial climb rate, feet per minute

Sikorsky CH-53E	2,500 ft
Westland Commando	2,020 ft
Aérospatiale AS 332M Super Puma	1,732 ft
Mil Mi-17 'Hip-H'	1,700 ft E
Boeing Vertol CH-46D Sea Knight	1,660 ft
Chinook HC.Mk 1	1,485 ft
Mil Mi-26 'Halo'	not quoted

Troops carried

Mil Mi-26 'Halo'	90
Sikorsky CH-53E	55
Chinook HC.Mk 1	44
Westland Commando	28
Mil Mi-17 'Hip-H'	28
Boeing Vertol CH-46D Sea Knight	25
Aérospatiale AS 332M Super Puma	25

The SIKORSKY CH-53

Sikorsky CH-53: heavy-lift hauler

Whether it be essential weaponry, fully-laden combat troops or a cargo of general supplies, the CH-53 can deliver the goods. Combining versatility with immense lifting power, this supreme hauler is an impressive asset in the vital transport role.

The CH-53A Sea Stallion represented a major upgrading in US assault transport strength when introduced into service. A significant external load can be carried in addition to the internal main cabin capacity.

In its latest guise as the CH-53E Super Stallion, Sikorsky's massive heavy-lift helicopter is undoubtedly one of the most powerful machines of its type currently in production anywhere in the world, whilst, with procurement expected to exceed the 150 mark, it is equally clear that the type will play an increasingly important role in years to come as it consolidates its position as the principal heavy-lift helicopter in service with both the US Navy and Marine Corps.

In point of fact, the CH-53E is just the latest example in a fairly long-line of S-65 developments, work on this project beginning well over 20 years ago. At that time Sikorsky had already established a solid reputation as a heavy helicopter manufacturer, types such as the piston-engined H-34 Choctaw and H-37 Mojave being in widespread service with various elements of the US armed forces. By the early 1960s, however, it was becoming apparent that these models were fast approaching obsolescence and would be unable to fulfil future requirements, especially in view of other new weapons and vehicles then under development.

Accordingly, the US Marine Corps turned its attention to finding a new heavy-lift/assault helicopter, subsequently revealing in late August 1962 that Sikorsky had been chosen to develop such a machine for service with the Marine Corps under the designation CH-53A. A key feature of the new helicopter design was the adoption of twin turbines, these being generally acknowledged to be far more reliable and certainly much more powerful than piston engines, with the result that the new machine's performance would be significantly better than that of the type it would replace, namely the Sikorsky CH-37C Mojave, or 'Deuce' as it was affectionately known.

Not surprisingly, the manufacturer incorporated much of the experience gained with the earlier S-64 although the S-65 design which resulted bore only a superficial resemblance to the gawky and ungainly Skycrane. Flown for the first time in mid-October 1964, the initial CH-53A began to enter service just under two years later, HMH-463 being the first USMC squadron to receive the type when it took delivery of its first example at Santa Ana on 20 September 1966.

After a brief period of work-up training, the Sea Stallion was deployed to the combat zone in South East Asia in remarkably short order, a four-aircraft detachment of HMH-463 beginning operations from the Marble Mountain Air Facility just to the south of Da Nang on 13 January 1967, the first instances of the CH-53A taking small arms fire occurring just four days later when two aircraft were hit: neither was seriously damaged and both were soon back in action again. Subsequently, on 25 January 1967, the CH-53A accomplished

the first of many helicopter retrievals when a USMC UH-34 which had suffered mechanical failure was recovered from the landing platform of a hospital ship and air-lifted to Marble Mountain for repair.

Despite being grounded briefly towards the end of January, the four CH-53As of the advanced echelon went on to accomplish 103 successful recoveries between then and 22 May, when the rest of the squadron arrived, bringing an additional 22 Sea Stallions. Statistically, the UH-34 topped the list of recoveries during this interval, no less than 72 being collected from various locations, but the HMH-463 detachment also retrieved 13

A general improvement in performance and troop capacity characterize the CH-53D, which gradually superseded the CH-53A. This dramatic view shows the dispensing of flares from rear-fuselage ports during overwater operations.

Boeing Vertol CH-46A Sea Knights and 16 Bell UH-1E Iroquois, throwing in a couple of USAF aircraft for good measure. Perhaps the most valuable aspect of the Sea Stallion's work, recovery operations such as these were often undertaken in areas where enemy forces were known to be active, and it was stated quite categorically that many of the machines which were airlifted to safety would otherwise have been lost. Clearly, the CH-53A was already showing a return on investment.

Following the arrival of the main body of the squadron, the scope and intensity of operations increased dramatically, HMH-463 Sea Stallions being called upon to perform all types of heavy-lift mission, these ranging from the movement of troops engaged in assault and pursuit operations through redeployment of artillery pieces from point to point to support the large number of fire bases which existed at the time.

In addition to demonstrating its prowess on the battlefield, the CH-53A was certainly no slouch when it came to flying qualities, being capable of much more than mere straight and level flight. Indeed, continued testing and evaluation

accomplished during the course of 1968 revealed many more aspects of this remarkable machine, a CH-53A with slightly modified General Electric T64-GE-6 engines establishing new unofficial payload and gross weight records for a production helicopter built outside the USSR on 17 February when it flew successfully at a gross weight of 23541 kg (51,900 lb).

Loops and rolls

A couple of months later, in April, another CH-53A made helicopter history when it completed the first automatic terrain clearance flight by this type of flying machine, but probably the most startling event of that year came on 23 October when, during the course of a flight test project intended to explore rotor system dynamics and manoeuvrability characteristics, a Sea Stallion successfully demonstrated unprecedented agility by completing a series of loops and rolls, an impressive achievement for any helicopter but all the more amazing when one recalls just how big the CH-53 really is. Production of the CH-53A eventually terminated after just under 150 had been

While the CH-53 can transport a huge variety of cargo both internally and externally, other roles include a limited rescue capability. This Israeli machine is seen winching aboard a downed pilot via the forward-fuselage hoist.

built, deliveries of an improved model known as the CH-53D getting under way in March 1969. The principal difference incorporated in the CH-53D concerned the engines, the much more powerful T64-GE-413 being fitted as standard, this being rated at 2927 kW (3,925 shp) as compared with the 2125 kW (2,850 shp) of the CH-53A's T64-GE-6 engines. Thus the CH-53D possesses the ability to airlift heavier loads and, although normally configured to take 38 troops in the assault role, the CH-53D can utilise a high-density cabin layout in which it can carry a maximum of 55 troops. Like its predecessor, the CH-53D was also committed to combat action in Vietnam at a fairly early stage in its operational career, many of the 120-odd examples that were eventually completed for service with the Marine Corps duly finding their way to South East Asia. Production of this model terminated in January 1972, but by then

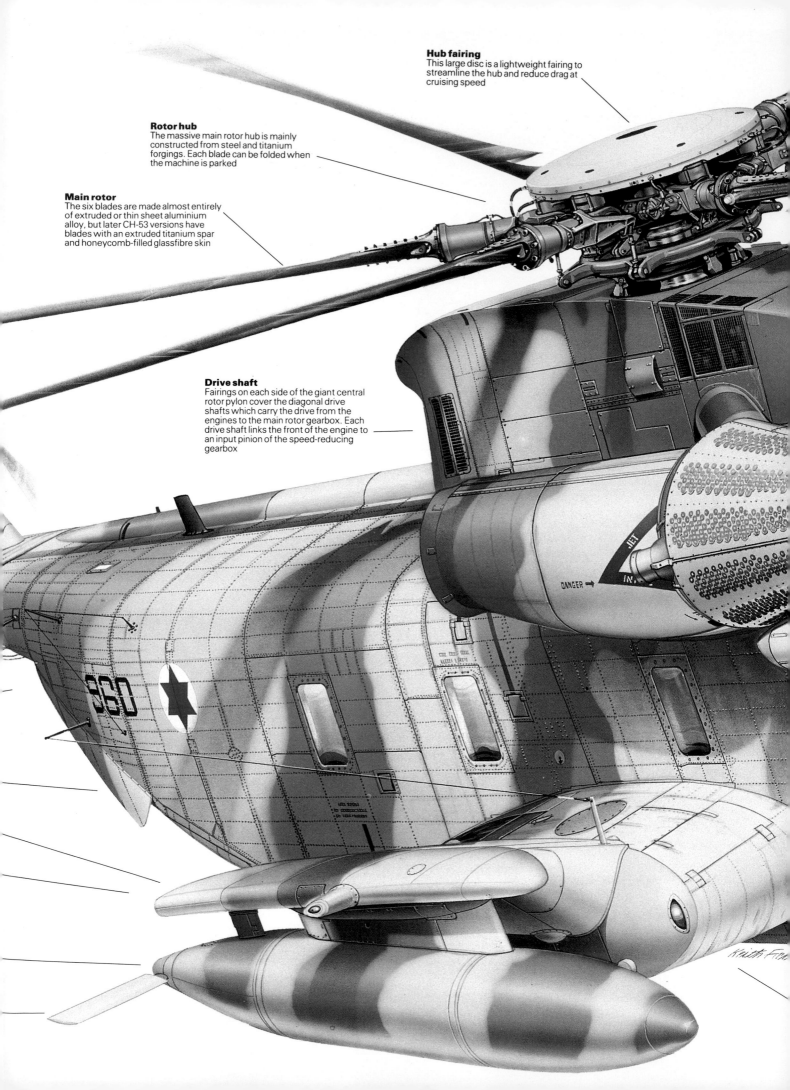

Hub fairing
This large disc is a lightweight fairing to streamline the hub and reduce drag at cruising speed

Rotor hub
The massive main rotor hub is mainly constructed from steel and titanium forgings. Each blade can be folded when the machine is parked

Main rotor
The six blades are made almost entirely of extruded or thin sheet aluminium alloy, but later CH-53 versions have blades with an extruded titanium spar and honeycomb-filled glassfibre skin

Drive shaft
Fairings on each side of the giant central rotor pylon cover the diagonal drive shafts which carry the drive from the engines to the main rotor gearbox. Each drive shaft links the front of the engine to an input pinion of the speed-reducing gearbox

DANGER ➡

JET
IN

360

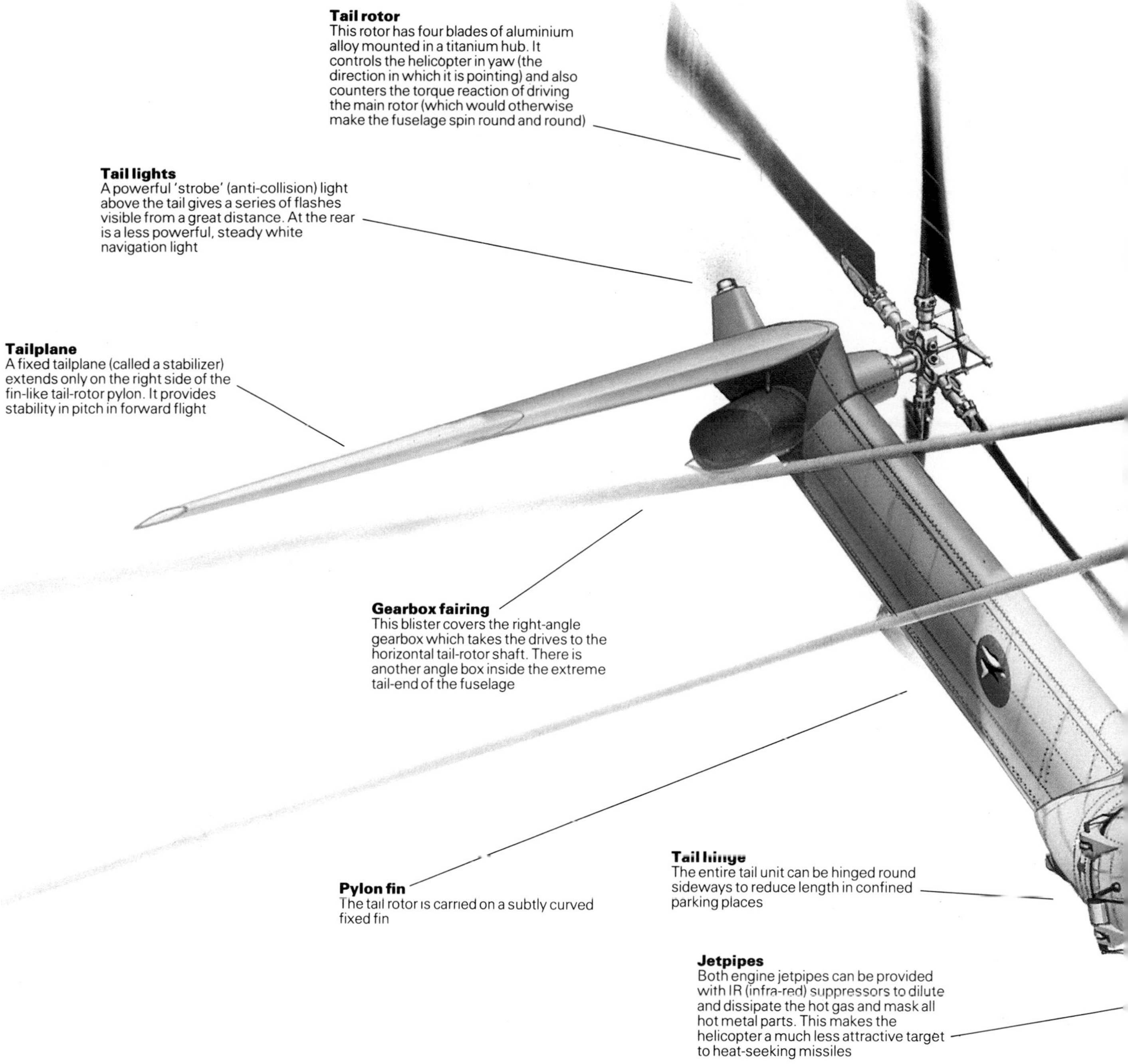

Tail rotor
This rotor has four blades of aluminium alloy mounted in a titanium hub. It controls the helicopter in yaw (the direction in which it is pointing) and also counters the torque reaction of driving the main rotor (which would otherwise make the fuselage spin round and round)

Tail lights
A powerful 'strobe' (anti-collision) light above the tail gives a series of flashes visible from a great distance. At the rear is a less powerful, steady white navigation light

Tailplane
A fixed tailplane (called a stabilizer) extends only on the right side of the fin-like tail-rotor pylon. It provides stability in pitch in forward flight

Gearbox fairing
This blister covers the right-angle gearbox which takes the drives to the horizontal tail-rotor shaft. There is another angle box inside the extreme tail-end of the fuselage

Pylon fin
The tail rotor is carried on a subtly curved fixed fin

Tail hinge
The entire tail unit can be hinged round sideways to reduce length in confined parking places

Jetpipes
Both engine jetpipes can be provided with IR (infra-red) suppressors to dilute and dissipate the hot gas and mask all hot metal parts. This makes the helicopter a much less attractive target to heat-seeking missiles

Ventral strakes
Fixed strakes like fences smooth out the airflow past the big rear cargo door and around the underside of the tapering rear fuselage

Pylon mounts
Special cantilever pylon mounts extend diagonally upwards from the tips of the sponsons to carry the auxiliary tanks

Drop tank lights
The drop tanks obscure the view of the left and right navigation lights, so these lights are duplicated on projections extended from the tips of the tank pylons

Drop tank
The Israeli CH-53s, like some other versions, can carry auxiliary jettisonable fuel tanks, each of 1703 litres (450 US gal/375 Imp gal) capacity

Fuel tank fins
Each tank is stabilized by down-sloping or swept-back tail fins

Sikorsky S-65C-3 (CH-53D)
Israeli Defence Force/Air Force

Sikorsky was actively engaged in improving the breed still further, a process which ultimately led to appearance of the CH-53E.

In the meantime, however, numerous other versions of the basic Sea Stallion had also appeared, these for the most part evolving from the CH-53A and CH-53D models. Some, such as the HH-53B and HH-53C, were dedicated to the task of combat search and rescue, being armed and armoured derivatives intended for service with the USAF's Aerospace Rescue & Recovery Service, and they compiled an impressive tally of 'saves' not only in Vietnam but also at various other operating locations around the world. Another model operated solely by the USAF is the CH-53C, which is perhaps most closely related to the USMC machines in that it is primarily intended for use as a cargo helicopter.

Helicopters of this type also formed part of the force assembled for the disastrous assault on Koh Tang Island following the seizure of the SS *Mayaguez* by Cambodian forces in May 1975 and, during the 14-hour long operation, three CH-53Cs were lost to the intense and often accurate ground fire encountered during the operation's insertion and retrieval phases. The surviving CH-53Cs are now used mainly to provide enhanced battlefield mobility to the USAF's Tactical Air Control System. Such work generally entails movement of mobile radars and control vans, the CH-53C's impresssive external lift capability being of great value.

German operations

In addition to US service, the CH-53 has also found favour with a handful of other air arms, West Germany being the major overseas customer. Essentially similar to the CH-53D, the CH-53G was acquired in fairly substantial numbers, West Germany's Heeresflieger (army air service) eventually receiving no less than 112, the first two of which were pattern aircraft manufactured by Sikorsky in the USA. Delivered during 1969, these two were followed by 20 aircraft asembled at Speyer from Sikorsky-supplied components, production thereafter entailing a roughly 50-50 split between components of US and West German origin. The prime contractor for this programme was VFW-Fokker, and the first CH-53G to be completed at Speyer made a successful maiden flight on 11 October 1971, deliveries to the Heeresflieger following soon afterwards and eventually terminating during 1975.

Aircraft of wholly US origin have also been supplied to the Iranian navy (RH-53D), the Israeli Defence Force/Air Force (CH-53D) and Austria (S-65-Oe), the last model being essentially similar to USAF HH-53s and undertaking rescue duties in the Alps as well as more conventional airlift tasks. However, both were eventually sold to the IDF/AF during the course of 1981. As far as the Iranian aircraft are concerned, these apparently operated

In addition to fitted main and auxiliary fuel tanks, the CH-53 can acquire additional fuel via the forward-extendable inflight-refuelling probe, and also via a hose attachment to ships with the CH-53 hovering above.

from Kharg Island at the head of the Persian Gulf on mine countermeasures tasks, but they are now believed to be inactive.

As noted earlier, the most recent development has been the three-engined CH-53E Super Stallion, a sub-type which is now well established in operational service with both the US Navy and the US Marine Corps. Company investigations into the possibility of producing a three-engined variant date back to the late 1960s, but it was not until 1973 that Sikorsky received the go-ahead to proceed with the construction of two prototypes under the terms of a $1.7 million cost-plus-fixed-fee contract.

Flown for the first time on 1 March 1974, the YCH-53E prototype was soon destroyed in a ground accident, but evaluation of the second YCH-53E, which first flew on 24 January 1974, soon revealed that it represented a major improvement over the earlier variants and it was subsequently ordered into quantity production during 1978. Once again the major customer has been the US Marine Corps, which has taken the lion's share of the aircraft delivered to date, using these to equip new heavy-lift helicopter squad-

Distinguishing features of the CH-53E include the addition of a third engine aft of the main rotor head in the port upper fuselage decking and the addition of a seventh main rotor blade, though the fuselage is essentially unchanged.

rons at both New River, North Carolina and Tustin, California (formerly Santa Ana). As far as the Marine Corps is concerned, the primary missions are largely unchanged from those of the CH-53A/D, encompassing assault, movement of artillery pieces and other bulky items, recovery of damaged or downed aircraft and helicopters, and general-purpose heavy airlift.

Additionally, the CH-53E has also been adopted in modest numbers by the US Navy and it now fulfils vertical offshore delivery duties with that service, examples of the type being employed by squadrons located in the principal overseas areas of Navy activity, namely the Mediterranean and the Western Pacific.

Sea Stallion and Super Stallion in service units and example aircraft

US Marine Corps

CJ-10, 157931/CJ-22
HMH-464 (CH-53E) 161184/
EN-05, 161260/EN-16
HMT-204 (CH-53A) no
examples known

1st Marine Aircraft Wing, Fleet Marine Force Pacific

Forward deployed in Japan; normally controls a single squadron at Futenma, Okinawa, on a rotational basis from ConUS

2nd Marine Aircraft Wing, Fleet Marine Force Atlantic

Base: New River, North Carolina
Squadrons and aircraft:
HMH-362 (CH-53D) 157150/YL-00, 156961/YL-24
HMH-461 (CH-53D) 156965/

3rd Marine Aircraft Wing, Fleet Marine Force Pacific

Base: Tustin, California
Squadrons and aircraft:
HMH-361 (CH-53A/D) no examples known
HMH-363 (CH-53A/D) 157157/YZ-21 ('D')
HMH-462 (CH-53A/D) 153286/YF-67 ('A'), 157143/YF-55 ('D')
HMH-465 (CH-53E) 161265/YJ-04, 162002/YJ-17
HMH-466 (CH-53E) no examples known
HMT-301 (CH-53A/E) 152406/SU-26 ('A'), 161997/SU-34 ('E')

1st Marine Brigade, Fleet Marine Force Pacific

Base: Kaneohe Bay, Hawaii
Squadron and aircraft:
HMH-463 (CH-53D) 157751/YH-00, 156671/YH-20

Marine Corps Development and Education Command

Base: Quantico, Virginia
Squadron and aircraft:
HMX-1 (V/CH-53D) 157930/MX-26 (CH-53D), 157755/– (VH-53D)

4th Marine Aircraft Wing (Reserve)

Base: Willow Grove, Pennsylvania
Squadron and aircraft:
HMH-772 (CH-53A) 153299/MT-401, 151688/MT-406

US Marine Corps CH-53s continue to wear an overall dark olive green camouflage, though lettering and national insignia have appeared in black in recent years. This is a CH-53D Sea Stallion of HMH-462.

US Navy

Anti-Submarine Warfare Wing Pacific (ASWWingPac)

Base: North Island, California
Squadron and aircraft:
HC-1 (CH-53E) 161542/UP-440, 161543/UP-441

Fleet Western Pacific (FAirWestPac)

Base: Cubi Point, Republic of Philippines
Squadron and aircraft:
VC-5 (CH-53E) no examples known

Fleet Air Mediterranean (FAirMed)

Base: Sigonella, Sicily
Squadron and aircraft:
HC-4 (CH-53E) 161532/HC-532, 161538/HC-538

Helicopter Tactical Wing One (HelTacWing-One)

Base: Norfolk, Virginia

Squadrons and aircraft:
HM-12 (CH-53E/RH-53D) 161534/DH-436 (CH-53E), 158751/DH-430 (RH-53D)

HM-14 (CH-53D/RH-53D)
158689/BJ-530 (RH-53D)
HM-16 (CH-53D/RH-53D)
158752/GC-633 (RH-53D)

US Navy Super Stallions are now wearing an overall dark grey colour scheme. This CH-53E wears the 'UP' code letters of HC-1 at NAS North Island, California.

US Air Force

601st TASS/601st TCW

Base: Sembach AB, West Germany
Aircraft: (CH-53C) 68-10932, 70-1630

1551st CCTS/1550th CCTW

Base: Kirtland AFB, New Mexico
Aircraft: (CH-53C) 68-10923, 70-1631

The small force of CH-53C Super Jollies have not escaped the US Air Force move towards a low-visibility colour scheme, this 601st TASS machine sporting the 'Euro One' camouflage colours and small national insignia.

West German Army (Heeresflieger)

Mittleres Heeresflieger Transportregimenten (MHFTR)

MHFTR-15
Base: Rheine-Bentlage
Aircraft: (CH-53G) 8469, 8478, 8491, 8499, 8512

MHFTR-25
Base: Laupheim
Aircraft: (CH-53G) 8415, 8446, 8454, 8464, 8496

MHFTR-35
Base: Niedermendig
Aircraft: (CH-53G) 8406, 8420, 8435, 8466, 8502

Heeresflieger Waffenschule (HFlWaS)
Base: Bückeburg
Aircraft: no examples known

Erprobungsstelle 61 (Est 61)
Base: Manching, Ingolstadt
Aircraft: (CH-53G) 8401

The sole European operator of the CH-53 is the German army, which has 107 CH-53Gs in use. All wear the prominent national insignia and four-number code. This example serves with MHFTR-35 as part of III Korps.

Israeli Defence Force/Air Force

Thirty-three S-65C-3s (basically CH-53Ds) were aquired via the United States Marine Corps' procurement programme. Two further machines of S-65C-2 configuration were acquired from Austria during 1981.

Standard IDF/AF camouflage colours identify the desert theatre of operations in which the force of CH-53Ds operate. As usual with IDF/AF aircraft, operating units and squadron insignia are almost impossible to verify.

Filter
Also called a particle separator, these large boxes separate out sand and other foreign matter from the engine inlet airflow. Extracted particles are discharged from a pipe on the outer side, visible on the nearside engine immediately in front of the red stencilled warning

Oil cooler
Inboard of each engine is a large air inlet admitting cooling air which is pumped by a fan through a high-capacity oil cooler. Helicopters need powerful cooling systems to dissipate the heat from the lubricating oil systems of the engines and gearboxes

Engine air inlets
Specially designed inlets provide adequate engine airflow even if the helicopter is moving sideways or backwards

Pitot tube
A pitot/static tube to measure airspeed is mounted above each side of the cockpit roof. Speed measurement in a hovering or slow-moving helicopter is difficult

Windscreen wipers
Pilot and co-pilot each have a powerful windscreen wiper. Transparent panels give a good view ahead, to the sides and almost vertically down past the pilots' feet

ILS
The CH-53 is one of the few helicopters with an instrument landing system to enable landings to be made in bad visibility to ILS-equipped airbases. This curved handle-like aerial (antenna) serves the glide slope ILS receiver which gives vertical guidance

Cockpit air intakes
These small grilles admit fresh air direct to the cockpit. In battle conditions they can be closed

Access panel
This panel can be unlatched and hinged upwards to provide complete access to the back of the cockpit instrument

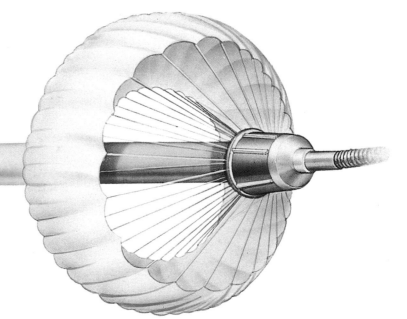

Inflight-refuelling
This can be retracted under the cockpit floor when not in use. It has to be very long and massive to keep the main rotor well clear of the tanker aircraft

Sponson
On each side is a large and capacious fairing called a sponson. It contains fuel tanks and, at the rear, the retracted twin-wheel main landing gears

Sponson lights
Navigation lights (bluish-green on the right, red on the left) are mounted on both sponsons

Rescue hoist
Most H-53 versions, including those of Israel, have this powerful rescue hoist with 250 ft (76.2 m) of cable. Not visible is the external cargo hook system for carrying heavy slung loads

Crew access
The main entry door is at the front on the right. There are no side doors to the cockpit, but the large side windows can be jettisoned for emergency escape

Equipment access
Large doors on each side of the nose give access to the radio and electronics bays, the probe mounting and other units

RESCUE

860

Specification:

Sikorsky CH-53E Super Stallion

Rotors

Main rotor diameter	24.08 m	(79 ft 0 in)
Tail rotor diameter	6.10 m	(20 ft 0 in)
Main rotor disc area	455.36 m²	(4,901.67 sq ft)
Tail rotor disc area	29.19 m²	(314.16 sq ft)

Fuselage and tail unit

Accommodation	three flightcrew and 55 troops	
Length overall, rotors turning	30.18 m	(99 ft 0.5 in)
Length, rotor and tail pylon folded	18.44 m	(60 ft 6 in)
Length of fuselage	22.35 m	(73 ft 4 in)
Height overall, tail rotor turning	8.66 m	(28 ft 5 in)
Height, rotor and tail pylon folded	5.66 m	(18 ft 7 in)

Landing gear

Retractable tricycle landing gear with twin-wheel main and nose units

Wheelbase	8.31 m	(27 ft 3 in)
Wheel track to centreline of shock struts	3.96 m	(13 ft 0 in)

Weights

Empty	15071 kg	(33,226 lb)
Maximum take-off with an external load	33339 kg	(73,500 lb)
Maximum external load	14515 kg	(32,000 lb)
Maximum internal load	13608 kg	(30,000 lb)

Powerplant

Three General Electric T64-GE-416 turboshafts		
Rating, each	3266 kW	(4,380 shp)

Sikorsky CH-53 recognition features

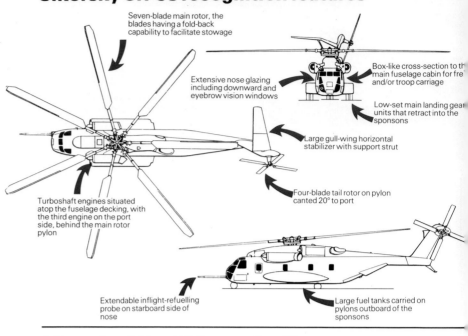

Seven-blade main rotor, the blades having a fold-back capability to facilitate stowage

Extensive nose glazing including downward and eyebrow vision windows

Box-like cross-section to th' main fuselage cabin for fre' and/or troop carriage

Low-set main landing gear units that retract into the sponsons

Large gull-wing horizontal stabilizer with support strut

Four-blade tail rotor on pylon canted 20° to port

Turboshaft engines situated atop the fuselage decking, with the third engine on the port side, behind the main rotor pylon

Extendable inflight-refuelling probe on starboard side of nose

Large fuel tanks carried on pylons outboard of the sponsons

Sikorsky CH-53 Super Jolly/Sea Stallion/ Super Stallion variants

CH-53A: original production model for service with USMC and still in front-line use today in modest quantities; about 140 built, some being supplied to USAF and USN, those with latter service being employed as interim mine countermeasures platform pending delivery of purpose-built RH-53D

CH-53C: transport version acquired by USAF; initially employed in South East Asia in support of Special Forces but today mainly serves as cargo helicopter with Tactical Control Wings, being used to position and support mobile radar units

CH-53D: updated assault helicopter for service with USMC, utilizing more powerful engines; about 125 delivered to USMC during 1969-72 period and most still in use today; 33 supplied to Israel

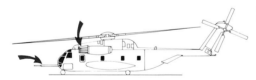

CH-53E: three-engined and much improved assault/general-purpose heavy-lift helicopter now in process of production for and delivery to USN/MC operational units; first flown in prototype form as YCH-53E in March 1974; extensive changes incorporated in this model have resulted in change of name to Super Stallion

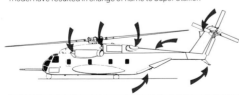

CH-53G: licence-built version produced by VFW-Fokker at Speyer, West Germany; total of 112 completed for service with Heeresflieger, first two being produced by parent company in USA and supplied as pattern/test aircraft; VFM-Fokker then assembled 20 from Sikorsky-supplied components, following up with a further 90 which featured an increasing proportion of locally-manufactured parts

Sikorsky CH-53E Super Stallion cutaway drawing key

1 Retractable inflight-refuelling boom
2 Refuelling boom fairing
3 Instrument compartment access door
4 Glideslope aerial
5 Fresh air intakes
6 Yaw control rudder pedals
7 Landing lamp
8 Downward vision windows
9 Nose undercarriage leg strut
10 Twin nosewheels
11 Radio and electronics bay, port and starboard
12 Cockpit floor level
13 Collective pitch control lever
14 Cyclic pitch control column
15 Co-pilot's armoured seat
16 Instrument panel shroud
17 Windscreen wipers
18 Windscreen panels
19 Rescue hoist/winch
20 Pitot tube
21 UHF aerial
22 Overhead control panel
23 Pilot's armoured seat
24 Cockpit eyebrow window
25 Flight leader's folding jump seat
26 Cockpit bulkhead
27 Jettisonable side window panel
28 Starboard side crew entry door

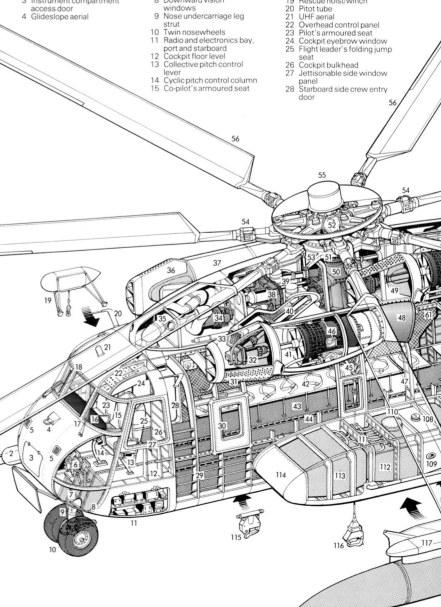

erformance:

aximum speed at sea level	170 kts	315 km/h (196 mph)
rvice ceiling	18,500 ft	(5640 m)
vering ceiling in		
round effect	11,550 ft	(3520 m)
vering ceiling out of		
round effect	9,500 ft	(2895 m)
f-ferry range in optimum		
uise condition	2076 km	(1,290 miles)
ial rate of climb	2,750 ft (838 m) per minute	

Service ceiling

- Sikorsky CH-53E 18,500 ft
- Mil Mi-26 'Halo' 15,100 ft
- CH-47D Chinook 15,000 ft
- Mil Mi-6 'Hook' 14,750 ft
- Super Frelon 10,170 ft

Payload (internal)

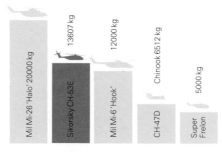

- Mil Mi-26 'Halo' 20000 kg
- Sikorsky CH-53E 13607 kg
- Mil Mi-6 'Hook' 12000 kg
- Chinook CH-47D 6512 kg
- Super Frelon 5000 kg

Speed at low altitude

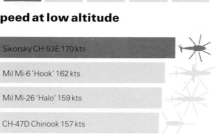

- Sikorsky CH-53E 170 kts
- Mil Mi-6 'Hook' 162 kts
- Mil Mi-26 'Halo' 159 kts
- CH-47D Chinook 157 kts
- Super Frelon 140 kts

Troops carried

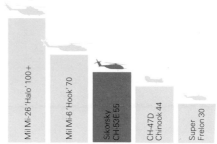

- Mil Mi-26 'Halo' 100+
- Mil Mi-6 'Hook' 70
- Sikorsky CH-53E 55
- CH-47D Chinook 44
- Super Frelon 30

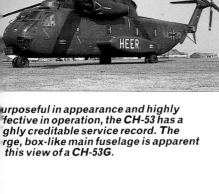

*urposeful in appearance and highly
fective in operation, the CH-53 has a
ghly creditable service record. The
rge, box-like main fuselage is apparent
this view of a CH-53G.*

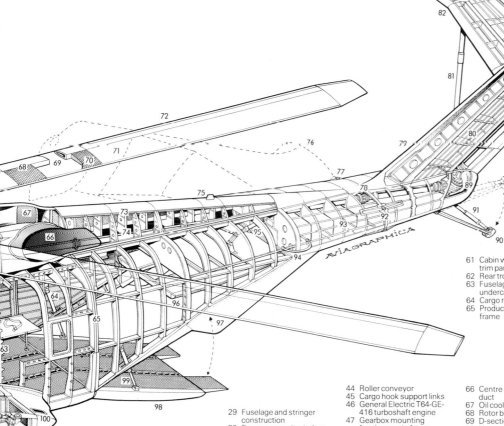

© Pilot Press Limited

29 Fuselage and stringer construction
30 Emergency exit window
31 Engine air intake particle-separator
32 Bevel drive gearbox
33 Engine oil cooler
34 Auxiliary power unit (APU)
35 Cabin heater unit
36 Starboard engine intake particle-separator
37 Engine cowlings, armoured on lower surface
38 Auxiliary gearbox
39 Hydraulic reservoirs
40 Gearbox drive shaft
41 Port engine transmission shaft
42 Folding troop seats, maximum 55 troops
43 Cargo loading floor
44 Roller conveyor
45 Cargo hook support links
46 General Electric T64-GE-416 turboshaft engine
47 Gearbox mounting fuselage main frame
48 Engine exhaust duct
49 Centre engine intake
50 Main transmission gearbox
51 Blade pitch control rotating swashplate
52 Rotor head mechanism
53 Blade pitch control links
54 Blade folding hinge points
55 Rotor head fairing
56 Seven-blade main rotor, 24.08 m (79 ft) diameter
57 Centre engine oil cooler
58 Maintenance handrail
59 Engine compartment firewall
60 Centre General Electric T64-GE-416 turboshaft engine
61 Cabin wall soundproofing trim panel
62 Rear troop seats
63 Fuselage/main undercarriage main frame
64 Cargo ramp hydraulic jack
65 Production break double frame
66 Centre engine exhaust duct
67 Oil cooler exhaust
68 Rotor blade cross-section
69 D-section titanium spar
70 Honeycomb trailing edge panel
71 Glass-fibre blade skin
72 Leading edge anti-erosion strip
73 Dorsal spine fairing
74 Tail rotor transmission shaft
75 Tacan aerial
76 Tail pylon folded position
77 Pylon hinge joint
78 Transmission shaft coupling
79 Glassfibre leading edge
80 Tailfin construction, canted 20° to port
81 Stabilizer bracing strut
82 Gull-wing horizontal stabilizer
83 Anti-collision light
84 Tail navigation light
85 Four-blade tail rotor, 6.1 m (20 ft) diameter
86 Tail rotor pitch control mechanism
87 Tail rotor gearbox
88 Final drive shaft
89 Bevel gearbox
90 Retractable tail bumper
91 Bumper hydraulic jack
92 Folding tail pylon latches
93 Tail boom construction
94 VOR/localizer aerial
95 Upper cargo door hydraulic jack
96 Upper cargo door, open position
97 Doorway side strakes
98 Cargo loading ramp, down position
99 Ramp hydraulic jack
100 Formation keeping light
101 Fuel jettison pipe
102 Main undercarriage leg strut
103 Twin mainwheels
104 Mainwheel bay
105 Hydraulic retraction jack
106 Maintenance platform walkway
107 Fuselage sponson main frame
108 Fuel filler cap
109 Port navigation light
110 Fuel tank access panel
111 Fuel system piping
112 Port main fuel tank: total internal capacity 3850 litres (1,017 US gal)
113 Secondary fuel tank
114 Sponson nose fairing
115 Two-point suspension cargo hooks
116 Single-point cargo hook: maximum external slung load 14606 kg (32,200 lb)
117 Auxiliary fuel tank pylon
118 Pylon navigation light
119 Auxiliary fuel tank, capacity 2461 litres (650 US gal)

The SIKORSKY SH-60 SEAHAWK

Seahawk: the multi-purpose mariner

While the world may be awestruck by the mighty naval forces deployed by the superpowers, such military might remains a highly vulnerable asset. The scourge of any surface vessel fleet is the submarine, hence the high degree of importance attached to securing an effective anti-submarine force. For the US Navy the latest asset is the SH-60B Seahawk, and this is a highly adaptable helicopter tasked with various duties.

The Sikorsky SH-3 Sea King was the first helicopter genuinely able to take off from a warship and fly a complete ASW mission, handling both the search and the attack tasks. A helicopter of this size cannot be carried by many frigates and destroyers, and in the 1960s the US Navy investigated the possibility of flying useful missions with a smaller helicopter. The result was the 1970 LAMPS programme for a Light Airborne Multi-Purpose System. As an interim LAMPS Mk I, the existing Kaman SH-2 Seasprite was adopted, but this does not have all the capability the US Navy wanted (though if the SH-2F enhancement programmes lead to re-engining with twin T700 engines the shortfall would be small). The definitive LAMPS Mk II proved to be beyond the Seasprite's capability, and despite Westland's offer of the naval Lynx as a fully capable alternative the Mk II requirement was cancelled. In its place a further upgraded Mk III requirement was written, and rather surprisingly a prime contract was awarded not to an aircraft company but to IBM, reflecting the overriding importance of the avionics systems.

Thus in the mid-1970s the position was

that IBM was managing the flight-control, navigation, mission search and weapon-delivery avionics, whilst the Navy considered which helicopters these should be packaged into. It so happened that at that time the US Army was evaluating candidate helicopters for its UTTAS, narrowing the field to the Boeing Vertol YUH-61A and Sikorsky YUH-60A, each powered by a pair of the specially designed General Electric T700 engine. These helicopters appeared highly suitable as a basis for the Navy LAMPS Mk III mission, and the Navy thus began its own evaluation. In late 1976 the Army picked the Sikorsky contender, and this certainly influenced the Navy's choice, not least because the planned 83 per cent commonality between the Army and Navy helicopters promised a significant reduction in unit price. The Navy followed the Army's lead in picking the Sikorsky in late summer 1977, and the new version was designated SH-60B Seahawk.

Seahawk structure

The basic helicopter closely resembles the UH-60A. The four-blade main rotor has hollow tubular titanium spars with glassfibre aerofoils stabilized by internal

As the LAMPS (Light Airborne Multi-Purpose System) Mk III platform, the SH-60B Seahawk will become an increasingly familiar sight aboard many US Navy vessels in the years to come. A total of 204 examples are on order.

honeycomb. Unlike the Army machine there is a rotor brake, and the blades are folded not manually but by electric power. The rest of the airframe is light-alloy stressed skin, with a fair amount of honeycomb construction. The large rectangular tailplane is driven by a hydraulic power unit to different angles appropriate to the flight condition in order to maintain trim, the setting in the hover being very sharply positive (leading edge upwards). The landing gear does not have to be as strong as that of the Army machine, and the tailwheel unit is totally different, being moved right forward under the fuselage, with twin wheels on a vertical strut which can be extended downwards for deck landing.

Development costs of the Seahawk have been reduced thanks to much airframe commonality with its UH-60A Black Hawk predecessor, but an obvious external difference is the pair of nose-mounted AN/ALQ-142 ESM housings.

The latter manoeuvre is assisted by a RAST device which via a cable hauls the helicopter firmly down on to the deck and them moves it under positive control into the ship's hangar, even in a rough sea.

The two main LAMPS Mk III missions are ASW and anti-ship surveillance and targeting. Sensors for the former mission include a Texas instruments APS-124 radar with a large aerial rotating about a vertical axis inside a flat-bottomed radome under the cockpit, a Texas Instruments ASQ-81(V) MAD with a red/yellow towed body extended on a cable from a housing on a pylon on the right side of the rear fuselage, and 125 sonobuoys ejected from a 5×5 (25-tube) Sikorsky pneumatic launcher firing to the left. Another very important installation is the Raytheon ALQ-142 ESM, with four receiver antennas (two under each side of the nose and the other two halfway down the flanks of the tapering rear part of the main fuselage, ahead of the tail boom) giving all-round coverage. These receive many kinds of hostile radio and radar transmissions, both for intelligence purposes and to assist detection and exact location of enemy targets. Among many other avionics items are a sonobuoy acoustic processor, main digital computer, digital data-link system (with antennas in ventral domes under the nose and tail boom) and various displays for the crew of three, the latter comprising the pilot, the tactical officer/co-pilot and, in the main cabin, the sensor operator.

Avionics suite

Of course, there are also extremely comprehensive avionics boxes for routine navigation and communications. Collins Radio provides the TACAN system and UHF DF radio, Teledyne Ryan the APN-217 Doppler navigation radar and Honeywell the APN-194(V) radar altimeter which gives a precise readout of height above the sea surface. The automatic flight-control and stabilization system incorporates such features as automatic capture of given heights and transition to and from an exact hover at a chosen height, irrespective of wind

strength. This is not used for dipping (dunking) sonar but is useful in the secondary role of SAR, for which there is also a powered hoist above the main sliding cabin door on the right side. Other secondary roles include vertrep (vertical replenishment of ships and beach-heads), medevac (medical evacuation of casualties), fleet support and communication relay.

In the primary ASW role the listening time on station is increased by no less than 57 minutes compared with that of the LAMPS Mk I SH-2F, while range, loiter time and overall endurance are all significantly increased, thanks to the capacity of 1368 litres (361 US gal) of the two crashproof tanks which fill the whole cross-section of the tapering rear part of the fuselage aft of the cabin. Operation is possible in all normal weather (except impossible conditions such as a hurricane), and the helicopter can operate completely on its own though it normally interfaces with its parent ship via the data-link. Standard ASW armament comprises two Mk 46 torpedoes, which in due course may be replaced by the Mk 50 advanced torpedo. In the anti-ship role it is expected that the standard weapon will be the Norwegian Kongsberg Vaapenfabrikk AGM-119 (Penguin Mk 2 Mod). This cruise missile, which unlike most anti-ship weapons has passive IR homing

East and west coast Light Helicopter Anti-Submarine Squadrons are receiving the SH-60B, principally for deployment aboard the 'Oliver Hazard Perry' class frigates. Here a Seahawk approaches the stern helicopter landing pad.

guidance, is an Americanized version whose special folding wings were designed by Grumman to suit the SH-60B application. Like the surface-launched Penguin Mk 2, the AGM-119 retains a tandem boost motor to permit firings while the helicopter is flying slowly or hovering. Typical range is 27 km (17 miles).

Export orders

The Royal Australian Navy has followed the US Navy and ordered eight. These are designated S-70B-2 RAWS, though they will be almost identical to the US Navy version. They will be embarked aboard 'Adelaide' class frigates, which are the same as the US 'Oliver Hazard Perry' class. Predictably this US machine has also been selected by Japan, to replace the SH-3A in the Japan Maritime Self-Defence Force. Sikorsky

Together the Seahawk and its frigate 'mother ship' make a highly effective operational team for the late 20th century US Navy. Note the colourful Magnetic Anomaly Detector (MAD) on its rear fuselage mounting.

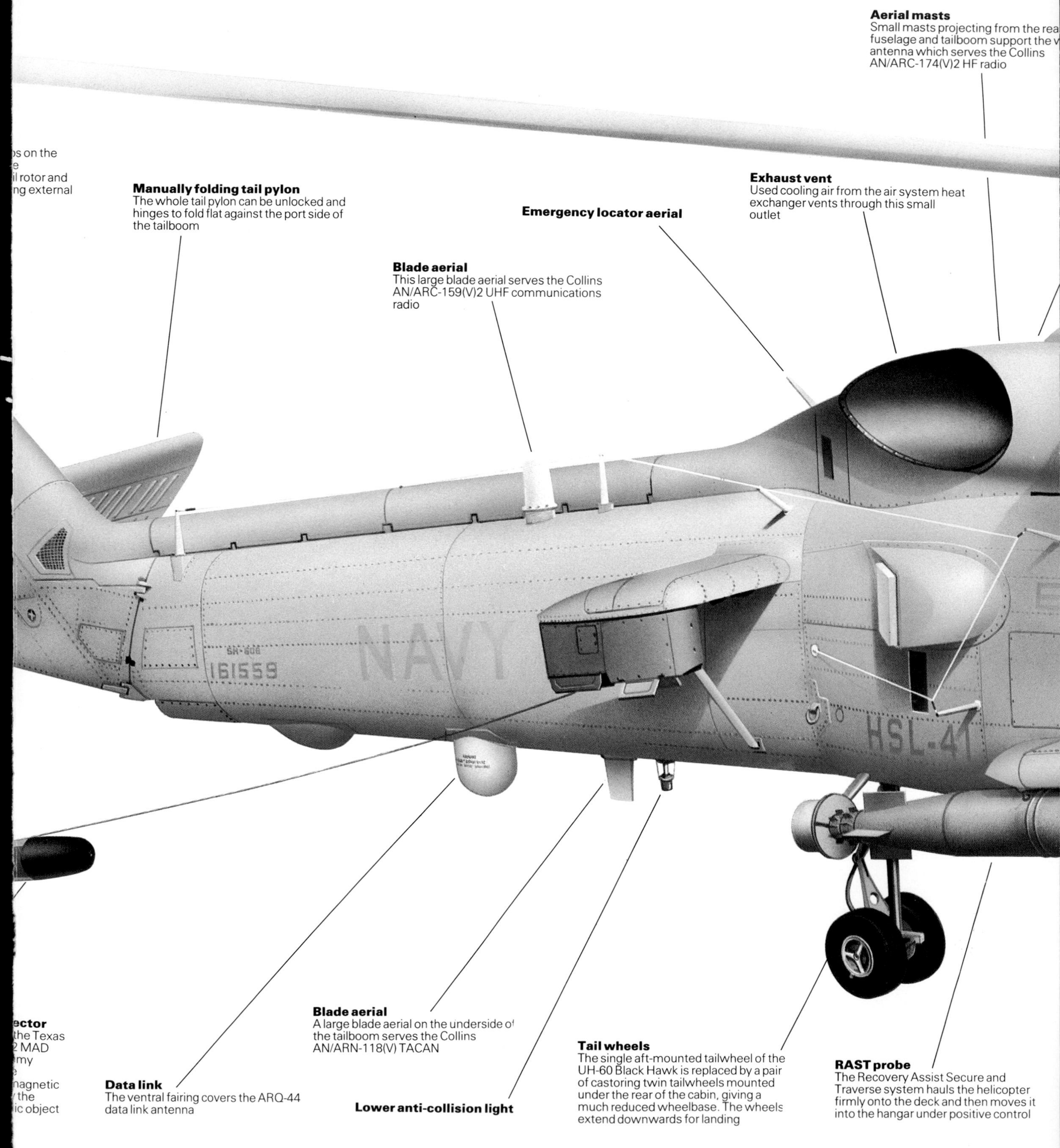

Aerial masts
Small masts projecting from the rea[r]
fuselage and tailboom support the v[ ]
antenna which serves the Collins
AN/ARC-174(V)2 HF radio

Exhaust vent
Used cooling air from the air system heat
exchanger vents through this small
outlet

Emergency locator aerial

Manually folding tail pylon
The whole tail pylon can be unlocked and
hinges to fold flat against the port side of
the tailboom

Blade aerial
This large blade aerial serves the Collins
AN/ARC-159(V)2 UHF communications
radio

[b]s on the
[ ]e
[i]l rotor and
[n]g external

NAVY

161559

HSL-41

SK-608

Blade aerial
A large blade aerial on the underside o[f]
the tailboom serves the Collins
AN/ARN-118(V) TACAN

Data link
The ventral fairing covers the ARQ-44
data link antenna

Lower anti-collision light

Tail wheels
The single aft-mounted tailwheel of the
UH-60 Black Hawk is replaced by a pair
of castoring twin tailwheels mounted
under the rear of the cabin, giving a
much reduced wheelbase. The wheels
extend downwards for landing

RAST probe
The Recovery Assist Secure and
Traverse system hauls the helicopter
firmly onto the deck and then moves it
into the hangar under positive control

[t]ector
[ ]the Texas
[ ]2 MAD
[r]my

[m]agnetic
[ ]the
[ni]c object

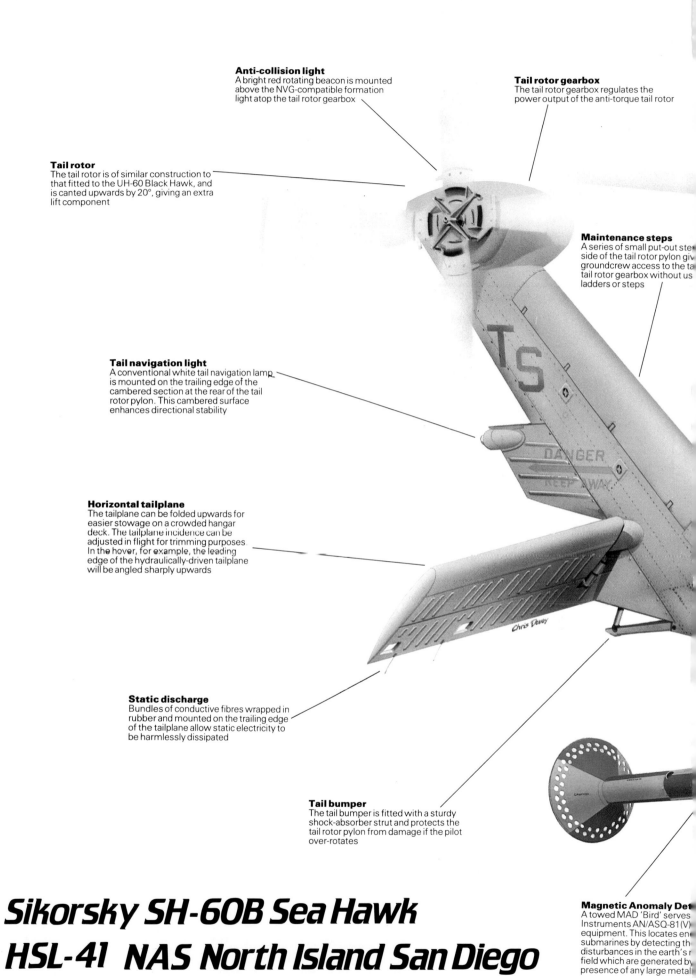

Anti-collision light
A bright red rotating beacon is mounted above the NVG-compatible formation light atop the tail rotor gearbox

Tail rotor gearbox
The tail rotor gearbox regulates the power output of the anti-torque tail rotor

Tail rotor
The tail rotor is of similar construction to that fitted to the UH-60 Black Hawk, and is canted upwards by 20°, giving an extra lift component

Maintenance steps
A series of small put-out ste[ ] side of the tail rotor pylon giv[ ] groundcrew access to the ta[ ] tail rotor gearbox without us[ ] ladders or steps

Tail navigation light
A conventional white tail navigation lamp is mounted on the trailing edge of the cambered section at the rear of the tail rotor pylon. This cambered surface enhances directional stability

Horizontal tailplane
The tailplane can be folded upwards for easier stowage on a crowded hangar deck. The tailplane incidence can be adjusted in flight for trimming purposes. In the hover, for example, the leading edge of the hydraulically-driven tailplane will be angled sharply upwards

Static discharge
Bundles of conductive fibres wrapped in rubber and mounted on the trailing edge of the tailplane allow static electricity to be harmlessly dissipated

Tail bumper
The tail bumper is fitted with a sturdy shock-absorber strut and protects the tail rotor pylon from damage if the pilot over-rotates

Magnetic Anomaly Det[ ]
A towed MAD 'Bird' serves [ ] Instruments AN/ASQ-81(V)[ ] equipment. This locates en[ ] submarines by detecting th[ ] disturbances in the earth's [ ] field which are generated by [ ] presence of any large metal[ ]

Sikorsky SH-60B Sea Hawk
HSL-41 NAS North Island San Diego

built two XSH-60J prototypes, which were sent to the Japanese licence-builder, Mitsubishi, for fitting out with largely Japanese (often licensed US) mission equipment and avionics. The first SH-60J is to fly in 1987, and Mitsubishi expects to deliver production SH-60Js, with a ring-laser gyro navigation system and several other avionics items developed in Japan. The definitive SH-60J, which will probably have a unit price considerably higher even than that of the SH-60B, is expected to enter service with the JMSDF 'in the early 1990s', with replacement of the SH-3A Sea King completed around 1995.

A special VIP transport version of the same basic helicopter has been prepared to replace the VH-3A Sea Kings as equipment of the Executive Flight Detachment at Andrews AFB, near Washington DC. The EFD is an element of US Marine Corps squadron HMX-1 but also includes Army personnel, and it has been traditional for at least one EFD helicopter to be an Army machine, though flying the same missions transporting the president of the USA, high-ranking officials and special visitors. There are eight VH-3As but the budget request is for nine VH-60s, with special interiors and of course no combat mission equipment. These helicopters would have some features of the SH-60 series and some of the Army UH-60.

A further very important Seahawk variant planned for the US Navy is the SH-60F. This was selected to replace the SH-3H Sea King as CV-Helo or, spelled out in full, the CV Inner Zone ASW helicopter. Unlike the SH-60B, the SH-60F will operate from aircraft-carriers, providing ASW protection for the inner zone of the carrier battle group. Though superficially resembling the SH-60B, the new subtype uses different sensors to detect, locate and classify hostile submarine targets. The main difference is that, instead of the sonobuoy storage and launch system, the SH-60F will be equipped with dipping (dunking) sonar. The very latest Bendix AQS-13F pattern will be carried, extended on a long cable below the centre of the fuselage and connected to analysers and displays in front of the sensor operator. It is also probable that no MAD will be carried, though a decision had not been taken on this point as this was written. Armament will include two Mk 46 torpedoes. There is no requirement as yet to fly the ASST mission, or be equipped with the AGM-119 Penguin missile.

Secondary duties

The SH-60F's secondary missions are plane guard and general SAR. Plane guard involves flying in formation with the parent carrier, astern and to one side of the landing approach, where the helicopter crew can see everything that happens to aircraft in the pattern. Should any aircraft go into the sea it is the helicopter's task to rescue the aircraft crew within seconds if possible. The SH-60F's interior will be slightly rearranged to facilitate SAR duties.

On 6 March Sikorsky received a $50.9 million contract for full-scale development of the SH-60F, as well as production options for 76 helicopters in five lots. The total US Navy requirement for the CV-Helo is 175 machines, and there seems little doubt that the whole force will be

delivered, probably before 1990. The prototype first flew on 19 March 1987 and, in view of the very high commonality with the SH-60B, it was expected that production SH-60F deliveries could begin in early 1988.

Future developments

Thus, Sikorsky already has commitments for some 400 helicopters of the Seahawk family. In the longer term more are likely to be ordered, though the machine's size, weight and, above all, extremely high price obviously militate against it in comparison with such rivals as the Lynx 3, Aérospatiale Dauphin/Panther and Soviet Kamov Ka-27/32. It remains to be seen what effect Sikorsky's partial ownership of Westland will have on the future prospects of the rival offerings from the two companies.

For the moment the most important prospect for future development of the entire UH-60/SH-60/HH-60 family is eventual re-engining with the Rolls-Royce/Turboméca RTM 322. This completely new turboshaft engine is in the 1565-kW (2,100-shp) class, and not only gives the whole H-60 family a marked increase in performance but offers other advantages resulting from the engine's extremely advanced design which dates from roughly 10 years later than the T700. At the same time General Electric, which currently has a monopoly in providing engines for all the H-60 variants as well as the McDonnell Douglas (Hughes) AH-64 Apache, will not lightly relinquish any of these important markets.

Nevertheless, there is no doubt that the

The broad cross-section of the Seahawk main cabin has been used to good effect by the US Navy. This area is the operational domain of the sensor operator and a wide range of operational equipment for ASW/ASST duties.

RTM 322 is a very impressive engine, and early in 1986 Rolls-Royce/Turboméca installed two in a Sikorsky S-70C, commercial version of the H-60 family, for flight development at Rolls-Royce's Bristol flight centre. By late 1986 the new engines had accumulated some 150 hours of flight time, with outstanding results. Certification is scheduled for 1987, and production of RTM 322 engines could begin in 1988.

Glossary

AFB Air Force Base
ASST Anti-Ship Surveillance and Targeting
ASW Anti-Submarine Warfare
DF Direction Finding
EFD Executive Flight Detachment
ESM Electronic Surveillance Measures
IR Infra-Red
MAD Magnetic Anomaly Detector
RAST Recovery Assist, Secure and Traverse
RAWS Role-Adaptable Weapon System
SAR Search And Rescue
TACAN TACtical Air Navigation
UHF Ultra High Frequency
UTTAS Utility Tactical Transport Aircraft System

A major development arising from the SH-60B is the SH-60F CV Inner Zone ASW helicopter, which is destined to replace the SH-3 fleet aboard US Navy aircraft carriers. They will have an integrated ASW avionics suite fitted.

SH-60B Seahawk in service

United States Navy

The US Navy has a total requirement for 204 Sikorsky SH-60B Seahawks, the first production example of which was handed over on 28 February 1983. The first operational squadron to equip with the type was HSL-41, this unit being tasked with Fleet Readiness training. Deliveries to the Navy are averaging two helicopters per month, these being deployed aboard frigates and destroyers from their land bases as required. The current requirement for the SH-60F stands at 175, the first of which should enter service during 1988, and the Navy has also ordered five (of an eventual total of 18) HCS helicopters for combat search and rescue/specialized warfare support duties.

Atlantic Fleet

HSL-40
Base: Mayport, Florida
Example aircraft:
162116/HK-400; 162125/
HK-402; 162126/HK-405;
162133/HK-411; 162130/
HK-414

HSL-42
Base: Mayport, Florida
Example aircraft:
162099/HN-420; 162100/
HN-424; 162113/HN-425;
162122/HN-432; 162104/
HN-435

HSL-44
Base: Mayport, Florida
Example aircraft:
162137/HP-440

Pacific Fleet

HSL-41
Base: North Island, California
Example aircraft:
161553/TS-00; 161557/
TS-04; 161560/TS-07;
161566/TS-13; 161569/
TS-16

HSL-43
Base: North Island, California
Example aircraft:
162093/TT-20; 162098/
TT-22; 162102/TT-24;
161570/TT-26; 162120/TT-32

HSL-45
Base: North Island, California
Example aircraft:
162134/TZ-40; 162329/TZ-42

Test Agencies

VX-1
Base: Patuxent River,
Maryland
Example aircraft:
162115/JA-40; 161561/
JA-41

**Naval Air Test
Center/Rotary Wing
Aircraft Test Directorate**
Base: Patuxent River,
Maryland
Example aircraft: 162107

Colourful is hardly the word to describe the operational camouflage scheme worn by US Navy Seahawks, as evidenced by this HSL-43 machine.

Two Sikorsky-built Seahawks have been supplied to the Mitsubishi company in Japan to act as test beds ahead of full-scale production. Both are designated XSH-60J, this being the first example delivered.

Australia

Confirmed order for eight S-70B-2 Seahawks on 9 October 1984 and a second batch of eight purchased in May 1986. Fifteen are to be assembled in-country by Hawker de Havilland. The aircraft are intended for operation by the Royal Australian Navy from 'Adelaide'-class guided missile frigates.

Japan

Intends to replace SH-3A/B Sea King with SH-60B with Japan Maritime Self-Defence Force from early 1990s onwards. Two XSH-60Js have been delivered to Mitsubishi at Nagoya for test purposes, with the first being due to fly after modification in 1987. Production in Japan will be undertaken by Mitsubishi.

Spain

Ordered six S-70Bs for delivery in 1988. These will serve with the Spanish naval air arm.

The nature of SH-60B Seahawk operations has led to several modifications to the airframe, including an automatic blade-folding facility. The entire airframe receives corrosion protection to counter the harsh effects of salt water.

Specification: SH-60B

Rotors

Main rotor diameter	16.36 m	(53 ft 8 in)
Main rotor disc area	210.14 m²	(2,262.0 sq ft)
Tail rotor diameter	3.35 m	(11 ft 0 in)

Fuselage and tail unit

Accommodation	pilot, co-pilot and sensor operator	
Length, rotors turning	19.76 m	(64 ft 10 in)
Length, rotors and tail pylon folded	12.47 m	(40 ft 11 in)
Height, rotors turning	5.18 m	(17 ft 0 in)
Tailplane span	4.38 m	(14 ft 4.5 in)

Landing gear

Wheelbase	4.83 m	(15 ft 10 in)
Wheel track	2.79 m	(9 ft 2 in)

Weights (estimated, ASW mission)

Empty	6191 kg	(13,648 lb)
Mission gross weight	9183 kg	(20,244 lb)
Internal fuel	1089 kg	(2,400 lb)

Powerplant

Two General Electric T700-GE-401 turboshaft engines
Rating, each	1260 kW	(1,690 shp)

SH-60 Seahawk recognition features

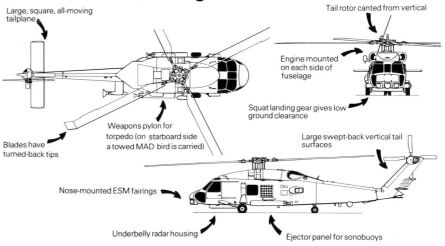

Large, square, all-moving tailplane

Tail rotor canted from vertical

Engine mounted on each side of fuselage

Squat landing gear gives low ground clearance

Large swept-back vertical tail surfaces

Weapons pylon for torpedo (on starboard side a towed MAD bird is carried)

Blades have turned-back tips

Nose-mounted ESM fairings

Underbelly radar housing

Ejector panel for sonobuoys

or blade
 main rotor blade consists of a
ex honeycomb core, graphite
g edge and root, and covering of
sfibre/epoxy. The drooped leading
 incorporates an anti-erosion
h, while a fixed tab is located on the
 part of the trailing edge. The
dual blade folding mechanism is
rically actuated

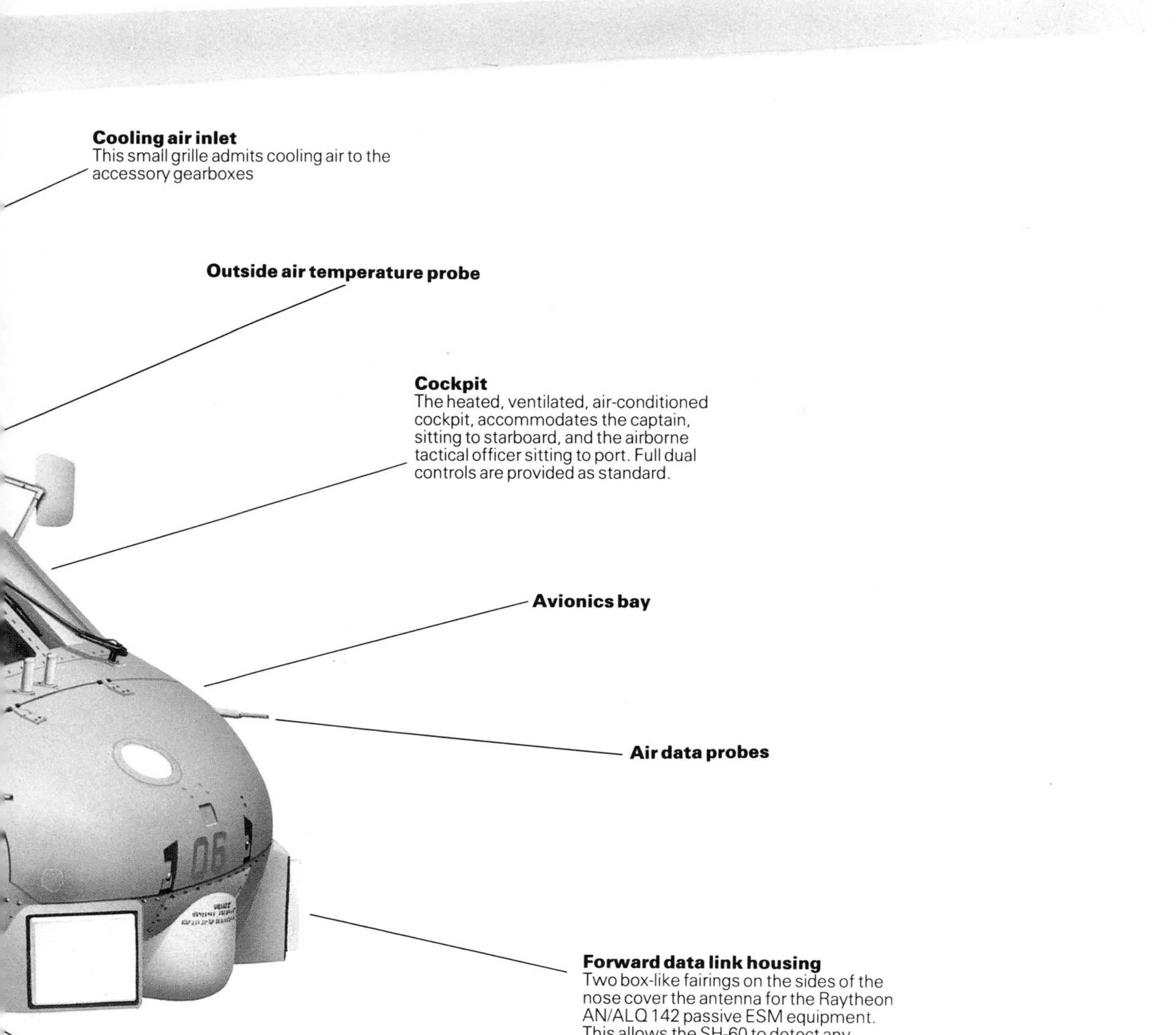

Cooling air inlet
This small grille admits cooling air to the
accessory gearboxes

Outside air temperature probe

Cockpit
The heated, ventilated, air-conditioned
cockpit, accommodates the captain,
sitting to starboard, and the airborne
tactical officer sitting to port. Full dual
controls are provided as standard.

Avionics bay

Air data probes

Forward data link housing
Two box-like fairings on the sides of the
nose cover the antenna for the Raytheon
AN/ALQ 142 passive ESM equipment.
This allows the SH-60 to detect any
hostile electro-magnetic emissions
while remaining 'silent' itself

Retractable landing/hover lamp

ntenna of the Texas Instruments
PS0124 Search Radar rotates
 a vertical axis and is covered by a
w ventral radome

ESM antenna
Aerials mounted on each side of the rear fuselage give rear hemisphere ESM coverage, while similar aerials on the nose take care of forward hemisphere coverage

Powerplant
The SH-60B is powered by a pair of 1,690-shp General Electric J700-GE-401 turboshafts, each one some 130-shp more powerful than the T-700-GE-700s used by the UH-60. The Sea Hawk, especially the new SH-60F, is an obvious candidate for the new-generation 2,100-shp Rolls-Royce Turboméca RJM 322. The new engine is already flying in a commercial S-70 at Filton, and is to be licence-built for the US Government by Pratt & Whitney

Rot
Eac
Nor
trail
glas
edg
she
oute
indi
elec

Torpedo
This SH-60B carries a Mk 46 anti-submarine torpedo. This will eventually be replaced by the Mk 50 advanced lightweight torpedo, and the more lethal British Sting Ray is already an alternative weapon. The small cylindrical box at the rear of the torpedo houses a stabilizing parachute

board weapons pylon
small stub pylon can carry various
ons, including torpedoes, depth
es and anti-ship missiles, such as
Ae Sea Skua and the Norwegian
sberg AGM-119 Penguin Mk 2 Mod
latter is a passive infra-red homing
missile, with a tandem boost
r to allow launch at low speeds or in
ver.

Cabin door
The main entrance door is located on the starboard side, and slides open to the rear. An electrically-powered rescue hoist is installed above the door. The window in the door can be jettisoned from inside the cabin, or simply pulled out from outside the aircraft

Sonobuoy launch tubes
Sonobuoys can be carried in 25 launch tubes mounted in the cabin under the main rotor. The buoys are pneumatically fired through apertures in the starboard side. No dipping sonar is carried by the SH-60B

Sensor operators station
The sensor operator sits behind the cockpit in the port side of the cabin. He is responsible for monitoring the radar, MAD, ESM and acoustics, the latter being processed by a Proteus acoustic processor and converter unit, and a Control Data AN/AYK-14 digital computer

Rada
The a
AN/A
aroun
shallo

Performance (estimated)

Maximum speed at 5,000 ft (1525 m)	126 kts; 233 km/h	(145 mph)
Service ceiling	19,000 ft	(5790 m)
Maximum range with internal fuel	600 km	(373 miles)
Vertical rate of climb per minute	700 ft	(213 m)

Weapon load

- Mil Mi-14 'Haze' 4000 kg E
- Westland Sea King HAS.Mk 2 2948 kg
- Westland Wessex HAS.Mk 1 1814 kg
- Aérospatiale SA 365N Dauphin 2 1600 kg
- Sikorsky SH-60B Seahawk 500 kg E
- Agusta-Bell AB 212ASW 490 kg
- Sikorsky SH-3D Sea King 381 kg

Maximum rate of climb per minute

- Sikorsky SH-3D Sea King 2,200 ft
- Westland Sea King HAS.Mk 2 2,020 ft
- Mil Mi-14 'Haze' 1,800 ft
- Westland Wessex HAS.Mk 1 1,750 ft
- Aérospatiale SA 365N Dauphin 2 1,515 ft
- Agusta-Bell AB 212ASW 1,300 ft
- Sikorsky SH-60B Seahawk 700 ft vertical

Speed at low altitude

- Aérospatiale SA 365N Dauphin 2 151 kts
- Sikorsky SH-3D Sea King 144 kts
- Westland Sea King HAS.Mk 2 140 kts
- Sikorsky SH-60B Seahawk 126 kts
- Mil Mi-14 'Haze' 124 kts
- Westland Wessex HAS.Mk 1 117 kts
- Agusta-Bell AB 212ASW 106 kts

Range

- Westland Sea King HAS.Mk 2 1230 km
- Sikorsky SH-3D Sea King 1005 km
- Aérospatiale SA 365N Dauphin 2 880 km
- Mil Mi-14 'Haze' 800 km
- Agusta-Bell AB 212ASW 667 km
- Westland Wessex HAS.Mk 1 628 km
- Sikorsky SH-60B Seahawk 600 km E

Service ceiling

- Aérospatiale SA 365N Dauphin 2 15,000 ft
- Sikorsky SH-60B Seahawk 15,000 ft E
- Sikorsky SH-3D Sea King 14,700 ft
- Westland Wessex HAS.Mk 1 14,100 ft
- Agusta-Bell AB 212ASW 14,000 ft E
- Mil Mi-14 'Haze' 14,000 ft E
- Westland Sea King HAS.Mk 2 14,000 ft E

Up on the flight deck the pilot occupies the right-hand seat, with the airborne tactical officer/back-up pilot nearest the camera. The pilot acts as the aircraft commander and controls all weapon launch. The principle responsibilities of the ATO include command of tactical operations, overall direction of the mission, selection and deployment of the sonobuoys, and monitoring of the ESM and radar.

S-70B/SH-60 Seahawk variants

Sikorsky S-70L: five prototypes built, plus one static test example; the first prototype flew on 12 December 1979; original mockup converted from UH-60A and used for non-flying ship compatibility trials

Sikorsky S-70B: a first batch of 18 Seahawks, designated SH-60B in US Navy service, were ordered in FY 1982, with 27 more being ordered in FY 1983; the US Navy's eventual requirement is for 204 SH-60Bs, to be deployed on 'Oliver Hazard Perry' class frigates and on 'Spruance' and Aegis destroyers; six have also been ordered by the Spanish navy

Sikorsky S-70B-2 RAWS: one Sikorsky-built prototype, followed by 15 assembled by de Havilland Australia; fitted with MEL Super Searcher radar and advanced new avionics equipment; the S-70B-2 RAWS (Role Adaptable Weapons System) will serve aboard the 'Adelaide' class guided missile frigates of the Royal Australian Navy

SH-60B: original model for US Navy for ASW and ASST roles, with various secondary missions, fulfilling LAMPS Mk III requirement; expected production 204

Sikorsky SH-60F: 'CV Inner Zone ASW helicopter' variant, with LAMPS III avionics, sensors and sonobuoys removed and replaced by an integrated ASW avionics suite, optimized for the close-in protection of the inner zone of a carrier battle group from submarine attack; 175 will replace the US Navy's carrier-borne SH-2 Sea Kings

Sikorsky XSH-60J: two Sikorsky-built Seahawks delivered to Mitsubishi at Nagoya for installation of Japanese avionics and mission equipment; will be followed by Japanese-built production aircraft to be designated SH-60J

Sikorsky HCS: September 1986 contract for initial production of five combat search and rescue and special warfare support helicopters, derived from SH-60F, for UD Navy; eventual total of 18 aircraft to be procured

Sikorsky MRR: medium-range recovery variant of SH-60F for US Coast Guard; two ordered in September 1986, of eventual requirement for 35 aircraft

An SH-60B Seahawk of HSL-41 flying near San Diego, California, close to its NAS North Island shore base. The aircraft carries a trailing MAD bird on the starboard fuselage side.

Sikorsky SH-60B Seahawk cutaway drawing key

1 Graphite epoxy composite tail rotor blades
2 Lightweight cross beam rotor hub
3 Blade pitch change spider
4 Anti-collision light
5 Tail rotor final drive bevel gearbox
6 Rotor hub canted 20 degrees
7 Horizontal tailplane folded position
8 Pull-out maintenance steps
9 Port tailplane
10 Tail rotor drive shaft
11 Fin pylon construction
12 Tailplane hydraulic jack
13 Cambered trailing edge section
14 Tail navigation light
15 Tailplane hinge joint (manual folding)
16 Handgrips
17 Static dischargers
18 Starboard tailplane construction
19 Towed magnetic anomaly detector (MAD)
20 Tail bumper
21 Shock absorber strut
22 Bevel drive gearbox
23 Tail pylon latch joint
24 Tail pylon hinge frame (manual folding)
25 Transmission shaft disconnect
26 Tail rotor transmission shaft
27 Shaft bearings
28 Tail pylon folded position
29 Dorsal spine fairing
30 UHF aerial
31 Tailcone frame and stringer construction
32 Magnetic compass remote transmitters
33 MAD detector housing and reeling unit
34 Tail rotor control cables
35 HF aerial cable
36 MAD unit fixed pylon
37 Ventral data link antenna housing
38 Lower UHF/TACAN aerial
39 Fuel jettison
40 Anti-collision light
41 Tie-down shackle

42 Tailcone joint frame
43 Air system heat exchanger exhaust
44 Engine exhaust shroud
45 Emergency locator aerial
46 Engine fire suppression bottles
47 IFF aerial
48 Port side auxiliary power unit (APU)
49 Oil cooler exhaust grille
50 Starboard side air conditioning plant
51 Engine exhaust pipe
52 HF radio equipment bay
53 Sliding cabin door rail
54 Aft AN/ALQ-142 ESM aerial fairing, port and starboard
55 Tailwheel leg strut
56 Fireproof fuel tanks, port and starboard, total capacity 361 US gal (1367 litres)
57 Starboard stores pylon
58 Castoring twin tail wheels
59 Torpedo parachute housing
60 Mk 46 lightweight torpedo
61 Cabin rear bulkhead
62 Passenger seat
63 Honeycomb cabin floor panelling
64 Sliding cabin door
65 Recovery Assist, Secure and Traverse (RAST) aircraft haul-down fitting
66 Ventral cargo hook, 6,000-lb (2722-kg) capacity
67 Floor beam construction
68 Spring-loaded door segment in way of stores pylon
69 Pull-out emergency exit window panel
70 Pneumatic sonobuoy launch rack (125 sonobuoys)
71 Rescue hoist/winch
72 General Electric T700-GE-401 turboshaft engine
73 Engine accessory equipment gearbox

74 Intake particle separator air duct
75 Engine bay firewall
76 Oil cooler fan
77 Rotor brake unit
78 Engine intake ducts
79 Maintenance step
80 Engine drive shafts
81 Bevel drive gearboxes
82 Central main reduction gearbox
83 Rotor control swash plate
84 Rotor mast
85 Blade pitch control rods
86 Bi-filar vibration absorber
87 Rotor head fairing
88 Main rotor head (elastomeric, non-lubricated, bearings)
89 Blade pitch control horn
90 Lead-lag damper
91 Individual blade folding joints, electrically actuated
92 Blade spar crack detectors
93 Blade root attachment joints
94 Main rotor composite blades
95 Port engine intake
96 Control equipment sliding access cover
97 Engine driven accessory gearboxes
98 Hydraulic pump
99 Flight control servo units
100 Flight control hydro-mechanical mixer unit
101 Cabin roof panelling
102 Radar operator's seat
103 AN/APS-124 radar console
104 Tie-down shackle
105 Gearbox and engine mounting main frames
106 Maintenance steps
107 Main undercarriage leg mounting
108 Shock absorber leg strut
109 Starboard mainwheel
110 Pivoted axle beam
111 Starboard navigation light
112 Cockpit step/main axle fairing
113 Forward cabin access panel
114 Collective and cyclic pitch control rods

115 Sliding fairing guide rails
116 Cooling air grille
117 Main rotor blade glass-fibre skins
118 Honeycomb trailing edge panel
119 Titanium tube blade spar
120 Rotor blade drooped leading edge
121 Leading edge anti-erosion sheathing
122 Fixed trailing edge tab
123 Cockpit eyebrow window
124 Rear view mirrors
125 Overhead engine throttle and fuel cock control levers
126 Circuit breaker panel
127 Pilot's seat
128 Safety harness
129 Crash resistant seat mounting
130 Pull-out emergency exit window panel
131 Flight deck floor level
132 Cockpit door
133 Boarding step
134 AN/APS-124 search radar antenna
135 Ventral radome
136 Retractable landing/hovering lamp
137 Downward vision window
138 Yaw control rudder pedals
139 Cyclic pitch control column
140 Instrument panel
141 Centre instrument console
142 Stand-by compass
143 ATO/co-pilot's seat
144 Outside air temperature gauge
145 Instrument panel shroud
146 Air data probes
147 Windscreen panels
148 Windscreen wipers
149 Hinged nose compartment access panel
150 Pitot tubes
151 Avionics equipment bay
152 Forward data link antenna
153 Forward AN/ALQ 142 ESM aerial housings

An SH-60B hovers gingerly above the helicopter pad as a member of the deck crew secures the Recovery Assist Secure and Traverse (RAST) haul-down gear. This is one of the features specifically fitted to the Seahawk to facilitate operations at sea, in an attempt to secure the helicopter once it has landed aboard decks which are often pitching and rolling.

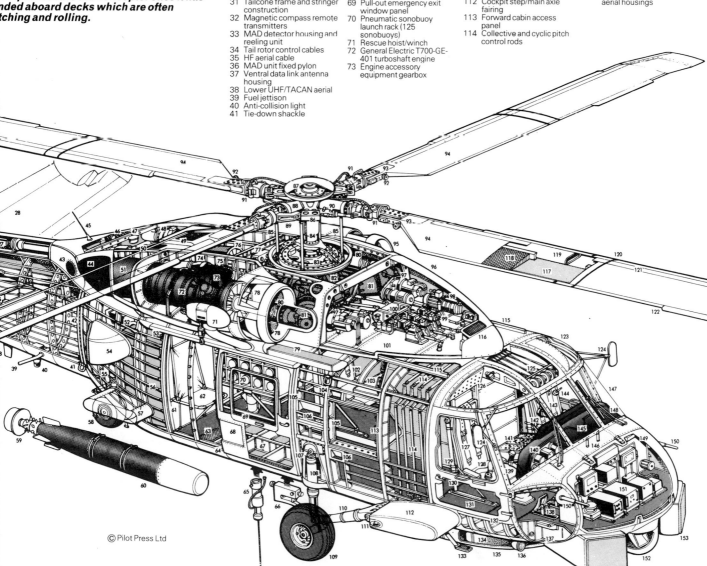

The SIKORSKY UH-60 BLACK HAWK

Sikorsky's Hawk Haulers

A crescendo of noise signals the arrival of the Black Hawks, disgorging troops and vital operational equipment set to engage the enemy. Such is the primary role of this highly important US Army helicopter, but it is only one among several performed by land-based models of the H-60 design.

Although the helicopter was used quite extensively during the Korean War, it was employed in that conflict principally as a SAR vehicle or for casualty evacuation, playing little or no part in the actual conduct of battle. In view of that, it is probably fair to say that the rotary-winged flying machine really came of age only a decade or more later, coincidentally in pretty much the same part of the world. Then, in South Vietnam, the helicopter played a quite major role with all four elements of the US armed forces, namely the Air Force, the Army, the Marine Corps and the Navy.

Naturally, each service had rather different operational requirements and, whilst some tasks overlapped, there were others that were the sole prerogative of just one service. Thus, whilst the Army and Marines used helicopters to move troops swiftly around the battlefield, the Navy machines were principally engaged in SAR from vessels operating in the Tonkin Gulf, whilst one role unique to the Air Force was that of recovering reconnaissance drones launched from the Lockheed DC-130 Hercules. Nevertheless, the helicopter usually seemed to be more than equal to the task, whatever the mission, and there is no doubt that the type matured rapidly as that long conflict dragged on.

As far as the Army was concerned, the ubiquitous Bell UH-1 Iroquois (more widely known as the 'Huey') was arguably the most versatile rotary-winged craft to see action in Vietnam and, indeed, variants of this highly successful machine also served with all the other services, albeit in rather smaller quantities. Needless to say, combat experience played a major part in the Huey's evolution, larger and more capable models making their debut as the war progressed. This same experience was to play a significant part in the development of what is now viewed as the Huey's successor, namely Sikorsky's UH-60A Black Hawk, a type that is now well established in service with the US Army and one that has been much in the news recently as a result of Sikorsky's fight to secure a chunk of Westland Helicopters.

As is so often the case with modern military aircraft and helicopters, the Black Hawk was a long time coming and the process of evolution may be traced back as far as October 1965, when the US Army first began to consider the question of acquiring a new model. At that time, the requirement was rather vague and it took several years for what eventually became known as the Utility Tactical Transport Aircraft System (UTTAS) to progress from the conceptual to the constructional phase. In fact, the gestation period was remarkably long for it was not until January 1972 that the Army issued an RFP to industry, this naturally being greeted warmly by quite a few manufacturers, for it could well result in several thousand examples of the successful design being ordered by the Army.

Role-versatility is a key factor in the UH-60's favour, with several operational configurations available. This machine carries prominent markings for its medical evacuation (medevac) role, while making full use of its external cargo hook to lift construction material.

In the event, the inevitable weeding-out process reduced the number of contenders quite significantly to a point where just two (those originating with Boeing Vertol and Sikorsky) were considered worthy of proceeding to the prototype stage. Consequently, on 30 August 1972, these two companies received contracts covering the construction of three prototypes for competitive evaluation by the Army, which would subsequently order the winning design into quantity production.

Sikorsky's contender, known by the company as the S-70, was given the service designation YUH-60A, the three prototypes covered by the Army contract taking to the air between mid-October 1974 and the end of February 1975. A ground test specimen and a fourth, company-funded, prototype were also com-

The deliberately compact dimensions of the Black Hawk allow for transport in several of the USAF's airlift aircraft, thus enabling the Army to receive its prime transport helicopter around the world to meet operational requirements in times of potential conflict.

pleted at about this time. Initial flight testing proved to be a quite exhaustive and lengthy process, but eventually culminated in an eight-month GCT programme which was accomplished between March and November 1976, this resulting in the Sikorsky Black Hawk being adjudged superior.

Army orders

Formal announcement of the decision to proceed with quantity production for the Army followed a fairly brief evaluation of the GCT findings and was made just two days before Christmas 1976, an initial contract for 15 UH-60As being awarded at the same time. Of greater long-term value to Sikorsky, though, was the revelation by the Army that it planned to purchase no fewer than 1,107 Black Hawks in due course, these all being earmarked to replace the UH-1 in the utility role, a vague mission definition which actually encompasses a multitude of functions ranging from casualty evacuation through troop transport to air cavalry support.

As far as the Black Hawk itself is concerned, it naturally embodied most of the breakthrough that had occurred in helicopter technology since the Iroquois first came on the scene in the latter half of the 1950s. For a start like the Huey it is turbine-powered, employing a pair of General Electric T700-GE-700 turboshaft engines, these being quite novel in that they feature a self-contained lubrication system and a built-in inlet particle separator. Rated at 1151 kW (1,543 shp) for normal continuous operation, they bestow a top speed of 160 kts (297 km/h; 184 mph) at sea level and permit loads of 11 infantrymen or 3629 kg (8,000 lb) of externally-slung cargo to be handled with ease. Thus, the UH-60 not only flies faster than the UH-1 but it does so with more payload, a fact which lets 15 Black Hawks accomplish the same amount of work as 23 Hueys.

Perhaps more important, though, in view of the literally vast numbers of Iroquois helicopters lost as a result of battle damage sustained in combat, is the fact that the Black Hawk incorporates a

number of measures aimed at enhancing its survivability. These include a fair amount of armoured protection for the pilots, extremely tough main rotor blades (they can take hits by 23-mm HE or incendiary shells without separating) and fire-proof main fuel tanks capable of absorbing hits by anything up to 12.7-mm (0.5-in) ammunition.

In addition, a fair measure of system redundancy has been built-in to the Black Hawk, whilst vulnerable features such as electrical and hydraulic systems are duplicated and widely separated so as to reduce the chance of losing both in the event that severe battle damage is sustained. The question of battle damage was actually a key aspect of the Army's original requirement, one of the contractual obligations stipulating that the UH-60A be able to fly for 30 minutes after sustaining a hit anywhere in the undersides and lower fuselage by a 7.62-mm (0.3-in) bullet fired from a range of just 300 ft (91 m). This was successfully demonstrated during the course of the flight test programme.

Minimum maintenance

Equally important, since the UH-60A may well be called upon to deploy to austere sites lacking in sophisticated support equipment, is the ability to sustain operations with the minimum of maintenance down-time. In fact, this aspect of the specification was particularly stringent but it has resulted in a

As a forerunner to the full-scale Night Hawk programme, the USAF procured 11 Black Hawks to act as trainers and project development machines. The majority of the examples, with their distinctive camouflage scheme, are in service with the 55th ARRS.

helicopter that requires only about one-quarter of the maintenance support demanded by the previous generation of turbine-powered types. As far as figures are concerned, the specification stipulated that no more than 2.8 man hours per flight be required for organizational maintenance and that routine preventative inspection and servicing requirements be met by a ratio of one man hour to each flight hour.

This was a tough set of figures, but the Army's insistence appears to have paid dividends, the Black Hawk displaying impressive levels of reliability in situations ranging from routine operations at a major Army installation with good support infrastructure to simulated combat in a variety of climatic conditions.

Entering service with the 101st Airborne Division at Fort Campbell, Kentucky in the summer of 1979, well over 600 examples of the UH-60A have now been delivered and, with production now

The large cabin door slides back to reveal the main cabin with seating for 11 fully-equipped infantrymen or a high-density arrangement for 14 troops. The cabin 'box' was specifically designed to remain largely intact in high-impact crash-landings.

Main rotor system
Designed to easily fold for stowage aboard US Air Force transport aircraft for deployment worldwide

Engines
Power is provided by two General Electric T700-GE-700 turboshafts each rated at 1,560 shp, giving a maximum speed of 269 km/h (145 kts) at mission take-off weight of 7,375 kg (16,260 lb)

Oil cooler exhaust
Shrouded against IR emissions, this cooler can be fitted with a Sanders ALQ-144 IR countermeasures set

Auxiliary Power Unit
For ground running and field starting, the Black Hawk is fitted with a Solar T62T-40-1 APU

Cabin floor
As a result of Operation 'Fury' (Grenada), the US Army has developed special floor matting which offers protection against small arms fire

Cabin doors
The large cabin doors slide back against the fuselage allowing exit and entry on each side; troops can deplane within six seconds. Heavier equipment can also be loaded

Troop seating
For some operations, troop webbing seating is retained with accommodation for an 11-man infantry squad; in war the seats are removed to increase capacity to 15 troops

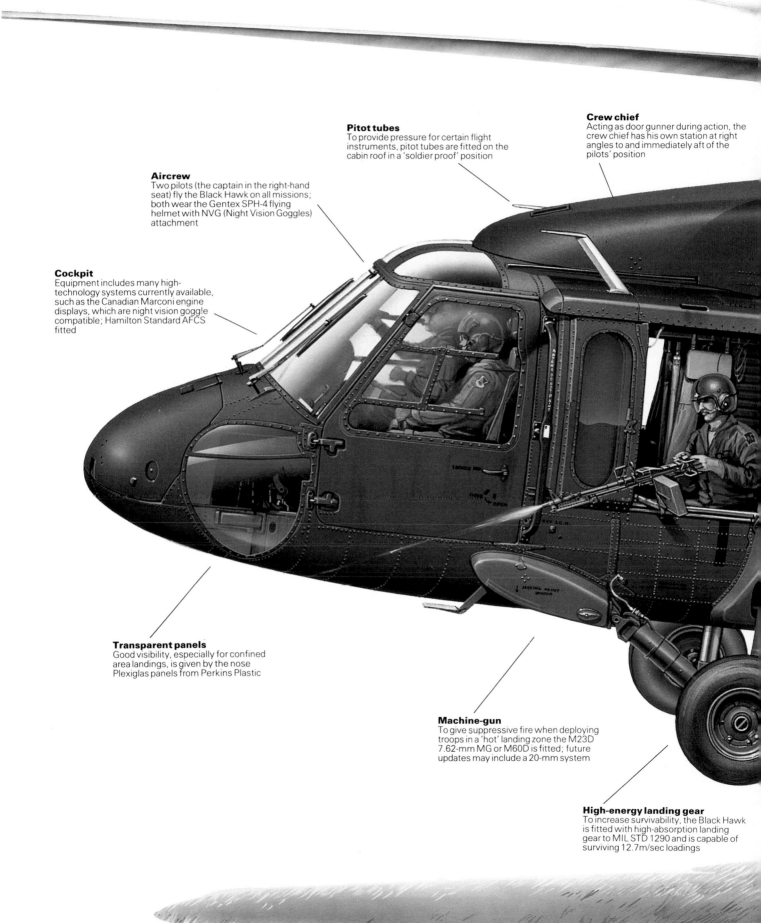

Pitot tubes
To provide pressure for certain flight instruments, pitot tubes are fitted on the cabin roof in a 'soldier proof' position

Crew chief
Acting as door gunner during action, the crew chief has his own station at right angles to and immediately aft of the pilots' position

Aircrew
Two pilots (the captain in the right-hand seat) fly the Black Hawk on all missions; both wear the Gentex SPH-4 flying helmet with NVG (Night Vision Goggles) attachment

Cockpit
Equipment includes many high-technology systems currently available, such as the Canadian Marconi engine displays, which are night vision goggle compatible; Hamilton Standard AFCS fitted

Transparent panels
Good visibility, especially for confined area landings, is given by the nose Plexiglas panels from Perkins Plastic

Machine-gun
To give suppressive fire when deploying troops in a 'hot' landing zone the M23D 7.62-mm MG or M60D is fitted; future updates may include a 20-mm system

High-energy landing gear
To increase survivability, the Black Hawk is fitted with high-absorption landing gear to MIL STD 1290 and is capable of surviving 12.7m/sec loadings

running at 10 per month, the numbers on charge continue to increase at a rapid rate. Initial deliveries were made to US-based units, but examples of the Black Hawk have also been deployed overseas, most notably to West Germany where the type now operates in conjunction with the Iroquois.

Action in Grenada

As well as those helicopters permanently based overseas, the Black Hawk has also operated in North Africa as part of the 'Bright Star' programme of military manoeuvres. Perhaps more importantly, its combat debut came in October 1983 when some UH-60As of the 82nd Airborne Division took part in the invasion of Grenada. By all accounts, the type acquitted itself well although there were a few casualties, a couple of aircraft apparently being destroyed when they collided.

Almost inevitably, the original Army model has spawned a number of derivatives, some for service with the original customer whilst others now fly with both the US Navy and US Air Force.

Looking at the Army sub-types first, this service plans to acquire a total of 77 EH-60As for communications jamming tasks, this model being fitted with specialized equipment able to locate, classify and disrupt enemy signals traffic. Development of the EH-60A began in the late 1970s under the codename 'Quick Fix II', and the type duly flew for the first time in prototype form during September 1981, being instantly recognizable by virtue of prominent dipole antennas on the aft fuselage sides and a retractable ventral whip antenna. Less visible differences concern the 816 kg (1,800 lb) of mission-related electronics located in the cabin.

Another electronic warfare version was the EH-60B 'SOTAS' (Stand-Off Target Acquisition System) which made its maiden flight in February 1981 and which was eventually abandoned later in that year. Had it gone ahead, it would have carried Motorola scanning equipment beneath the cabin, this being lowered in flight and rotated so as to provide full-hemisphere coverage. Fitment of the

antenna necessitated a revised landing gear arrangement, this being designed to retract rearwards.

As far as the US Navy is concerned, the SH-60B Seahawk is significantly different in that it is optimized for anti-submarine warfare. Accordingly, it will be examined in detail later.

The third US customer for a variant of the S-70 is the Air Force, which is to acquire a total of 90 HH-60A Night Hawks for combat SAR tasks. Deliveries are expected to get under way in 1988, this service having originally proposed the procurement of a full-system all-weather variant known as the HH-60D backed up by the less capable HH-60E.

Air force hybrid

In the event, neither model was proceeded with, the USAF instead opting for the HH-60A which made its maiden flight in February 1984 and which will feature a sophisticated avionics suite encompassing a FLIR sensor, terrain-following radar, terrain-avoidance radar and ground mapping radar. Basically a marriage of a modified UH-60A airframe with the SH-60B's more powerful T700-GE-701 engines, the HH-60A will also employ the Seahawk's transmission system, rotor brake and rescue hoist. Other changes required by the SAR mission include the addition of stub wings on which will be mounted a pair of 875-litre (231-US gal) auxiliary fuel tanks, whilst this version will also be able to refuel in flight.

Designed specifically to airlift an infantry squad into hostile territory quickly and with good survivability rates, the Black Hawk is a worthy successor to the UH-1 Huey within US Army forces worldwide. Note the deflected tailplane, keeping the fuselage at an optimum angle in the hover.

Pending delivery of its own purpose-built HH-60As, the USAF is currently operating a total of 11 UH-60As, these mainly being employed on training duties.

Despite the fact that the Iroquois found a ready market for overseas sales, the Black Hawk has thus far proved rather less popular although this may well have something to do with the fact that large numbers of surplus Hueys are readily available at far less cost. Whatever the reason, the only overseas air arms which have opted to buy the basic UH-60A are those of the Philippines and Switzerland, these nations respectively ordering two and three aircraft.

Glossary
FLIR Forward-Looking Infra-Red
GCT Government Competitive Test
RFP Request For Proposals
SAR Search and Rescue
SOTAS Stand-Off Target Acquisition System
UTTAS Utility Tactical Transport Aircraft System

After many trials and tribulations, the USAF HH-60 Night Hawk combat rescue helicopter programme is now under way, with 90 HH-60As on order. External fuel tanks and an inflight-refuelling probe increase mission radius and loiter time.

Sikorsky H-60 in service

US Army

To date, US Army contracts for the Sikorsky UH-60A Black Hawk cover 930 machines, though this figure is likely to rise to as many as 1,715 by the 1990s. Approximately 700 examples have been delivered and are in service with a large number of front-line, National Guard and Army Air Reserve units, these being deployed within the continental USA, South Korea, Hawaii, Panama and West Germany. Within the US Army in Europe (USAREUR) forces based in West Germany, approximately 150 UH-60As are in service, principal role being troop transport and medical evacuation. It is envisaged that 205 Black Hawks will be committed to USAREUR by 1992, replacing more of the large Bell UH-1H force. Typical force structure at present is 15 UH-60As in a Combat Aviation Company, within a Combat Aviation Brigade, and a single UH-60A within the brigade's Air Cavalry Squadron. Two existing Corps Aviation Companies, each with 15 Black Hawks, are set to be redesignated Combat Support Aviation Companies during 1987, their parent Combat Aviation Groups attaining brigade status. Three Attack Helicopter Battalions will be added to each brigade, their inventory including a total of nine UH-60As per brigade.

A Sikorsky UH-60A Black Hawk assigned to the 82nd Airborne Division for casualty evacuation duties in Grenada.

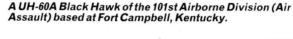

US Air Force

Though plans are well advanced for the procurement and introduction of a substantial number of HH-60A combat rescue helicopters into service during the late 1980s, current USAF operation of the H-60 models is restricted to nine UH-60A Black Hawks assigned to the 55th ARRS, 39th ARRW at Eglin AFB, Florida, primarily to serve as lead-in trainers for the HH-60 force. Two additional machines were set aside to become full scale development prototypes for the HH-60D.

A UH-60A Black Hawk of the 101st Airborne Division (Air Assault) based at Fort Campbell, Kentucky.

Philippine Air Force

Two Sikorsky S-70A-5s are in service with the PAF, this being a tactical utility version of the UH-60A, though their current operational status is unclear.

To date, USAF UH-60s and HH-60s have worn 'European One' camouflage. Illustrated is the first HH-60A Night Hawk.

Specification: UH-60A Black Hawk

Rotors

Main rotor diameter	16.36 m	(53 ft 8 in)
Tail rotor diameter	3.35 m	(11 ft 0 in)
Main rotor disc area	210.05 m²	(2,261 sq ft)

Fuselage and tail unit

Accommodation	three-man crew plus up to 11 troops	
Length overall, rotors turning	19.76 m	(64 ft 10 in)
Length, fuselage	15.26 m	(50 ft 0.75 in)
Length, rotors and tail pylon folded	12.60 m	(41 ft 4 in)
Height overall, tail rotor turning	5.13 m	(16 ft 10 in)
Tailplane span	4.38 m	(14 ft 4.5 in)

Landing gear

Non-retractable tailwheel landing gear with single wheel on each unit

Wheelbase	8.83 m	(28 ft 11.75 in)
Wheel track	2.71 m	(8 ft 10.5 in)

Weights

Empty	4819 kg	(10,624 lb)
Maximum take-off	9185 kg	(20,250 lb)
Maximum external load (on hook)	3629 kg	(8,000 lb)
Internal fuel load	1340 litres	(354 US gal)

Powerplant

Two General Electric T700-GE-700 turboshafts		
Rating, each	1163 kW	(1,560 shp)

UH-60A recognition features

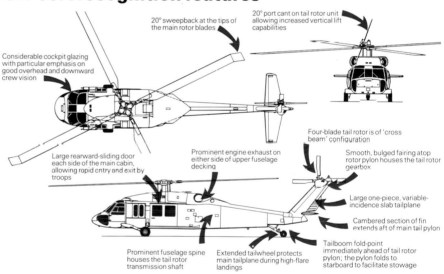

20° sweepback at the tips of the main rotor blades

20° port cant on tail rotor unit allowing increased vertical lift capabilities

Considerable cockpit glazing with particular emphasis on good overhead and downward crew vision

Four-blade tail rotor is of 'cross beam' configuration

Smooth, bulged fairing atop rotor pylon houses the tail rotor gearbox

Large rearward-sliding door each side of the main cabin, allowing rapid entry and exit by troops

Prominent engine exhaust on either side of upper fuselage decking

Large one-piece, variable-incidence slab tailplane

Cambered section of fin extends aft of main tail pylon

Prominent fuselage spine houses the tail rotor transmission shaft

Extended tailwheel protects main tailplane during high-flare landings

Tailboom fold-point immediately ahead of tail rotor pylon; the pylon folds to starboard to facilitate stowage

Sikorsky H-60 variants

UH-60A Black Hawk: initial production model for service with US Army in utility tactical transport role, being capable of carrying 11 fully-equipped troops as well as a crew of three; approximately 700 now delivered with manufacture continuing towards the planned total of 1,715; nine delivered to USAF for training duties pending availability of forthcoming HH-60A rescue version

EH-60A Black Hawk: specialized variant to perform battlefield ECM tasks with US Army, and instantly recognizable by virtue of dipole antenna array; first flown in prototype form as **YEH-60A** on 24 September 1981, current Army planning anticipating procurement of 77 production examples as part of on-going SEMA (Special Electronics Missions Aircraft) programme

HH-60A Night Hawk: combat search-and-rescue version for service with USAF, which intends to buy 90 for delivery from 1988; will possess ability to perform SAR by day or night at treetop height over a radius of 463 km (287 miles) and without recourse to inflight-refuelling or escort support

EH-60B Black Hawk: specialized version developed for Army's SOTAS (Stand-Off Target-Acquisition System) and first flown in February 1981; project terminated in September 1981

SH-60B Seahawk: anti-submarine warfare/anti-ship missile defence model now being delivered for use aboard US Navy surface combatants; present planning anticipates procurement of just over 200; features sophisticated array of sensors, sonobuoys and electronic equipment plus towed MAD (Magnetic Anomaly Detector)

SH-60C Seahawk: planned Navy model to equip carrier-borne ASW squadrons which presently use the SH-3H Sea King; deliveries are expected to begin in about 1988

HH-60D Night Hawk: initial all-weather combat SAR variant proposed for service with USAF; abandoned in favour of HH-60A

HH-60E Night Hawk: less capable variant of SAR helicopter, originally to be operated alongside full-system HH-60D model; abandoned in favour of HH-60A

HH-60A recognition features

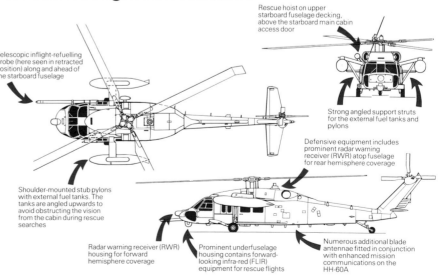

Rescue hoist on upper starboard fuselage decking, above the starboard main cabin access door

Telescopic inflight-refuelling probe (here seen in retracted position) along and ahead of the starboard fuselage

Strong angled support struts for the external fuel tanks and pylons

Defensive equipment includes prominent radar warning receiver (RWR) atop fuselage for rear hemisphere coverage

Shoulder-mounted stub pylons with external fuel tanks. The tanks are angled upwards to avoid obstructing the vision from the cabin during rescue searches

Radar warning receiver (RWR) housing for forward hemisphere coverage

Prominent underfuselage housing contains forward-looking infra-red (FLIR) equipment for rescue flights

Numerous additional blade antennae fitted in conjunction with enhanced mission communications on the HH-60A

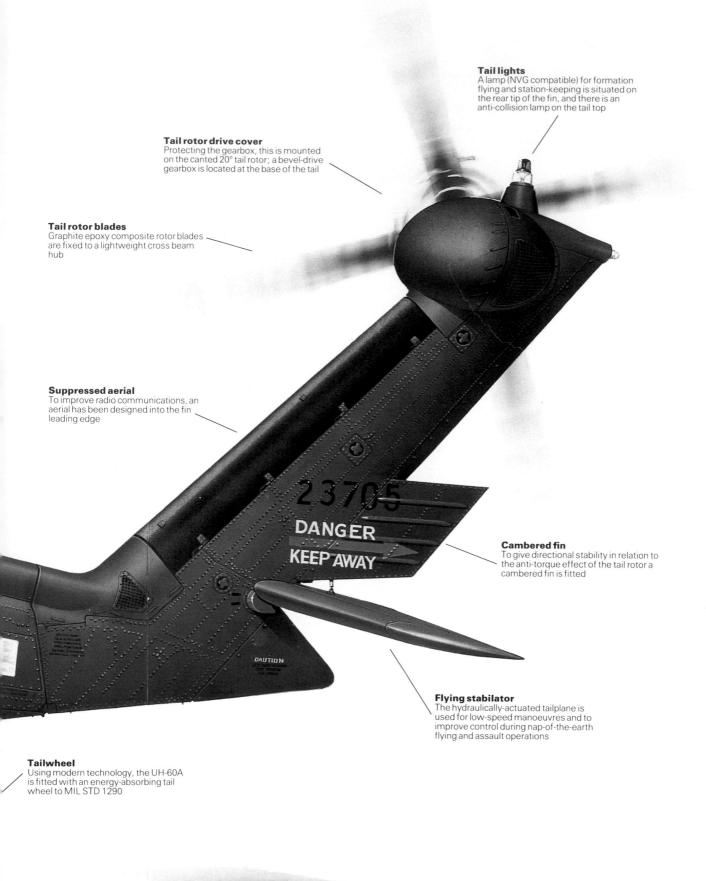

Tail lights
A lamp (NVG compatible) for formation flying and station-keeping is situated on the rear tip of the fin, and there is an anti-collision lamp on the tail top

Tail rotor drive cover
Protecting the gearbox, this is mounted on the canted 20° tail rotor; a bevel-drive gearbox is located at the base of the tail

Tail rotor blades
Graphite epoxy composite rotor blades are fixed to a lightweight cross beam hub

Suppressed aerial
To improve radio communications, an aerial has been designed into the fin leading edge

Cambered fin
To give directional stability in relation to the anti-torque effect of the tail rotor a cambered fin is fitted

Flying stabilator
The hydraulically-actuated tailplane is used for low-speed manoeuvres and to improve control during nap-of-the-earth flying and assault operations

Tailwheel
Using modern technology, the UH-60A is fitted with an energy-absorbing tail wheel to MIL STD 1290

23705

DANGER

KEEP AWAY

CAUTION

Keith Fretwell.

Main rotor blades
Composite glassfibre main rotor blades
are wrapped around a titanium main spar
with drooped leading edge and fixed
trailing edge tabs

Engine exhaust
The T700 engine exhausts can be fitted
with IR-suppression kits to reduce the
signature on to which enemy shoulder-
launched SAMs could be 'locked'

Sikorsky UH-60A Black Hawk
203rd Aviation Company
223rd Aviation Battalion (Corps)
US Army in Europe

UNITED STATES ARMY

Tactical radio aerial
Amongst the US Government-furnished
radio sets are VHF/AM, VHF/FM and
UHF/FM, together with SIF/IFF

Above: The ESSS pylons can carry four external fuel tanks, these consisting of two 870-litre (230 US-gal) tanks on the outboard pylons and two 1703-litre (450 US-gal) tanks inboard.

Above: Weapons trials with the Black Hawk and the External Stores Support System (ESSS) units have included the carriage and live firing of the Hellfire anti-armour missile, 16 of which can be carried.

Above: The UH-60A Black Hawk cockpit is designed for two-pilot operation with full dual controls. The centre console between the pilot's armour-plated seats carries radio communication and systems controls.

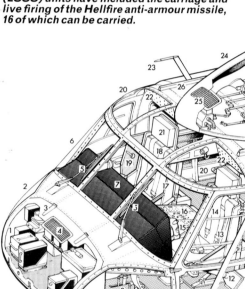

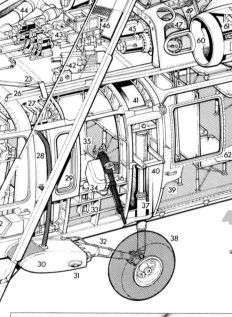

Left: Another distinctive Black Hawk variant, which will not enter production, is the EH-60B, which was designed as a component within the Army's Stand-Off Target Acquisition System. The long underfuselage housing contains the antenna for the Motorola radar, with retractable landing gear.

Above: The EH-60A is easily distinguished by the fuselage dipole antenna arrays and the underfuselage whip aerial, these forming par of the Quick Fix II radio jamming and ECM suite.

Sikorsky UH-60A Black Hawk cutaway drawing key

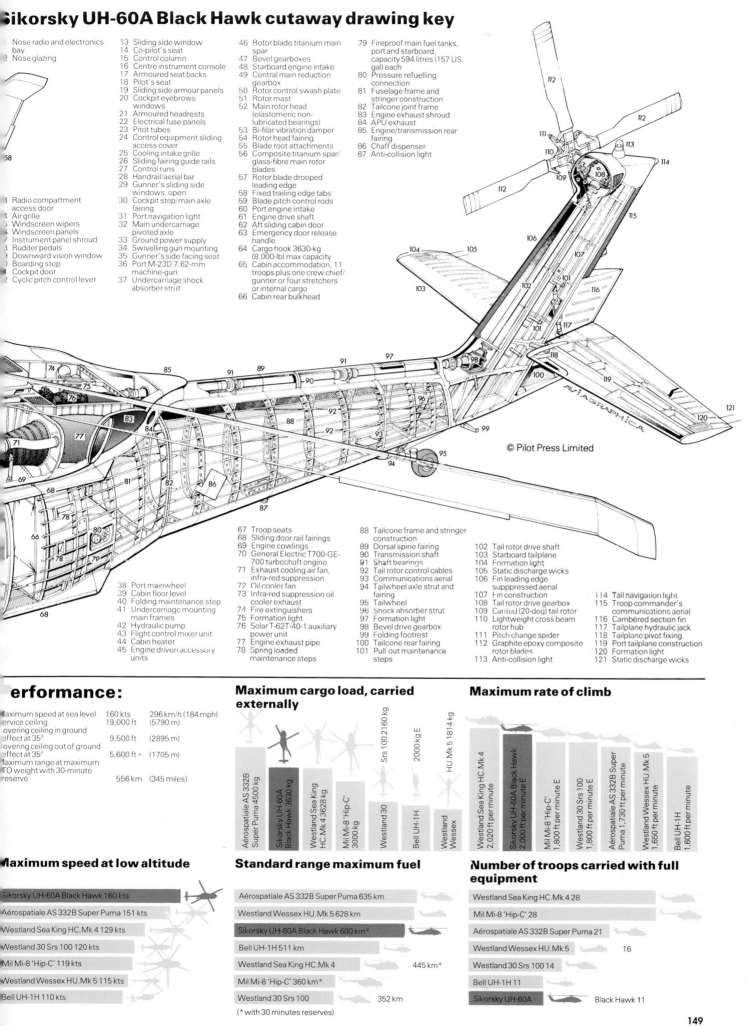

1 Nose radio and electronics bay
2 Nose glazing
3 Radio compartment access door
4 Air grille
5 Windscreen wipers
6 Windscreen panels
7 Instrument panel shroud
8 Rudder pedals
9 Downward vision window
10 Boarding step
11 Cockpit door
12 Cyclic pitch control lever
13 Sliding side window
14 Co-pilot's seat
15 Control column
16 Centre instrument console
17 Armoured seat backs
18 Pilot's seat
19 Sliding side armour panels
20 Cockpit eyebrows windows
21 Armoured headrests
22 Electrical fuse panels
23 Pitot tubes
24 Control equipment sliding access cover
25 Cooling intake grille
26 Sliding fairing guide rails
27 Control runs
28 Handrail/aerial bar
29 Gunner's sliding side windows, open
30 Cockpit step/main axle fairing
31 Port navigation light
32 Main undercarriage pivoted axle
33 Ground power supply
34 Swivelling gun mounting
35 Gunner's side facing seat
36 Port M-23D 7.62-mm machine-gun
37 Undercarriage shock absorber strut

46 Rotor blade titanium main spar
47 Bevel gearboxes
48 Starboard engine intake
49 Central main reduction gearbox
50 Rotor control swash plate
51 Rotor mast
52 Main rotor head (elastomeric non-lubricated bearings)
53 Bi-filar vibration damper
54 Rotor head fairing
55 Blade root attachments
56 Composite titanium spar/glass-fibre main rotor blades
57 Rotor blade drooped leading edge
58 Fixed trailing edge tabs
59 Blade pitch control rods
60 Port engine intake
61 Engine drive shaft
62 Aft sliding cabin door
63 Emergency door release handle
64 Cargo hook 3630-kg (8,000-lb) max capacity
65 Cabin accommodation, 11 troops plus one crew chief/gunner or four stretchers or internal cargo
66 Cabin rear bulkhead

79 Fireproof main fuel tanks, port and starboard, capacity 594 litres (157 US gal) each
80 Pressure refuelling connection
81 Fuselage frame and stringer construction
82 Tailcone joint frame
83 Engine exhaust shroud
84 APU exhaust
85 Engine/transmission rear fairing
86 Chaff dispenser
87 Anti-collision light

67 Troop seats
68 Sliding door rail fairings
69 Engine cowlings
70 General Electric T700-GE-700 turboshaft engine
71 Exhaust cooling air fan, infra-red suppression
72 Oil cooler fan
73 Infra-red suppression oil cooler exhaust
74 Fire extinguishers
75 Formation light
76 Solar T-62T-40-1 auxiliary power unit
77 Engine exhaust pipe
78 Spring loaded maintenance steps

38 Port mainwheel
39 Cabin floor level
40 Folding maintenance step
41 Undercarriage mounting main frames
42 Hydraulic pump
43 Flight control mixer unit
44 Cabin heater
45 Engine driven accessory units

88 Tailcone frame and stringer construction
89 Dorsal spine fairing
90 Transmission shaft
91 Shaft bearings
92 Tail rotor control cables
93 Communications aerial
94 Tailwheel axle strut and fairing
95 Tailwheel
96 Shock absorber strut
97 Formation light
98 Bevel drive gearbox
99 Folding footrest
100 Tailcone rear fairing
101 Pull out maintenance steps

102 Tail rotor drive shaft
103 Starboard tailplane
104 Formation light
105 Static discharge wicks
106 Fin leading edge supppressed aerial
107 Fin construction
108 Tail rotor drive gearbox
109 Canted (20-deg) tail rotor
110 Lightweight cross beam rotor hub
111 Pitch change spider
112 Graphite epoxy composite rotor blades
113 Anti-collision light

114 Tail navigation light
115 Troop commander's communications aerial
116 Cambered section fin
117 Tailplane hydraulic jack
118 Tailplane pivot fixing
119 Port tailplane construction
120 Formation light
121 Static discharge wicks

© Pilot Press Limited

Performance:

Maximum speed at sea level	160 kts	296 km/h (184 mph)
Service ceiling	19,000 ft	(5790 m)
Hovering ceiling in ground effect at 35°	9,500 ft	(2895 m)
Hovering ceiling out of ground effect at 35°	5,600 ft	(1705 m)
Maximum range at maximum TO weight with 30-minute reserve	556 km	(345 miles)

Maximum cargo load, carried externally

- Aérospatiale AS 332B Super Puma 4500 kg
- Sikorsky UH-60A Black Hawk 3630 kg
- Westland Sea King HC.Mk 4 3628 kg
- Mil Mi-8 'Hip-C' 3000 kg
- Westland 30 Srs 100 2160 kg
- Bell UH-1H 2000 kg E
- Westland Wessex HU.Mk 5 1814 kg

Maximum rate of climb

- Westland Sea King HC.Mk 4 2,020 ft per minute
- Sikorsky UH-60A Black Hawk 2,000 ft per minute E
- Mil Mi-8 'Hip-C' 1,800 ft per minute E
- Westland 30 Srs 100 1,800 ft per minute E
- Aérospatiale AS 332B Super Puma 1,730 ft per minute
- Westland Wessex HU.Mk 5 1,650 ft per minute
- Bell UH-1H 1,600 ft per minute

Maximum speed at low altitude

- Sikorsky UH-60A Black Hawk 160 kts
- Aérospatiale AS 332B Super Puma 151 kts
- Westland Sea King HC.Mk 4 129 kts
- Westland 30 Srs 100 120 kts
- Mil Mi-8 'Hip-C' 119 kts
- Westland Wessex HU.Mk 5 115 kts
- Bell UH-1H 110 kts

Standard range maximum fuel

- Aérospatiale AS 332B Super Puma 635 km
- Westland Wessex HU.Mk 5 628 km
- Sikorsky UH-60A Black Hawk 600 km*
- Bell UH-1H 511 km
- Westland Sea King HC.Mk 4 445 km*
- Mil Mi-8 'Hip-C' 360 km*
- Westland 30 Srs 100 352 km

(* with 30 minutes reserves)

Number of troops carried with full equipment

- Westland Sea King HC.Mk 4 28
- Mil Mi-8 'Hip-C' 28
- Aérospatiale AS 332B Super Puma 21
- Westland Wessex HU.Mk 5 16
- Westland 30 Srs 100 14
- Bell UH-1H 11
- Sikorsky UH-60A Black Hawk 11

The AEROSPATIALE
ALOUETTE II/III

Alouette II & III: lightweight larks

The Alouette has been France's most successful helicopter design, exported in vast numbers to numerous customers and licence-built by India and Yugoslavia. Radical new gunship variants have been designed and built in Yugoslavia and South Africa, further extending the service life of this versatile family.

This Gendarmerie Alouette III is seen hovering over typical French Alpine scenery; it is fitted with a rescue hoist above the main port door. The sturdy and robust Alouette has sufficient performance in reserve to make mountain flying possible.

The Alouette (lark) story began with the Sud-Est SE.3101, the first all-French helicopter designed and built after World War II. This single-seat experimental machine was powered by a 63.4-kW (85-hp) Mathis piston engine and first flew in June 1948. The company then produced the two-seat SE.3110, powered by a 149-kW (200-hp) Salmson 9NH piston engine, and then the three-seat SE.3120, designed mainly for agricultural purposes and the first of the line to be named Alouette.

The first of two SE.3120 prototypes, also powered by the Salmson 9NH engine, flew on 31 July 1952. In the following July this type set a new world closed circuit record by staying airborne for 13 hours 56 minutes.

The adoption of Turboméca's 268-kW (360-shp) Artouste I turboshaft led to a redesign of the airframe for the production model. The SE.3130 prototype first flew on 12 March 1955, and the resultant Alouette II had the distinction of being the first turboshaft-powered helicopter to enter production anywhere in the world. Three months later the type proved its potential by setting a new helicopter altitude record of 8209 m (26,932 ft). In layout the Alouette II followed contemporary light helicopter design, with a bubble-style Plexiglass cabin and open-framework fuselage and tail boom. The engine was positioned horizontally above the centre fuselage to drive the articulated three-blade main rotor and two-blade tail rotor. The standard skid landing gear was replaced by a quadricycle wheeled landing gear for shipboard operations.

Two prototypes were followed by three pre-production aircraft built in 1956, and the Alouette II was granted a French certificate of airworthiness on 2 May 1957. In that year Sud-Est merged with Sud-Aviation, and the production version of the five-seat Alouette II was redesignated SE.313B. Sud was itself taken over by SNIA (Société Nationale Industrielle Aérospatiale) in 1970.

Mass production at Marseilles/Marignane started in response to initial orders from the French forces, and the first delivery was made to the Armée de l'Air on 1 May 1956. By 1958 the Armée de l'Air was operating 19 of the type in Algeria. The Alouette II was soon in great demand internationally because it offered a major leap forward in performance, payload and reliability. The sturdy Alouette II was thus a success from the start. The type was particularly suitable for high-altitude operations, and an Artouste-powered Alouette in 1958 set a helicopter altitude record of 36,027 ft (10981 m) for all classes and a height record of 31,440 ft (9583 m) in the 1000/1750-kg (2,205/3,858-lb) category.

The Alouette II became the first foreign helicopter to be granted US certification and, in 1961, the type was being produced at the rate of 16 per month. Some 924 Artouste-powered Alouette IIs were produced for customers in 33 countries, 22 of which put the aircraft into military service. The French services, in particular the Aviation Légère de l'Armée de Terre (ALAT), acquired 363 Alouettes and the German armed forces bought 267.

Other principal military operators of

This view of a Belgian army Alouette II shows off the 'lattice tail' of the earlier aircraft. The Belgian army uses the Alouette II largely for observation and reconnaissance duties, in four mixed squadrons.

Aérospatiale SA 316B Alouette III
No. 16 Squadron
South African Air Force

Pilot
The Alouette III is flown from the right-hand seat of the three forward seats, the second pilot sitting in the middle of the airframe

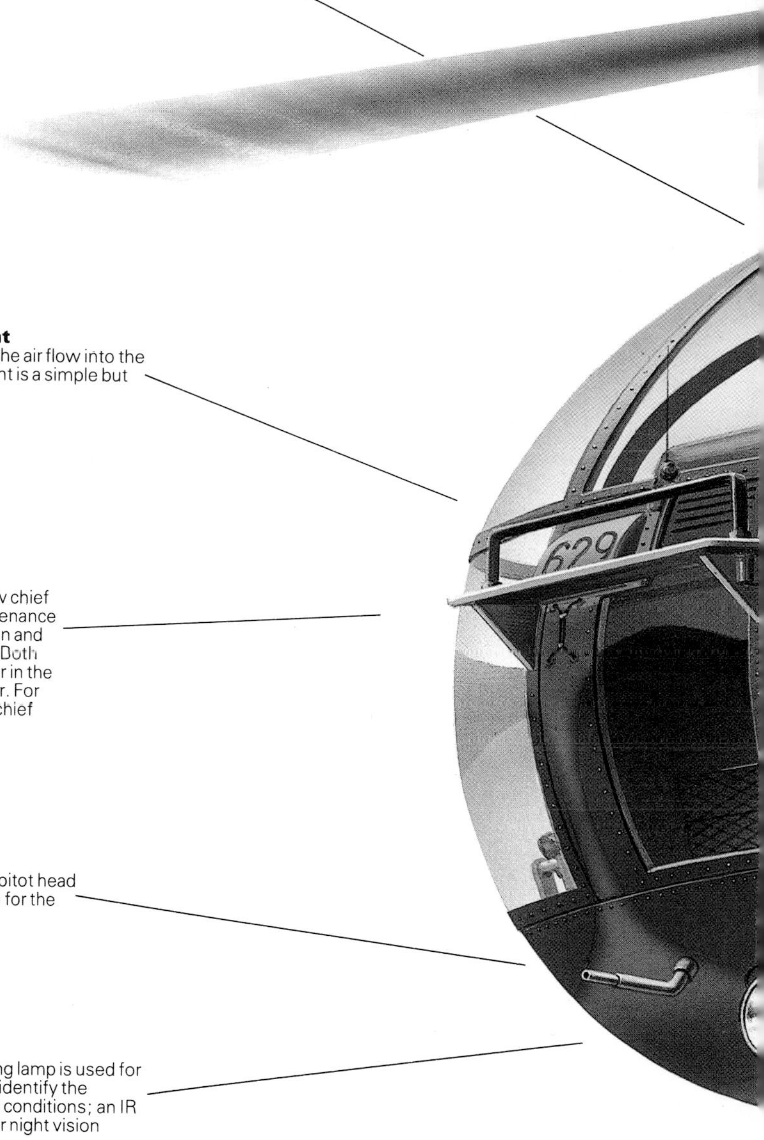

Cockpit air vent
Used to regulate the air flow into the cockpit, the air vent is a simple but effective device

Crew chief or 'Tech'
The flight technican (tech) or crew chief is responsible for the basic maintenance of the helicopter, acts as crewman and would man any armament fitted. Both he and the pilot wear body armour in the otherwise unarmoured helicopter. For operational area flying, the crew chief sits facing aft

Pitot head
Carried under the cabin, the pitot head provides air data information for the helicopter's instruments

Landing lamp
The retractable landing lamp is used for night landings and to identify the helicopter in low light conditions; an IR shield can be fitted for night vision goggle compatibility

Port navigation light
In non-tactical situations, the port (red) and starboard (green) lights are illuminated in low light conditions

Nose landing wheel
This is part of the landing gear arrangement, which ensures easy ground mobility

aroused the interest of the French forces, who needed a fast, well-armed machine for the war in Algeria. Military trials were carried out with various weapons fits, including wire-guided missiles and pivot-mounted guns.

Able to fly at about 113 kts (210 km/h; 130 mph), the Alouette III was well suited to the armed forces' requirements, but the Algerian conflict ended before the type entered service. Initial deliveries were mainly to overseas customers, starting with three examples for the Burmese air force in 1961. This was followed by others to the South African Air Force and the Rhodesian Air Force. The French ALAT and Aéronavale took only 11 such helicopters between them from the initial production batch, and other early military customers included Peru and the Danish navy.

South Africa was one of the first operators of the Alouette III, and still has about 100 machines in service. The type has taken the brunt of the fighting during airborne assaults in South West Africa (Namibia) and Angola, and has played a crucial role in every big cross-border operation, fulfilling a host of roles including target-spotting, airborne control, SAR and fire support.

The SAAF operates three types of Aérospatiale helicopter: the Alouette III, the Puma and a small number of the Super Frelon for SAR. Eight Alouette IIs have been withdrawn, and it is the small Alouette III which has seen most of the action, as an indispensible tool in South Africa's counter-insurgency war.

At the end of 1970 the SA.316B version with strengthened transmission was introduced and, two years later, the SA.316C went into production with the new 649-kW (870-shp) Artouste IIID turboshaft derated to 447 kW (600 shp). Another variant, which adopted an Astazou XIV turboshaft of the same power rating, was designated the SA.319B. This last version had much higher capabilities, with a 25 per cent reduction in fuel consumption. A navalized version of the Alouette III Astazou was developed to deal with small surface craft such as fast torpedo-boats. It can be equipped with an autostabilization system, ORB 31 surveillance radar, APX-Bézu 260 gyro-stabilized sight and two AS.12 wire-guided missiles. For the ASW role, it can carry two Mk.44 homing torpedoes beneath the fuselage, or one torpedo and MAD gear in a streamlined container which is towed behind the helicopter on a 50-m (164-ft) cable. For air-sea rescue a hoist (capacity 225 kg; 496 lb) is mounted on the port side of the fuselage.

French producton of the Alouette III

ended in 1983, by which time Aérospatiale had delivered 1,455 such helicopters to 74 countries, of which some 60 or more operated the type in military service. Production has also been extended to India and Romania under licence. HAL of India named the aircraft Chetak, and has built nearly 300 for home military and government orders. A few have been exported to a small number of countries including the USSR.

The SA.316B version is produced in Romania by Intreprinderea de Constructii Aeronautice (ICA) as the IAR-316B, and more than 200 have been built, including a number exported via Aérospatiale to Pakistan, Algeria and Angola.

Communist development

During the early 1980s, ICA of Romania also began development of its own light attack and liaison helicopter and the result employs much of the IAR-316B's dynamic system and other components of the locally-produced Alouette III. The new IAR-317 Airfox is a low-cost ground-attack helicopter, and features a slimmed down tandem-seat cockpit, with an elevated pilot position behind the weapons operator. The IAR-316B's main landing gear, rear fuselage, tail unit and Artouste IIIB powerplant are retained. Armament fits include podded machine-guns, unguided rockets or six anti-tank missiles. In addition, two 7.62-mm (0.3-in) machine-guns are built in, one on each side of the front cockpit. The prototype Airfox first flew at the ICA Brasov factory in April 1984.

South African Air Force pilots have long cried out for their own attack helicopter, but the strict international arms embargo has put paid to South Africa

buying any such machines on the open market. So the South Africans have set about building their own, and again it is based on the Alouette III. The Alpha XH1 light attack helicopter was developed by the Atlas Aircraft Corporation in direct response to the arms restrictions.

Design of the XH1 began in March 1981 to fulfil a requirement for the SAAF. Atlas took the locally manufactured rotor and transmission system of the SA.316B, together with a Turboméca powerplant, and married these components to a new fuselage. The tail boom is based closely on that of the Alouette III. The cockpit is in the traditional gunship style with the weapons operator seated in front of and below the pilot, with side entry doors and extensive glazing. Below the front fuselage is a turret-mounted 20-mm GA.1 cannon, slaved to the weapons operator's helmet sight. Alternative weapons can be carried on stub pylons. The prototype first flew on 3 February 1985, under conditions of great secrecy, and its existence was not publicly announced until March 1986, but there is no suggestion that the Alpha XH1 is close to service entry.

Both the Alouette II and the Alouette III have acquitted themselves extremely well for many years in numerous countries around the world. Where reliability and ease of maintenance are key factors, these two important helicopter types will continue to soldier on for some time to come.

Glossary
AAC Army Air Corps
ASW Anti-Submarine Warfare
C of G Centre of Gravity
ESBA Eastern Sovereign Base Area
MAD Magnetic Anomaly Detection
SAM Surface-to-Air Missile
SAR Search-And-Rescue

Alouette II/Lama/Alouette III in service

Algeria
Algeria formed an air force almost immediately after the departure of the colonial French in 1962, and has six SA.316Bs in its helicopter inventory.

Angola
The FAPA (Angolan People's Air Force), which has seen action against South African forces, operates 20 SA.316Bs and has six more on order. The air force also flies one SA.315B and six Romanian-built IAR-316Bs, and has 24 more of the latter on order.

Argentina
The Fuerza Aérea Argentina's SAR squadron operates eight Lamas and the army a further six. The navy has a fleet of nine Alouette IIIs.

Austria
A component of the Austrian army, the Austrian air arm is organized as three flying regiments each with a helicopter squadron. Twenty-one Alouette IIIs are operated by Hubschraubergeschwader 2 and 3 for SAR and liaison.

Bangladesh
The single helicopter squadron of the Bangladesh Defence Force Air Wing operates four ex-Indian SA.316Bs alongside Soviet-supplied Mil Mi-4s and Mi-8s.

Belgium
Nearly 90 Alouette IIs were supplied to the Landmacht (army) for liaison, observation and pilot training, with the first of 39 SE.313Bs delivered in 1959 and the first SA.318Cs in 1967. Seventy-one survive with the light aviation squadrons. No. 17 Squadron became famous for its 'Blue Bees' demonstration team. The Zeemacht (navy) operates three SA.316Bs (M1 to M3).

Bolivia
The Bolivian air force SAR squadron operates eight Helibras HB.315Bs and has three more on order.

Brazil
Helibras-assembled HB.315B Gaviãos (SA.315B Lamas) are in service with the Força Aérea Brasileira (six) and with the Force Aeronavale (three).

Burkina Faso
The air force has two SA.316Bs.

Burma
The Burmese air force was the first customer for the Alouette III in 1961, and still has 10 SA.316Bs on strength for liaison duties.

Burundi
The air arm of the Burundi forces is concerned with internal security and operates three SA.316Bs.

Cameroun
This ex-French colony's air force, known as the Armée de l'Air du Cameroun, has a small helicopter fleet including two Alouette IIs, one Lama and one Alouette III.

Chad
The Escadrille Tchadienne, the air arm of Chad, has a small rotary-wing element comprising four SA.330 Pumas and 10 SA.316Bs.

Chile
The FAC's search-and-rescue squadron based at Temuco operates six Aérospatiale Lamas, while the Chilean army's air arm has 13 SA.315Bs for rescue operations in the Andes. The navy has eight SA.319Bs.

Colombia
Colombia's air force has an effective and substantial SAR capability in the form of 27 Lamas and six Kaman HH-43 Huskies.

Congo
The Congolese air force was formed after the departure of the colonial power in 1960, and operates a mixed fleet of mainly French and Soviet types, including three SA.318C Alouette IIs.

Djibouti
Another former French colony, Djibouti established an air force in the late 1970s. One SE.313B operates alongside two AS.355Fs.

Dominican Republic
The Fuerza Aérea Dominicana has an unusually large assortment of helicopters used for liaison, light transport and SAR, including two SA.318Cs and one SA.316C.

Ecuador
The Ecuadorean air force operates four SA.315Bs and four SA.316Bs, while the navy has a pair of the later SA.319B. The army inventory includes two Lamas and one SA.316B.

Eire
The Irish Army Air Corps has long been an operator of the faithful Alouette III, eight machines equipping No. 1 Support Wing at Baldonnel.

El Salvador
Transport plays an important role in the bitter fighting in El Salvador, and the air force's three Lamas and two Alouette IIIs are no doubt heavily utilized.

Ethiopia
The combat-experienced Ethiopian air force comprises a miscellany of Soviet and Western types, including five SA.316Bs

France
About 40 Alouette IIs remain in service with the Armée de l'Air, along with 50 Alouette IIIs. The ALAT has nearly 140 Alouette IIs and 70 Alouette IIIs on strength, while 13 Alouette IIs and 37 Alouette IIIs are in the Aéronavale inventory. Both Alouette IIs and IIIs are also in service with the Gendarmerie and various official bodies, including the Securité Civile, the customs, and the fire service.

Gabon
This former French colony maintains close links with the Armée de l'Air and operates mainly French equipment, including one SA.316B and three SA.319Bs.

West Germany
The West German army's Heeresflieger was second only to the French armed forces in the number of Alouette IIs ordered. About 107 SE.313Bs and 53 SA.318Cs remain in service.

Greece
The Greek navy has a small air arm comprising only two squadrons. One of these operates four SA.319Bs for liaison.

Guinea Bissau
This small ex-Portuguese colony operates a mixed fleet of helicopters, including one SE.313B and two SA.316Bs.

Guyana
The para-military Guyana Defence Force, whose main base is at Timehri East Bank near Demarara, operates two SA.319Bs alongside two Bell Jet Rangers and three Bell 212s.

India
The Indian air force's large helicopter fleet includes a mixture of French and HAL-built Alouettes. Current estimates are 60 SA.316Bs, 70 HAL Cheetahs and 120 HAL Chetaks. The Indian navy operates one SA.316B and 16 Chetaks on ASW duties.

Belgium

This is one of 90 Alouette IIs supplied to Belgium for liaison, training and observation duties. About 70 remain in service with four squadrons.

Chile

This Artouste-engined, Helibras-built SA.315B Lama was one of at least 16 delivered to the Chilean army.

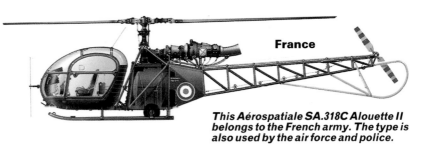

Eire

Eire's Alouette IIIs perform a number of vital roles, and serve with the Baldonnel-based No. 1 Support Wing.

France

This Aérospatiale SA.318C Alouette II belongs to the French army. The type is also used by the air force and police.

India

The Indian Air Force operates a large number of Alouette variants, many of them licence-built by HAL. This aircraft is in fact a HAL Chetak.

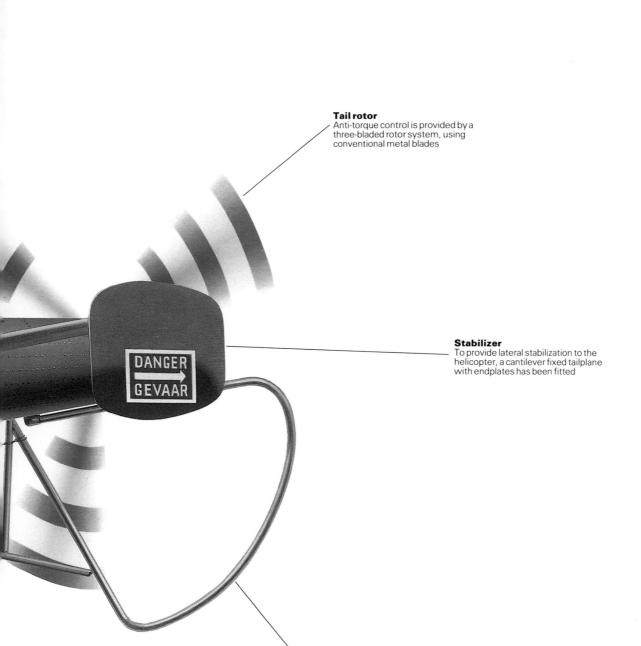

Tail rotor
Anti-torque control is provided by a three-bladed rotor system, using conventional metal blades

Stabilizer
To provide lateral stabilization to the helicopter, a cantilever fixed tailplane with endplates has been fitted

DANGER
GEVAAR

Tail guard
To prevent heavy, operational-style landings from interfering with the tail rotor, a tubular steel guard is fitted, together with a tailboom bracing strut

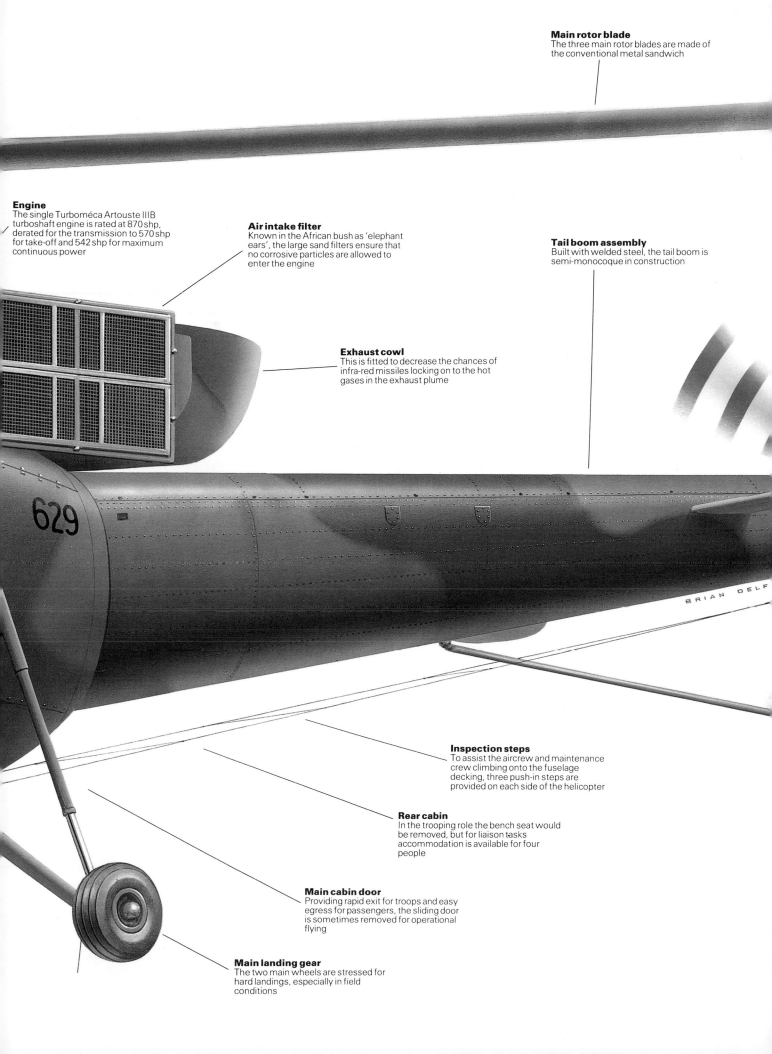

Main rotor blade
The three main rotor blades are made of the conventional metal sandwich

Engine
The single Turboméca Artouste IIIB turboshaft engine is rated at 870 shp, derated for the transmission to 570 shp for take-off and 542 shp for maximum continuous power

Air intake filter
Known in the African bush as 'elephant ears', the large sand filters ensure that no corrosive particles are allowed to enter the engine

Tail boom assembly
Built with welded steel, the tail boom is semi-monocoque in construction

Exhaust cowl
This is fitted to decrease the chances of infra-red missiles locking on to the hot gases in the exhaust plume

Inspection steps
To assist the aircrew and maintenance crew climbing onto the fuselage decking, three push-in steps are provided on each side of the helicopter

Rear cabin
In the trooping role the bench seat would be removed, but for liaison tasks accommodation is available for four people

Main cabin door
Providing rapid exit for troops and easy egress for passengers, the sliding door is sometimes removed for operational flying

Main landing gear
The two main wheels are stressed for hard landings, especially in field conditions

629

BRIAN DELF

Indonesia

All three of Indonesia's armed forces are equipped in part with Alouettes. The TNI-AU (air force) has three Alouette IIs, The TNI-AD (army) operates six Alouette IIIs, and the ALRI (naval air arm) has a further six Alouette IIIs.

Iraq

Iran's opponent in the protracted Gulf War, Iraq has a substantial air force comprising equipment supplied mostly from the Eastern bloc and by France. Iraq is reported to have 11 helicopter squadrons and about 40 SA.316B Alouette IIIs equipped with AS.12 air-to-surface missiles.

Ivory Coast

The Force Aérienne de Côte d'Ivoire relies mainly on French equipment. The air force's small helicopter fleet includes one Alouette II and two Alouette IIIs.

Jordan

The Royal Jordanian air force operates a squadron of 12 Alouette IIIs for utility transport from the King Abdullah air base near Amman.

Laos

The single helicopter squadron of the Air Force of the Laotian Liberation Army has a mix of Soviet and Western types. Two SE.313Bs are thought to soldier on.

Lebanon

Civil war and the occupation of Lebanon by foreign forces has reduced the effectiveness of the Force Aérienne Libanaise. The helicopter squadron once operated both Alouette IIs and IIIs, but only four SA.316Bs remain.

Liberia

The Liberian Army/Air Reconnaissance Unit, which has no combat aircraft, has a small helicopter element of three HAL Chetaks.

Libya

One of the largest and most potent air arms in Africa is operated by Libya, whose oil wealth has bought aircraft from various sources. The air force's four helicopter squadrons have a mixture of French, Italian and Soviet machines, including four SA.316Bs. The Libyan army also operates 10 Alouette IIIs.

Malawi

Designed for internal security and transport, the Malawi Air Wing has no combat aircraft, and its rotary-wing assets include one SA.316B for training and liaison.

Malaysia

The Royal Malaysian air force remains a major Alouette III operator, with about 24 machines in service for liaison with No. 3 Squadron at Kuala Lumpur and No. 5 Squadron at Labuan.

Netherlands

A-218

The Dutch armed forces remain a major user of the Alouette III. This aircraft is one of those used for observation, liaison and training by the army.

Mexico

SAR is one of the Mexican air force's most important tasks, and for this purpose there is a special squadron wth five SA.316Bs. The naval air arm's helicopter squadron includes four SA.319Bs.

Mozambique

Mozambique inherited a number of Portuguese aircraft in 1979, but has since developed a useful air capability with the aid of Cuba, East Germany and the USSR. The air force's one helicopter squadron operates four Alouette III armed helicopters left by the Portuguese.

Netherlands

About 67 SA.316Bs remain in service with the Dutch armed forces, but the most famous are those of the Royal Netherlands air force's 'Grasshoppers' display team, which gave its first demonstration in 1973.

Nicaragua

The Fuerza Aérea Sandinista, Nicaragua's air force, has in recent years turned to the Eastern bloc for its equipment, but among its Soviet- and Western-supplied helicopter fleet are two Alouette IIIs.

Nigeria

Nigeria's air force has, unlike the air arms of many other African countries, a substantial helicopter force. Ten SA.316Bs are used for SAR and for training/liaison.

Pakistan

All three of Pakistan's armed forces utilize the versatile Alouette III. The PAF's No. 12 Squadron operates 13, the army has 21, and the navy musters four SA.316Bs.

Peru

Aérospatiale types form a major part of the Peruvian armed forces' equipment, but many have a humanitarian role to play. The air force's rotary-wing assets fall under the command of Grupo 3, based at Callao with four squadrons. One operates the Alouette III and Lama for SAR. The army operates seven Alouette IIs for observation, and the navy inventory includes a pair of SA.319Bs.

Portugal

The Fôrça Aérea Portuguesa (Portuguese air force) was a major European operator of both the Alouette II and Alouette III. About 30 SA.316Bs are in service in the liaison and utility roles, and are based at Tancos.

Romania

One of the smaller air arms in the Warsaw Pact, the air force of the Romanian Socialist Republic has an expanding rotary-wing regiment and includes two French types built under licence. Some 50 IAR-316Bs and 90 IAR-330 Pumas are in service, while two Alouette II Astazous are thought to have been withdrawn.

Saudi Arabia

The pro-Western monarchy of Saudi Arabia turned to France and Italy to supply its helicopter needs. The RSAF's rotary-wing force is based at Taif, No. 14 Squadron's Alouette IIIs being tasked with training and SAR.

Senegambia

The Senegambia air force was formed after the union of Senegal and the Gambia in 1981. The French-supplied helicopter force of five machines includes two Alouette IIs.

Aérospatiale SA 316B Alouette III cutaway drawing key

1. FM homing antennas, port and starboard
2. Pitot head
3. Instrument access panel
4. Cockpit ventilating air intake
5. Antenna mounting
6. Downward view windows
7. Curved windscreen panels
8. Standby compass
9. Instrument panel shroud
10. Pilot's instrument console
11. Weapons system control panel
12. Centre control pedestal
13. Yaw control rudder pedals
14. Landing lamp
15. Floor beam construction
16. Levered suspension nose landing gear leg strut
17. Non-retracting castoring nosewheel
18. Port navigation light
19. Door jettison linkage
20. Cyclic pitch control colur
21. Central power and engin condition levers
22. Collective pitch control lever
23. Control column handgrip
24. Missile hand controller
25. Safety harness
26. Starboard jettisonable cockpit door
27. Outside air temperature guage
28. Starboard sliding cabin door
29. Cabin roof glazing
30. APX-Bezu 260 gyro-stabilized sight
31. Retractable sight control and binocular viewer

Alouette II/Alouette III variants

SE.3120: Alouette I powered by a 149-kW (200-hp) Salmson 9NH radial engine.
SE.3130: two prototype Alouette IIs, powered by the 268 kW (360 shp) Turboméca Artouste I turboshaft, were followed by three pre-production aircraft.
SE.313B: designation of Alouette IIs after Sud-Est merged with Ouest Aviation in 1957, becoming renamed Sud-Aviation; 924 built before production switched to the SA.318C.

SE.3140: Alouette II development powered by a 298-kW (400-shp) Turboméca Turmo II engine, but did not reach production stage.
SA.3180: Alouette II derivative powered by the more economical Astazou IIA and featuring a new centrifugal clutch.
SA.318C: production version of the SA.3180.

SE.3160: Alouette III powered by one 649-kW (870-shp) Turboméca Artouste IIIB turboshaft, derated to 410 kW (550 shp).
SA.316A: production version of the SE.3160.
SA.316B: featured strengthened main and tail rotor transmissions and could carry more payload. Produced in Romania as the IAR-316B and in India by HAL as the Chetak.
SA.316C: Artouste IIID powered variant built in limited numbers.
SA.319B: direct development of the SA.316B and powered by a more efficient and more economical 649-kW (870-shp) Turboméca Astazou XIV turboshaft, derated to 447 kW (600 shp).

SA.315B: the Lama combined a strengthened Alouette II airframe with the SA.316B's engine and dynamic parts. Assembled in Brazil as the Hélibras Gaviao, and produced in India by HAL as the Cheetah.

Specification: SE.313B Alouette II

Rotors

Main rotor diameter	10.20 m	(33 ft 5.6 in)
Main rotor disc area	81.71 m²	(879.58 sq ft)
Tail rotor diameter	1.81 m	(5 ft 11.3 in)

Fuselage and tail unit

Accommodation	pilot and four passengers, or two litters and one attendant	
Length overall, rotors turning	12.05 m	(39 ft 6.4 in)
Length, blades folded	9.70 m	(31 ft 9.9 in)
Height overall	2.75 m	(9 ft 0.3 in)

Landing gear

Standard twin-skid landing gear (or quadricycle wheeled landing gear for shipboard operations)

Skid track	2.00 m	(6 ft 6.7 in)

Weights

Empty	895 kg	(1,973 lb)
Maximum take-off	1600 kg	(3,527 lb)
Internal fuel capacity	580 litres	(128 Imp gal)

Powerplant

One Turboméca Artouste IIC6 turboshaft
Rating 395 kW (530 shp) derated to 268 kW (360 shp)

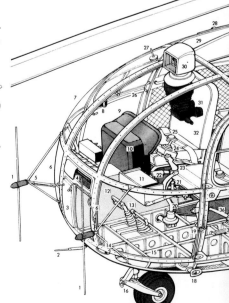

Main rotor and transmission
The SA 316B model has a transmission rated at 570 shp, the main rotor carrying three conventional honeycomb blades

Wire cutter
Some helicopters have a wire-cutter fitted to prevent catastrophic damage from wires and power lines. The second cutter is under the fuselage

VHF/AM whip aerial
This is a standby communications set for the helicopter in tactical situations

Cabin step
For normal trooping and liaison tasks the cabin step helps access to the cabin; some versions have the step removed and a gun position is fitted, firing sideways and aft

VHF/FM radio aerial
The VHF/FM radio provides air-to-air and general air traffic line-of-sight communications; the control boxes are in the cockpit console

Anti-collision lights
Standard flashing orange anti-collision lights are used for normal peacetime flying operations

The British Army mainly uses its Cyprus-based Alouette IIs for pilot training, UK and German based AAC helicopter pilots doing a short 'hot and high' course with No. 6 Flight. Eight are in use, and no replacement is in sight.

the Alouette II included Austria, Belgium and Switzerland. In the UK the AAC received 17 machines. The Alouette's good high-altitude performance was put to use by No. 8 Flight, AAC, in Kenya where several mountain rescues were carried out. AAC machines have also served in British Guyana, West Germany, Uganda, Zanzibar, Tanganyika, Jamaica and, of course, Cyprus.

The size of the Alouette II makes it ideal for observation, liaison, medevac and training, but for a more offensive role some Alouettes have been equipped with AS.11 or AS.12 missiles for anti-tank capability, while the French Aéro-navale's machines have carried Mk 44 anti-submarine torpedoes. Apart from the usual roles, British Alouettes have been used for underslung resupply and troop-lift to UN forces in Cyprus and in support of police marksmen to arrest big game poachers in Kenya. During late 1964 XR232 was used in trials on Salisbury Plain to evaluate SS.11 anti-tank missile suitability for the Westland Scout.

A development of the Alouette II, the SE.3140 with a 298-kW (400-shp) Turboméca Turmo II engine, was announced in May 1957 but did not go into production. Another derivative, powered by the more economical 395-kW (530-shp) Turboméca Astazou IIA turboshaft engine and featuring a new centrifugal clutch, was more successful. The prototype SA.3180 first flew on 31 January 1961, and after trials an extension of the Alouette II's French airworthiness certificate was granted on 18 February 1964.

Production as the SA.318C began during that year, with first deliveries follow-ing in 1965. An initial 15 Alouette II Astazous were built for the ALAT. The SA.318C was of similar appearance but had a slightly higher level speed and longer range, and could lift heavier loads, but this aircraft was less suitable for high-altitude operations. A licence to produce the Alouette II was also granted to Saab of Sweden and to Republic Aviation of the USA, but few were built.

By the spring of 1975, when production of the Alouette II ended, 382 SA.318Cs had been built, bringing total production to more than 1,300. The Alouette II has been used by 126 civil and military operators in 46 countries, by any criteria an outstanding achievement.

'Hot and high'

Sud capitalized on the enormous success of the Alouette II to produce the SA.315B Lama in response to an Indian air force requirement for an aircraft capable of operating in the Himalayas. The Lama married the airframe of the Alouette II to the derated Artouste IIIB engine and the rotor system of the SA.316B Alouette III. This provided exceptional 'hot and high' and slung-load performance, increasing the normal gross weight to 1950 kg (4,299 lb) and allowing the Lama to carry up to 1135 kg (2,502 lb) on the hook. High-altitude capability was more than confirmed on 21 June 1972 when a

Lama established a world absolute height record of 40,820 ft (12442 m).

Aérospatiale has sold SA.315Bs to a handful of military customers, including Chile. In addition the helicopter has been produced since 1972 by Hindustan Aeronautics Ltd in India as the Cheetah. More than 150 have been built by HAL, most of them entering service with the Indian forces. The type is also assembled by Helibras in Brazil under the name Gavião.

The Alouette III, originally designated the SE.3160, was a natural development of the Alouette II, but featured an extensively-glazed and widened cabin to accommodate seven. The dynamic components were derived from those of the Alouette II, but the more powerful 410-kW (550-shp) Artouste III turboshaft was introduced with an extended-diameter main rotor and three-blade tail rotor. The centre section and tail boom were covered, and tricycle landing gear was fitted.

The prototype (F-ZWVQ) made its first flight on 28 February 1959, and in June 1960 the new aircraft reached 15,781 ft (4810 m) on Mont Blanc. It immediately

Eight float-equipped Alouette IIIs were delivered to the Danish naval air service, but have been replaced by a similar number of Westland Lynx HAS.Mk 80s. Several other nations have operated amphibious versions of the Alouette III.

South Africa

An unarmed Alouette III of the South African Air Force. About 100 are in use, serving with Nos 16, 17 and 22 Squadrons and No. 87 AFS.

South Africa

South Africa has the most powerful air arm in southern Africa, and helicopter operations play a key role, particularly in the insurgency war in northern South West Africa (Namibia). The SAAF has a fleet of about 100 Alouette IIIs.

Spain

The FAMET, the air component of the Spanish army, has a substantial helicopter force contributing much to the army's battlefield mobility, logistic resupply and anti-tank capability. The impressive line-up includes three SA.319Bs.

Sweden

In Swedish military use the Alouette II is designated the HKP-2 and operates with floats as well as conventional skid landing gear. All three services have operated the HKP-2, the air force since 1956.

Switzerland

A major European operator of Alouettes, the Swiss Flugwaffe's *Leichtefliegerstaffeln* (light aviation squadrons) Nos 1 to 4 operate both types for SAR and liaison. Twenty-six SA.313Bs and 76 SA.316Bs remain in service.

Togo

France has supplied the four helicopters which form the rotary-wing element of the Togolese air force, in the form of one SA.315B, two SA.318Cs and one SA.330 Puma.

Tunisia

One of the poorer Arab states, Tunisia maintains a relatively small air force. The TRAF's single helicopter squadron possesses five Alouette IIs and seven Alouette IIIs.

United Arab Emirates

The UAE is a federation of seven Gulf states, and the air force is an amalgamation of three separate forces. The helicopter unit includes up to seven Alouette IIIs for liaison.

United Kingdom

The Army Air Corps ordered 17 Alouette IIs, of which eight remain in service in Cyprus with one held in reserve. These aircraft are expected to soldier on until at least 1995.

United Kingdom

An aged Aérospatiale Alouette II of No. 16 Flight, Army Air Corps, based in Cyprus for training and UN/garrison support duties.

Venezuela

As many as 26 Alouette IIIs are in service with the Venezuelan armed forces. The FAV's liaison and reconnaissance group at Barcelona has a substantial fleet of helicopters, including 14 SA.316Bs, while the army has a squadron of SA.316Bs for observation.

North Yemen

The mixture of equipment in the Yemen Arab Republic Air Force reflects North Yemen's attempt to strike a balance between Eastern and Western influences. The helicopter unit contains two Alouette IIIs alongside Italian- and Soviet-supplied types.

Yugoslavia

Helicopters play a vital communications role in Yugoslavia, where the Gazelle is built under licence. Four squadrons operate helicopters, one of them equipped with up to 20 Alouette IIIs.

Zaïre

The Zaïrean air force has a small helicopter element which includes seven Alouette IIIs.

Zambia

The Zambian air force's utility helicopter squadron operates eight Alouette IIIs, while five Alouette IIs are thought to have been withdrawn.

Zimbabwe

The air force of Zimbabwe has two helicopter squadrons for liaison and light transport (Nos 7 and 8) and is thought to have up to six Alouette IIs and 10 Alouette IIIs still in service. A further 30 SA.316Bs are reported to be in storage.

32 Pilot's seat
33 Co-pilot/weapons officer's seat
34 Sliding side window panel
35 Port jettisonable cockpit door
36 Collective pitch control lever
37 Seat mounting rails (three-abreast front seat row)
38 Boarding step
39 Lower fuselage 'raft' section skin panelling
40 Port sliding cabin door
41 Passenger/cargo loading door
42 Door hatches/stretcher handle apertures
43 Door latches
44 Troop carrying folding seats (four)
45 Fixed backrest
46 Control rod linkages
47 Sliding door top rail
48 Cabin rear sloping bulkhead
49 Trim/insulating panelling
50 First aid kit
51 Anti-collision light
52 VHF aerial
53 Cabin roof skin panelling
54 Rotor head control rods
55 Main transmission gearbox
56 Swash plate mechanism
57 Blade pitch angle control rods
58 Torque scissor links
59 Rotor head hinge fitting
60 Lifting fitting
61 Hydraulic drag hinge dampers
62 Bracing cables
63 Three-blade main rotor
64 Blade root attachment joints
65 Blade pitch angle control horn
66 Engine inlet filter screen
67 Starboard engine inlet
68 Accessory equipment gearbox
69 Generator
70 Engine transmission shaft
71 Rotor brake
72 Transmission oil cooler
73 Oil tank
74 Oil cooler air duct
75 Gearbox mounting deck
76 Fuel tank, capacity 575 litres (126.5 Imp gal)
77 Electrical system equipment
78 Equipment loading deck
79 Sliding cabin door bottom rail
80 Missile system avionics equipment
81 Position of fuel filler on starboard side
82 Welded steel tube centre fuselage framework
83 Gearbox mounting struts
84 Non-structural skin panelling
85 Fireproof engine mounting deck
86 Angled tail rotor transmission shaft
87 Engine reduction gearbox
88 Ignition control unit
89 Port engine bellmouth air inlet
90 Rear engine mounting strut
91 Tailpipe negative pressure cooling air duct
92 Engine combustion section
93 Turboméca Artouste IIIB turboshaft engine
94 Engine exhaust duct
95 Tailboom top decking/access panel
96 Tail rotor transmission shaft
97 Transmission shaft bearings
98 Tail rotor control cables
99 Starboard fixed tailplane
100 Endplate tailfin
101 Three-blade tail rotor
102 All-metal tail rotor blades
103 Blade pitch control mechanism
104 Right-angle final drive gearbox
105 Tail navigation light
106 Steel tube tailskid/rotor protector
107 Port fixed tailplane
108 Port endplate tailfin
109 Tailplane bracing struts
110 Main rotor blade balance weights
111 Aluminium alloy blade spar
112 Moltoprene foam trailing edge filler
113 Bonded aluminium alloy rotor blade skin panels
114 Tailboom frame and stringer construction
115 Upper longeron
116 Tailboom attachment joints
117 68-mm folding fin aircraft rocket (FFAR)
118 Matra 18×68 rocket launcher pack
119 Missile pylon adaptor
120 Missile launch rail
121 AS.12 wire guided air-to-surface missile (two)
122 Port mainwheel
123 Shock absorber leg strut
124 Trailing axle beam
125 Hydraulic brake pipe
126 Tie-down point
127 Axle beam pivot fixing
128 Weapons pylon mount
129 Detachable missile pylons
130 AS.11 wire guided air-to-surface missiles (four)

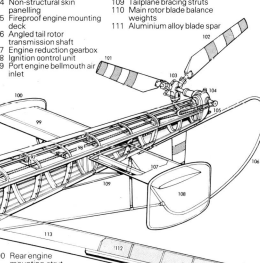

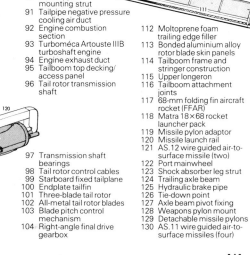

© Pilot Press Ltd

Alouette II and III warload

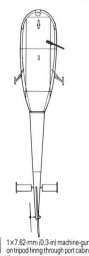 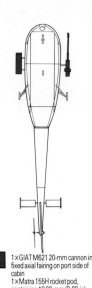 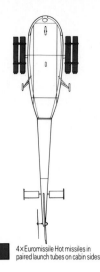 

■ 4 × Aérospatiale AS.11 anti-tank missiles in pairs on fuselage sides

■ 2 × Aérospatiale AS.12 air-to-surface missiles on cabin sides

■ 1 × 7.62-mm (0.3-in) machine-gun on tripod firing through port cabin door

■ 1 × GIAT M621 20-mm cannon in fixed axial fairing on port side of fuselage
1 × Matra 155H rocket pod, containing 18 68-mm (2.68-in) unguided rockets on starboard side

■ 4 × Euromissile Hot missiles in paired launch tubes on cabin sides

■ 1 × Mk 44 torpedo on port side of cabin
□ 1 × Crouzet DHAX-3 MAD bird and winch pod on starboard side of cabin
1 × OMERA ORB-31 search radar in nose-mounted radome

Alouette II anti-armour
The AS.11 has largely been superseded by the HOT missile in French army service, but remains an armament option for both the Alouette II and the Alouette III. British Westland Scouts used the missiles against bunkers and strongpoints during the Falklands war.

Alouette II anti-shipping
The AS.12 is a much bigger missile than the AS.11, with wire-transmitted command to line of sight guidance and optical flare tracking. The missile has a much larger warhead and is suitable for use against ships or fortifications.

Alouette III SAAF armed reconnaissance
South African Alouettes are used for a variety of operational roles and are used frequently on 'externals'. Their only armament consists of a temporary machine-gun mounting in the cabin, although aircrew almost inevitably carry personal weapons.

Alouette III close air support/COIN
The Alouette III could alternatively carry two rocket pods, with one on each side of the fuselage. Rockets are a useful area weapon, with good incendiary characteristics, and are particularly useful against dispersed vehicles and other soft targets.

Alouette III anti-armour
The Euromissile HOT is a tube-launched, optically remote-guided anti-tank missile with a hollow-charge warhead. The French army operate HOT-armed Gazelles and Alouettes. An alternative anti-tank weapon is the FN ETNA TMP-5 twin 7.62-mm (0.3in) machine-gun pod.

Alouette III anti-submarine
Naval Alouette III variants can carry a pair of Mk 44 torpedoes, or one torpedo and a towed magnetic anomaly detector on a 50-m (164-ft) cable, housed in a streamlined winch pod on the starboard fuselage side. A 225-kg (496-lb) capacity rescue hoist can also be installed.

Specification: SA.316B Alouette III

Rotors
Main rotor diameter	11.02 m	(36 ft 1.9 in)
Main rotor disc area	95.38 m²	(1,026.7 sq ft)
Tail rotor diameter	1.91 m	(6 ft 3.3 m)

Fuselage and tail unit
Accommodation: pilot and two passengers side-by-side at the front of the cabin, and up to four passengers or two litters at the cabin rear

Length overall, rotors turning	12.84 m	(42 ft 1.5 in)
Length, fuselage	10.03 m	(32 ft 10.9 in)
Height overall	3.00 m	(9 ft 10.1 in)

Landing gear
Fixed tricycle landing gear with single mainwheels and steerable single nosewheel
Wheel track	2.60 m	(8 ft 6.4 in)

Weights
Empty	1143 kg	(2,520 lb)
Maximum take-off	2200 kg	(4,850 lb)
Internal fuel capacity	575 litres	(126 Imp gal)
External load	750 kg	(1,653 lb)

Powerplant
One Turboméca Artouste IIIB turboshaft
Rating: 649 kW (870 shp) derated to 425 kW (570 shp)

Alouette III recognition features

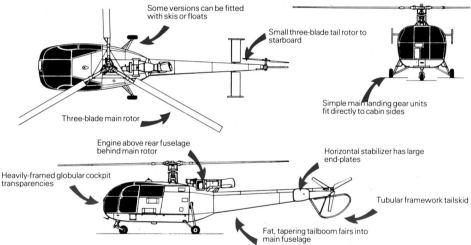

Some versions can be fitted with skis or floats

Small three-blade tail rotor to starboard

Three-blade main rotor

Simple main landing gear units fit directly to cabin sides

Engine above rear fuselage behind main rotor

Heavily-framed globular cockpit transparencies

Horizontal stabilizer has large end-plates

Tubular framework tailskid

Fat, tapering tailboom fairs into main fuselage

Performance SE.313B Alouette II
Maximum speed at sea level	100 kts	185 km/h (115 mph)
Cruising speed	89 kts	164 km/h (102 mph)
Service ceiling	7,055 ft	(2150 m)
Range with 390-kg (860-lb) payload	300 km	(186 miles)
Range with maximum fuel	565 km	(351 miles)

Performance SA.316B Alouette III
Maximum speed at sea level	113 kts	210 km/h (130 mph)
Cruising speed	100 kts	185 km/h (115 mph)
Service ceiling	10,500 ft	(3200 m)
Hovering ceiling out of ground effect	4,920 ft	(1500 m)
Range with maximum fuel at sea level	495 km	(308 miles)

Maximum speed at optimum altitude
- Aérospatiale SA 360C Dauphin 148 kts
- Aérospatiale/Westland SA 342L Gazelle 140 kts
- Bell OH-58A Kiowa 120 kts
- MBB BO 105 P (PAH-1) 119 kts
- Aérospatiale SA 318C Alouette II Astazou 110 kts
- Aérospatiale SA 316B Alouette III 100 kts
- Bell 47G-4A Trooper 91 kts
- Schweizer/Hughes Model 300C 82 kts

Maximum payload
- Aérospatiale SA 360C Dauphin 1300 kg
- Aérospatiale SA 316B / Alouette III 750 kg
- Aérospatiale/Westland SA 342L Gazelle 700 kg
- SA 318C Alouette II / Astazou 600 kg
- MBB BO 105 P (PAH-1) 580 kg E
- Bell 47G-4A / Trooper 455 kg
- Schweizer/Hughes Model 300C 408 kg
- Bell OH-58A Kiowa 310 kg

Range with maximum payload
- Aérospatiale/Westland SA 342L Gazelle 710 km
- Aérospatiale SA 360C Dauphin 680 km
- MBB BO 105 P (PAH-1) 575 km
- Aérospatiale SA 316B Alouette III 495 km
- Bell OH-58A Kiowa 490 km
- Bell 47G-4A Trooper 380 km
- Schweizer/Hughes Model 300C 373 km
- Aérospatiale SA 318C Alouette II Astazou 100 km

Service ceiling
- Bell OH-58A Kiowa 18,900 ft
- MBB BO 105 P (PAH-1) 13,780 ft
- Aérospatiale/Westland SA 342L Gazelle 13,450 ft
- Aérospatiale SA 360C Dauphin 13,000 ft
- Bell 47G-4A Trooper 11,200 ft
- Aérospatiale SA 318C Alouette II Astazou 10,800 ft
- Aérospatiale SA 316B Alouette III 10,500 ft
- Schweizer/Hughes Model 300C 10,200 ft

Maximum rate of climb, feet per minute
- Bell OH-58A Kiowa 1,780 ft
- MBB BO 105 P (PAH-1) 1,770 ft
- Aérospatiale SA 360C Dauphin 1,770 ft
- Aérospatiale/Westland SA 342L Gazelle 1,535 ft
- Aérospatiale SA 318C Alouette II Astazou 1,300 ft
- Alouette II 850 ft
- Aérospatiale SA 316B 800 ft
- Trooper 800 ft
- Bell 47G-4A
- Schweizer/Hughes Model 300C 750 ft

The AEROSPATIALE WESTLAND GAZELLE

Gazelle: battlefield lightweight

The Anglo-French Gazelle has proved a useful and popular light battlefield helicopter, fast and manoeuvrable and with the capacity to carry a useful range of anti-tank weapons. Combat-proven in the Middle East and the Falklands, only its fragility has generated any real criticism.

This SA 342M Gazelle demonstrator carries a 20-mm cannon mounted to starboard, and an unguided rocket pod to port. The Gazelle can carry a substantial warload but has proved very vulnerable to ground fire.

As sprightly as its name suggests, the Gazelle is one of the world's leading army helicopters. Equipped for observation, liaison or anti-tank missions with today's light but hard-hitting guided missiles, the Gazelle has been employed in combat by at least five of its 22 military users, and its popularity is attested by the fact that assembly has been undertaken at four plants in Europe and Africa. The subject of continual upgrading by its designers, the Gazelle is receiving yet further improvements at the hands of its two major operators, ensuring that worthwhile service will be obtained well into the next decade.

Alouette replacement

Such success was confidently expected when Sud Aviation began work on a replacement for its rapid-selling Alouette II light helicopter during the mid-1960s. The expertise accumulated by the French helicopter industry in earlier ventures was well employed in design of the new machine, which was intended to offer the advantages of being faster and more manoeuvrable than its predecessor. Turboméca, the local turboshaft engine manufacturer, provided part of the formula with a more powerful motor then on the drawing board, but the breakthrough came in design of the helicopter's dynamic components.

The Gazelle (and all subsequent French helicopters) benefited from a 1964 agreement with Bölkow of West Germany for joint development of a glass-fibre rotor blade and an associated rigid rotor head. Accepted today as the norm, composite-material rotors ushered in a breakthrough in blade construction through their ability to combine lightness with strength, resistance to damage (including small-calibre gunfire), reduced maintenance requirements and greatly extended fatigue life. Similar simplicity and strength (not to mention a high degree of agility) is offered by a rotor head which dispenses with the complex mechanisms providing for secondary blade movement. In the event, however, complete rigidity was abandoned in the prototype stage, leaving today's Gazelle with a compromise (semi-articulated) head, which has flap hinges but no drag hinges.

A further (and most obvious) innovation is the inset fan which replaces the more traditional type of helicopter tail rotor. This system, known as the 'fenestron' in allusion to its window-like appearance in the fin, reflected the designers' plan for directional stability to be achieved at cruising speed without the need for a balancing moment at the tail. The auxiliary rotor was thus shrouded, so that it would not be in the airflow when disengaged after take-off. These aspirations proved slightly optimistic when flight tests showed that turbulence around the fan was resulting in poor responses to control movements. As well as being used for landing, take-off and hovering (as intended), the fan is now powered in cruising flight, although the 5 per cent saving in power it allows shows that the fenestron's development effort was not entirely wasted.

More usual aspects of the Gazelle's design include a cockpit and cabin based on a semi-monocoque frame including two longitudinal box sections, upon which is mounted a light alloy carrier frame for the windows and doors. Alloy honeycomb panels are used liberally in the central and rear sections of the cabin, whereas the boom and tail surfaces are produced from sheet metal. Extensive glazing is provided for the pilot and observer, whilst a bench in the cabin can be removed for the accommodation of light cargo as an alternative to three passengers. Forward-opening doors for the two crew members interconnect with larger doors hinged at the rear for access to the cabin. The usual army skid landing gear is standard on all Gazelle versions.

Continued improvement

What was originally known as the Sud X-300 had become the SA 340 by the time of its maiden flight on 7 April 1967. Its intended 336-kW (450-shp) Oredon turboshaft had been cancelled by Turboméca, so initially it was forced to make do with the 268 kW (360 shp) offered by an Astazou II until uprated versions of that engine became available. A proving airframe with conventional rotors, the SA 340 was followed on 12 April 1968 by a more representative prototype with rigid rotor and fenestron. Here problems began. Having tested the new rotor in a four-blade configuration on an Alouette, Sud discovered serious control deficiencies in a three-blade layout, forcing a change to semi-articulation and the revised designation SA 341.

One of the Soko licence-built Gazelles of the Yugoslav air force runs up in front of a line of Soviet-built Mil Mi-8 'Hip' transport helicopters. Yugoslav Gazelles can carry 'Sagger' anti-tank missiles and 'Grail' air-to-air missiles for self-defence and anti-helicopter use.

This aircraft became the Sud Gazelle in July 1969, but only until 1 January 1970 when Sud was absorbed into the new Aérospatiale. Before series-built aircraft could be released, yet more unexpected difficulties arose. Again, it was as the result of testing aspects of the design in isolation, then expecting them to work together in harmony. Production Gazelles featured an Astazou III powerplant maximum-rated at 440 kW (590 shp), a longer cabin, and two rear cabin access doors and a larger tail unit, resulting in a delay of a year before most of the ground resonance and transmission vibration they prompted could be eliminated.

Rightfully, France's army aviation (Aviation Légère de l'Armée de Terre, or ALAT) is the major Gazelle operator, flying the helicopter in its original and uprated forms. The early Gazelles for both home use and export employed an Astazou III and were limited to a take-off weight of 1800 kg (3,968 lb), but on 11 May 1973 Aérospatiale flew a prototype of the SA 342, introducing a 640-kW (858-shp) Astazou XIVH. Accordingly, take-off weight rose to 1900 kg (4,189 lb) in the resultant export SA 342K, this becoming an SA 342L when fitted with an improved fenestron, and SA 342M in similar configuration for ALAT. The last-mentioned also specified automatic engine start-up capability, in which form its powerplant is known as the Astazou XIVM. Most recently, in 1985, Aérospatiale has offered a boosted maximum weight of 2000 kg (4,409 lb) in the SA 342L$_1$ which also has the continuous rating of the Astazou XIV increased from 426 kW (571 shp) to 441 KW (592 shp).

French army service

ALAT continues to operate most of the original 170 SA 341F Gazelles it received from 1973 onwards as Alouette II replacements in the observation, liaison and training roles. Many have been updated since the last was delivered in 1977, and there are at present three different standards of modification. First, in anticipation of later developments, plans were

announced to convert 110 to SA 341M standard with the addition for four Euromissile HOT anti-tank missiles on outrigger pylons, and an associated roof-mounted sight. SA 341Ms entered service in September 1978, but because of its limited maximum weight the aircraft was regarded only as an interim model and the conversion target reduced to 40.

A further 62 SA 341Fs are in the process of modification to SA 341F/Canon standard including, predictably enough, a GIAT M.621 20-mm cannon for armed escort duties. Only one M.621 is installed, on the starboard side, and it is on a level with the forward skid support leg, rather than being mounted on the HOT outrigger pylons. The weapon, which can fire at either 300 or 740 rounds per minute, has no external sight. However, a simplified version of the M334 roof-mounted sighting system employed by HOT-armed SA 342s (see below) is being installed in SA 341Fs dedicated to reconnaissance. Having acquired information via this magnifying equipment, the observer will be able to report his finding to base via a second VHF/FM radio with which the reconnaissance Gazelle is also being equipped.

In February 1980, ALAT began receiving the first of a planned 158 SA 342Ms, armed with four HOTs. As well as the uprated engine, the SA 342M also has a

During the Falklands war, British Army and Royal Marines Gazelles were extensively used and a number were lost. Those operated by No. 3 CBAS were armed with rocket pods and door-mounted machine guns, but most were unarmed and used for recce and casevac tasks.

Crouzet Nadir self-contained navigation system, SFIM PA 85G autopilot, Decca 80 Doppler, night flying equipment and provision for an exhaust deflector. The last-mentioned, an upturned duct for the hot gas (providing a measure of protection against heat-seeking SAMs), replaces the normal exhaust duct only in combat situations. (It has been installed, for example, on the Gazelles which form part of the French intervention force facing Libyan-backed anti-government guerrillas in Chad since 1984.) Most closely connected with the 4000-m (4,375-yard) range HOT is a SFIM APX M397 sight mounted atop the cockpit, above the gunner's seat on the port side. A variant of the APX M334 series, the sight is gyro-stabilized and has magnifications of ×2.5 and ×10.

Most of the RAF's Gazelles are concentrated at RAF Shawbury, where No. 2 FTS and a Central Flying School detachment use them for helicopter pilot and instructor training. Pilots destined for the Harrier also do a short course on the Gazelle.

Pilot-in-command
Under current Army Air Corps instructions, the pilot-in-command flies the helicopter from the right-hand seat and is responsible for the flight envelope and safety of the helicopter

Cockpit instrument pedestal
The AH.Mk 1 has limited instrumentation, mainly connected with general flight indicators, radio controls and the lightweight navigation aid. The small size of the panel allows for good visibility from the cockpit. The instruments are night vision goggle compatible

Mk III helmet
Current aircrew helmets are being replaced by the Mk IV series, manufactured by Helmets Limited; Army Air Corps helmets will be fitted with night vision goggles and Racal Acoustic boom microphones

Observation aid fairing
All front-line AH.Mk 1s are being fitted with the Ferranti AF 532 observation aid for seeking and identifying possible targets for artillery, fighter ground attack and (primarily) helarm (armed helicopter) attacks

Observer/second pilot
Until recently, this member of the aircrew has been the junior of the two crew, but under a new policy guideline the left-hand seat will soon be filled with the captain of the aircraft

Rear passenger seats
Bench-type seats for three people are provided; behind is additional kit stowage space. These seats are removed and the left-hand forward seat folded forward for stretcher carriage

Cabin doors
The AH.Mk 1 is fitted with a large cabin door on each side for front-seat crew and smaller, inter-locking doors behind for passengers and baggage

Harness release/forward seats
The front seat aircrew have a harness system which allows for movement on inertia reel or is locked for take-off and landing. Armoured seats are currently being delivered to BAOR units

External supply
External power and intercom sockets are found here, protected by a flap. The system is rarely used operationally

Aérospatiale (Westland) Gazelle AH.Mk 1
No.656 Squadron
Army Air Corps

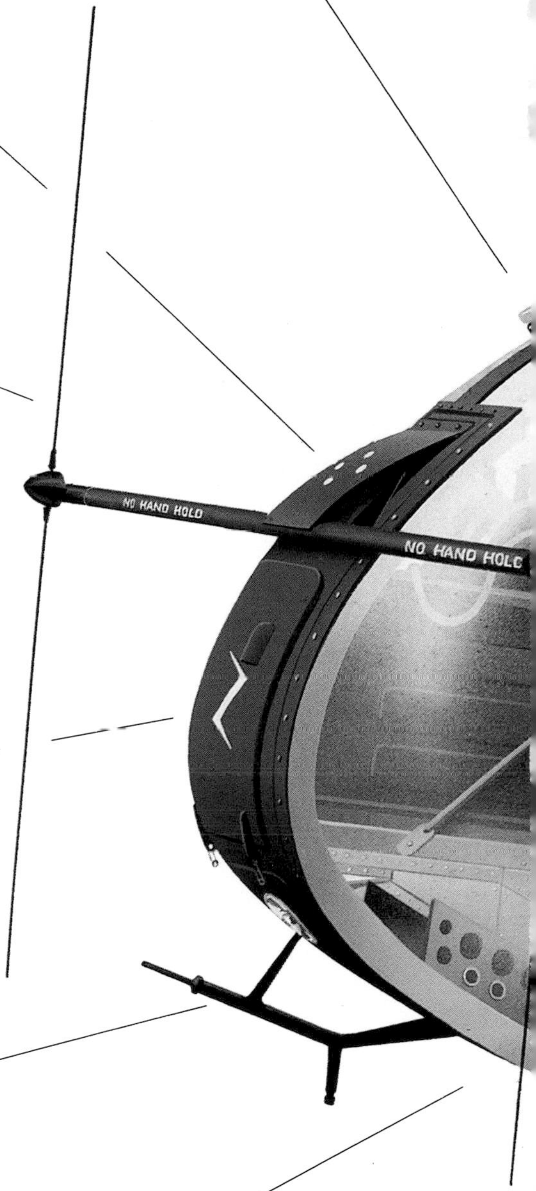

Slip indicator
Not shown on this illustration is the sprung wire slip indicator, topped with a red string which assists the pilot during slow speed and hover flight manoeuvres by giving relative wind direction

Cabin air intake
Because the VHF homer was a post-design modification, the efficiency of the cabin cool-air intake has been degraded and side vents are frequently used

VHF/FM homer
The ARC 340 has twin dipole aerials for radio homing; direction indication is given in the cockpit on the attitude indicator. The same radio has a communications serial under the tailcone

Battery access
Panel access is given to the Gazelle's main 24-volt nickel-cadmium battery (immediately forward of the cockpit pedestal)

Pitot-static head
This provides data for the pressure-responsive instruments — ASI, altimeter, and vertical speed indicator. It is heated by a 28-volt DC system

Yaw pedals
XX444 has its left-hand cyclic and collective controls removed, but the yaw pedals are retained; these pedals (duplicated for the pilot on the right-hand side) control the fenestron pitch angle

UHF homing aerials
Not shown are two UHF/AM homing aerials, which have two metallized strips on the transparency adjacent to the aerials to provide additional ground planes. UHF communications aerials are in the tailcone and tailfin

British production

Under the terms of a 1967 agreement also involving joint adoption of the Aérospatiale Puma and Westland Lynx, the UK's Army Air Corps (AAC) became a large-scale operator of Gazelles assembled by Westland. First deliveries were made in 1973, and when the British line closed in February 1984 it had contributed 282 to the sales total. All except 12 (10 civilian and two Qatar police) were for home military use, including pilot training models for the Fleet Air Arm and RAF. (To be pedantic, there were two UK lines, the Yeovil facilities transferring to Weston-super-Mare in 1977 to build the last 92.) Westland also was assigned 65 per cent of all Gazelle parts fabrication on a man-hours basis, this share reducing in line with subsequent changes in military orders and currency rates.

The AAC operates the survivors of 212 Gazelle AH.Mk 1s acquired for observation and liaison, a few of them purchased on behalf of the Royal Marines. They, too, have exhaust deflectors available for emergency fitment, and a few have received uprated models of the Astazou engine, known as the Mk IIIN2. Assigned to units at home and in West Germany, as well as farther afield in Belize, Central America, they functioned in unarmed roles until hastily given provision for carrying a Matra 68-mm (2.68-in) SNEB rocket pod on each outrigger at the start of the 1982 Falklands war. In all, 17 were assigned to the Royal Marines and No. 656 Squadron, AAC, for the period of hostilities, and these also had an armed escort and reconnaissance option with a general-purpose machine-gun in the cabin doorway. Three losses, including two to small arms, lend some support to allegations that the Gazelle is not sufficiently robust for the battlefield.

In spite of this, the AAC is planning to uprate 67 of its Gazelles to SA 342 standard as target-finders for its anti-tank Westland Lynx helicopters. In this scouting role, they will be assisted by a Doppler-based navigation system and a roof-mounted Ferranti AF532 optical sight. The AF532 is based on the Lynx's weapon sight and, like its French counterpart, has ×2.5 and ×10 magnification options. Since January 1983, units supporting the British Army of the Rhine in West Germany have included six TOW-Lynx squadrons each with four scouting Gazelles attached (Nos 651, 652, 653, 654, 659 and 662), plus three all-Gazelle reconnaissance squadrons (Nos 661, 663

and 669). The AAC is considering giving the manoeuvrable Gazelle an anti-helicopter role in BAOR, armed with air-launched versions of the new Shorts Javelin infantry SAM.

Gazelles abroad

Of the 1,195 Gazelles sold (and 1,138 delivered) by 1 January 1986, the majority of exports have come from the French assembly line, all but 170 of them for military use. The original (Astazou III-powered) military SA 341H model was sold far and wide before supplanted by the uprated SA 342K and SA 342L, some of them armed with four or six HOTs, or the 20-mm GIAT M.621. Iraq's SA 342Ls are most likely to have been amongst the armed helicopters used against Iranian troops in the Gulf War since 1980, and Syrian Gazelles were in action during the 1982 Israeli invasion of Lebanon (losing several of their number as a result, one being captured intact by the Israelis). Those of the Moroccan air force (with HOT and cannon) have fought the Polisario guerrillas in the disputed territory of Western Sahara.

Different armament is to be found in Yugoslavia, where 212 Gazelles are being built by Soko at Mostar. An initial agreement of 1971 covered 21 French-built helicopters and a licence for 112 SA 341Hs, and this was followed in 1982 by a further arrangement to build 100 SA 342Ls with Yugoslav-assembled Astazou engines. In military service, they can be fitted with two Soviet-designed AT-3 'Sagger' anti-tank missiles on each outrigger and, more recently, an air-launched SA-7 'Grail' infantry SAM (mounted in the middle of each 'Sagger' pair) for anti-helicopter combat.

For diversity of weapons, however,

This French army Gazelle mounts a pair of Matra Mistral tube-launched short-range air-to-air high-velocity guided missiles. The weapon is not yet in service in its air-to-air version, but is developed from the shoulder-launched SATCP surface to air missile.

Egypt is difficult to beat. Gazelles with HOT and 20-mm cannon are accompanied by those equipped to fire the older Aérospatiale AS.12 air-to-surface missile in the anti-shipping role. Following a series of trails held in 1981, it is possible that other Egyptian Gazelles may receive the Hughes BGM-71 TOW as an alternative to HOT for tank-busting. Egypt is also the site of the most recently established Gazelle assembly line, the first of an initial batch of 30 having been delivered from Factory No. 36 at Helwan in December 1983. A steady if subdued demand (49 were ordered worldwide in 1985) will keep the three remaining Gazelle assembly lines ticking over for some time to come. The Gazelle may not meet the standards of battle-worthiness demanded from the current generation of combat helicopter, but in all other respects it is highly regarded as a swift, manoeuvrable and indispensable adjunct to modern army operations.

Glossary
AAC Army Air Corps
ALAT Aviation Légère de l'Armée de Terre
BAOR British Army of the Rhine
SAM Surface-to-Air Missile

An ALAT SA 342 Gazelle pops up above the treeline to fire a HOT missile at an armoured target. HOT is a Franco-German heavy anti-tank weapon, tube-launched and wire-guided. It employs automatic command to line-of-sight guidance and infra-red tracking.

Gazelle in service
MAJOR OPERATORS
France
Aviation Légère de l'Armée de Terre

France uses armed and unarmed versions of the Gazelle for a variety of army co-operation and support tasks, including that of the anti-tank role.

1 Régiment d'Hélicoptères de Combat
Base: Phalsbourg
Aircraft: SA 342M (three flights), SA 341F/Canon (one flight), SA 341F (one flight)

2 Régiment d'Hélicoptères de Combat de Corps d'Armée
Base: Friedrichshafen
Aircraft: SA 342M (three flights forming), SA 341F/Canon (one flight)

3 Régiment d'Hélicoptères de Combat
Base: Etain-Rouvres
Aircraft: SA 342M (three flights), SA 341F/Canon (one flight), SA 341F (one flight)

4 Régiment d'Hélicoptères de Commandement, de Manoeuvre et de Soutien
Base: Nancy
Aircraft: SA 341F (one flight)

5 Régiment d'Hélicoptères de Combat
Base: Pau
Aircraft: SA 342M (three flights), SA 341F/Canon (one flight), SA 341F (one flight)

6 Régiment d'Hélicoptères de Combat de Corps d'Armée
Base: Compiègne
Aircraft: SA 342M (three flights forming), SA 341F/Canon (one flight)

7 Régiment d'Hélicoptères de Combat de Corps d'Armée
Base: Nancy
Aircraft: SA 342M (three flights forming), SA 341F/Canon (one flight)

Escadron ALAT du Tchad
Base: N'djamena, Chad
Aircraft: SA 342M, SA 341F

Ecole de Spécialisation
Base: Dax
Aircraft: SA 341F

The French army uses HOT and cannon-armed Gazelles, as well as unarmed aircraft.

United Kingdom

The British Army uses its Gazelles primarily for reconnaissance and communications flying, often in conjunction with armed Lynx helicopters; a few were armed for participation in the Falklands war. The Royal Marines aircraft are used for similar duties. Royal Air Force and Royal Navy Gazelles are used mainly for training.

Army Air Corps

BRITISH ARMY OF THE RHINE (BAOR)

1 Regiment
Base: Hildesheim
Role: Anti-tank/reconnaissance
Units: No. 651 Sqn, No. 652 Sqn (Gazelle, Lynx), No. 661 Sqn (Gazelle only)

3 Regiment
Base: Soest
Role: Anti-tank/reconnaissance
Units: No. 653 Sqn, No. 662 Sqn (Gazelle, Lynx), No. 663 Sqn (Gazelle only)

4 Regiment
Base: Detmold
Role: Anti-tank/reconnaissance
Units: No. 654 Sqn, No. 659 Sqn (Gazelle, Lynx), No. 669 Sqn (Gazelle only)

No. 664 Squadron
Base: Minden
Role: Communications

No. 7 Flight
Base: RAF Gatow, West Berlin

No. 12 Flight
Base: RAF Wildenrath
Role: Communications

UK AND ABROAD

No. 655 Squadron (Gazelle, Lynx)
Base: Aldergrove, Ballykelly
Role: Anti-tank/reconnaissance/communications

No. 656 Squadron (Gazelle, Lynx)
Base: Netheravon
Role: Anti-tank/reconnaissance/communications in support of 1 Brigade UKMF (UK Mobile Force)

No. 657 Squadron (Gazelle, Lynx)
Base: Oakington
Role: Anti-tank/reconnaissance/communications

No. 658 Squadron (Gazelle, Scout)
Base: Netheravon
Role: Anti-tank/reconnaissance/communications in support of 5 Brigade (Airborne) and ACE (Allied Command Europe) Mobile Force

No. 7 Regiment (Gazelle, Agusta A 109)
Base: Netheravon (A 109 detachment at Hereford)
Role: Communications/Special Duties (Gazelles form semi-autonomous unit, No. 2 Flight)

No. 3 Flight
Base: Topcliffe
Role: Communications

No. 25 Flight
Base: Belize
Role: Reconnaissance/communications/support

No. 29 Flight
Base: BATUS (British Army Training Unit, Suffield), Canada
Role: Communications/support

Garrison Air Squadron (Gazelle, Scout)
Base: Port Stanley, Falkland Islands
Role: Anti-tank/reconnaissance/communications

Advanced Rotary Wing Squadron, Army Air Corps Centre
Base: Middle Wallop
Role: Aircrew training

Development and Trials Squadron, Army Air Corps Centre
Base: Middle Wallop
Role: Evaluation of tactics and equipment

Royal Marines

3 Commando Brigade Air Squadron (Gazelle, Lynx)
Base: RNAS Yeovilton
Role: Anti-tank/reconnaissance/support/communications

Royal Air Force

No. 32 Squadron (Gazelle, BAe 125, Andover)
Base: RAF Northolt
Role: VIP transport/communications

No. 2 Flying Training School (Gazelle, Wessex)
Base: RAF Shawbury
Role: Rotary-wing pilot training

Central Flying School (helicopter) Detachment
Base: RAF Shawbury
Role: Instructor training

Gazelle AH.Mk 1s serve at the Army Air Corps Centre at Middle Wallop.

Royal Navy

No. 705 Squadron
Base: RNAS Culdrose (HMS *Seahawk*)
Role: Pilot training

XW855

Left: The Royal Navy uses the Gazelle for basic helicopter pilot training; its Gazelles equip No. 705 Sqn at RNAS Culdrose. The squadron also provides aircrew and helicopters for the Sharks display team.

Above: The Gazelle HCC.Mk 4 is used by No. 32 Sqn for VIP transport duties; three more aircraft have been converted from HT.Mk 3s. Most RAF Gazelles are used by No. 2 FTS at Shawbury for rotary-wing pilot training.

OTHER OPERATORS

Abu Dhabi
Received 10 SA 342Js for training duties at Maqatra from 1982 onwards.

Angola
Purchased six SA 342Ls in 1985.

Burundi
Received two SA 342Ls, armed with 20-mm GIAT M621 cannon, in 1982.

Cameroun
Has four SA 342Ls in use from a 1981-82 delivery, armed with HOTs.

Chad
Received one SA 341H in 1975.

Egypt
Obtained four SA 342Ks, followed by 50 SA 342Ls, including 24 armed with HOT, 12 with 20-mm cannon and 12 with AS.12 ASMs for anti-shipping operations. A further 36 SA 342Ls (24 HOT and 12 cannon) included 30 assembled locally. Further orders are believed to have been placed.

SA 342L

Two SA 342Ls were delivered to the Irish Air Corps for communications, training and support duties.

Eire
Has two SA 342Ls, delivered in 1979 and 1981, in service with the Irish Air Corps.

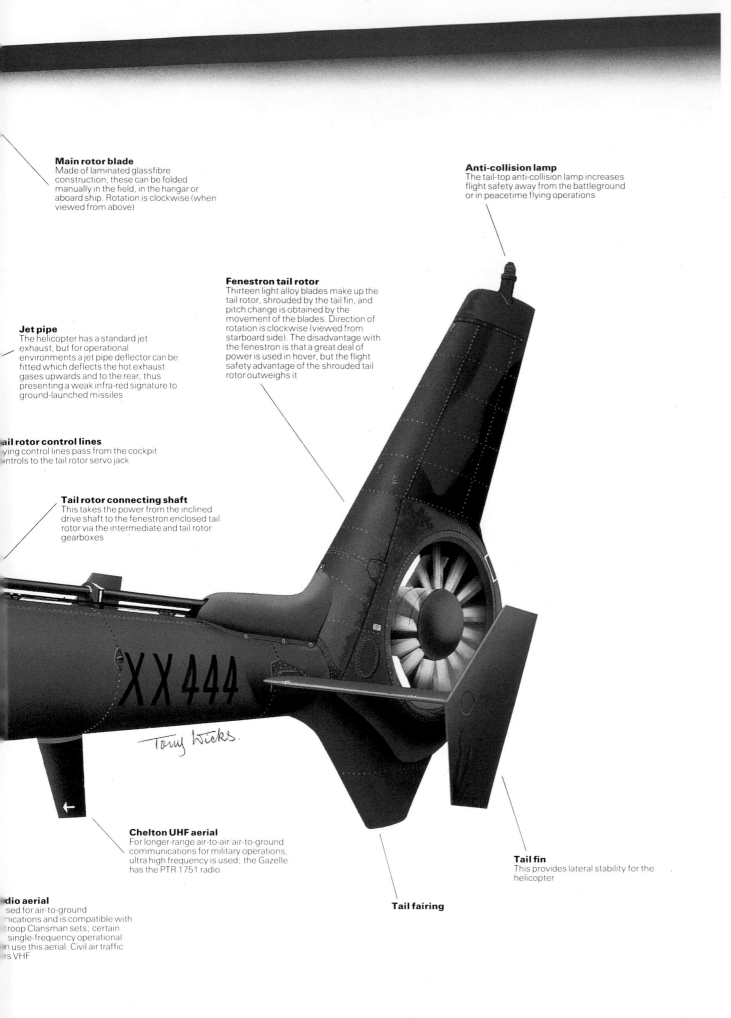

Main rotor blade
Made of laminated glassfibre construction, these can be folded manually in the field, in the hangar or aboard ship. Rotation is clockwise (when viewed from above)

Anti-collision lamp
The tail-top anti-collision lamp increases flight safety away from the battleground or in peacetime flying operations

Fenestron tail rotor
Thirteen light alloy blades make up the tail rotor, shrouded by the tail fin, and pitch change is obtained by the movement of the blades. Direction of rotation is clockwise (viewed from starboard side). The disadvantage with the fenestron is that a great deal of power is used in hover, but the flight safety advantage of the shrouded tail rotor outweighs it

Jet pipe
The helicopter has a standard jet exhaust, but for operational environments a jet pipe deflector can be fitted which deflects the hot exhaust gases upwards and to the rear, thus presenting a weak infra-red signature to ground-launched missiles

ail rotor control lines
ying control lines pass from the cockpit ntrols to the tail rotor servo jack

Tail rotor connecting shaft
This takes the power from the inclined drive shaft to the fenestron enclosed tail rotor via the intermediate and tail rotor gearboxes

XX444

Tony Wicks.

Chelton UHF aerial
For longer-range air-to-air/air-to-ground communications for military operations, ultra high frequency is used; the Gazelle has the PTR 1751 radio

Tail fin
This provides lateral stability for the helicopter

Tail fairing

dio aerial
sed for air-to-ground
nications and is compatible with
roop Clansman sets; certain
single-frequency operational
n use this aerial. Civil air traffic
s VHF

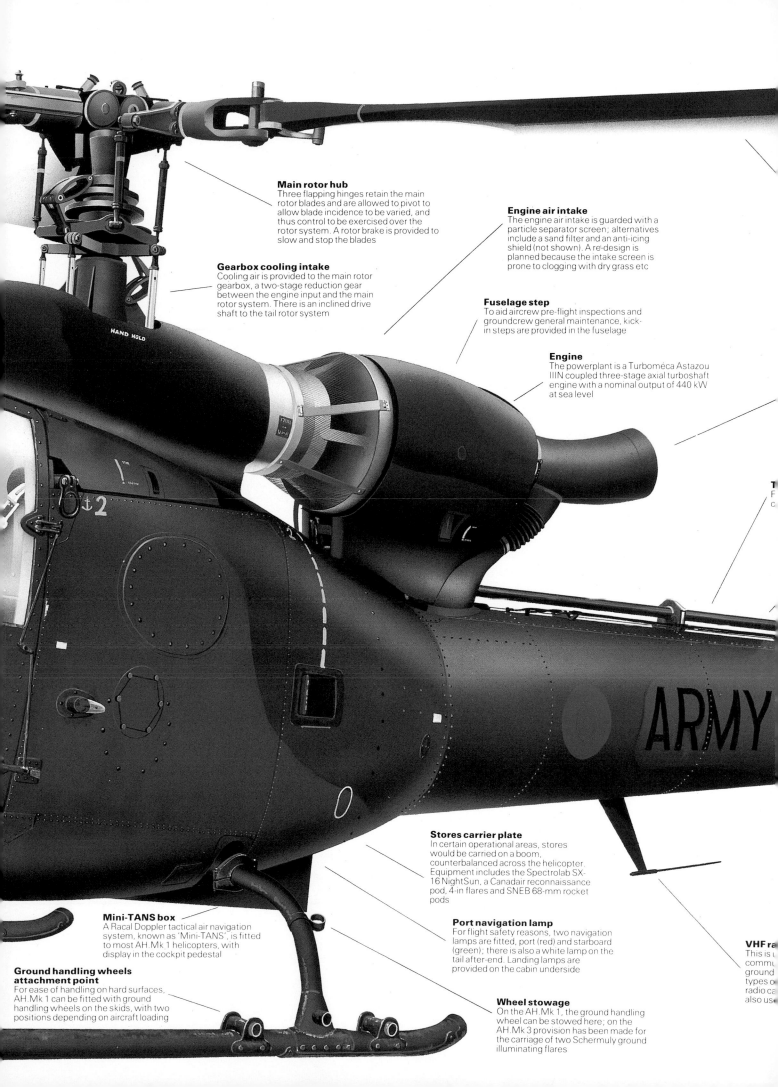

Main rotor hub
Three flapping hinges retain the main rotor blades and are allowed to pivot to allow blade incidence to be varied, and thus control to be exercised over the rotor system. A rotor brake is provided to slow and stop the blades

Engine air intake
The engine air intake is guarded with a particle separator screen; alternatives include a sand filter and an anti-icing shield (not shown). A re-design is planned because the intake screen is prone to clogging with dry grass etc

Gearbox cooling intake
Cooling air is provided to the main rotor gearbox, a two-stage reduction gear between the engine input and the main rotor system. There is an inclined drive shaft to the tail rotor system

Fuselage step
To aid aircrew pre-flight inspections and groundcrew general maintenance, kick-in steps are provided in the fuselage

Engine
The powerplant is a Turboméca Astazou IIIN coupled three-stage axial turboshaft engine with a nominal output of 440 kW at sea level

HAND HOLD

ARMY

Stores carrier plate
In certain operational areas, stores would be carried on a boom, counterbalanced across the helicopter. Equipment includes the Spectrolab SX-16 NightSun, a Canadair reconnaissance pod, 4-in flares and SNEB 68-mm rocket pods

Mini-TANS box
A Racal Doppler tactical air navigation system, known as 'Mini-TANS', is fitted to most AH.Mk 1 helicopters, with display in the cockpit pedestal

Port navigation lamp
For flight safety reasons, two navigation lamps are fitted, port (red) and starboard (green); there is also a white lamp on the tail after-end. Landing lamps are provided on the cabin underside

VHF ra
This is
commu
ground
types o
radio ca
also us

Ground handling wheels attachment point
For ease of handling on hard surfaces, AH.Mk 1 can be fitted with ground handling wheels on the skids, with two positions depending on aircraft loading

Wheel stowage
On the AH.Mk 1, the ground handling wheel can be stowed here; on the AH.Mk 3 provision has been made for the carriage of two Schermuly ground illuminating flares

Gabon
Was assigned five SA 342Ls as part of a French aid package in 1985.

Guinea
Has received a single SA 342.

Iraq
Had received 40 HOT-armed SA 342Ls by the end of 1977 followed by 20 more in 1980-1.

Jordan
Received eight SA 341Hs in 1975-6.

Kenya
Took delivery of one SA 342K.

Kuwait
Has 24 SA 342Ks delivered between 1974 and 1976, half armed with HOTs and half flying in the liaison and observation roles. Further batches of SA 342Ls followed in 1977 and 1983.

Lebanon
Has four SA 342Ls received in 1980. These are equipped to carry SS.11 or SS.12 anti-tank missiles, or a 20-mm cannon.

Libya
Claims to have received 40 Gazelles, but no corroboration is available.

Morocco
Assigned combat roles to 24 SA 342Ls delivered in 1982 with HOT and cannon armament. A further three SA 342Ks and three SA 342Ls were delivered to the Gendarmerie in 1976-7.

A missile-armed Gazelle of the Iraqi a force, which has use the type in the war against Iran. No details have emerge concerning the type war service, howeve

Some of the Gazelles delivered to Kuwait were equipped to carry HOT missiles, while others were delivered unarmed for liaison duties.

Morocco has received a total of 30 Gazelles of various marks, six of them being delivered to the Gendarmerie. The aircraft delivered to the Moroccan air force had HOT and cannon armament.

Gazelle variants

SA 340: two prototypes; first with conventional rotors and T-tail; second fitted with rigid main rotors and fenestron; Astazou II powerplant of 268 kW (360 shp)

SA 341: four pre-production helicopters with enlarged cabin, semi-articulated rotors, 440-kW (590-shp) Astazou III and 1800-kg (3,968-lb) maximum weight

SA 341B: British Army Corps **Gazelle AH.Mk 1**; 212 built

SA 341C: Royal Navy (Fleet Air Arm) **Gazelle HT.Mk 2**; 40 built

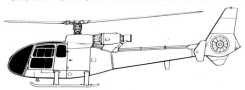

SA 341D: Royal Air Force **Gazelle HT.Mk 3**; 29 built

SA 341E: Royal Air Force **Gazelle HCC.Mk 4** VIP transport; one built (plus three conversions from HT.Mk 3)

SA 341F: French army light aviation model; 170 built; later conversions of 40 to **SA 341M** (HOT) and 62 to **SA 341F/Canon** (20-mm M.621)

SA 341G: initial civilian model, with Astazou III

SA 341H: initial military export model, with Astazou III

SA 342J: uprated civilian model with 640-kW (858-shp) Astazou XIVH and 1900-kg (4,189-lb) maximum weight

SA 342K: uprated military export model

SA 342L: military export model with improved fenestron; current

SA 342L₁ version has Astazou XIVM and 2000-kg (4,409-lb) maximum weight

SA 342M: current production (158 planned) for French army light aviation, with 640-kW (858-shp) Astazou XIVM and HOT ATMs

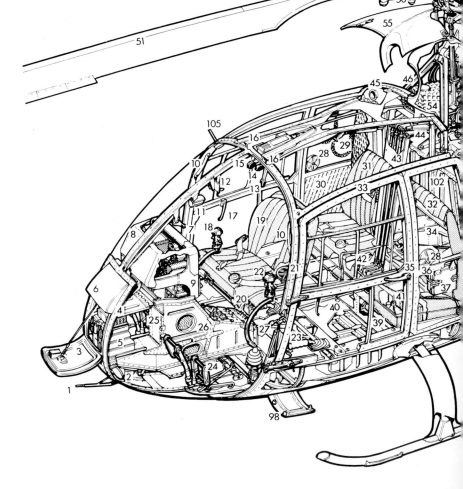

Qatar
has four Gazelles, two Westland-built aircraft being delivered to the Police Air Wing in 1974, and a further pair of SA 342s supplied to the air force from France in 1983.

Qatar
has four Gazelles, two Westland-built aircraft being delivered to the Police Air Wing in 1974, and a further pair of SA 342s supplied to the air force from France in 1983.

Rwanda
received six SA 342Ls, the first four being delivered in mid-1983.

Senegambia
has one SA 341H, delivered to Senegal in 1973.

Syria
accepted delivery of 50 HOT-armed SA 342Ls from 1976, and 5 more were later ordered to replace losses, including several in the 1982 conflict with Israel.

Yugoslavia
has 21 French-built SA 341Hs, supplied in 1973-4, and these were followed by 112 built locally. A licence for production of 100 SA 342Ls was granted in 1982.

Aérospatiale (Westland) SA 341 Gazelle cutaway drawing key

Syria lost a number of its Gazelles during the 1982 war with Israel, at least one being captured and painted in Israeli markings.

1 Pitot head
2 Landing light
3 Battery access panel (open)
4 Circuit breaker panel
5 Battery
6 Cabin ventilating air intake
7 Cabin ventilating air control lever
8 Instrument panel shroud
9 Instrument panel
10 Handgrip (assisting entry/exit)
11 Standby compass
12 Rear view mirror
13 Transmission brake control lever
14 Fuel flow control lever
15 Fuel shut-off lever
16 Cabin heating system ducts
17 Door pull (both forward doors)
18 Pilot's cyclic pitch stick
19 Pilot's seat
20 Collective lever with control box
21 Tail-rotor control cable relay
22 Co-pilot's cyclic pitch stick
23 Co-pilot's collective pitch stick
24 Co-pilot's directional control assembly
25 Pilot's directional control assembly
26 Control pedestal and radio control panel
27 Left hand front door jettison lever
28 Ventilator with rotational adjuster
29 Roof mounted intercom connectors

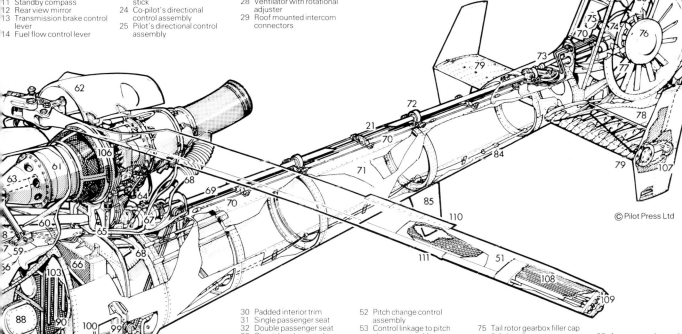

© Pilot Press Ltd

30 Padded interior trim
31 Single passenger seat
32 Double passenger seat
33 Circuit breaker panel
34 Cargo compartment access (seat squab can be raised and seat base/cushion hinged forward into floor recess)
35 Left hand front door
36 Left hand rear door
37 First aid kit stowage (inner face of door)
38 Left hand rear door jettison linkage
39 Hinged passenger seat base/cushion
40 Passenger seat floor recess
41 Dynamotor and transmitter/receiver
42 Mixing unit (rotor controls)
43 Main rotor controls and guard panel
44 Transmission platform main rotor control linkage
45 Stale air extractor duct
46 Main gearbox mounting 'V' strut
47 Engine to main gearbox coupling
48 Main gearbox
49 Main rotor head (semi-articulated)
50 Friction type drag damper
51 Bölkow-type rotor blades
52 Pitch change control assembly
53 Control linkage to pitch change assembly
54 Hydraulic pack (master hydraulic pump)
55 Right hand main gearbox cowling (open for access)
56 Mounting plate damper (main gearbox)
57 Transmission platform
58 Transmission disc-brake
59 Main gearbox mounting rear strut
60 Transmission shaft (main gearbox to intermediate gearbox)
61 Reduction gear housing
62 Starboard engine cowling (open for access)
63 Clutch and free-wheel unit
64 Fuel flow control assembly
65 Engine mounting strut with rubber dampers
66 Oil cooler
67 Intermediate gearbox
68 Oil cooler warm air extraction duct
69 Transmission shaft to tail-rotor gearbox
70 Hydraulic lines to tail-rotor gearbox
71 Tail boom
72 Transmission shaft bearing
73 Tail rotor control rod
74 Tail rotor gearbox
75 Tail rotor gearbox filler cap (lubricant)
76 Tail rotor hub
77 Tail rotor blades
78 Main stabilizer ventral fin
79 Stabilizer/tailplane
80 Tail rotor hub/fairing support strut
81 Tail beacon
82 Upper UHF aerial
83 Navigation light
84 Conduit for tail electronics leads
85 Lower UHF/VHF aerial
86 Securing (anchorage) ring
87 Fuel tank (upper compartment of centre section)
88 Fuel tank access panel
89 Honeycomb sandwich centre section structure
90 Oil cooler compartment air intake mesh grill
91 Distribution box
92 Port side navigation light
93 Landing gear damper (hydraulic)
94 Medical kit container with securing hook
95 Port access panel to cargo compartment
96 Attachment lug for wheel (towing)
97 Landing gear
98 Access panel to under-floor section
99 Foot hold with anti-slip surface (to aid access to cowling/transmission platform)
100 Hand hold (to aid access to cowling/transmission platform)
101 Main stabilizer fin (heavily cambered to offload rotor)
102 Forward bulkhead
103 Aft bulkhead
104 Passenger safety belt anchorage point
105 Air temperature (exterior) gauge
106 Turboméca Astazou III turboshaft
107 Honeycomb and wood end-plate fin structure (metal skinned)
108 Honeycomb structure of main rotor blade(s)
109 Adjustable weights assembly (fine balance dynamically) in tip of each main rotor blade
110 Tab on main lift area of main rotor blade(s)
111 Polyurethane band on leading edge of main rotor blade(s)

Gazelle warload

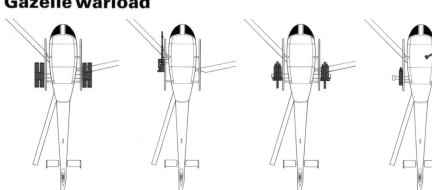

■ 4×Euromissile HOT anti-tank missiles	■ 1×GIAT M.621 20-mm cannon	■ 4×AT-3 'Sagger' ATMs 2×SA-7 'Grail' AAMs	■ 2×Matra SNEB 68-mm rocket pods 1×7.62 GPMG mounted in rear cabin, firing from port door

Anti-tank

Although a third HOT can be fitted to each outrigger pylon, the normal configuration for French army light aviation SA 341Ms and SA 342Ms is a total of four missiles. HOT indicates Haut subsonique Optiquement téléguidé tiré d'un Tube (high subsonic, optically-guided, tube-launched), wire-guided missile with a range of up to 4000 m (4,375 yards) which can penetrate up to 800 mm (31.5 in) of solid armour.

Armed escort

The SA 341F/Canon model of French army light aviation, as well as several export helicopters, is armed with a single GIAT (Groupement Industriel de Armements Terrestres) M.621 cannon mounted to starboard. This fires 100-gram (3.53-oz) projectiles at either 300 or 740 rounds per minute with a muzzle velocity of between 980 and 1030 m (3,215 and 3,379 ft) per second. Light weight (47 kg/104 lb) and low recoil forces make the M.621 an ideal helicopter weapon.

Battlefield multi-role

Yugoslavia is the first to apply two different types of missile simultaneously to the Gazelle. The Soviet-designed AT-3 'Sagger' anti-tank missile is a wire-guided weapon with a range of up to 3000 m (3,280 yards) and capable of penetrating 400 mm (15.75 in) of armour. Two SA-7 'Grails' provide an anti-helicopter capability, this missile having begun its career in the USSR as a hand-held SAM with optical guidance and infra-red terminal homing.

Armed reconnaissance (Falklands)

During the Falklands War a number of No. 3 Commando Brigade Air Squadron Gazelles were armed with SNEB rocket pods and a general-purpose machine-gun. The gun proved inaccurate, but an excellent morale booster, and has been fitted on other occasions. The rocket installation was a more hasty modification, using Chinagraph pencil lines for sighting, and did not prove successful.

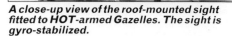

A close-up view of the roof-mounted sight fitted to HOT-armed Gazelles. The sight is gyro-stabilized.

An Aérospatiale-operated Gazelle demonstrator fires a HOT tube-launched, wire guided missile.

Specification: SA 342M Gazelle

Rotors
Main rotor diameter	10.50 m	(34 ft 5.4 in)
Tail rotor diameter	0.695 m	(2 ft 3.4 in)
Main rotor disc area	86.59 m²	(932.08 sq ft)

Fuselage and tail unit
Accommodation	pilot, observer and (liaison role only) up to three passengers	
Length overall	11.97 m	(39 ft 3.3 in)
Length of fuselage	9.53 m	(31 ft 3.2 in)
Height overall	3.19 m	(10 ft 5.6 in)

Landing gear
Fixed twin-skid landing gear		
Skid track	2.015 m	(6 ft 7.3 in)

Weights
Empty	991 kg	(2,184 lb)
Maximum take-off	1900 kg	(4,188 lb)
Internal fuel load	425 litres	(937 lb)

Powerplant
One Turboméca Astazou XIVM turboshaft		
Maximum rating	604 kW	(858 shp)

Gazelle recognition features

Small tailplane with angular end-plates

Large three-bladed main rotor

Long, streamlined 'raindrop' cockpit canopy with large side doors

Flimsy-looking twin-skid landing gear

Fully enclosed fenestron tail rotor

Long, narrow tail boom

Armament carried on stub pylons on fuselage sides

Performance:

Maximum cruising speed at sea level	140 kts	(260 km/h; 161 mph)
Service ceiling	13,450 ft	(4100 m)
Maximum range	710 km	(440 miles)
Initial rate of climb	1,535 ft	(468 m) per minute

Maximum external load
- Westland AH.Mk 1 Lynx 1,360 kg
- Aérospatiale SA 316B Alouette III 750 kg
- Aérospatiale SA 342L Gazelle 700 kg
- Westland AH.Mk 1 Scout 680 kg
- Hughes 500MD Defender 550 kg
- Messerschmitt-Bölkow-Blohm BO 105 CB 500 kg
- Bell OH-58A Kiowa 400 kg E

Maximum rate of climb
- Aérospatiale SA 342L Gazelle 2,010 ft per minute
- Bell OH-58A Kiowa 1,780 ft per minute
- Westland AH.Mk 1 Lynx 1,760 ft per minute
- Westland AH.Mk 1 Scout 1,670 ft per minute
- Hughes 500MD Defender 1,650 ft per minute
- Messerschmitt-Bölkow-Blohm BO 105 CB 1,375 ft per minute
- Aérospatiale SA 316B Alouette III 850 ft per minute

Speed at high altitude
- Aérospatiale SA 342L Gazelle 142 kts
- Westland AH.Mk 1 Lynx 140 kts
- Messerschmitt-Bölkow-Blohm BO 105 CB 130 kts
- Bell OH-58A Kiowa 120 kts
- Hughes 500MD Defender 119 kts
- Westland AH.Mk 1 Scout 114 kts
- Aérospatiale SA 316B Alouette III 113 kts

Range at optimum altitude
- Messerschmitt-Bölkow-Blohm BO 105 CB 657 km
- Westland AH.Mk 1 Lynx 630 km
- Westland AH.Mk 1 Scout 510 km
- Bell OH-58A Kiowa 481 km
- Aérospatiale SA 316B Alouette III 480 km
- Hughes 500MD Defender 428 km
- Aérospatiale SA 342L Gazelle 360 km

Maximum number of passengers
- Westland AH.Mk 1 Lynx 10
- Hughes 500MD Defender 6
- Aérospatiale SA 316B Alouette III 6
- Aérospatiale SA 342L Gazelle 4
- Westland AH.Mk 1 Scout 4
- Messerschmitt-Bölkow-Blohm BO 105 CB 4
- Bell OH-58A Kiowa 3

The MBB
BO 105

MBB BO 105:
Battlefield Bantamweight

The Messerschmitt-Bölkow-Blohm BO 105 has been one of Germany's most successful aircraft programmes, with almost 1,000 helicopters exported to 34 countries. Small, highly manoeuvrable, reliable and fast, the BO 105 has proved to be a useful general-purpose light helicopter.

A BO 105 demonstrator carries a load of eight TOW anti-tank missiles, equipped with a stabilized roof-mounted sight above the left hand seat and a sophisticated Doppler navigation system. TOW-equipped BO 105s are in service with Sweden.

Providing front-line defence against Warsaw Pact penetration of West Germany's borders with East Germany and Czechoslovakia, the BO 105P anti-tank helicopter is a key element in the defence of the NATO Central Region. Carefully controlled numbers of the helicopter have been exported, and several nations have undertaken licence production of West Germany's first commercially successful helicopter.

After World War II the Messerschmitt company amalgamated with the Bölkow und Hamburger Flugzeugbau GmbH to form Messerschmitt-Bölkow-Blohm GmbH, known now throughout the world as MBB. The company started the development of its own helicopter line in the early 1960s, and designed the BO 102 non-flying trainer helicopter for the embryo Heeresflieger (West German army aviation). This work led to the BO 103 prototype and the cancelled BO 104 two-seat observation helicopter.

The BO 105 was initially a civil helicopter development for a multiple array of tasks, and designed with twin-engined safety in mind. At the same time, the Bundeswehr (West German armed forces) defined a replacement for its Aérospatiale Alouette II liaison and scout helicopters, which had been delivered when the Heeresflieger was formed in 1956. Moreover, given the growing threat posed by the imbalance of tank forces (in favour of the Warsaw Pact) ranged on each side of the inner German border, the Bundes-

This Colombian navy BO 105CB, pictured before delivery, is equipped with a search radar in its streamlined nose, and is fitted with flotation bags on the skids. Several Latin American navies use the BO 105, from ships and from shore bases.

wehr decided to develop a helicopter which could carry anti-tank missiles.

The first flight of the BO 105 V2 took place on 16 February 1967, the type being powered by two 280-kW (375-shp) Allison 250-C18 turboshaft engines and reportedly using the three-blade main rotor system of the Westland Scout. Despite the destruction of the first prototype (BO 105 V1) during ground tests, the helicopter was obviously worth further development. The type was tested against contemporary designs, and in 1974 the BO 105 was selected as a scout helicopter (designated BO 105M or VBH) and in 1975 as an anti-tank helicopter (BO 105P or PAH-1).

Development work on the PAH-1 got under way in 1977, with the Allison 250-C20B powerplant selected to give a maximum take-off power of 313 kW (420 shp) per engine through a main rotor transmission from ZF Germany.

Although a relatively small aircraft, the BO 105P has a maximum gross weight of 2400 kg (5,291 lb) and its operational role is envisaged as the carriage of six Euromissile HOT anti-tank missiles, which have SACLOS wire-guidance, to engage tanks at ranges from 1500 to 4000 m (1,640 to 4,375 yards) using the direct-view-optics APX M397 stabilized daylight-only sight manufactured by SFIM. The sight is mounted on the port side of the cabin roof and operated by the helicopter's commander; the missile selector is positioned on the port door surround, and the aiming selector is mounted on the right side of the operator, who uses a folding arm rest. The SFIM sight is used for observation, detection, acquisition and identification of the target as well as for target tracking. The sight has two field

of view options: ×3.2 magnification for observation and acquisition, and ×10.8 for target tracking. The sight is linked to an IR localizer which measures the individual missile deviation relative to the optical axis and line-of-sight. The actual manual tracking of the missile and tank is a feat for a well-trained operator, even with the HOT-1's relatively slow velocity of 240 m (787 ft) per second. There is now an improved HOT-2, which began firing trials with the Heeresflieger in April 1986, and this variant is faster and more lethal.

Doppler navigation is provided by the SEL ASN-128 system, whose keyboard and display are mounted on the central cockpit console. Future improvements include a lighter fire-control system (the current model is developed from that of the Leopard 1 main battle tank), an uprated engine (including a better combustion chamber) and a laser rangefinder module for the sight. Eventually the sight will be night capable and the instruments compatible with night-vision goggles.

Improved reliability

The needs of the military helicopter are more exacting than those of civil counterparts, and both the PAH-1 and the unarmed VBH have special features which allow for more time between overhauls and 'on condition' maintenance. In addition, for the military user MBB has developed reinforced transmission and rotor components, and an improved tail rotor design, the object being reliability rather than survivability. The increase in the provision of tail rotor authority is vital because the tactical performance of the PAH-1 is linked to extended times hovering in amongst the trees in an ambush or fire position; the helicopter must also remain within the HOT missile firing constraints during the maximum 17 seconds time of flight of the missile to the target.

Three types of BO 105 have been delivered to the Spanish army aviation (FAMET) for service as scout/observation helicopters, anti-tank missile carriers and close support gunships. All three types were manufactured under licence from MBB by Construcciones Aeronauticas SA (CASA) at Madrid. The scout/observation version is basically similar to the Heeresflieger's VBH, but has a different radio fit. The BO 105ATH is equipped with the

HOT missile and SFIM sight like its German counterpart. The most unusual variant is the BO 105GSH which uses the Rheinmetall MK 20 Rh 202 20-mm cannon in an under-fuselage mounting requiring the adoption of high skid landing gear. The GSH variant has a wartime role of close escort and support of both the anti-tank and the troop-helicopters operated by FAMET. The task also includes 'riding shotgun' for the service's Boeing Vertol Chinook unit.

Sweden has also adopted the standard-production BO 105CB as its anti-tank helicopter, but has opted for the Saab-Emerson HeliTOW missile system to arm the 20 anti-tank helicopters ordered in late 1984. The first deliveries are to be made in December 1986, with the first unit forming by July 1987. The Saab-Emerson system uses the tried and tested Hughes Aircraft Company TOW anti-tank missile but links it to one of the Saab-Pilkington Helios family of direct-view optical sights.

A number of other countries have acquired the BO 105 helicopter in the past 15 years, but all have adopted versions for scouting, observation, patrol and training duties. An early customer was the Royal Netherlands air force, which operates about 30 of the original 105C version, powered by two 298-kW (400-shp) Allison 250-C20 turboshafts. These helicopters are about to undergo a major update programme, although it is not clear at present if they will be armed with HOT missiles as an interim measure pending introduction of the Dutch army's anti-tank helicopter force in the mid-1990s. Operational maintenance of the Dutch BO 105Cs is pooled with that of the West German police, which also operates the type. Three BO 105Cs are also used for light transport by the Peruvian air force, and the first model assembled in Chile was displayed to the world at FIDA '86 in March 1986. Chilean BO 105s are also used by the Carabinieros (military police) for fast response ambulance work.

The Chilean-assembled helicopters will be used for SAR, which is another role carried out by several nations using the BO 105. Typical are the Nigerian air force, which reportedly has 24 still in service, and the Swedish air force, which has taken delivery of four BO 105CBS SAR helicopters.

South American navies have also put the BO 105 to sea. In 1973 MBB began extensive rolling-platform tests with a company demonstrator helicopter at RAE Bedford, England, to prove the design was capable of taking the rolling environment of a ship's flight deck at ±10°. The inherent handling qualities of the rigid rotor make the helicopter easier to control in such conditions than a more conventional type. Tests were carried out in the North Sea with vessels as small as 175 tonnes. The result of the tests was certification of the BO 105 for maritime operations in sea conditions up to sea state 4, with the ship pitching ±3.5° and rolling ±5°.

The Mexican navy has taken delivery of six BO 105CB helicopters for use aboard coastal and fisheries protection corvettes and a further six helicopters were ordered in September 1985 for use ashore. The Mexican helicopters are fitted with nose-

mounted search radar and a rescue winch. A typical SAR mission lasts about 3 hours, and a standard profile comprises a 160-km (100-mile) transit at 1,500 ft (457 m) to a search area, followed by a 30-minute search and rescue operation (including winching), and then by the return to the parent ship with two survivors and a 30-minute fuel reserve available.

When first forming a national naval air arm in the early 1980s, the Colombian government looked at its peculiar two-ocean naval force and decided to opt for a maritime reconnaissance/liaison helicopter which could be operated ashore or from the flight deck of small naval craft. After some consideration the BO 105CB was selected for the task and two helicopters were ordered, with a pilot and groundcrew training package developed by MBB in West Germany. The sort of mission profile envisaged by the Colombian navy is maritime reconnaissance at best endurance speed, flying at 1,500 ft and lasting about 3.9 hours (with a 30-minute fuel reserve at the return in case of a fouled deck). MBB has produced a long-range auxiliary fuel tank which can fitted in place of the rear seat assembly, giving a mission take-off weight of 2300 kg (5,071 lb) including a crew of two (pilot and maritime observer).

Naval uses have been incorporated into the mission profile of BO 105s manufactured under licence in Indonesia under the designation NBO 105 by IPTN Indonesian Aircraft Industry (formerly PT Nurtanio). The NBO 105s are used for navy, air force and army liaison, and for training and transport tasks, and the type is also in service with the gendarmerie, forestry service and national SAR or-

This 'Giraffe'-camouflaged BO 105 is an MBB-operated demonstrator, equipped with an Ophelia mast-mounted sight. These allow helicopters to stay low even during missile launch, perhaps behind a screen of trees.

ganization.

Another Far Eastern licensee (where production has now been completed) is the Philippine Aircraft Development Corporation (PADC) which has been involved in military assembly of the helicopter for the Philippine armed forces.

To the west of the Philippines, the Brunei Defence Force has operated six BO 105C models on liaison and paramilitary tasks for some years. It is understood that the Sultan was so impressed with the helicopter that he ordered one of the larger BO 105CBS helicopters for his own personal use.

Special missions

There is a wide variety of special mission equipment which can be fitted to the BO 105 series in addition to the TOW, HeliTOW and HOT anti-tank missile systems already mentioned. The MPDS has been specially developed for the BO 105 and it features a variety of external store possibilities. Amongst the weapons which can be fitted are unguided folding-fin rockets from 50-mm to 81-mm (2-in to 3.2-in) calibre, machine-gun pods from 7.62-mm to 12.7-mm (0.3-in to 0.5-in) calibre, and cannon. Other equipment includes the Spectrolab Nightsun search-

Spain operates both missile- and gun-armed versions of the BO 105, and an unarmed variant is used for observation and reconnaissance. The gunship version is used to escort support helicopters and anti-tank BO 105s.

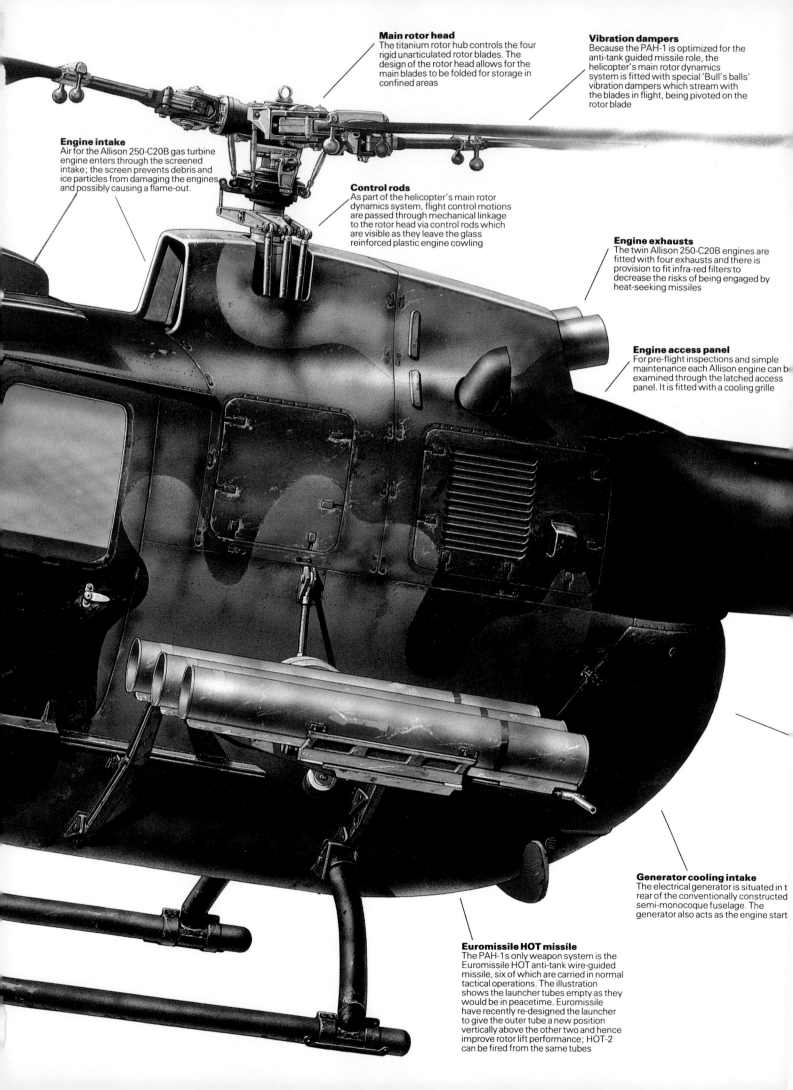

Main rotor head
The titanium rotor hub controls the four rigid unarticulated rotor blades. The design of the rotor head allows for the main blades to be folded for storage in confined areas

Vibration dampers
Because the PAH-1 is optimized for the anti-tank guided missile role, the helicopter's main rotor dynamics system is fitted with special 'Bull's balls' vibration dampers which stream with the blades in flight, being pivoted on the rotor blade

Engine intake
Air for the Allison 250-C20B gas turbine engine enters through the screened intake; the screen prevents debris and ice particles from damaging the engines and possibly causing a flame-out.

Control rods
As part of the helicopter's main rotor dynamics system, flight control motions are passed through mechanical linkage to the rotor head via control rods which are visible as they leave the glass reinforced plastic engine cowling

Engine exhausts
The twin Allison 250-C20B engines are fitted with four exhausts and there is provision to fit infra-red filters to decrease the risks of being engaged by heat-seeking missiles

Engine access panel
For pre-flight inspections and simple maintenance each Allison engine can be examined through the latched access panel. It is fitted with a cooling grille

Generator cooling intake
The electrical generator is situated in the rear of the conventionally constructed semi-monocoque fuselage. The generator also acts as the engine start

Euromissile HOT missile
The PAH-1s only weapon system is the Euromissile HOT anti-tank wire-guided missile, six of which are carried in normal tactical operations. The illustration shows the launcher tubes empty as they would be in peacetime. Euromissile have recently re-designed the launcher to give the outer tube a new position vertically above the other two and hence improve rotor lift performance; HOT-2 can be fired from the same tubes

Pilot
Sitting in the right-hand seat, the pilot of the PAH-1 can be a junior officer but is more likely to be a non-commissioned officer. His role is to manoeuvre the helicopter tactically but safely, especially keeping the machine in a tactical position during missile engagement and subsequent 'bug-out'

SFIM APX M397 sight
The direct view optical sight of the PAH-1 is manufactured by SFIM in France, with certain Federal German sub-components. The sight is used to locate, identify, track and engage enemy armoured targets, using a line-of-sight commander system which allows minimal course changes to the HOT missile to be calculated and transmitted to the missile via the wire command link. It is daylight-capable only

Main cabin door
The main cabin door slides aft for access. The PAH-1's cabin has been designed to accommodate two pilots for regular tactical operations and only one folding spare seat is fitted. There is space however for the Talissi laser missile simulator control panels, used for certain pre-live firing training exercises

Aircraft commander
All PAH-1 helicopters have the aircraft commander sitting in the port seat with control of the sight and the HOT missile system firing controls; from this position he can also attend to the radios and navigation systems. There are dual controls

Battery access
For ground operations, external power is plugged into the electrical system; in flight the electrical system is powered by a generator and for stand-alone operations the battery provides systems power

HOT firing controls
Specially-designed fold-down arms for the HOT missile system have been incorporated behind the two pilots, and on the port side of the cabin is the missile firing selection switch, attached to the cabin door post

Landing lamp housing
For night and foul-weather operations, the helicopter is fitted with a high luminance landing lamp which can be used for identification and flight safety during airfield circuit

Cabin air intake
To provide the aircrew with outside air ventilation, a regulated underfuselage duct is fitted to the BO 105. There is also an engine-linked warm air system for winter operations

Anti-collision light
As part of the ground and flight safety regime for peacetime air operations, the PAH-1 is fitted with orange anti-collision lamps, including this underfuselage light. At all times when the engine is running, the lamp is illuminated unless the helicopter is acting tactically during an exercise

Landing gear skid
For tactical operations, the PAH-1 is fitted with skids; in addition to being stressed for heavy landings, the skids are relatively light. There is no provision for ground handling wheels, as the German airfields have specially designed carts

light (with an IR fitting for use with night-vision goggles), FLIR sensor pods and reconnaissance cameras.

Airframe fixed equipment for the MPDS include symmetrical fittings on each side of the fuselage, and weapons can be launched or released using a trigger mounted in the left- and/or right-hand cyclic stick. Detachable fittings for MPDS include the multi-purpose pylon arrangement with its emergency release unit, and a sight support for the pilot (right-hand side) mounted to the frame of the cockpit to carry an optical reflex sight (or Mono-HUD such as those manufactured by Thomson-CSF and GEC Avionics). The system requires special airframe electrical connectors and vibration dampers ('bull's balls') fitted to the main rotor blade roots.

There exists an option for the helicopter to be fitted with naval weapon systems for the anti-submarine and anti-surface vessel warfare role. For ASW, special systems have been perfected to allow for the use of a Crouzet, Texas Instruments or CAE Electronics MAD for area detection of large submarines, and such equipment is used in conjunction with smoke marker floats. A dipping sonar has yet to be fitted to the BO 105, although trials are currently under way for a lightweight system with an operator's panel inside the cockpit. Active and passive sonobuoys can be dropped from the helicopter, but there is no provision for an onboard processor as a result of weight and space considerations. For offensive ASW operations MBB has designed a torpedo delivery system to carry one or two lightweight ASW torpedoes such as the Whitehead Motofides A 244/S system developed for the Italian navy.

Advanced cockpit

The BO 105 has been extensively tested by MBB and the West German development agency to improve the potential of advanced cockpits, visual aids and navigation systems for updates and even future helicopter designs. The company has sponsored a number of programmes to improve the helicopter and develop new systems for its use. There is considerable market potential in certifying a helicopter with an assortment of weapons, hence the programme to certificate the BO 105 for the TOW anti-tank missile using the British Aerospace TRS.

Another sighting system which has been tested in the BO 105 is the SFIM-developed Ophelia MMS, which uses the main rotor mast as a base. A BO 105 with this equipment could be used for reconnaissance, scouting, observation, fire control, anti-tank missile, border patrol and other related roles because the system provides an unrestricted 360° view without extensive structural modification to the fuselage; the required modification of the rotor head is minimal. The use of the MMS with its line-of-sight some 1.1 m (3.6 ft) above the rotor disc allows for observation from the heli-

copter whilst it remains masked behind cover with only the low-profile optics ball above the cover. For night and adverse-weather operations, the MMS would be fitted with a thermal imaging package, FLIR or LLLTV. The thermal image can be displayed inside the helicopter as a head-up image or on a cockpit/mission management system such as the Racal RAMS.

Besides the mast-mounted and cabin roof systems already mentioned, MBB has undertaken trials with nose-mounted sensor systems, including the Martin Marietta PNVS, a slaved gimbal mounting which displays in a helmet-mounted system, thus allowing the pilot to move his head towards a target and see the image even in darkness or fog conditions. The helmet CRT display receives the signals of the outside world's image via electro-optical sensors. MBB's Dynamic Division has developed its own PISA system, which consists of a wide-angle sensor providing night vision capability for orientation and observation purposes. The system depends on an infra-red thermal imager with Sprite detectors, a single-axis steering mechanism for azimuth, a symbol generator and a display panel for the cockpit console.

The variety of mission packages available for the BO 105 makes it one of the

Heeresflieger BO 105Ms demonstrate nap-of-the-earth flying, using a riverbank to provide a degree of terrain-masking. One hundred of these light observation helicopters have been delivered to replace the elderly Alouette IIs previously used.

most versatile combat helicopters on the market and in service. It is probable that the type will continue in production until at least the end of the decade, and with some of the updating equipment mentioned above will remain viable into the 21st century.

Glossary

ASW Anti-Submarine Warfare
CRT Cathode Ray Tube
FLIR Forward-Looking Infra-Red
IR Infra-Red
LLLTV Low-Light-Level TV
MAD Magnetic Anomaly Detection
MMS Mast-Mounted Sight
MPDS Multi-Purpose Delivery System
NVG Night Vision Goggles
Ophelia Optique Plateforme HELIcoptère Allemand (German helicopter optical platform)
PAH PanzerAbwehrHubschrauber (anti-tank helicopter)
PISA Pilot's Infra-red Sighting Ability
PNVS Pilot's Night Vision Sensor
RAE Royal Aircraft Establishment
SACLOS Semi-Automatic Command to Line Of Sight
SAR Search And Rescue
TRS TOW Roof Sight
VBH VerBindungsHubschrauber (liaison helicopter)

A Heeresflieger BO 105P (PAH-1) is seen armed with six Euromissile HOT anti-tank missiles, showing off its stabilized roof sight. Two hundred and twelve PAH-1s have been delivered to the German army.

BO 105 in service

Royal Brunei Armed Forces Air Wing

No. 2 Squadron, based at Brunei airport, uses half a dozen gun- and rocket-armed MBB BO 105Cs. A further BO 105CBS is operated, alongside a Sikorsky S-76, for VIP use, mainly by the Sultan himself. The BO 105Cs are serialled from AMDB-123 to AMDB-128.

Canadian Coast Guard/Garde Cotière Canadienne

The Coast Guard operates a small fleet of civil-registered BO 105CBs. Further deliveries are possible from a Canadian production line, to be set up at Fort Erie.

Ciskei Defence Force

The Ciskei Defence Force is thought to operate two BO 105Cs and a single VIP MBB BK117.

Chilean air force (Fuerza Aerea de Chile)

The paramilitary police force was the first Chilean operator of the BO 105, operating six BO 105Cs serialled between C-9 and C-14 and a BO 105S serialled C-15, but further aircraft have been ordered for the air force, army and navy. A proposed narrow-fuselaged gunship version was revealed in mock-up form at the recent FIDA 86 exhibition.

Colombian navy (Armarda de Colombia)

BO 105LSs are used by Colombia's embryonic naval air arm for ASW and SAR duties from its frigates

German Army Aviation (Heeresflieger)

100 BO 105Ms were delivered to the Heeresflieger as Alouette II replacements, for light observation and liaison duties. Procurement of a further 212 BO 105Ps (PAH-1) have been delivered for anti-tank duties. They are equipped with a stabilized roof-mounted sight, HOT missiles and an improved Tactical Navigation System. Each of Germany's three corps has an aviation command with three helicopter regiments, one equipped with the PAH-1. Every regiment comprises three Staffeln. Each division has a liaison company, equipped with the BO 105M. The Border Guard operates four BO 105s, as do many Federal Police and Medevac organizations.

Indonesian National Armed Forces (Tentara Nasional Indonesia)

The surviving BO 105Cs from the 16 German-built machines originally procured (HH-1501 to HH-1516) have been supplemented in air force service by Nurtanio-built NB-105s (including HS-7051). Further indigenous machines are in service with the army, navy and police.

Iraqi air force (Al Quwwat al Jawwiya al Iraqiya)

20 BO 105Ps armed with unidentified anti-tank missiles are under construction for this air arm by CASA in Spain. None are believed to have yet entered front-line service.

Mexican Navy (Aviación de la Armada de Mexico)

Six ship-based BO 105s are used for maritime patrol, fishery protection and anti-smuggling duties from 'Halcon' class corvettes.

Royal Netherlands air force, light aircraft group

(Koninklijke Luchtmacht Groep Lichte Vliegtuigen)

The survivors of 32 BO 105Cs delivered remain in service with No. 298 Squadron at Soesterberg and No. 299 Squadron at Deelen; they are serialled between B-37 and B-80. Five civil-registered BO 105Cs (PH-RPR, S, U, V, and W) serve with the Rijkspolitie (State Police).

The Brunei defence force operates six BO 105Cs for various military duties, while a single BO 105CBS is used by the Sultan as a personal VIP transport.

The BO 105 is being assembled in Chile for use by civilian and military customers, including the police. A single-pilot gunship conversion has been mooted.

The Heeresflieger operates 100 BO 105Ms for light observation duties and 212 BO 105Ps, with HOT missiles and roof-mounted sights, in the anti-tank role

The Dutch army uses 29 BO 105s, largely in the light observation role. They augment a larger force of Alouette IIIs.

Federal Nigerian air force

Four BO 105Cs, serialled 500-503, have been supplemented by 20 BO 105Ds serialled from 504 to 523.

The cockpit of the BO 105 is compact and well laid out, with all essential flight and engine instruments on the T-shaped panel, along with navigational aids and weapons controls where appropriate. Full dual controls are fitted as standard, with standard left-handed combined collective pitch/throttle levers and a cyclic pitch stick. Rudder pedals control the pitch, and therefore the thrust, of the tail rotor. All-round view from the well-glazed bubble cockpit is superb.

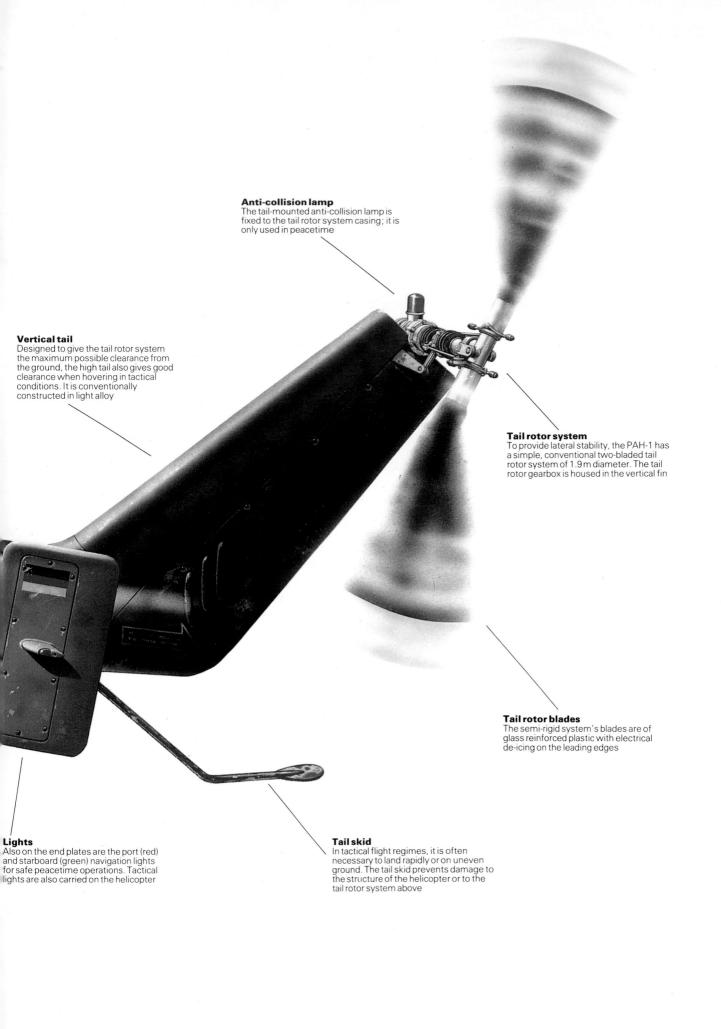

Anti-collision lamp
The tail-mounted anti-collision lamp is
fixed to the tail rotor system casing; it is
only used in peacetime

Vertical tail
Designed to give the tail rotor system
the maximum possible clearance from
the ground, the high tail also gives good
clearance when hovering in tactical
conditions. It is conventionally
constructed in light alloy

Tail rotor system
To provide lateral stability, the PAH-1 has
a simple, conventional two-bladed tail
rotor system of 1.9m diameter. The tail
rotor gearbox is housed in the vertical fin

Tail rotor blades
The semi-rigid system's blades are of
glass reinforced plastic with electrical
de-icing on the leading edges

Lights
Also on the end plates are the port (red)
and starboard (green) navigation lights
for safe peacetime operations. Tactical
lights are also carried on the helicopter

Tail skid
In tactical flight regimes, it is often
necessary to land rapidly or on uneven
ground. The tail skid prevents damage to
the structure of the helicopter or to the
tail rotor system above

Main rotor blades
The PAH-1 is fitted with four glass fibre reinforced plastic main rotor blades which give a main rotor diameter of 9.82 m. A rotor brake is fitted to the PAH-1 and blades have the WMI electrical de-icing system on the leading edge

Tail boom
The light alloy, semi-monocoque tail boom contains the tail rotor shaft, with its gearbox assembly at the end, at the base of the tail fin. the PAH-1/BO 105P tail boom is on a design modified from the original civil version

Stabilizer
Built of conventional light alloys, the horizontal stabilizer is fitted with end plates which carry HF/FM radio aerials for tactical communications

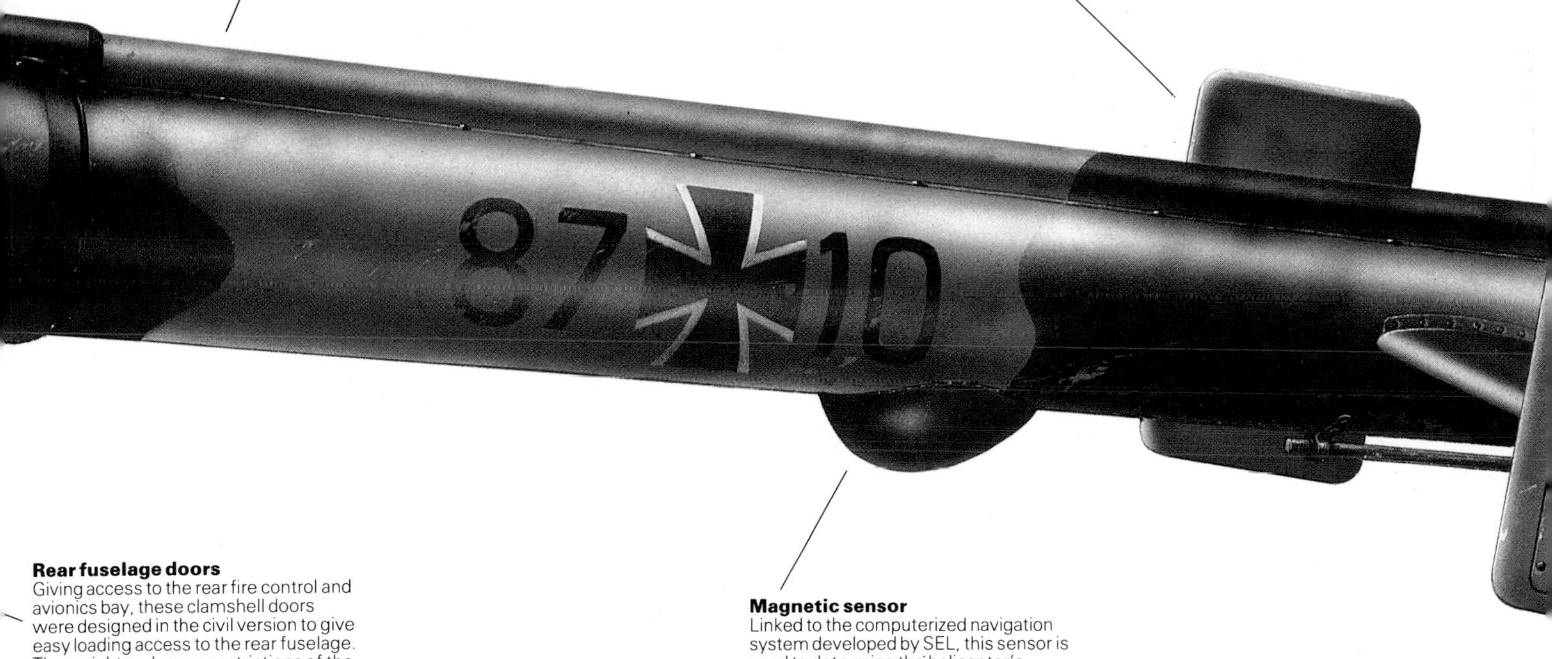

Rear fuselage doors
Giving access to the rear fire control and avionics bay, these clamshell doors were designed in the civil version to give easy loading access to the rear fuselage. The weight and space restrictions of the fire control system in the PAH-1 mean that no stores may be carried here

Magnetic sensor
Linked to the computerized navigation system developed by SEL, this sensor is used to determine the helicopter's position in relation to the Earth's magnetic field. The SEL tactical navigation system's display is situated in the cockpit

Messerschmitt-Bölkow-Blohm BO 105P (PAH-1)
6th Regiment
West German Army Aviation (Heeresflieger)

Peru

Three were delivered in the early 1980s presumably for liaison and police support duties.

Philippine air force

(Hukbong Himpapawid ng Pilipinas)
Ten BO 105Cs are in use for liaison duties. A further six serve in support of the army, and two serve with the navy, which passed on two aircraft to the paramilitary police force.

Republic of Sierra Leone Military Forces Air Wing

MBB BO 105C GS-A-1 is the sole military aircraft in use in the republic

Spanish Army Aviation

(Fuerzas Aeromoviles del Ejercito de Tierra)
The Batallon de Ataque at Ciudad Real operates a company of 28 HOT-armed CASA-built BO 105s in the anti-tank role and 18 cannon-armed aircraft for armed reconnaissance. A further 14 of these versatile helicopters are used for training and light observation duties.

Swedish air force (Flygvapen)

Four SAR-configured BO 105 CBSs (local designation HKP-9B) have been delivered to F6 at Karlsborg and F7 at Satenas for IFR SAR duties.

Swedish army air corps (Armeflygkar)

20 BO 105 CBs equipped with Saab/Emerson HeliTOW missile systems and sophisticated night sights, are being delivered to the army for anti-tank duties.

This FAMET BO 105GSH carries a 20-mm cannon under the fuselage. Observation and anti-tank variants are also used by FAMET.

One of four BO 105CBS helicopters delivered to the Flygvapen for SAR duties. A further 20 BO 105CBs are being delivered to the army for use in the anti-tank role.

Specification: MBB BO 105P (PAH-1)

Rotors

Main rotor diameter	9.84 m	(32 ft 3.4 in)
Tail rotor diameter	1.90 m	(6 ft 2.8 in)
Main rotor disc area	76.05 m²	(818.62 sq ft)

Fuselage and tail unit

Accommodation	two flightcrew and one passenger	
Length overall, rotors turning	11.86 m	(38 ft 10.9 in)
Length excluding main rotor	8.56 m	(28 ft 1 in)
Height overall, to top of rotor mast	3.00 m	(9 ft 10.1 in)

Landing gear

Two non-retractable tubular skids		
Skid track	2.53 m	(8 ft 3.6 in)

Weights

Empty	1673 kg	(3,688 lb)
Maximum take-off	2400 kg	(5,291 lb)
Useful load	691 kg	(1,523 lb)
Usable fuel load	294 kg	(648 lb)

Powerplant

Two Allison 250-C20B turboshafts		
Rating, take-off (each)	313 kW	(420 shp)
Rating, maximum continuous (each)	298 kW	(400 shp)

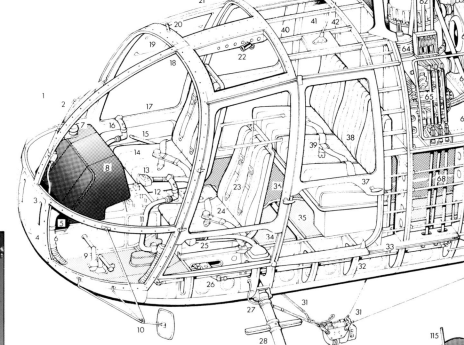

The BO 105 prototype was originally fitted with the main rotors and rotor head of a Westland Scout, but this soon gave way to a purpose-designed four-bladed main rotor with a rigid, hingeless titanium head.

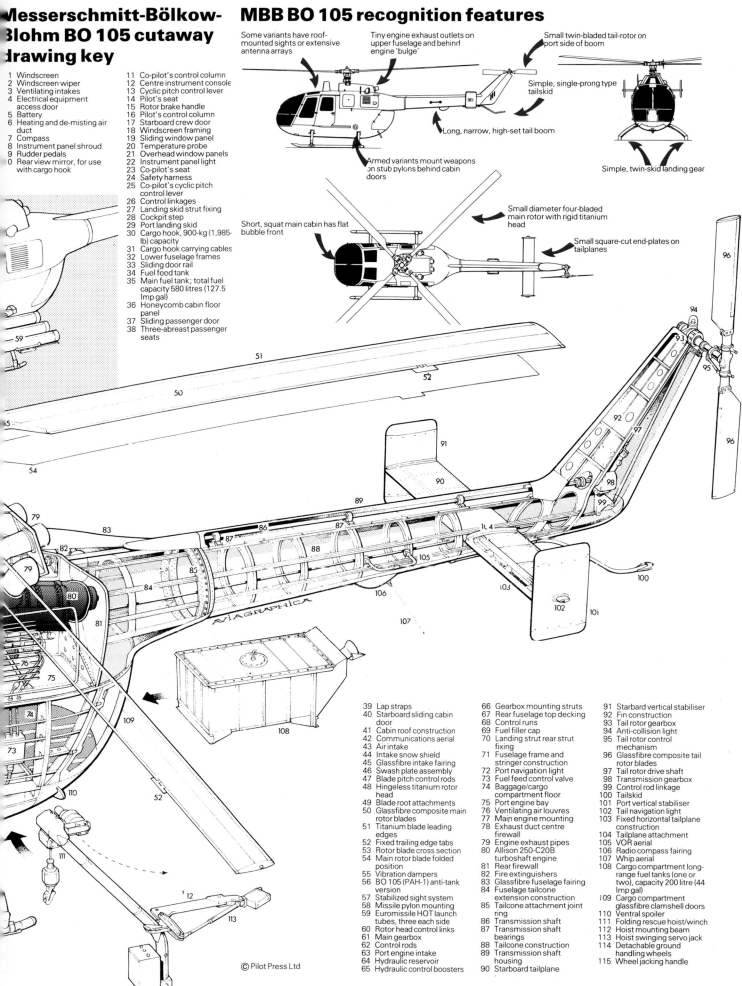

Messerschmitt-Bölkow-Blohm BO 105 cutaway drawing key

1 Windscreen
2 Windscreen wiper
3 Ventilating intakes
4 Electrical equipment access door
5 Battery
6 Heating and de-misting air duct
7 Compass
8 Instrument panel shroud
9 Rudder pedals
10 Rear view mirror, for use with cargo hook
11 Co-pilot's control column
12 Centre instrument console
13 Cyclic pitch control lever
14 Pilot's seat
15 Rotor brake handle
16 Pilot's control column
17 Starboard crew door
18 Windscreen framing
19 Sliding window panel
20 Temperature probe
21 Overhead window panels
22 Instrument panel light
23 Co-pilot's seat
24 Safety harness
25 Co-pilot's cyclic pitch control lever
26 Control linkages
27 Landing skid strut fixing
28 Cockpit step
29 Port landing skid
30 Cargo hook, 900-kg (1,985-lb) capacity
31 Cargo hook carrying cables
32 Lower fuselage frames
33 Sliding door rail
34 Fuel feed tank
35 Main fuel tank; total fuel capacity 580 litres (127.5 Imp gal)
36 Honeycomb cabin floor panel
37 Sliding passenger door
38 Three-abreast passenger seats

MBB BO 105 recognition features

Some variants have roof-mounted sights or extensive antenna arrays

Tiny engine exhaust outlets on upper fuselage and behind engine 'bulge'

Small twin-bladed tail-rotor on port side of boom

Simple, single-prong type tailskid

Long, narrow, high-set tail boom

Armed variants mount weapons on stub pylons behind cabin doors

Short, squat main cabin has flat bubble front

Small diameter four-bladed main rotor with rigid titanium head

Small square-cut end-plates on tailplanes

Simple, twin-skid landing gear

39 Lap straps
40 Starboard sliding cabin door
41 Cabin roof construction
42 Communications aerial
43 Air intake
44 Intake snow shield
45 Glassfibre intake fairing
46 Swash plate assembly
47 Blade pitch control rods
48 Hingeless titanium rotor head
49 Blade root attachments
50 Glassfibre composite main rotor blades
51 Titanium blade leading edges
52 Fixed trailing edge tabs
53 Rotor blade cross section
54 Main rotor blade folded position
55 Vibration dampers
56 BO 105 (PAH-1) anti-tank version
57 Stabilized sight system
58 Missile pylon mounting
59 Euromissile HOT launch tubes, three each side
60 Rotor head control links
61 Main gearbox
62 Control rods
63 Port engine intake
64 Hydraulic reservoir
65 Hydraulic control boosters
66 Gearbox mounting struts
67 Rear fuselage top decking
68 Control runs
69 Fuel filler cap
70 Landing strut rear strut fixing
71 Fuselage frame and stringer construction
72 Port navigation light
73 Fuel feed control valve
74 Baggage/cargo compartment floor
75 Port engine bay
76 Ventilating air louvres
77 Main engine mounting
78 Exhaust duct centre firewall
79 Engine exhaust pipes
80 Allison 250-C20B turboshaft engine
81 Rear firewall
82 Fire extinguishers
83 Glassfibre fuselage fairing
84 Fuselage tailcone extension construction
85 Tailcone attachment joint ring
86 Transmission shaft
87 Transmission shaft bearings
88 Tailcone construction
89 Transmission shaft housing
90 Starboard tailplane
91 Starbard vertical stabiliser
92 Fin construction
93 Tail rotor gearbox
94 Anti-collision light
95 Tail rotor control mechanism
96 Glassfibre composite tail rotor blades
97 Tail rotor drive shaft
98 Transmission gearbox
99 Control rod linkage
100 Tailskid
101 Port vertical stabiliser
102 Tail navigation light
103 Fixed horizontal tailplane construction
104 Tailplane attachment
105 VOR aerial
106 Radio compass fairing
107 Whip aerial
108 Cargo compartment long-range fuel tanks (one or two), capacity 200 litre (44 Imp gal)
109 Cargo compartment glassfibre clamshell doors
110 Ventral spoiler
111 Folding rescue hoist/winch
112 Hoist mounting beam
113 Hoist swinging servo jack
114 Detachable ground handling wheels
115 Wheel jacking handle

© Pilot Press Ltd

MBB BO105 warload

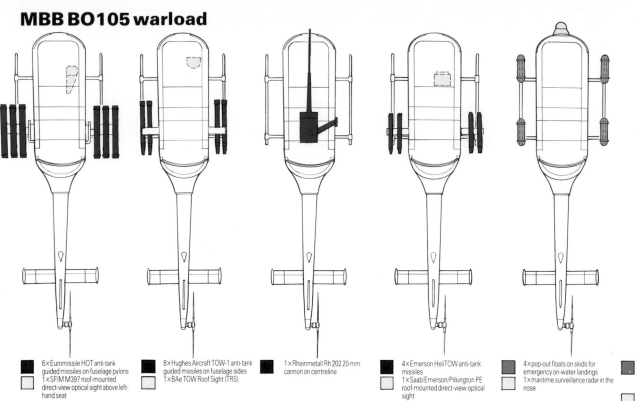

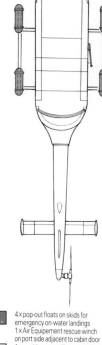

■ 6×Euromissile HOT anti-tank guided missiles on fuselage pylons	■ 8×Hughes Aircraft TOW-1 anti-tank guided missiles on fuselage sides	■ 1×Rheinmetall Rh 202 20-mm cannon on centreline	■ 4×Emerson HeliTOW anti-tank missiles	■ 4×pop-out floats on skids for emergency on-water landings	■ 4×pop-out floats on skids for emergency on-water landings
☐ 1×SFIM M397 roof-mounted direct-view optical sight above left-hand seat	☐ 1×BAe TOW Roof Sight (TRS)		☐ 1×Saab/Emerson/Pilkington PE roof-mounted direct-view optical sight	☐ 1×maritime surveillance radar in the nose	☐ 1×Air Equipement rescue winch on port side adjacent to cabin door ☐ 1×maritime surveillance radar in the nose

Heeresflieger daylight attack

Heeresflieger MBB BO105s can be fitted with a thermal imager for night operations, and there have been proposals to fit a laser designator. An improved sighting system will be required before any self-defence air-to-air missile can be fitted (the General Dynamics Stinger has been proposed in this role).

Maximum firepower anti-tank

This configuration has been demonstrated to Belgium, the Netherlands and Sweden. Eight TOW missiles give the BO105 a mighty punch, but only at the cost of some fuel, thereby reducing range and endurance. No service users have equipped their BO105s in this configuration so far.

Spanish army close support

The gun is used for fire suppression and against soft targets, especially during escort missions in support of HOT-armed BO105s or assault transport helicopters. A reflector gunsight is usually employed, but a head-up display is under consideration.

Swedish anti-tank missiles

The MBB BO105CB is scheduled to enter Swedish army service during 1986 or 1987. The small HeliTOW system was chosen for its lightness, and because it is jointly manufactured in Sweden. EW and ECM equipment are sure to be added, and an air-to-air missile like the Matra Mistral, Shorts Javelin or the General Dynamics Stinger may also be procured.

Maritime reconnaissance

Unarmed BO105s are embarked on various Colombian warships but are interim equipment until armed helicopters can be procured. MBB has investigated the fitting of torpedoes and dipping sonar to demonstrators.

Maritime surveillance and rescue

Six BO105s were delivered to the Mexican navy for maritime patrol, fishery protection and anti-smuggling duties from 'Halcon' class corvettes. They are equipped with extensive maritime equipment and have folding rotor blades, a washing system to remove salt deposits, and deck lashing points.

MBB BO 105 variants

BO 105C: original production variant for commercial and military service, powered by two Allison 250-C20 engines; built for the Royal Netherlands air force (32), Philippines armed forces (14), Nigerian air force (24), Peru (4), Spanish army (30) and Brunei (6) for military liaison and training roles; four were also delivered to the West German border guard for observation tasks
BO 105CB: powered by two Alllison 250-C20B engines and equipped for IFR/IMC operations; Swedish version armed with Emerson Saab HeliTOW system; 20 on order for delivery from late 1986 until March 1987. Colombian (2) and Mexican (6) versions equipped with Bendix weather radar and pop-out floats for overwater/naval operations; naval rescue version has a radius of action of 160 km (100 miles)
BO 105CBS: VIP variant with slightly longer fuselage, and delivered for the personal use of the Sultan of Brunei; four have

been delivered to Sweden for SAR
BO 105D: commercial version; 20 delivered to the Nigerian air force
BO 105M: German military version of the BO 105CB used for training and liaison tasks by the Heeresflieger as **VBH**; 100 built; type used by reigning world helicopter free-style champion, Hauptmann Charly Zimmermann
BO 105P: German anti-tank version, armed with six Euromissile HOT wire-guided missiles and equipped with the SFIM M397 direct vision optical sight; known as **PAH-1**, and 212 delivered 1980-4; upgrading plans include the provision of night-firing capability and self-defence missiles
CASA BO 105: Spanish co-produced version of the BO 105P; 28 remain in service with the Spanish FAMET armed with HOT missiles, 18 with Mk 20 Rh 202 20-mm cannon, and 14 as light

observation variants
NBO 105: Indonesian licence-built variant which continues in production for the Indonesian military and government agencies; 110 had been completed by February 1986, some for naval service with pop-out floats; none armed at present; many assembled from kits, but now co-produced with German factory

---

Performance

Maximum speed at sea level	130 kts 241 km/h	(150 mph)
Maximum cruising speed at sea level	118 kts 219 km/h	(136 mph)
Rate of climb at sea level	1,930 ft	(588 m) per minute
Hovering ceiling out of ground effect	5,200 ft	(1585 m)
Service ceiling	14,000 ft	(4267 m)
Range at sea level	318 km	(198 miles)
Endurance at sea level	2.1 hours	

Troops carried/weapon load

Bell AH-1J SeaCobra 0/1243 kg
Agusta A 129 Mangusta 0/1000 kg
PZL Swidnik (Mil) Mi-2 8/800 kg
Westland Lynx AH. Mk 1 10/600 kg E
Alouette III 6/500 kg E
SA 319B
Gazelle 4/500 kg
SA 342L₁
MBB BO 105 P (PAH-1) 0/500 kg E
500MD McDonnell Douglas Defender 6/425 kg E

Service ceiling

McDonnell Douglas 500MD Defender 13,800 ft
MBB BO 105 P (PAH-1) 13,790 ft
Aérospatiale SA 342L₁ Gazelle 13,450 ft
PZL Swidnik (Mil) Mi-2 13,125 ft
Agusta A 129 Mangusta 12,000 ft E
Westland Lynx AH.Mk 1 11,600 ft E
Aérospatiale SA 319B Alouette III 11,000 ft E
Bell AH-1J SeaCobra 10,550 ft

Maximum cruising speed at optimum altitude

Bell AH-1J SeaCobra 180 kts
Agusta A 129 Mangusta 140 kts
Aérospatiale SA 342L₁ Gazelle 140 kts
Westland Lynx AH.Mk 1 140 kts
McDonnell Douglas 500MD Defender 119 kts
MBB BO 105 P (PAH-1) 119 kts
Aérospatiale SA 319B Alouette III 118 kts
PZL Swidnik (Mil) Mi-2 108 kts

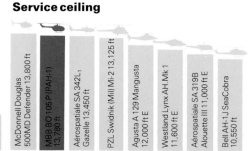

Range with maximum payload

Agusta A 129 Mangusta 750 km E
Aérospatiale SA 342L₁ Gazelle 710 km
Aérospatiale SA 319B Alouette III 605 km
Bell AH-1J SeaCobra 577 km
MBB BO 105 P (PAH-1) 570 km E
Westland Lynx AH.Mk 1 540 km
McDonnell Douglas 500MD Defender 428 km
PZL Swidnik (Mil) Mi-2 170 km (5% reserves)

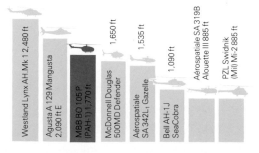

Initial rate of climb, feet per minute

Westland Lynx AH.Mk 1 2,480 ft
Agusta A 129 Mangusta 2,090 ft E
MBB BO 105P (PAH-1) 1,770 ft
McDonnell Douglas 500MD Defender 1,650 ft
Aérospatiale SA 342L₁ Gazelle 1,535 ft
Bell AH-1J SeaCobra 1,090 ft
Aérospatiale SA 319B Alouette III 885 ft
PZL Swidnik (Mil) Mi-2 885 ft

The MIL
Mi-24 'HIND'

Mil Mi-24 'Hind' The Devil's Chariot

The toughest and most capable gunship helicopter in the world, the Mil Mi-24 'Hind' is feared by all who face it, whether they be NATO ground forces, hapless Iranians in the Hawizah marshes or the brave mujahideen tribesmen of Afghanistan. It combines considerable firepower with the ability to carry eight fully combat-ready troops, a feat no Western helicopter can perform.

The business end of a 'Hind-D': the Mi-24 is second only to the Mi-8 'Hip-E' in terms of firepower for a helicopter. The rocket pods each carry 32 S-5 57-mm rockets, which can carry a varied array of warheads, including chemical.

Mikhail L. Mil's design bureau created the Mi-24, also known as the A-10, in the mid-1960s and delivered the first example soon after Mil's death in 1970. Though based on the mass-produced Mi-8 transport, the new helicopter was in no sense merely a new variant; there is not a single major part common to both. This demonstrates yet again that even when an excellent basic type already exists, the Soviet procurement machine prefers the massive extra costs of a totally 'clean sheet of paper' design. Compared with the Mi-8 the Mi-24 is smaller, and has more power, retractable landing gear and totally new interior arrangements.

Whereas in the West the helicopter was in the early to mid-1960s regarded merely as a useful utility and rescue machine, with limited transport and naval capabilities, in the Soviet Union it was by 1965 recognized as one of the supreme military vehicles. It was regarded as the exact airborne counterpart to the tank and armoured personnel carrier, being able to roam swiftly over the battlefield, to take out enemy strongpoints and pockets of resistance, and to occupy and hold ground. What was needed was a new helicopter designed from the start not for utility transport but for battlefield carriage of a squad of eight armed troops (if necessary with special portable weapons) and packing the biggest offensive punch possible. Missions were to include anti-armour with both the helicopter's own weapons and those of its troops, anti-helicopter using guns and missiles, and escort of assault transport helicopters.

Early exercises showed a 'correlation between tank and helicopter losses of 12:1 or even 19:1 in the helicopter's favour'.

The prototype is believed to have flown in 1970. The more powerful TV3 engines turn smaller rotors in the same direction as those of the Mi-8 but at higher speed and, except for the initial batch, the new helicopter has the tail rotor on the other (left) side of the tail. The totally new fuselage was very carefully tailored to the mission requirements, with the cabin amidships accessed on each side by a large door divided into upper and lower portions which both open outwards, one up and the other down. It was a requirement that the last man should be out within two seconds of the first, and this is easily met, with exit only on the chosen side. At the front is arranged a capacious cockpit for four, comprising pilot, co-pilot, tactical navigator and forward observer.

On test the early A-10 (Mi-24) helicopters proved themselves fully able to meet all requirements, with excellent agility for so large a machine and with speed higher than that of any other helicopter in use anywhere. One of the early A-10 prototypes with low-powered TV2-117A engines (flown by a female crew) even set speed records at up to 180.5 kts (334.46 km/h; 207.826 mph), and a later A-10 with the production TV3 engine pushed this up to 198.8 kts (368.4 km/h; 228.9 mph). Combined with fighter-like agility, this is very remarkable for a helicopter with a loaded weight much heavier than that of a Sea King.

The new battle helicopter, taken for granted by its operators as their 'flying tank', was first seen by the West at East German airfields in 1974. It was dubbed 'Hind', but it was then realized there was a pre-production version with simpler horizontal wings without the missile launchers, so the standard version was called the 'Hind-A' and the pre-production type the 'Hind-B'. Then 'Hind-C' was added to describe a supposed model without the nose gun and chin sight. But the NATO name-givers were hardly ready for what appeared in 1975: a totally new 'Hind' with a gunship-type forward fuselage. This showed that a major re-design had taken place not later than about 1971, and as expected this new model became the standard production type.

The obvious change is the replacement of the big four-man flight deck by tandem cockpits, with the weapon operator in front and the pilot behind and at a higher level. The previous cockpit had had access via an upward-hinged pilot door and a larged outward-bulged aft-sliding

One of the main roles for the Mil Mi-24 will be the coverage of amphibious landings, where their heavy firepower will be used to suppress the defences on the beachhead. These two 'Hind-Ds' are flying over a 'Polnocny' class amphibious assault ship.

Oil cooler
Large amounts of unwanted heat have to be dissipated from the gearboxes and engines. This is done by the lubricating oil, which is cooled in a fan-powered duct above the engines

Engine inlets
The air inlets to the two turbine engines are protected by large dished covers which form powerful vortices to centrifuge out sand, abrasive dust and other solid matter which would rapidly wear out the engines

Debris chute
Solid matter extracted from the engine airflow is ejected overboard via a pipe configured to prevent the debris being caught up again in the engine air

Air inlet
This ram inlet supplies fresh air to the air-conditioning system. The cockpits and cabin can be heated or cooled, and supplied with filtered fresh air in the most adverse conditions

Nose landing gear
The nose leg had to be lengthened on the gunship versions to make room for the sensors under the nose. When the unit is retracted the wheels partly project, to cushion a crash landing

Cabin door
Troops can enter or leave at the highest rate because there is a huge door on both sides. The doors are split into upper and lower hinged sections, the lower part having a full-width step

Keith Fretwell

31

Mil Mi-24 `Hind-D´ Assault Helicopter Squadron, 16th Air Army, Group of Soviet Forces, Germany

Pilot's cockpit
The pilot sits above and to the rear of th[e] WSO and has totally different instruments and controls. The canopy i[s] fixed, and the pilot enters via steps and door on the right side

Seats
Both crew seats in this Mi-24 are armoured and specially arranged to absorb shocks in a violent vertical descent, in conjunction with controlled collapse of the surrounding structure

SRO-3 IFF
Identification friend or foe is the task of the standard family of SRO-3 electronic systems (called 'Odd Rods' by NATO). The system interrogates discerned targets and, in the absence of a 'friendly' automatic electronic reply, indicates them as potentially hostile

Gunner's cockpit
The front cockpit is occupied by the gunner, or WSO (weapon-systems officer). The canopy, not bulletproof, opens to the right

Windscreen
Both forward windscreens (US, windshields) are optically flat, for undistorted vision, and made of multiple thick layers of glass and plastics to be bulletproof against strikes up to 23-mm calibre

Air-data probe
This long boom carries precise instrumentation to measure airspeed at very low speeds, angle of yaw (sideways travel) and angle of attack (angle of the oncoming airflow in the vertical plane). This is needed for accurate weapon delivery

Pitot heads
Twin pitot heads measure oncoming ram air pressure and static (local atmospheric) pressure, the difference being presented to the pilot as indicated airspeed. The heads are electrothermally de-iced

Gun
All 'gunship' Mi-24 versions have a four-barrel 12.7-mm rapid-fire rotary cannon, power-aimed according to the 'looking' direction of the undernose sensors. Ammunition is loaded through the twin nose doors above it

Boarding steps
Like the pilot's on the right side, the gunner has three steps to assist easy boarding. The upper two are of the 'kick in' type

Visual sensors
This big chin turret houses an LLTV (low-light TV) and there is abundant evidence that, contrary to what Washington has long insisted, it also contains a FLIR (forward-looking infra-red). The latter detects anything colder or hotter than its surroundings, such as anything with an engine

Radar
This neat radar provides all-weather and night target detection and ranging, and is especially associated with the AT-2 'Swatter' missiles which can be fired under all conditions

Armour
At this location is a fragment-stopping transverse bulkhead. Both cockpits have side armour

Latest identified version of the Mi-24 is the 'Hind-E', which deletes the gun turret in favour of a twin-barrel cannon arrangement on the starboard side. The sensors in the nose are much larger than on the 'Hind-D' and are presumably far more capable.

The Mi-24 exhibits the classic gunship cockpit, with the weapons systems officer in the front cockpit, and the pilot sitting above and behind him. The probe protruding from the front of the cockpit is the air data probe, with highly sensitive instruments for seeking targets.

rear door, both on the left side. Instead the new cockpits had individual fighter-type canopies, the front canopy being hinged to open sideways and the rear canopy incorporating a large rear-hinged door on the right side, with access via a fixed step. Even more startling than the new crew arrangement was the profusion of sensors and aiming devices which took some sorting out.

The weapon wings and EO sensor are unchanged from those of the 'Hind-A', but the nose has been transformed. One feature that was immediately identifiable was the chin turret armed with a gun of previously unknown type, a 12.7-mm four-barrel Gatling-type weapon firing at 6,000 rpm, with selectable lower rates when preferred. This is right in the tip of the underside of the nose, where it can fire in azimuth anywhere within an arc of 180°, and in elevation from horizontal to vertically downwards. Immediately to the rear of this turret are the two sensors, an LLTV and (usually) radar or FLIR. For many years NATO insisted the Soviet Union could not have an FLIR, without explaining why so obvious a sensor should have been omitted. By the time the new gunship helicopter got into production the wing sensor had been changed to a laser, associated with the new anti-armour missile known to NATO as the AT-6 'Spiral', which homes on laser light reflected by the illuminated target. This missile is fired straight from its storage tube and is estimated to have an effective range of up to 5000 m (5,470 yards) at 1000 km/h (621 mph), a performance which eclipses even that of the Hughes TOW, longest-ranged of Western anti-tank missiles. Each 'Spiral' is estimated to have a launch weight of 32 kg (70.5 lb).

Weapon-aiming aid

What was not immediately noticed was that the new gunship, called 'Hind-D', introduced a long rod projecting ahead of the front windshield to provide super-accurate air data for weapon-aiming computer input. This rod is actually a precision pitot head with two-axis vanes to give the relative wind (which for a helicopter in battle can be almost anything). Even less obvious was the total redesign of the Mi-24 to give it dramatically greater survivability in land warfare. The rotor

blades were redesigned, the previous aluminium rear pockets being replaced by high-tensile duplicated steel spars and glassfibre skin. The hub is a titanium forging which resists 20-mm cannon strikes. The windscreens resist 20-mm armour-piercing hits and the canopies are bulletproof. Almost all critical airframe parts, previously made of aluminium alloy, were redesigned in titanium or steel. The amount and quality of armour carried was appreciably increased, and the fuel tanks were made self-sealing and explosion-proof. The result was a helicopter officially described as 'more difficult to shoot down than any other'.

Production of the 'Hind-D' was stepped up, not only in the Far East at Arsenyev but also at a factory at Rostov-on-Don. The combined output has averaged 15 per month for the past 10 years, with 1,800 and possibly as many as 2,700 Mi-24s delivered by the spring of 1985. Some hundreds have been exported, to Warsaw Pact and client states.

High-standard equipment

From the start the Mi-24 has been extremely popular with its crews, being impressive to fly without requiring the physical effort common to Soviet helicopters. Equipment is lavish, and on the 'Hind-D' includes a full-authority electronic autopilot and stability-augmentation system, ADF, pictorial map display, comprehensive RWR and threat-warning display, GIK-1 gyrocompass, RV-5 radar altimeter, SRO-2 IFF installation, and extremely complete communications including those for direct link with front-line troops, and with a high degree of security. The entire impression given by the Mi-24 is of rock-solid safety and lavish equipment, to a standard considerably higher than that of the original models with the four-seat cockpit.

Mi-24s did very well indeed in many large-scale exercises in which their capabilities were explored, but it was not until the war in Afghanistan that they really got their act together. This was in part because the Sukhoi Su-25 'Frogfoot' fixed-wing machine was also deployed for the first time, and whereas an Mi-24 cannot effectively work with a Mikoyan-Gurevich MiG-21 or MiG-27, it can co-operate beautifully with an Su-25. Together they became a greatly feared team that caused, and still causes, severe casualties to the Afghan resistance fighters. The tremendous combination of varied firepower, coming in carefully

timed waves from different directions, presents terrifying problems to the basically small-arms equipped tribesmen, who find themselves up against the latest technology for smashing armour. Smaller numbers of Mi-24s fight for Iraq against Iran, though not deployed in the same way as the Soviet/Afghan gunships, and these are noteworthy mainly for their amazing ability to withstand withering ground fire, though several have, in fact, been shot down.

By 1980 at the latest the 'Hind-E' was fast becoming an important version in Eastern Europe. (It must be understood that the actual designations of the different versions are unknown.) The 'Hind-E' has a massive GSh-23L, or a close relative, attached to the right side of the fuselage firing ahead. This big twin-barrel 23-mm cannon replaces the chin turret, and though it means the gunner has to aim the whole helicopter it gives a major increase in firepower and range. What is not yet known is how far the gun can fire accurately without wasting ammunition (which is probably about 500 rounds). The underside of the nose is a smooth fairing, and the general appearance of the helicopter is less lumpy; but details of changes in the sensors are unknown.

From the start of design it was planned that the squad of troops carried would be able to deploy their own battlefield missiles, but the 'Hind-E' carries the AT-6 'Spiral' which is too big and heavy to be fired by infantry. It would be logical, however, for reload missiles to be carried in racks in the cabin and for pairs of troops to clip the fresh rounds on to the launchers, at some hull-down location out of harm's way among friendly forces. Reloading of Mi-24s has not been seen in films released to the West, but it is something the Mi-24 could do that is beyond the capability of Western helicopters such as the Bell AH-1 and Hughes AH-64.

Glossary

ADF Automatic Direction-Finding equipment
EO Electro-Optical
FLIR Forward-Looking Infra-Red
IFF Identification Friend or Foe
LLTV Low-Light TV
MMS Mast-Mounted Sight
RWR Radar Warning Receiver

Mil Mi-24 'Hind' performance

Maximum speed, clean	173 kts	320 km/h	(199 mph)
Maximum speed with weapons	156 kts	290 km/h	(180 mph)
Initial rate of climb per minute	750 m		(2,461 ft)
Service ceiling	4500 m		(14,764 ft)
Combat radius, maximum ordnance	160 km		(99 miles)

Service ceiling

- AH-64A Apache 20,000ft
- UH-60A Blackhawk 19,000ft
- AS.332 Super Puma 15,090ft
- Mi-8 'Hip' 14,760ft
- Mi-24 'Hind-D' 14,764ft
- Bell AH-1S 12,200ft
- Agusta A.129 10,800ft
- Westland Lynx 10,600ft
- Bell AH-1T 7,400ft

Max rate of climb at sea level

- UH-60A Blackhawk 2770 ft/min
- AH-64A Apache 2500 ft/min
- Westland Lynx 2480 ft/min
- Mi-24 'Hind-D' 2460 ft/min
- Agusta A.129 2090 ft/min
- Bell AH-1T 1785 ft/min
- AS.332 Super Puma 1732 ft/min
- Bell AH-1S 1620 ft/min

Combat radius

- AS.332 Super Puma 300km
- UH-60A Blackhawk 250km
- Agusta A.129 250km
- AH-64A Apache 230km E
- Westland Lynx 212km
- Mi-8 'Hip' 200km E
- Bell AH-1T 200km
- Bell AH-1S 200km
- Mi-24 'Hind-D' 160km

Speed at sea level

- Mi-24 'Hind-D' 173kt
- AH-64A Apache 162kt
- UH-60A Blackhawk 160kt
- AS.332 Super Puma 151kt
- Bell AH-1T 149kt
- Agusta A.129 149kt
- Westland Lynx 140kt
- Mi-8 'Hip' 140kt
- Bell AH-1S 123kt

Weapons load / troops carried

	Weapons load	troops carried
Mi-8 'Hip'	6,000-lb E	28
AH-64A	4,000-lb E	nil
Mi-24	3,000-lb E	8
Bell AH-1T	3,300-lb E	nil
Bell AH-1S	2,523-lb	nil
Westland Lynx	2,500-lb E	9
Agusta A.129	2,205-lb	nil
UH-60A Blackhawk	nil	14
AS.332 Super Puma	nil	25

Key

18 Weapons systems officer's seat
19 Sighting unit, stowed
20 Upward hinged canopy cover
21 Twin barrel externally mounted 23-mm GSh23-L cannon
22 Pilot's armoured windscreen panel
23 Windscreen wiper
24 Instrument panel shroud
25 Cyclic pitch control column
26 Collective pitch control lever
27 Yaw control rudder pedals
28 Nose undercarriage leg strut
29 Twin nosewheels
30 Air conditioning system fresh air intake
31 Nosewheel bay, semi-retracted housing
32 Control rod linkages
33 Pilot's armoured seat
34 Safety harness
35 Anti-fragmentation cockpit lining
36 Pilot's cockpit canopy cover
37 Starboard side entry door
38 'Hind-A' nose section
39 Boarding steps
40 Pitot tube
41 Ventral radome
42 Single-barrel 12.7-mm machine-gun
43 Armoured windscreen panels
44 Weapons systems officer's seat
45 Flat plate pilots' windscreen panels
46 Weapons officer's entry hatch
47 Pilot and co-pilot/engineer's seats, side-by-side
48 Sliding entry hatch
49 Engine air intake vortex type dust/debris extractors
50 Debris ejection chute
51 Generator cooling air scoop
52 Starboard engine cowling/work platform
53 Engine accessory equipment gearbox
54 Isotov TV3-117 turboshaft engine
55 Oil cooler intake
56 Oil cooler fan
57 Engine/gearbox drive shaft
58 Exhaust port
59 Main cabin door upper segment, open
60 Main cabin seating (8 fully-armed troops)
61 Door lower segment, open
62 Boarding step
63 Ventral aerial cable
64 Underfloor fuel tanks
65 Cabin window panels
66 Gearbox mounting fuselage main frames
67 Cabin rear bulkhead
68 Gearbox mounting deck
69 Main reduction gearbox
70 Gearbox support struts
71 Rotor head hydraulic control jacks (3)
72 Rotor head fairing
73 Swash plate mechanism
74 Blade pitch control rods
75 Blade root attachments
76 Titanium rotor head
77 Hydraulic drag dampers
78 Hydraulic reservoir
79 Electric blade leading edge de-icing
80 Blade root cuffs
81 Five-bladed main rotor
82 Starboard side APU intake
83 Auxiliary power unit (APU)
84 APU exhaust duct
85 Rotor head tail fairing
86 Hollow section steel rotor blade spar
87 Honeycomb trailing edge
88 Titanium leading edge anti-abrasion sheathing
89 Aerial lead-in
90 HF aerial cable
91 VHF aerials
92 Anti-collision light
93 Rotor blade fixed tab
94 All-moving tailplane
95 Bevel drive gearbox
96 Tail rotor drive shaft
97 Final drive right-angle gearbox
98 Three-bladed tail rotor
99 Glass-fibre tail rotor blades
100 Titanium leading edge sheathing
101 Blade pitch control mechanism
102 Cambered tail rotor pylon
103 Tail navigation light
104 'Odd-rods' IFF aerial
105 Tail bumper
106 Tailplane control jack
107 Tailboom
108 Tail rotor transmission shaft
109 RV-5 radar altimeter aerial
110 Tailboom frame and stringer construction
111 GIK-1 gyromagnetic compass unit
112 ILS aerial
113 Rear radio and electronics equipment bay
114 Ventral access door
115 Wing pylon tail fairings
116 Formation light
117 Port stub wing
118 Mainwheel bay
119 Wing stores pylons
120 Main undercarriage leg door
121 Shock absorber strut
122 Aft retracting mainwheel leg strut
123 Port mainwheel
124 Laser designator
125 Port navigation light
126 Wing tip missile pylon
127 AT-2 Swatter launch rails
128 AT-2 Swatter air-to-ground/anti-tank missile
129 UV-32 rocket pod (32 × 57-mm rockets)
130 AT-6 Spiral air-to-ground/anti-tank missile
131 Folding fins
132 AT-6 Spiral launch tube
133 Radar director pod associated with 'Spiral'-armed 'Hind-E'

AVIA GRAPHICA

The MIL Mi-8/Mi-I7 and Mi-I4

Mil Mi-8/14/17: 'Hip', 'Haze', Hurrah!

Although less glamorous than the dedicated Mi-24 'Hind' gunship, the Mi-8/14/17 family are the most important helicopters in Warsaw Pact service, and have also been exported in staggering numbers. Used for every conceivable role, the 'Hip' and 'Haze' are growing old gracefully, and will give many years' more useful service.

Demonstrating its amphibious capability, a Polish Mi-14 'Haze-A' takes off from the water. The Polish navy uses 15 Mi-14s for ASW, patrol and mine countermeasures duties, alongside five standard transport 'Hips'.

If any one weapon came to symbolize US military activities in Vietnam it was the helicopter. The conflict in South Vietnam was a 'helicopter war': despite the contributions of all the various weapons systems used, it would have been virtually impossible to wage the ground war in South East Asia without the helicopter. The deployment of two helicopter companies in December 1961 was the first major symbol of US combat capability in Vietnam, and the arrival of the helicopter gunship signalled the first overt use of US military might against the Viet Cong.

The airmobile concept and the later success of UH-1Bs equipped with TOW anti-tank missiles in Vietnam heralded a new era in warfare. But the US Army's massive scale of airmobile operations also had a profound influence on Soviet military thinking with regard to the development and tactical deployment of helicopters. The experience gained and the lessons learned by the USA in South East Asia evoked a new awareness of the potential of helicopters, and this has now been put into well-honed practice by the USSR and its allies around the world.

The importance placed on assault transport helicopters and gunships by the Soviet military is clearly demonstrated by the vast numbers of Mil Mi-8 'Hips' and growing numbers of Mil Mi-24 'Hinds' available to tactical commanders. The emergence of the armed transport helicopter and deadly helicopter gunship has been rapid, and is now a prime concern for NATO. At least 1,600 Mi-8s (out of a production total of 8,100) now support the Soviet armies in the field.

The Mi-8 came from the design bureau of the brilliant Soviet helicopter pioneer Mikhail Leontyevich Mil, who died in 1970. A string of mass-produced and record-breaking helicopters remains the testament to his engineering and design skills. The Mi-8, a turbine-powered development of the Mi-4 'Hound' (itself a shock to the West), was first seen in public at Tushino in 1961 and was powered by a single 2013-kW (2,700-shp) Soloviev turbine mounted above the cabin roof. Although the fuselage was new, with the pilots' seats at the front instead of over the cabin, the helicopter employed the rotor hub, rotor blades, transmission and boom of the Mi-4. The second prototype, which flew in September 1962, was powered by two 1044-kW (1,400-shp) Isotov TV2 turboshafts, and the production version was given a five-bladed main rotor in place of the four-blade rotor inherited from the 'Hound'.

The Mi-8's fuselage is a conventional all-metal semi-monocoque structure of the pod and boom type. The tricycle landing gear is non-retractable, with a steerable twin-wheel nose unit which is locked in flight, and a single wheel on each main unit. Two pilots sit side-by-side in the cockpit, which also has provision for a flight engineer's seat. The standard passenger version has 28 four-abreast tip-up seats with a centre aisle, a wardrobe and luggage compartment, or 32 seats and bulkheads that are removable for the carriage of cargo. The Mi-8T has cargo tie-down rings on the floor, a winch of 200-kg (441-lb) capacity, an external cargo sling system with a capacity of 3000 kg (6,614 lb), and 24 tip-up seats along the side walls of the cabin. Clamshell freight doors and hook-on ramps facilitate vehicle loading, while a passenger airstair is standard on the commercial version. The Mi-8 Salon (a VIP version for 11 passengers) was demonstrated at the Paris air show in 1971.

The principal civil operator is Aeroflot, the Soviet international and domestic carrier, which is the world's largest airline. The Soviet 'national economy' task, which includes agricultural support and aeromedical flights, amounts to 14 million flying hours a year, of which nearly half is performed by Mi-8s. Aeroflot also operates in support of Soviet activities in the Antarctic, where Mi-8s are used for ice patrol and reconnaissance, rescue operations and the movement of supplies and equipment. These Mi-8s are also available as a military reserve, with provision for carrying strap-on weapons.

NATO allocated the reporting names 'Hip-A' and 'Hip-B' to the prototypes, and at the spectacular 1967 Domodedovo air display the 'Hip' appeared in military colours. Military production was under way, and no time was lost in taking advantage of the Americans' hard-won experience of Vietnam. The 'Hip' became the standard Soviet utility/assault helicopter (able to carry 24 armed troops) and was well to the fore in the Soviet development of the airmobile concept. Outriggers with two pylons were added on each side of the cabin to carry four UV-32-57 packs, each containing 32 55-mm (2.17-in) S-5 air-to-surface rockets. This version was designated 'Hip-C', but by 1979 a more

An Mi-8 'Hip-E' of Hübschraubergeschwader 'Ferdinand von Schill', Luftstreitkrafte und Luftverteidigung, looses off a salvo of 57-mm rockets. Even during peacetime, these aircraft come under direct Soviet command.

Specification and recognition points

(estimated) Mil Mi-24 'Hind-D'

Rotors and Wings

Main rotor diameter	17.00 m	(55 ft 9.3 in)
Tail rotor diameter	3.90 m	(12 ft 9.5 in)
Main rotor disc area	226.98 m²	(2443.27 sq ft)
Auxiliary wings, span	7.50 m	(24 ft 7.3 in)

Fuselage and Tail Unit

Length overall, excluding rotors	18.50 m	(60 ft 8.3 in)
Height	4.25 m	(13 ft 11.3 in)
Horizontal stabilizer span	3.44 m	(11 ft 3.4 in)
Width of fuselage, maximum	2.04 m	(6 ft 8.3 in)

Landing Gear

Wheelbase	4.63 m	(15 ft 2.3 in)
Wheel track	3.44 m	(11 ft 3.4 in)

Weights

Empty	6500 kg	(14,330 lb)
Take-off	10500 kg	(23,149 lb)
External weapons	1275 kg	(2,811 lb)

Large five-bladed rotor

Slightly tapering anhedral stub wings shoulder-mounted on fuselage

Twin engine intakes of circular section, box-mounted on cabin roof

Cannon mounted in nose turret

Cabin accommodating missile reloads and/or troops

Missile rails permanently mounted on wingtips

Stabilizer/tailplane on each side of boom

Separate, stepped pilot's and gunner's cockpits except on earliest variants

Various sensors on chin

Three-bladed tail rotor usually mounted on port side of boom

Hind may be confused with Aérospatiale Puma, Hughes AH-64, Apache, Mil Mi-28 Havoc and various attack and transport helicopters

Mil Mi-24 'Hind' variants

Mi-24 'Hind-A': second production version, introducing auxiliary wings with considerable anhedral and four underwing hardpoints, plus wingtip stations for anti-tank missiles; tail rotor moved from right to left side of fin

Mi-24 'Hind-B': initial production version built in small numbers only, with tail rotor on right side of fin, auxiliary wings without anhedral or dihedral and only four underwing hardpoints

Mi-24 'Hind-C': basically similar to late production 'Hind-A', but without the nose gun and wingtip missile rails

Mi-24 'Hind-D': basically similar to late production 'Hind-A', but developed as a dedicated gunship; more powerful TV3-117 engines and revised forward fuselage with separate cockpit for the gunner (forward); four-barrel 12.7-mm (0.5-in) machine-gun in a turret beneath the nose, and an extensive sensor fit to ensure accurate weapon delivery

Mi-24 'Hind-E': developed version of 'Hind-D', but equipped to carry the AT-6 'Spiral' laser-homing anti-tank missile instead of the AT-2 'Swatter', and with a larger sensor pod beneath the left side of the nose

Mi-24 'Hind-?': version of 'Hind-E' with revised nose contours and the undernose gun turret replaced by a 23-mm cannon pack on the right side of the fuselage

A-10: record-setting version of Mi-24, with 'Hind-A/C' forward fuselage and TV3-117 powerplant; has set FAI accredited speed record of 368.4 km/h (228.9 mph) over a 15/25-km (9.32/15.53-mile) course

Mil Mi-24 cutaway drawi

1 Low speed precision airspeed sensors
2 Sensor boom
3 'Odd-rods' IFF aerial
4 Armoured windscreen panel
5 Windscreen wiper
6 Weapons officer's instrument panel
7 Pitot tubes
8 Formation light
9 Ammunition loading doors
10 Four-barrel 12.7-mm rotary cannon
11 Cannon swivelling mounting
12 Forward-looking infra-red (FLIR) and low-light television (LLTV) sensor housing
13 Ventral sensor pack
14 Radar director unit associated with AT-2 Swatter-armed 'Hind-D'
15 Boarding steps
16 Cockpit section armoured skin panelling
17 Canopy latch

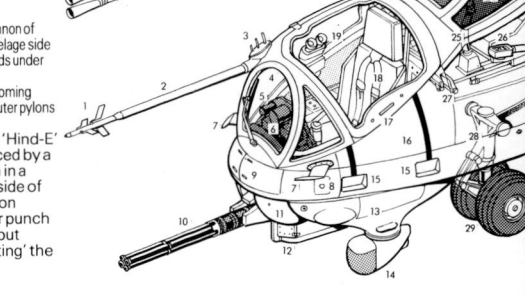

© Pilot Press Limited

Mil Mi-24 warload

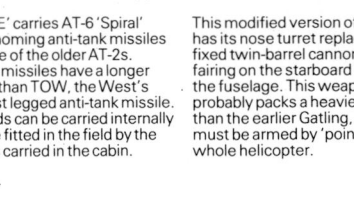

Close air support, 'Hind-A'

■ 1 × 12.7-mm gun in nose, firing through 60° arc
4 × UV-32-57 rocket pods under stub wings
4 × AT-2 'Swatter' radio-guided anti-tank missiles on outer pylons

'Hind-A' was the first major production variant and a small number remain in service. Some of these have been seen in Afghanistan although they may have been relegated to support duties.

Anti-armour, 'Hind-D'

■ 1 × 12.7-mm four barrel Gatling gun in undernose turret
4 × UV-32-57 rocket pods under stub wings
4 × AT-2 'Swatter' radio-guided anti-tank missiles on outer pylons

'Hind-D' introduced the four barrel Gatling-type gun in a turret which can rotate through 180° and traverse from the horizontal to vertically downwards. As on all 'Hind' variants the wing tip missile rails are fixed and extra rocket pods cannot be carried.

Anti-armour, 'Hind-E'

■ 1 × 12.7-mm four barrel Gatling gun in undernose turret
4 × UV-32-57 rocket pods under stub wings
4 × AT-6 'Spiral' laser-homing anti-tank missiles on outer pylons

'Hind-E' carries AT-6 'Spiral' laser-homing anti-tank missiles in place of the older AT-2s. These missiles have a longer range than TOW, the West's longest legged anti-tank missile. Reloads can be carried internally and be fitted in the field by the troops carried in the cabin.

Anti-armour, 'Hind-?'

■ 1 × fixed twin barrel cannon of unknown calibre in fuselage side
4 × UV-32-57 rocket pods under stub wings
4 × AT-6 'Spiral' laser-homing anti-tank missiles on outer pylons

This modified version of 'Hind-E' has its nose turret replaced by a fixed twin-barrel cannon in a fairing on the starboard side of the fuselage. This weapon probably packs a heavier punch than the earlier Gatling, but must be armed by 'pointing' the whole helicopter.

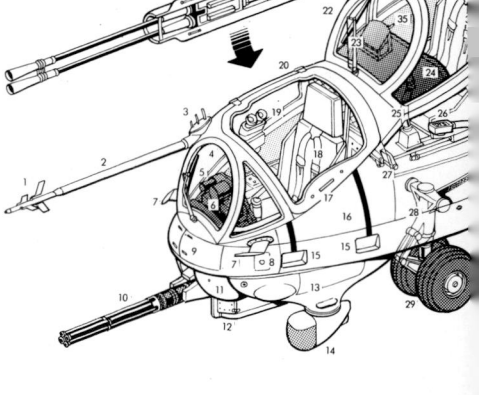

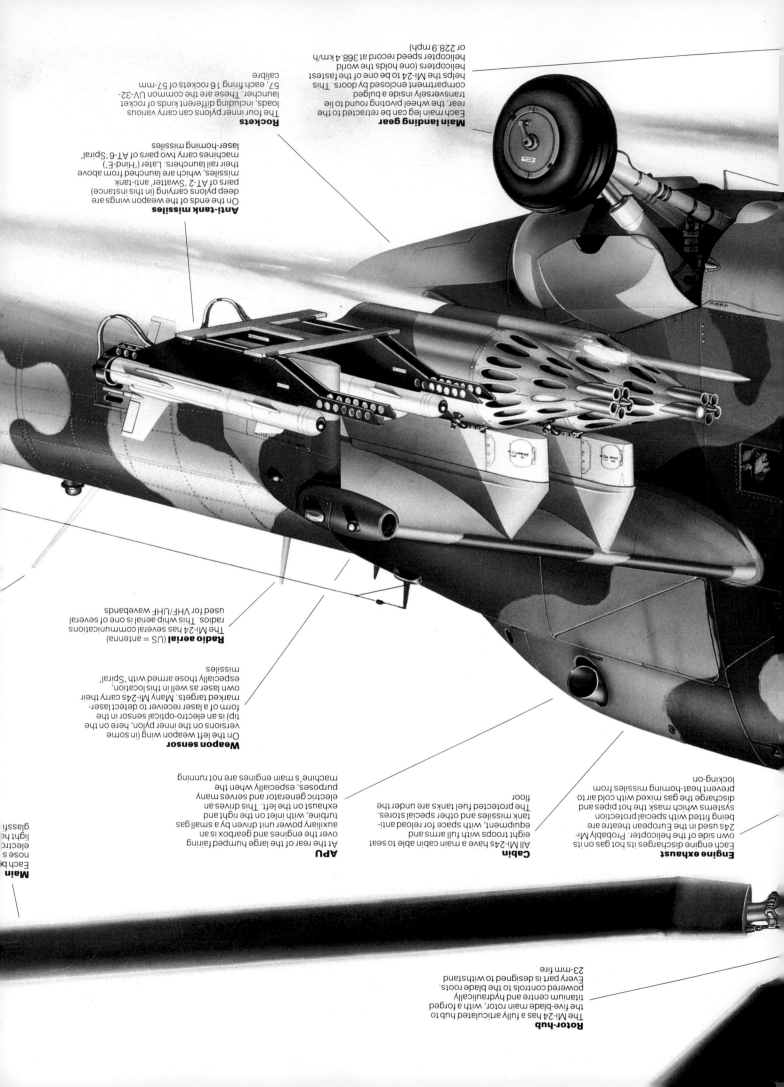

Main landing gear
Each main leg can be retracted to the rear, the wheel pivoting round to lie transversely inside a bulged compartment enclosed by doors. This helps the Mi-24 to be one of the fastest helicopters (one holds the world helicopter speed record at 368.4 km/h or 228.9 mph)

Rockets
The four inner pylons can carry various loads, including different kinds of rocket launcher. These are the common UV-32-57, each firing 16 rockets of 57-mm calibre

Anti-tank missiles
On the ends of the weapon wings are deep pylons carrying (in this instance) pairs of AT-2 'Swatter' anti-tank missiles, which are launched from above their rail launchers. Later ('Hind-E') machines carry two pairs of AT-6 'Spiral' laser-homing missiles

Radio aerial (US = antenna)
The Mi-24 has several communications radios. This whip aerial is one of several used for VHF/UHF wavebands

Weapon sensor
On the left weapon wing (in some versions on the inner pylon, here on the tip) is an electro-optical sensor in the form of a laser receiver to detect laser-marked targets. Many Mi-24s carry their own laser as well in this location, especially those armed with 'Spiral' missiles

APU
At the rear of the large humped fairing over the engines and gearbox is an auxiliary power unit driven by a small gas turbine, with inlet on the right and exhaust on the left. This drives an electric generator and serves many purposes, especially when the machine's main engines are not running

Cabin
All Mi-24s have a main cabin able to seat eight troops with full arms and equipment, with space for reload anti-tank missiles and other special stores. The protected fuel tanks are under the floor

Engine exhaust
Each engine discharges its hot gas on its own side of the helicopter. Probably Mi-24s used in the European theatre are being fitted with special protection systems which mask the hot pipes and discharge the gas mixed with cold air to prevent heat-homing missiles from locking-on

Main b
nose s
electr
light h
glassf
Each b

Rotor-hub
The Mi-24 has a fully articulated hub to the five-blade main rotor, with a forged titanium centre and hydraulically powered controls to the blade roots. Every part is designed to withstand 23-mm fire

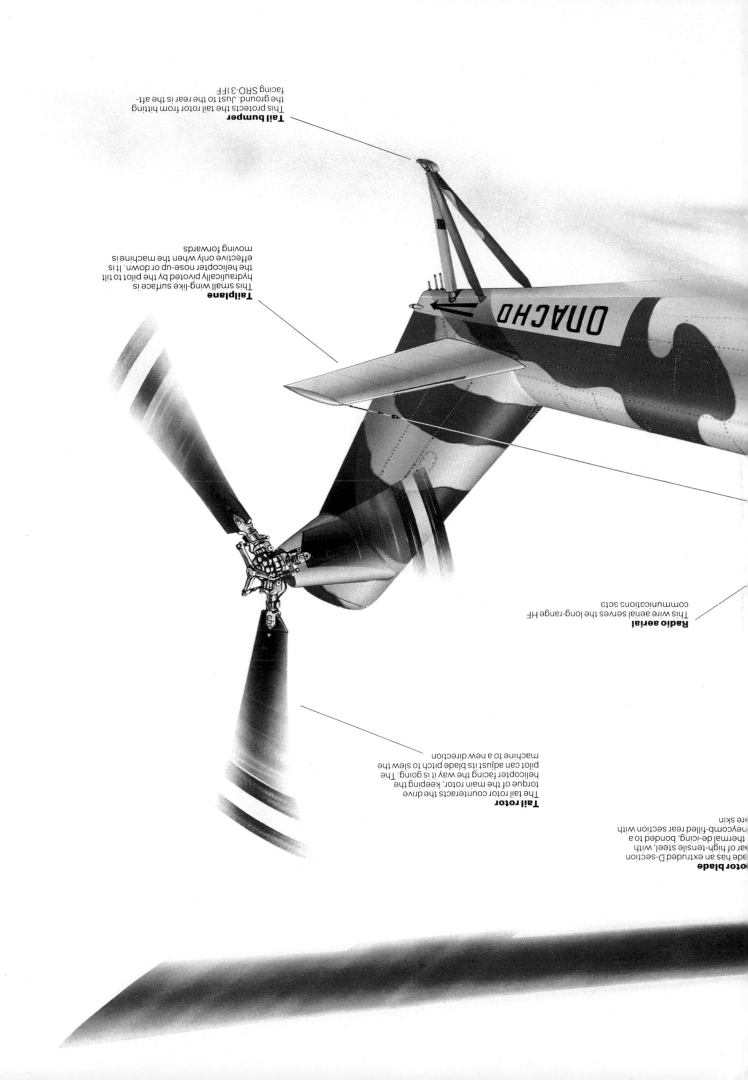

Tail bumper
This protects the tail rotor from hitting the ground. Just to the rear is the aft-facing SRO-3 IFF

Tailplane
This small wing-like surface is hydraulically pivoted by the pilot to tilt the helicopter nose-up or down. It is effective only when the machine is moving forwards

Radio aerial
This wire aerial serves the long-range HF communications acts

Tail rotor
The tail rotor counteracts the drive torque of the main rotor, keeping the helicopter facing the way it is going. The pilot can adjust its blade pitch to slew the machine to a new direction

...otor blade
...ade has an extruded D-section
...ar of high-tensile steel, with
...thermal de-icing, bonded to a
...neycomb-filled rear section with
...re skin

Mil Mi-24 'Hind' in service

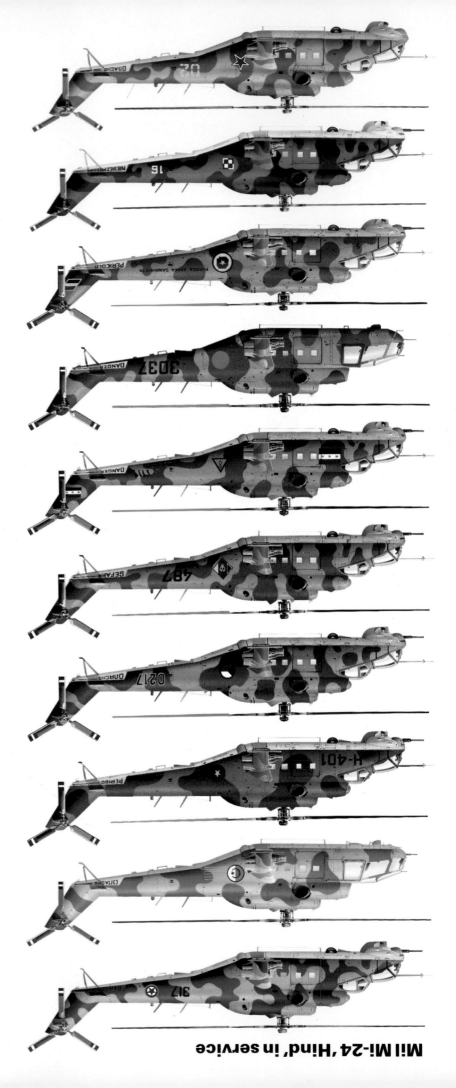

Soviet Union

Over 1,000 'Hinds' are in service with the Soviet forces, most of them under the command of the army and directly controlled by ground units. Among them is the 'Hind-E' version, with a heavy-calibre cannon in place of the rotary-gun in the nose (illustrated). Foreign deployments include Czechoslovakia, East Germany, Poland and, of course, Afghanistan.

Poland

Poland operates a dozen 'Hind-Ds' on anti-tank duties, alongside Mi-8s and Mi-2s (built in Poland). In common with East Germany, Poland is also host to large numbers of Soviet Mi-24 units.

Nicaragua

The current inventory of the Fuerza Aérea Sandinista is difficult to ascertain, but several 'Hind-Ds' are believed to have been delivered. If this is the case, they would be of great use against the Contra guerillas operating against the Sandinista government.

Libya

Libya has enjoyed good relations with Moscow, especially over the supply of arms. Along with vast numbers of fixed-wing combat aircraft, it has received at least 25 'Hinds', including some of the early 'Hind-As'.

Iraq

Over 40 'Hinds' have been delivered to Iraq. These have seen a great deal of action over the battlefields of the Gulf War. Iraq maintains good relations with both East and West, and the 'Hinds' have been fighting alongside Aérospatiale Gazelles and MBB BO 105s.

East Germany

Thirty 'Hind-Ds' have been delivered to the East German air force and these operate in concert with Mil Mi-8 'Hip-F' gunships. In addition to these aircraft, the Soviet Union operates eight squadrons of 'Hinds' in East Germany.

Czechoslovakia

Czechoslovakia was an early recipient of the 'Hind-D' due to its important position on the Central Front. The total is thought to be 22, supplemented by Mil Mi-4s and Mi-8s.

Angola

Mil Mi-24s were received in 1982-3 to supplement Mil Mi-8s supplied earlier. These are not thought to have seen action against South African forces. Authorities in Johannesburg claim that a further 16 Mi-25 export aircraft were delivered in 1984.

Algeria

This 'Hind-A' is typical of the 40-plus supplied to Algeria. Some 'Hind-Ds' have also been supplied. These serve alongside other types such as the Aérospatiale Puma, Mil Mi-4 and Mi-8.

Afghanistan

About 40 Mil Mi-24 'Hind-As' and 'Hind-Ds' have been supplied to the Afghan air force. These have seen widespread action against the mujahideen rebels, in both the gunship and assault roles. It is thought that many Soviet air force aircraft fly with Afghan markings in the interest of world opinion.

Mil Mi-8 series in service

Afghanistan
The Afghan Republican air force operates about 40 Mi-8 'Hip-C' and 'Hip-E' variants alongside its elderly Mi-4 'Hounds' and Mi-24 'Hind' helicopter gunships. The aircraft are co-located and operated in conjunction with Soviet Mi-8s.

Algeria
Algeria's substantial helicopter fleet is substantially Soviet-equipped, and includes 12 Mi-8s. These aircraft may eventually be replaced by Aérospatiale Super Pumas.

Angola
Forty Mi-8s and 11 Mi-17s have been delivered to the Angolan air force, which was established in 1976 with the aid of Cuban and Soviet advisers.

Bangladesh
The helicopter squadron of the Bangladesh Defence Force Air Wing operates a dozen Mi-8s in addition to 31 other helicopters.

Bulgaria
The Bulgarian air force was supplied with six Mi-8s to supplement its helicopter force of elderly Mi-2s and Mi-4s. The navy has a dozen Mi-14s for ASW duties.

China
China has a massive helicopter force, including an estimated 400 Mi-1s, 500 Mi-2s and 300 Mi-4s. The air force also operates 30 Mi-8s.

Cuba
The Cubans' entire helicopter inventory has been supplied by the USSR. The air force operates 20 Mi-8 'Hip-Cs', 20 Mi-8 'Hip-Fs', 16 Mi-17 'Hip-Hs' and 14 Mi-14s.

Czechoslovakia
Like all Warsaw Pact countries, Czechoslovkia is reliant upon the Soviets for helicopters. The air force has 30 Mi-8s and more than 30 Mi-17s, while the Border Guard operates a further 10 Mi-8s.

East Germany
More than 40 Mi-8s are in service with the East German air force and a further five with the navy. More than 20 Mi-14s have also been delivered to the navy.

Egypt
Egypt, once heavily dependent on the USSR for military equipment, still operates about 50 Mi-8s. The Egyptians had between 120 and 140 'Hips' at the beginning of the Yom Kippur War in 1973 and by the end had lost 40 or 50, some to their own fire. The navy has 10 Mi-8s.

Ethiopia
The small but experienced Ethiopian air force has nine Mi-8s and also 10 huge Mi-6 'Hooks'.

Finland
The Finnish air force helicopter flight at Utti has operated Mi-8s since 1973 and has six in service, including two Mi-8Ps distinguishable by their large rectangular windows. Three Mi-8s have been transferred to the Frontier Guard.

Guinea-Bissau
A single Mi-8 'Hip-C' was presented by the USSR to the little West African republic of Guinea-Bissau. This acquisition was important from both the practical and prestige points of view.

Guyana
The current status of the Mi-8s delivered to Guyana by sea during 1985 is unknown.

Hungary
The Hungarian air force operates a mix of Kamov Ka-26s and a variety of Mil types, including 30 Mi-8s, in support of the Warsaw Pact.

India
The Indian Air Force operates about 60 Mi-8s for transport duties, and also has 10 Mil-17s for evaluation. Thirty further 'Hip' variants are thought to be on order. The aircraft equip Nos 105, 109, 110, 118, 119 and 121 Squadrons. No. 109 Squadron has a VIP role.

Iraq
About 60 Mi-8s are in service with the Iraqi air force and have seen a great deal of action in the Gulf War. Iraq maintains good relations with both East and West, and has an impressive mixture of helicopters.

Israel
A number of Mi-8s have been seen in Israeli markings, and are presumably captured Egyptian or Syrian machines used for evaluation and propaganada purposes.

Laos
Ten Mi-8s and an equal number of the early Mi-24 'Hind-As' have been delivered to the Laotian air force by the USSR.

Libya
Libya has enjoyed good relations with Moscow, especially over the supply of arms. Along with vast numbers of fixed-wing aircraft, the air force has received 10 Mi-8s and 12 Mi-14s.

Madagascar
The Madagascar air force is designed to provide this ex-French colony with internal security only. The country's political allegiance is to the Eastern bloc and its equipment, which includes two Mi-8s, reflects its affiliation to the USSR.

Mali
Mali is a[...] for arms[...] a single M[...]

Mon
The air f[...] is organiz[...] Mi-8s.

Moza
Mozamb[...] the depar[...] helicopte[...] 11 Mi-8s

potent variant, the 'Hip-E', had become the world's most heavily-armed helicopter with six UV-32-57 packs housing 192 rockets, four AT-2 'Swatter' anti-tank guided missiles on rails above the rocket packs, and a nose-mounted 12.7-mm (0.5-in) machine-gun. Even when fully fuelled and armed, the 'Hip-E' can still lift 12-14 troops, though operations at maximum gross weight allow little power for manoeuvre at low speed and in the hover.

Other military versions in use include the 'Hip-D' and 'Hip-G', which have been developed for command and control duties. The 'Hip-D' is similar to the 'Hip-C' but features canisters on the outer stores racks and added antennae for the battlefield communications-relay role, while the 'Hip-G' has rearward inclined antennae projecting from the rear of the cabin and from the undersurface of the tailboom, though intended for the same task as the 'Hip-C'. The 'Hip-F' is an export version of the 'Hip-E' and is equipped with six AT-3 'Saggers' in place of the four 'Swatters'. This version first entered service with the East German 'Adolf von Lützow' Combat Helicopter Regiment. The 'Hip-J' is an ECM version identifiable by additional small boxes on the sides of the fuselage, fore and aft of the main landing gear legs. The 'Hip-K' is a communications-jamming ECM version with a large antennae array on each side of the cabin.

Export success

Some 1,600 Mi-8s are in service with the USSR's Frontal Aviation, 900 with Transport Aviation and a further 100 with Naval Aviation. Mi-8s have also been exported to 39 other countries and have tasted combat in several theatres of action. During the first evening of the Yom Kippur War in 1973 a force of about 100 'Hips' carrying crack 18-man Egyptian commando teams crossed the Suez Canal to attack Israeli oilfields and to hinder the movement of reinforcements. The commandos were supported by 'Hips' armed with rockets and bombs, while others were modified to carry two

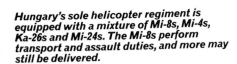

fixed heavy machine-guns and up to six light machine-guns to provide suppressive fire around LZs. Napalm bombs were also reported to have been rolled out through the clamshell doors on to Israeli positions along the canal. Egyptian 'Hips' were also used for resupply and medevac duties. The Syrians employed about a dozen 'Hips' to deliver commandos 2440 m (8,000 ft) up Mount Hermon to capture an Israeli observation post.

In the bitter Ogaden war, the Soviet commander of the Ethopian forces used 'Hips' to airlift troops and light armoured vehicles over a mountain and place them behind forward Somali positions. And earlier, in 1974, two Soviet 'Hips' operated from the deck of the ASW helicopter cruiser *Leningrad* as they helped sweep mines from the southern end of the Suez Canal. More recently 'Hips' have been used both for troop transport and as gunships in the protracted Afghanistan conflict. During the month following the Soviet invasion of Christmas 1979, Mi-8s (some of them from Aeroflot) provided logistic support, and 'Hips' have been in the thick of the fighting ever since.

Like the Huey 'slicks' and 'hogs' of Vietnam, troop-carrying 'Hips' are usually escorted by the more heavily-armed Mi-24 'Hind-D' gunships. It has been claimed in the USA that both these helicopters have been used to wage chemical and biological warfare against the Afghan guerrillas, with loads gener-

Hungary's sole helicopter regiment is equipped with a mixture of Mi-8s, Mi-4s, Ka-26s and Mi-24s. The Mi-8s perform transport and assault duties, and more may still be delivered.

ally fired in 55-mm rocket rounds. But Mi-8s have also been put to humanitarian use. During 1985, for instance, Soviet and Polish 'Hips' took part in famine-relief operations in drought-stricken Ethiopia. The Polish Relief Helicopter Squadron arrived at Assab aboard the MV *Wislica* with 100 tons of food and equipment. Three days later the Mi-8Ts were assembled and began airlifting supplies for distribution to the starving in the desert. In Finland, the Mi-8s of the Finnish air force (Suomen Ilmavoimat) and the Frontier Guard (Rajavartiolaitos) have added a useful dimension to the country's communications network, particularly through the country's long, hard winters when overland routes are blocked by snow or floods.

When the Soviets sought a suitable replacement for the ageing ASW version of the Mi-4 'Hound' they looked no further than the versatile 'Hip', although the conversion proved to be a lengthy

Egypt retains large numbers of Soviet aircraft from the days when it was a major Soviet client. Present allegiances are reflected by the USAF C-5 Galaxy and Egyptian Sea King behind this ageing 'Hip'.

affair. The project began about 1968 and the first flight of the Mi-14 (given the reporting name 'Haze-A' by NATO) did not take place until 1973, indicating some major stumbling blocks. This long overdue ASW helicopter serves only with shore-based elements of Naval Aviation, as it is far too big to use the elevators of the 'Kiev' class carriers and it would be unthinkable for them to remain on deck during a lengthy voyage.

The Mi-14 has shorter engine nacelles than the Mi-8, indicating the use of the uprated TV3-117 turboshafts found on the Mi-17 and Mi-24, and the tail rotor has been relocated to the port side of the fin. Other new features include a boat-shaped hull (for emergency amphibious operations) with a sponson on each side at the rear of the cabin, and a small float under the boom. The landing gear is fully retractable. A Doppler radar box is housed under the forward part of the boom, while additional equipment includes a search radar beneath the nose and a MAD 'bird' stowed in the angle of the fuselage/boom junction. Torpedoes and depth charges are carried in an enclosed bay at the bottom of the hull.

Friendly users

About 120 Mi-14s are operated by the Soviet naval air force, which has retired its fleet of obsolete Mi-4s from shore-based ASW units. The 'Haze-A', which has a crew of four or five, is also in service with the naval forces of Bulgaria, Cuba, East Germany, Libya, Poland, Romania and Syria.

The 'Haze-B' is a mine countermeasures version, and is identifiable by a fuselage strake and pod on the starboard side of the cabin, and deletion of the sonar 'bird'. About 10 are in service with the Soviet navy.

A more powerful and modernized development of the Mi-8 is the Mi-17 medium-lift helicopter, which is powered by two 1417-kW (1,900-shp) Isotov TV3-117MT turboshafts. SSSR-17718, in Aeroflot markings, was first displayed in the West at the Paris air

show in 1
turboshaft
rate, and
weight fr
13000 kg (2
engine is
crease in t
An APU is
inlets can
operations

The mili
known as t
been mad
slovakia an
supplied to

Meanwh
of life for m
SA, France
copter tur
adaptation
Aérospatial
Mi-8, whos
not entirely
held with a
mers, inclu
Pakistan. W
Makila wou
normal per
bient tempe
not plan t
altitude op
available p
the main t
increase cos

The Sovie
Mi-17 to hig

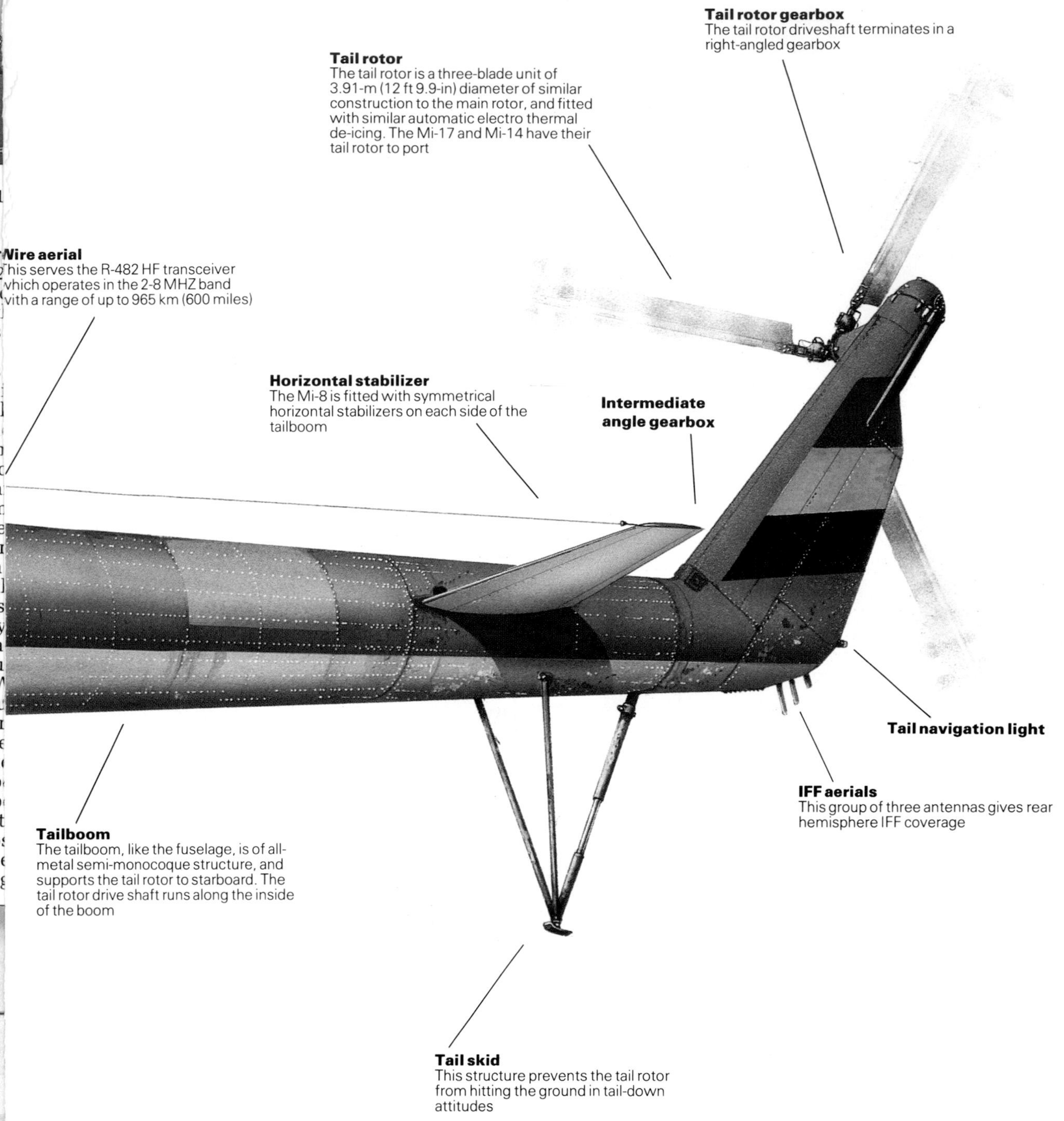

Tail rotor gearbox
The tail rotor driveshaft terminates in a right-angled gearbox

Tail rotor
The tail rotor is a three-blade unit of 3.91-m (12 ft 9.9-in) diameter of similar construction to the main rotor, and fitted with similar automatic electro thermal de-icing. The Mi-17 and Mi-14 have their tail rotor to port

Wire aerial
This serves the R-482 HF transceiver which operates in the 2-8 MHZ band with a range of up to 965 km (600 miles)

Horizontal stabilizer
The Mi-8 is fitted with symmetrical horizontal stabilizers on each side of the tailboom

Intermediate angle gearbox

Tail navigation light

IFF aerials
This group of three antennas gives rear hemisphere IFF coverage

Tailboom
The tailboom, like the fuselage, is of all-metal semi-monocoque structure, and supports the tail rotor to starboard. The tail rotor drive shaft runs along the inside of the boom

Tail skid
This structure prevents the tail rotor from hitting the ground in tail-down attitudes

il Mi-8 `Hip-C´
ngolan Air Force
orca Aerea Popular de Angola e
efesa Anti Avioes)

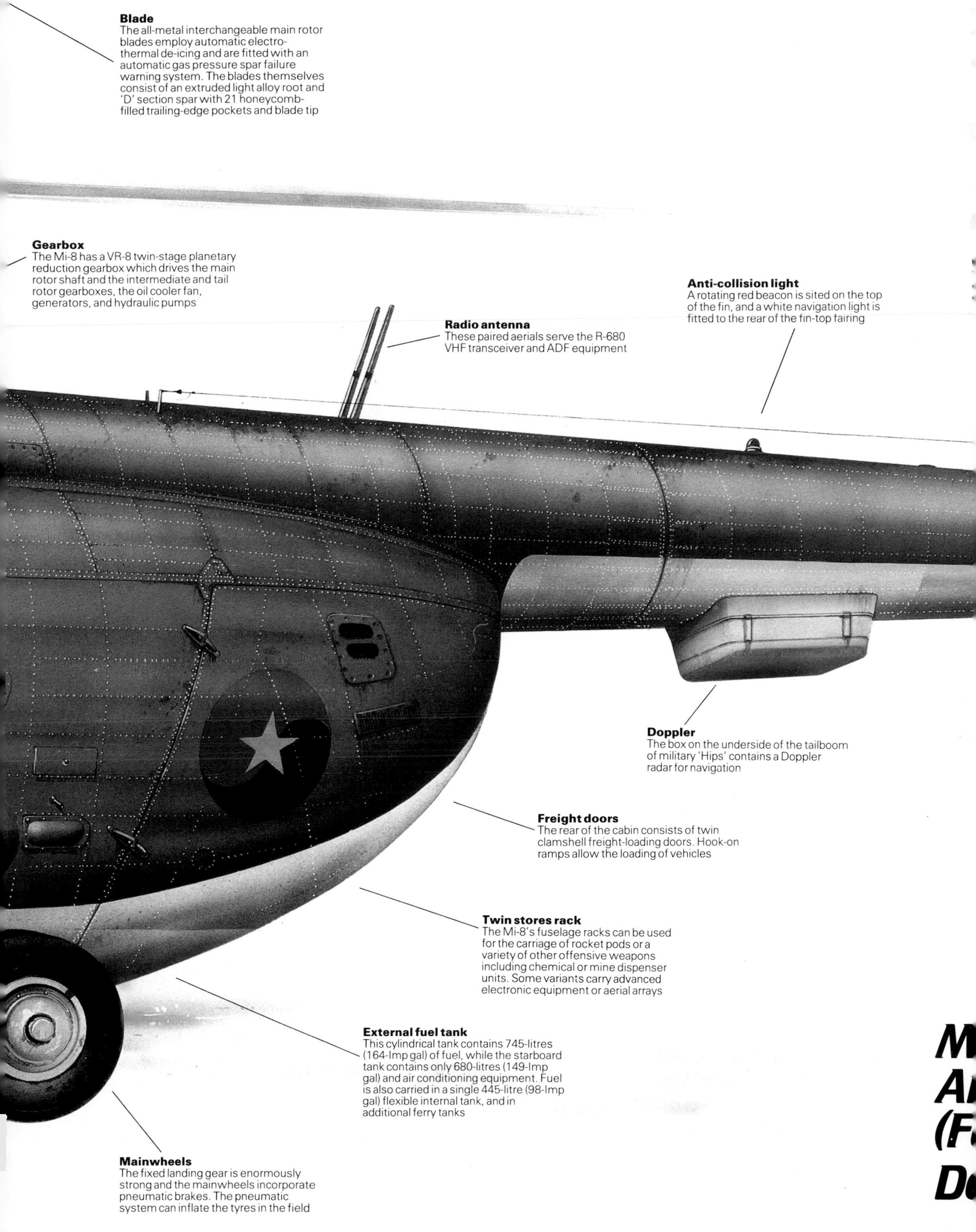

Blade
The all-metal interchangeable main rotor blades employ automatic electro-thermal de-icing and are fitted with an automatic gas pressure spar failure warning system. The blades themselves consist of an extruded light alloy root and 'D' section spar with 21 honeycomb-filled trailing-edge pockets and blade tip

Gearbox
The Mi-8 has a VR-8 twin-stage planetary reduction gearbox which drives the main rotor shaft and the intermediate and tail rotor gearboxes, the oil cooler fan, generators, and hydraulic pumps

Anti-collision light
A rotating red beacon is sited on the top of the fin, and a white navigation light is fitted to the rear of the fin-top fairing

Radio antenna
These paired aerials serve the R-680 VHF transceiver and ADF equipment

Doppler
The box on the underside of the tailboom of military 'Hips' contains a Doppler radar for navigation

Freight doors
The rear of the cabin consists of twin clamshell freight-loading doors. Hook-on ramps allow the loading of vehicles

Twin stores rack
The Mi-8's fuselage racks can be used for the carriage of rocket pods or a variety of other offensive weapons including chemical or mine dispenser units. Some variants carry advanced electronic equipment or aerial arrays

External fuel tank
This cylindrical tank contains 745-litres (164-Imp gal) of fuel, while the starboard tank contains only 680-litres (149-Imp gal) and air conditioning equipment. Fuel is also carried in a single 445-litre (98-Imp gal) flexible internal tank, and in additional ferry tanks

Mainwheels
The fixed landing gear is enormously strong and the mainwheels incorporate pneumatic brakes. The pneumatic system can inflate the tyres in the field

M
Ai
(Fa
Dc

Nicaragua

The inventory of the Fuerza Aérea Sandinista includes 11 Mi-8s and 16 Mi-24 gunships which have been in action against the Contra guerrillas opposing the Sandinista government.

North Korea

The North Korean army operates 20 Mi-8s and a similar number of Mi-4s, together with 87 Hughes 300C, 500D and 500 E models.

North Yemen

A dozen Mi-8s are operated by the Yemen Arab Republic air force, which has also received helicopters from France and Italy in order to strike a balance between Eastern and Western influences.

Pakistan

Like neighbouring India, Pakistan has sought to steer a fairly neutral course between East and West and so purchases aircraft from various sources. The army operates a mix of French-, US- and Soviet-supplied helicopters, including 10 Mi-8s.

Peru

Peru has modern and well-equipped armed forces and is a force to be reckoned with in South America. The Fuerza Aérea del Peru has six Mi-8s and five Mi-6s for transport, plus 12 Mi-24 'Hinds', while the army's strength includes 38 Mi-8s.

Poland

The Polish air force (Polskie Wojska Lotnicze) is the largest Warsaw Pact air arm after that of the USSR, and is organized along standard Soviet lines. Its large helicopter force includes 28 Mi-8s, while the land-based navy air units operate 12 Mi-8s and 15 Mi-14s for ASW and SAR duties.

Romania

Romania has one of the smaller air forces of the Warsaw Pact countries, and its helicopter fleet of 19 Mi-8s, 14 Mi-4s and 10 Mi-2s is being strengthened by IAR-316Bs and IAR-330s.

Somalia

Somalia is still rebuilding its forces after the bitter Ogaden war with Ethiopia, and has turned to Agusta to supplement its four Mi-4s and two Mi-8s.

South Yemen

Unlike its northern neighbour, the air force of the South Yemen People's Republic is strong and wholly Soviet-equipped. The helicopter squadron operates three Mil types in the form of three Mi-4s, eight Mi-8s and 12 Mi-24s.

Sudan

The Sudan air force has a mix of aircraft supplied by the East and the West. The helicopter force was based on 15 Mi-8s, but these are now largely unserviceable. Much of their work has been taken on by IAR-330 Pumas and MBB BO 105s.

Nicaraguan Mi-8s have been used in the assault role, backed up by Mi-24 'Hind-D' gunships, against the Contras.

This Mi-8 'Hip-C' wears the markings of the Yemen Arab Republic Air Force.

The Peruvian air force, uses six Mi-8s while the army operates more than 30.

The Polish navy used 15 Mi-14 'Haze-As' for ASW tasks.

Mil Mi-8 'Hip' variants

Mi-8 'Hip-A': original prototype with single 2013-kW (2,700-shp) Solovyev turboshaft and four-blade main rotor

Mi-8 'Hip-B': second prototype, introducing now-standard Isotov twin-turbine powerplant

Mi-8 'Hip-C': basic assault transport, with twin rack for stores on each side of cabin able to carry total of 128 55-mm rockets in four packs, or other weapons

Mi-8 'Hip-D': developed for airborne communications role; similar to 'Hip-C', but with canisters on outer stores racks and added antennae

Mi-8 'Hip-E': standard helicopter of Soviet army support forces, with one trainably mounted 12.7-mm machine-gun in nose, triple stores rack on each side of cabin (able to carry up to 192 rockets) and four 'Swatter' anti-tank missiles on rails above racks

Mi-8 'Hip-F': export version of 'Hip-E', with six 'Saggers' in place of 'Swatters'

Mi-8 'Hip-G': airborne communications version featuring rearward-inclined antennae projecting from rear of cabin and from undersurface of boom

Mi-8 'Hip-J': ECM version identifiable by additional small boxes on sides of fuselage, fore and aft of main landing gear legs

Mi-8 'Hip-K': communications-jamming ECM version with large antennae array on each side of cabin

Mi-14 'Haze-A': much-developed land-based ASW version with more powerful TV3 turboshafts and uprated transmission, a boat hull with retractable wheeled landing gear, and a mass of role equipment including radar, MAD and internally-carried weapons

Mi-14 'Haze-B': specialized mine-countermeasures version of the Mi-14

Mi-17 'Hip-H': much-improved version of the Mi-8 with the powerplant and uprated transmission of the Mi-14 together with structural and avionic developments

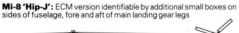

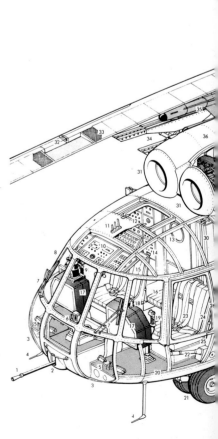

Syria

Syria has strengthened its air force since the Israeli invasion of southern Lebanon in 1982, and can call upon a formidable helicopter force to transport troops and equipment. The helicopter regiments comprise 50 Mi-8s, together with 10 Mi-6s, 8 Mi-14s, 35 Mi-24 'Hind-Ds' and other types.

Uganda

The three Uganda Army Air Force Mi-8s are almost certainly grounded due to lack of spares and the general economic dislocation of Uganda, if they were not destroyed in the civil war or Tanzanian invasion.

USSR

Frontal Aviation's helicoptr force is comprised entirely of Mil types, including 1,600 Mi-8 'Hip-Cs' and 'Hip-Hs' plus 150 of the uprated Mi-17. Transport Aviation also has a mix of Mil helicopters, including about 900 Mi-8s, while Naval Aviation operates about 100 Mi-8s and 120 Mi-14s on ASW duties.

Vietnam

The Vietnamese People's Air Force is one of the larger air arms in east Asia and its equipment is a mix of Soviet and US types, the latter abandoned in South Vietnam. About 60 Mi-8s are in service.

Yugoslavia

Yugoslavia, although a communist country, sits precariously on the fence between East and West. The make-up of its forces reflects its independence to choose its own equipment, which includes 29 Mi-8s for transport and ASW duties.

Zambia

After independence from the UK in 1964, the Zambian air force relied initially on British aid but has in recent years turned to other countries for equipment. The helicopter squadron operates mostly Agusta-Bell types, but also has 11 Mi-8s for transport.

This Mi-8 'Hip-E' is armed with AT-2 'Swatter' anti-tank missiles, six rocket pods and a nose-mounted 12.7-mm machine-gun

This Mi-14 'Haze-A' belongs to the Soviet navy, which also uses a specialized mine-countermeasures variant, 'Haze-B'.

Mil Mi-8TP 'Hip E' cutaway drawing key

1 12.7-mm machine-gun barrel
2 Flexible gun mounting
3 Downward vision windows
4 Pitot heads
5 Yaw control rudder pedals
6 Gunsight
7 Windscreen wipers
8 Windscreen panels
9 Weapon systems officer's sighting unit
10 Overhead switch panels
11 'Odd-Rods' IFF aerials
12 Cockpit roof hatch
13 Main cabin doorway
14 Radio and electrical equipment racks
15 Co-pilot/weapons systems officer's armoured seat
16 Gunner's folding seat
17 Instrument consoles
18 Stand-by compass
19 Cyclic pitch control column
20 Cockpit floor level
21 Twin nosewheels
22 Collective pitch control lever
23 Safety harness
24 Pilot's armoured seat
25 Adjustable seat mounting
26 Sliding cockpit side window panel
27 Ground power and intercom sockets
28 Batteries (two)
29 Cockpit rear bulkhead
30 Control rod ducting
31 Engine air intakes
32 Main rotor blade hollow steel spar boom
33 Honeycomb trailing edge panels
34 Starboard missile launch rails (two)
35 AT-2 'Swatter' air-to-surface missile
36 Hinged engine cowling panel/work platform
37 Engine bay fireproof bulkhead
38 Accessory equipment gearbox
39 Generator
40 Generator cooling air duct
41 Isotov TV2-117A turboshaft engine
42 Engine mounting deck
43 Starboard side folding troop seats, maximum 24 troops
44 Rescue hoist/winch
45 Main cabin loading deck
46 Port folding troop seats
47 Cabin wall mounted heating duct
48 Entry doorway
49 Folding entry steps
50 Sliding main entry door
51 Door latch
52 Port external fuel tank, total fuel capacity 1870 litres (411.4 Imp gal)
53 Centre-section underfloor fuel cell
54 Sliding door rail
55 Engine exhaust duct
56 Engine/gearbox drive shaft
57 Oil cooler
58 Oil cooler air intake
59 Five-blade main rotor
60 Blade root attachment joints
61 Hydraulic drag dampers
62 Rotor head hydraulic reservoir
63 Blade pitch control rods
64 Swashplate mechanism
65 Rotor head tail fairing
66 Main reduction gearbox
67 Hydraulic rotor head control jacks (three)
68 Gearbox mounting struts
69 Control rod linkage
70 Gearbox mounting deck
71 Fuselage upper longeron
72 External stores pylons mounting struts
73 Gearbox mounting fuselage main frames
74 Cabin window panels
75 Main landing gear shock absorber leg strut
76 Fuselage frame and stringer construction
77 Control system access hatch
78 Engine/gearbox bay aft fairing
79 Cooling air exit louvres
80 Aerial mast
81 VHF aerial
82 Tailboom attachment joint ring frame
83 Anti-collision light
84 Tail rotor transmission shaft
85 Shaft bearings
86 HF aerial cable
87 Starboard variable incidence tailplane
88 Bevel drive gearbox
89 Tail rotor drive shaft
90 Final drive right-angle gearbox
91 Tail rotor pitch control mechanism
92 Three-blade tail rotor
93 Tail rotor pylon
94 Pylon tail fairing
95 Tail navigation light
96 Port variable incidence tailplane
97 Fixed tail bumper
98 Tailboom frame and stringer construction
99 Doppler aerial fairing
100 Aft clamshell doors, open
101 Hydraulic door jack
102 Vehicle loading ramps
103 Ramp toe-plate
104 AT-2 'Swatter' air-to-surface missile
105 Missile launch rails
106 Missile firing control unit
107 Port stores pylons (three)
108 UV-32-57 rocket launcher 32×55-mm folding-fin rockets

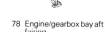

© Pilot Press Ltd

Mi-8 'Hip' warload

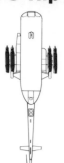

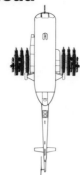

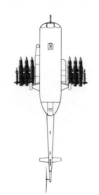

■ 4×UV-32-57 pods suspended beneath the outriggers for a total of 128 55-mm (2.17-in) unguided rockets

■ 1×trainably mounted DShK 12.7-mm (0.5-in) single-barrel machine-gun in the nose
6×UV-32-57 pods suspended beneath the outriggers for a total of 192 55-mm (2.17-in) unguided rockets
4×AT-2 'Swatter' radio-command to line of sight guided anti-tank missiles on launch rails mounted above the outriggers

■ 1×trainably mounted DShK 12.7-mm (0.5-in) single-barrel machine-gun in the nose
6×UV-32-57 pods suspended beneath the outriggers for a total of 192 55-mm (2.17-in) unguided rockets
4×AT-3 'Sagger' optically-sighted wire-guided anti-tank missiles on launch rails mounted above the outriggers

■ 144×PFM-1 anti-personnel liquid explosive minelets in two dispersal units mounted beneath the outriggers

■ 2×unidentified torpedoes in belly weapons bay
□ 1×retractable sonar unit in starboard rear of boat hull
1×towed MAD 'bird' normally stowed against rear of cabin
1×unidentified search radar with large undernose radome

■ ?×unidentified mines in belly weapons bay
□ 1×retractable sonar unit in starboard rear of boat hull
1×towed MAD 'bird' normally stowed against rear of cabin
1×unidentified search radar with large undernose radome

Armed transport ('Hip-C')
In the transport role the 'Hip' can accommodate up to 32 fully armed troops on forward-facing 4-abreast seating. If the 3000-kg (6,614-lb) external sling is to be used, 24 tip-up seats along the cabin floor are employed. Twelve stretchers can be carried in the medevac role.

Soviet close air support ('Hip-E')
Its ability to carry six UV-32-57 rocket pods, in addition to anti-tank missiles, makes the 'Hip' the world's most heavily armed helicopter. The AT-2 is still in widespread use, and has proved useful against caves and guerrilla strongpoints in Afghanistan. It may have terminal IR homing.

Export close air support ('Hip-F')
The AT-3 has been widely exported and has been seen on Mi-24 'Hind', Mi-2 'Hoplite' and even Yugoslav Gazelle helicopters. It is simple, but highly effective, against armoured or soft targets. Some export customers use 'Hip-Cs' in the close support role, fitting two UV-32-57 rocket pods on makeshift pylons.

Anti-personnel ('Hip-H')
The Mi-17 'Hip-H' has enhanced hot-and-high performance, and has been used in Afghanistan. Rocket pods and door-mounted machine-guns can be used to supplement a range of anti-personnel weapons including chemical and nerve agents, and various incendiary devices.

Anti-submarine ('Haze-A')
The Mi-14 is a shore-based anti-submarine helicopter with a crew of four or five, and equipped with a range of sensors and weapons. Sonobuoys, flares and smoke floats can be launched from chutes in the rear fuselage, to augment the radar, sonar and magnetic anomaly detector.

Mine warfare
The Mi-14 can be used to sow or (in 'Haze-B' form) to clear mines. 'Haze-A' has now almost completely replaced the elderly Mi-4 in Soviet navy service, and has been exported to a number of customers including Poland, Bulgaria, Cuba, Libya, Romania and East Germany.

Specification: Mi-8 'Hip'

Rotors
Main rotor diameter	21.29 m	(69 ft 10.2 in)
Tail rotor diameter	3.91 m	(12 ft 9.9 in)
Main rotor disc area	356.0 m²	(3,832.08 sq ft)

Fuselage and tail unit
Length overall, excluding rotors	18.17 m	(59 ft 7.4 in)
Height	5.65 m	(18 ft 6.4 in)
Width of fuselage	2.50 m	(8 ft 2.4 in)

Landing gear
Fixed tricycle landing gear with single-wheel main units and twin wheel nose unit
Wheelbase	4.26 m	(13 ft 11.7 in)
Wheel track	4.50 m	(14 ft 9.2 in)

Weights
Empty, civil passenger version	6799 kg	(14,989 lb)
civil cargo version	6624 kg	(14,603 lb)
military versions (typical)	7260 kg	(16,006 lb)
Maximum take-off, vertical	12000 kg	(26,455 lb)
Internal fuel load	1459 kg	(3,216 lb)

Powerplant
Two Isotov TV2-117A turboshafts
Rating, each	1268 kW	(1,700 shp)

Mi-8 'Hip' recognition features

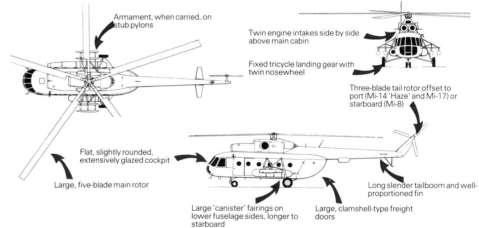

Armament, when carried, on stub pylons

Twin engine intakes side by side above main cabin

Fixed tricycle landing gear with twin nosewheel

Three-blade tail rotor offset to port (Mi-14 'Haze' and Mi-17) or starboard (Mi-8)

Flat, slightly rounded, extensively glazed cockpit

Large, five-blade main rotor

Long slender tailboom and well-proportioned fin

Large 'canister' fairings on lower fuselage sides, longer to starboard

Large, clamshell-type freight doors

Performance:

Maximum speed at 3,280 ft (1000 m) at 11100 kg (24,471 lb)	140 kts	260 km/h (162 mph)
Maximum speed at sea level at 11100 kg (24,471 lb)	135 kts	250 km/h (155 mph)
at 12000 kg (26,455 lb)	124 kts	230 km/h (143 mph)
with 2500 kg (5,512 lb) of slung cargo	97 kts	180 km/h (112 mph)
Service ceiling	14,765 ft	(4500 m)

Range
cargo version at 3,280 ft (1000 m) with standard fuel and 5% reserves		
normal AUW	465 km	(289 miles)
maximum AUW	445 km	(277 miles)
with 28 passengers at 3,280 ft (1000 m) with 20-minute fuel reserves	500 km	(311 miles)

External load
Aircraft	Load
Boeing Vertol CH-46D Sea Knight	4535 kg
Aérospatiale AS 332M Super Puma	4500 kg
Sikorsky UH-60A Black Hawk	3630 kg
Westland Commando Mk 2	3628 kg
Puma HC.Mk 1	2500 kg
Mil Mi-8 'Hip'	3000 kg
Aérospatiale (Westland)	2000 kg E
Bell UH-1H Iroquois	
Westland Wessex	
HU.Mk 5	1814 kg

Initial rate of climb, in feet per minute
Westland Commando Mk 2	2,020 ft
Sikorsky UH-60A Black Hawk	2,000 ft E
Mil Mi-8 'Hip'	1,800 ft E
Aérospatiale AS 332M Super Puma	1,730 ft
Boeing Vertol CH-46D Sea Knight	1,660 ft
Westland Wessex HU.Mk 5	1,650 ft
Bell UH-1H Iroquois	1,600 ft
Aérospatiale (Westland) Puma HC.Mk 1	1,400 ft

Maximum cruising speed at optimum altitude
Sikorsky UH-60A Black Hawk	160 kts
Aérospatiale AS 332M Super Puma	151 kts
Aérospatiale (Westland) Puma HC.Mk 1	143 kts
Boeing Vertol CH-46D Sea Knight	140 kts
Mil Mi-8 'Hip'	124 kts
Westland Wessex HU.Mk 5	115 kts
Westland Commando Mk 2	112 kts
Bell UH-1H Iroquois	110 kts

Range with internal fuel
Aircraft	Range	
Aérospatiale AS 332M Super Puma	635 km	
Aérospatiale (Westland) Puma HC.Mk 1	630 km	
Westland Wessex HU.Mk 5	628 km	
Sikorsky UH-60A Black Hawk	600 km	30 minutes reserves
Bell UH-1H Iroquois	511 km	
Mil Mi-8 'Hip'	500 km	20 minutes reserves
Westland Commando Mk 2	445 km	30 minutes reserves
Boeing Vertol CH-46D Sea Knight	383 km	10% reserves

Number of troops carried
Aircraft	Troops
Westland Commando Mk 2	28
Mil Mi-8 'Hip'	28
Boeing Vertol CH-46D Sea Knight	25
Aérospatiale AS 332M Super Puma	25
Westland Wessex HU.Mk 5	16
Aérospatiale (Westland) Puma HC.Mk 1	16
Bell UH-1H Iroquois	14
Sikorsky UH-60A Black Hawk	11

The KAMOV
Ka-25 and Ka-27

Kamov `Hormone´ and `Helix´: compact co-axials

When the Soviet helicopter carrier 'Moskva' made its first appearance in 1968, its complement consisted entirely of Kamov Ka-25 'Hormones'. These versatile helicopters are now being augmented by the later Ka-27 'Helix', and both types serve in large numbers from shore bases, various warships, and the 'Kiev'-class carriers.

This hovering Kamov Ka-25 'Hormone-A' is employing a dipping sonar to try and detect a hostile submarine. The aircraft can use depth charges or torpedoes in the anti-submarine warfare role.

Nikolai I. Kamov (1902-73) was the world's leading pioneer of co-axial helicopters. Machines of this configuration have two main rotors which turn in opposite directions about the same vertical axis, being driven by co-axial shafts. Thus, the drive torque to either rotor cancels out the drive torque to the other, so no tail rotor is needed. Moreover, the required rotor disc area can be obtained with a rotor diameter much less than usual, and both these features make for a compact helicopter ideally suited to shipboard operation.

The Kamov family

Kamov's first naval helicopters were small single-seaters with inflatable pontoon alighting gear and a 41-kW (55-hp) piston engine. Later he developed the Ka-15 and Ka-18, with 209-kw (280-hp) piston engine, but the great leap came with the so-called Ka-20, which was demonstrated carrying two dummy missiles in 1961. This machine was appreciably bigger than the Ka-18, and powered by two turboshaft engines each of (671-kW) 900 hp. By 1962 this had been developed into the Ka-25, since built in substantial numbers as the standard multi-role shipboard helicopter of the Soviet navy, and in particular of the AV-MF (naval aviation).

In general design the Ka-25 family of helicopters is conventional. Each rotor is fully articulated, the blades being attached to flapping and drag hinges with oil lubrication, and with provision for automatic blade folding to reduce dimensions to those of a ship's hangar. The blades of most Ka-25s are of aluminium alloy, with an extruded spar and lightweight trailing-edge pockets filled with light ribs and stabilizers. There has to be a large vertical clearance between the upper and lower rotors to allow for the fact that each blade climbs and sinks as it goes round each revolution, as in all conventional helicopters.

The fuselage is a normal light-alloy semi-monocoque, with an almost unobstructed interior. In the nose is the cockpit, the full width of the helicopter and seating two pilots side-by-side, with a sliding door on each side. The main cabin to the rear has a doorway leading to the cockpit and a giant sliding door at the rear on the left side. The interior arrangement depends on the sub-type of helicopter and its mission. At the rear, the cabin section is connected to the tapering boom which carries the tail. The latter is unusual, because while it has no rotor it does possess a tailplane with elevators, as well as three fins and two rudders. The outer fins, on the ends of the tailplane, are sharply

toed inwards to enhance directional stability. The rudders are used for directional control in translational (cruising) flight; they can also be used in the rotor downwash in hovering flight, but they are then rather less effective.

One of the more unusual features is the landing gear. This resembles that of the Sikorsky S-55 in that there are four units, essentially one at each corner of the main fuselage. The nose units have vertical oleo struts, and the lower fork fittings carrying the wheels can castor. Each main unit has a vertical leg which is carried well outboard on upper and lower pairs of vee-struts. All elements are pivoted together so that each leg and wheel can swing freely in a nearly vertical plane. Such movement is reacted by a long diagonal oleo shock strut joining the top of the vertical leg to the top of the fuselage. In most versions it is possible to raise the wheels right up out of the 'line of sight' of the chin-mounted radar, to avoid obstructing the latter's operation. The main wheels have both normal and sprag (locking) brakes, and all four units can be fitted

The Kamov Ka-27 'Helix-A' is slowly replacing 'Hormone-A' in the ASW role. About 16 are usually carried by each 'Kiev'-class carrier, and a pair can be carried by 'Udaloy'-class guided missile destroyers.

with rapid-inflating flotation bags for emergency alighting on water (for example, following double engine failure or running out of fuel). The Ka-25 is not intended for normal amphibious operation, though examples have been recovered after water landings and, after overhaul, returned to operational service.

Fuel is housed mainly under the cabin floor. Pumps transfer the fuel to the high-pressure pump on each engine. Each GTD-3BM engine is a single-shaft turbine unit made in Poland and in some ways resembling the US General Electric T58 engine. Left and right engines are almost identical except for having handed jet-pipes turned outwards to exhaust through a large-diameter circular stack in line with the rotor mast. Careful provisions are made for all-weather operation, with inlets heated by raw alternating current, and the inlet guide vanes and central bullet fairing de-iced by hot air bled from the compressor. At the rear is the main gearbox, which joins the left and right engines to the rotor drive shaft. Behind this is the oil radiator, air being forced through this under all flight conditions by a large fan driven from the main gearbox.

Flight equipment

Flight equipment includes comprehensive avionics for flight-control and auto-stabilization, for overwater navigation and for various specific missions. The largest avionic item is usually a search radar, carried under the nose with a direct link to a display in the cockpit or, in some versions, in the main cabin. The original AV-MF version, called 'Hormone-A' by NATO, is an ASW version. This carries a crew of four, two being mission crew in the cabin. Equipment includes 'Big Bulge' I/J-band search radar, a secure data-link to surface vessels, IFF and reply interrogator, precise radar altimeter giving exact height above the sea, the 'Tie Rod' EO sensor, sonobuoys for detecting submerged submarines (dropped from three-buoy canisters on each side of the fuselage), a MAD sensor carried on the end of a towing/sensor cable, and dye markers under the rear fuselage.

Armament

Anti-submarine torpedoes or nuclear depth charges can be carried along the ventral centreline or in a shallow weapon bay under the fuselage. Most 'Hormone-A' helicopters have a shallow bay with two doors which can house two 450-mm (17.7-in) torpedoes. A few of these helicopters have specially deep bays, reportedly to house one or two wire-guided torpedoes.

It is possible to carry an auxiliary fuel tank on each side of the cabin, plumbed into the helicopter's fuel system to extend range. When these tanks, or weapons, are not carried it is possible to take on board up to 12 passengers.

'Hormone-B' is the NATO name for a special electronics version, whose primary mission is to acquire distant OTH targets for cruise missiles launched from Soviet warships. Among the types of missile involved are SS-N-3 'Shaddock', SS-N-12 'Sandbox' and SS-N-19, all of which have range capability far exceeding that of the targeting radar carried by surface ships or submarines. This helicopter has a larger and more spherical main radome and a cylindrical drum radome under the rear of the cabin, as well as special data-link communications to pass the target data to the missile after launch.

SAR and plane guard

'Hormone-C' is the NATO name for the SAR and utility version, configured basically for transport. It is generally similar to the 'Hormone-A' but with all ASW sensors (except radar) and weapons removed, and with a 300-kg (661-lb) hoist fitted for rescue. Some of this type have a four-pronged Yagi-type antenna projecting ahead of the nose, probably serving an all-weather ship landing system. Some 'Hormone-Cs' have been seen in high-

The 'Hormone' is frequently used as a camera platform, photographing NATO warships for intelligence purposes. The helicopter can carry a variety of weapons on pylons on the cabin sides.

contrast red/white colour scheme, whereas operational versions are painted in low-visibility shades of grey.

Total production of all versions was probably 500, ending in about 1975. An estimated 460 were supplied to the AV-MF, of which about 190 remained operational in early 1987. In addition 17 were supplied to Vietnam, some to Yugoslavia, nine to Syria and five (ex-AV-MF) to the Indian navy's No. 333 Squadron for deployment aboard three 'Kashin II' class destroyers.

New generation

Compared with the Ka-25, the Ka-27 in production today offers more than twice the capability for only slightly greater bulk. The key to its development (by a new design team, led by S.V. Mikheev, Kamov's successor) lies in the availability of a completely new engine, the Isotov TV3-117V. This engine was already extremely experienced in a series of Mil helicopters, and with a basic contingency rating of 1659 kW (2,225 hp) gives well over double the power of the engines used in the Ka-25. Mikheev's engineers found that, without any significant change in rotor diameter, they could absorb this far greater power in the new machine by designing new high-efficiency rotor

'Hormone' crews, dressed in bulky immersion suits, race to their aircraft during a rapid response ASW exercise. The aircraft are capable of autonomous operation.

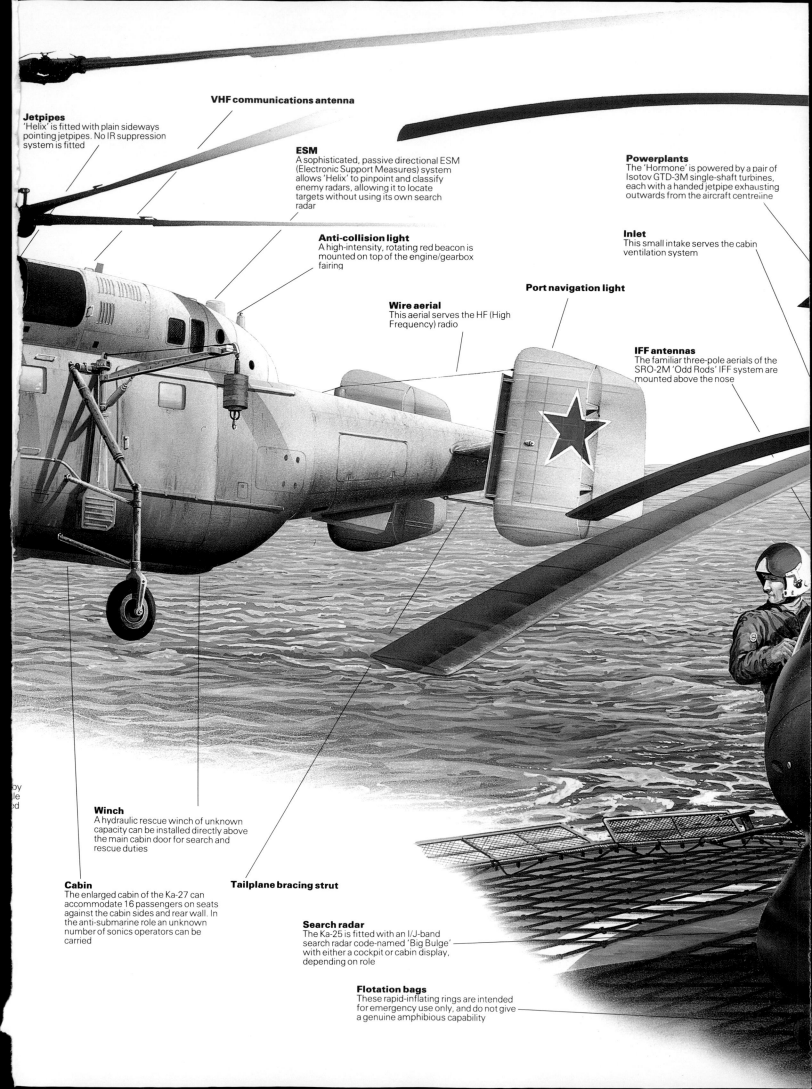

Jetpipes
'Helix' is fitted with plain sideways pointing jetpipes. No IR suppression system is fitted

VHF communications antenna

ESM
A sophisticated, passive directional ESM (Electronic Support Measures) system allows 'Helix' to pinpoint and classify enemy radars, allowing it to locate targets without using its own search radar

Anti-collision light
A high-intensity, rotating red beacon is mounted on top of the engine/gearbox fairing

Wire aerial
This aerial serves the HF (High Frequency) radio

Port navigation light

Powerplants
The 'Hormone' is powered by a pair of Isotov GTD-3M single-shaft turbines, each with a handed jetpipe exhausting outwards from the aircraft centreline

Inlet
This small intake serves the cabin ventilation system

IFF antennas
The familiar three-pole aerials of the SRO-2M 'Odd Rods' IFF system are mounted above the nose

Winch
A hydraulic rescue winch of unknown capacity can be installed directly above the main cabin door for search and rescue duties

Cabin
The enlarged cabin of the Ka-27 can accommodate 16 passengers on seats against the cabin sides and rear wall. In the anti-submarine role an unknown number of sonics operators can be carried

Tailplane bracing strut

Search radar
The Ka-25 is fitted with an I/J-band search radar code-named 'Big Bulge' with either a cockpit or cabin display, depending on role

Flotation bags
These rapid-inflating rings are intended for emergency use only, and do not give a genuine amphibious capability

Engine intakes
The engines are fitted with plain, circular intakes which are electrically de-iced but are not fitted with filters or particle separators

Rotor blade
'Helix' is fitted with composite blades. Each blade consists of a spar with plies and filament winding in carbon and glassfibre. Thirteen trailing edge pockets are filled with nylon honeycomb, and skinned with an aramid fibre similar to Kevlar. An abrasion-resistant leading edge strip of unknown composition is fitted. The blades employ electrical de-icing

IFF antenna
Aerials for the SRO-2M 'Odd Rods' IFF transponder are located on the nose, in front of the windscreen, and above the tailboom

Powerplant
The Ka-27 is powered by a pair of Isotov TV3-117Vs giving about twice the power output of the engines fitted to the Ka-25. The engine has been thoroughly tried and tested in several helicopters designed by the Mikhail Mil OKB. A redesigned gearbox and transmission have been fitted to absorb the greater power

Intake air temperature sensor

Cockpit
Helix is usually fitted with full hydraulic dual controls for its two pilots. The crew sits slightly behind the pilots. The controls have no manual reversion and a new automatic flight control system is fitted

Probe
This air data sensor probe gathers pitot-static and dynamic pressure information for the flight instruments, the tactical navigation system, and the autopilot unit

Radar warning receiver
This antenna serves the passive radar warning receiver

Search radar
The new radar fitted to the 'Helix' has a larger, but shallower, scanner than that fitted to 'Hormone'. No details are known of its performance, and no NATO reporting name has been published

Lamp
This housing contains the ventral lamp, which can be used for landing, or during search and rescue work

Nose undercarriage
The nosewheel units consist of long-stroke vertical oleo struts and fully castoring nosewheels. This gives adequate ground clearance for the radome, and allows easy deck handling

Stores box
'Helix' dispenses with the clumsy underfloor weapons bay fitted to 'Hormone' and instead drops sensors from large boxes on the cabin sides. These are thought to contain between 10 and 12 sonobuoys

Fuselage fuel tanks
Most internal fuel capacity is provided tanks under the cabin floor. A removab weapons bay under the fuselage is us for the stowage of various types of torpedoes, some of them wire-guided and depth charges, conventional or nuclear

Kamov Ka-25 `Hormone-A´ and Ka-27 `Helix´ Soviet Naval Aviation

Rotor blade

Each blade is thought to consist of an aluminium D-spar with light honeycomb-filled rear pockets. A nitrogen crack detection system is fitted and the blades can be automatically folded from the cockpit. The blades are de-iced by liquid alcohol, which is metered to the blade root, then distributed down the leading edge by centrifugal force

Avionics bay

Various avionics equipment is housed in the capacious tailboom, probably including the ADF equipment. A twin, gyromagnetic compass unit is housed in a fairing immediately below the boom

s
arge square tailfins are fitted with
e, fixed slats which enhance
ctional stability

Tail fins

The two outer tail fins are toed in for directional stability. They are fitted with rudders, which are used for directional control in translational and cruising flight, but are ineffective in the hover. The tailplane is also fitted with elevators

Cabin door

Access to the cabin is via a large forward sliding door

Rear undercarriage

The rear undercarriage is carried well outboard from the fuselage, giving a surprisingly wide track. Sprag-type, positive locking brakes are fitted

Cockpit doors

On both 'Helix' and 'Hormone' the pilots enter the cockpit through separate, rearward-sliding doors, which are frequently left open in flight. Footsteps and grab handles make cockpit access easier

Auxiliary fuel tanks

'Strap-on' fuel tanks can be carried on the cabin sides, although this prevents the carriage of dye markers, smoke floats, or air-to-surface missiles on their usual cabin-mounted pylons

Tony Wicks.

Engine intakes
The engines are fitted with plain, circular intakes which are electrically de-iced but are not fitted with filters or particle separators

Rotor blade
'Helix' is fitted with composite blades. Each blade consists of a spar with plies and filament winding in carbon and glassfibre. Thirteen trailing edge pockets are filled with nylon honeycomb, and skinned with an aramid fibre similar to Kevlar. An abrasion-resistant leading edge strip of unknown composition is fitted. The blades employ electrical de-icing

IFF antenna
Aerials for the SRO-2M 'Odd Rods' IFF transponder are located on the nose, in front of the windscreen, and above the tailboom

Powerplant
The Ka-27 is powered by a pair of Isotov TV3-117Vs giving about twice the power output of the engines fitted to the Ka-25. The engine has been thoroughly tried and tested in several helicopters designed by the Mikhail Mil OKB. A redesigned gearbox and transmission have been fitted to absorb the greater power

Intake air temperature sensor

Cockpit
Helix is usually fitted with full hydraulic dual controls for its two pilots. The crew sits slightly behind the pilots. The controls have no manual reversion and a new automatic flight control system is fitted

Probe
This air data sensor probe gathers pitot-static and dynamic pressure information for the flight instruments, the tactical navigation system, and the autopilot unit

Radar warning receiver
This antenna serves the passive radar warning receiver

Search radar
The new radar fitted to the 'Helix' has a larger, but shallower, scanner than that fitted to 'Hormone'. No details are known of its performance, and no NATO reporting name has been published

Lamp
This housing contains the ventral lamp, which can be used for landing, or during search and rescue work

Nose undercarriage
The nosewheel units consist of long-stroke vertical oleo struts and fully castoring nosewheels. This gives adequate ground clearance for the radome, and allows easy deck handling

Stores box
'Helix' dispenses with the clumsy underfloor weapons bay fitted to 'Hormone' and instead drops sensors from large boxes on the cabin sides. These are thought to contain between 10 and 12 sonobuoys

Fuselage fuel tanks
Most internal fuel capacity is provided tanks under the cabin floor. A removab weapons bay under the fuselage is us for the stowage of various types of torpedoes, some of them wire-guided and depth charges, conventional or nuclear

Kamov Ka-25 'Hormone-A' and Ka-27 'Helix' Soviet Naval Aviation

blades. It has thus been possible to lift loads roughly 50 per cent heavier in a greatly enlarged cabin, whilst still operating from the decks and hangars tailored to the Ka-25.

The new rotor blades are made entirely of advanced composite materials. The D-shaped leading edge and main spar are filament-wound from carbon fibre plastics and GRP (glass reinforced plastics). The pockets along the rear of the blade are of a fibre-reinforced material similar to Kevlar (aramid fibre), the interior being filled with Nomex honeycomb. Each blade has much greater chord than those of the Ka-25, and a single tab is fitted to the trailing edge, adjustable on the ground. The hub is machined from forgings in titanium and steel, and the hinges are so arranged that the blades can be folded by hand aboard the ship. The entire leading edge of each blade is de-iced by an electric heater mat all the time the engines are running, and the heat also prevents icing of the droop stops or hub hinges. Each blade has a pair of dumb-bell-type anti-vibration masses on its inboard section, and the upper rotor carries navigation lights on its tips.

Longer fuselage

The Ka-27's fuselage is generally similar to that of the Ka-25, but is much longer, overall length increasing from 9.75 m (32 ft 0 in) to 11.30 m (37 ft 1 in). The entire underpart is made watertight, though alighting on water is still done only in emergency. Large amounts of titanium and bonded sandwich are used in the structure, and in the entire tail boom and tail skins. The tail has no central fin, and the twin fins are toed in more sharply than before (about 25°). To avoid any tendency of the fins to stall at extreme sideways angles of attack each carries a large slat along the inside of its leading edge.

The engine hump along the top looks very much like that of the Ka-25, despite the great increase in power. Electricity and bleed air are again used for inlet anti-icing, and a new feature is a synchronizer to tie both engines as nearly as possible to the same output speed and drive torque. The same system automatically opens the throttle fully on either engine following failure of the other. At the rear, on the centreline, is the fan-assisted oil cooler. Alongside, on the right, is another addition, a gas-turbine APU to provide hydraulic, air and electric power when the main engines are not running and also start the main engines (it is believed, electrically). The usual underfloor tanks are augmented by vertical scabbed-on tanks on each side of the fuselage. If auxiliary tanks are needed they are carried inside the cabin.

First deployment

The Ka-27 and its civil Ka-32 counterpart were probably designed about 1977, and the first was seen on the then-new missile destroyer *Udaloy* in 1981. By early 1987 the number built of all Ka-27 and Ka-32 versions was probably about 150, and because of the importance of its civil version the total production is likely to exceed the 500-odd of its predecessor. As before, the assembly line is believed to be at Ulan-Ude, in the Trans-Baikal region.

Again, as before, there are believed to

be three main AV-MF versions of the Ka-27. The first, dubbed 'Helix-A' by NATO, is the ASW variant. This carries a full spectrum of anti-submarine sensors and weapons, including a completely new search radar in the chin position, much larger boxes of sonobuoys on each side, and greatly upgraded EW and ESM equipment. As this was written, in early 1987, little was known of the weapons carried, though the choices are likely to be wider than in the case of the Ka-25. In the civil Ka-32 the cockpit is arranged for a pilot and navigator, and this is probably the case with the 'Helix-A'. In the main cabin from one to three mission and sensor operators manage the ASW systems and the attack, usually in partnership with the parent vessel (but the Ka-27 is designed also to be capable of autonomous operation).

Infantry assault

'Helix-B' is the reporting name of an infantry assault version, serving with the Soviet Marines. Few details were available in early 1987, but this helicopter is said by the US Department of Defense to have 'different undernose equipment'. It is certainly able to carry 16 troops with weapons and personal equipment. The third variant, 'Helix-C', is the utility transport, with a rescue hoist, used mainly in

The 'Hormone-A' is operated by a crew of three, with pilot and co-pilot side by side on the flight deck and a crewman in the rear cabin. He operates the sensors and acts as a winchman and camera operator.

the SAR and plane-guard role (first seen attending *Novorossiysk*). It has always been seen with the scabbed-on external tanks, and the 300-kg hoist above the main cabin door. This model, like other variants, appears likely to find a market in India (which already operates 'Helix-A') and several other countries having a need for versatile maritime helicopters.

Glossary
APU Auxiliary Power Unit
ASW Anti-Submarine Warfare
EO Electro-Optical
ESM Electronic Support Measures
EW Electronic Warfare
IFF Identification Friend or Foe
MAD Magnetic Anomaly Detector
OTH Over The Horizon
SAR Search And Rescue

This winch-equipped 'Helix-C' is used for plane-guard duties on board the 'Kiev'-class carrier Novorossiysk, providing essential SAR support for the Yakovlev Yak-38 'Forger' fighters carried by the ship.

Kamov 'Hormone' and 'Helix' in service

India
Five ex-AV-MF Kamov Ka-25 'Hormone-As' were delivered to the Indian navy during the 1970s and equip INAS No. 333 Squadron for use on 'Godavari' class frigates and 'Kashin II' class destroyers. Eighteen 'Helix' helicopters allegedly designated Ka-28 were delivered in 1985, and may include 'Helix-C' variants.

Syria
Between five and nine ex-AV-MF 'Hormone-As' supplement the Syrian navy's force of 12 Mil Mi-14 'Haze' ASW helicopters for coastal ASW duties.

USSR
About 190 Ka-25 'Hormone' variants are thought to be in front-line service with the AV-MF, of about 460 delivered. Some ex-AV-MF aircraft have been exported, while others serve in various support roles. About 50 Kamov Ka-27 'Helix' helicopters had entered service by the spring of 1987. Both 'Helix' and 'Hormone' can be carried individually or in pairs on various classes of frigate, destroyer and cruiser, or in larger numbers on the 'Kiev' class carriers and 'Moskva' class anti-submarine cruisers.

Vietnam
Unconfirmed reports indicate that the Vietnam People's Navy operates 17 Kamov Ka-25s from some of its Soviet, Chinese and US-built warships.

Yugoslavia
The tiny Yugoslav navy operates some 10 ASW-configured Kamov Ka-25s, alongside a larger number of Mil Mi-8s and Aérospatiale Gazelles.

A Ka-25 'Hormone-A' of the AV-MF. Operational 'Hormones' wear an overall grey colour scheme.

Some 'Hormone-Cs' wear colourful markings and are used for second-line duties, including search and rescue.

Four Ka-25 'Hormone-Cs' of the AV-MF lands on board Moskva. They would usually operate singly or in pairs.

A Ka-27 'Helix-A' of the AV-MF based on the 'Kiev'-class carrier Novorossiysk.

Kamov 'Hormone' and 'Helix' warload

☐ ASW radar (NATO reporting name 'Big Bulge') under nose
'Tie-Rod' downward looking electro-optical sensor

■ 2×wire-guided torpedoes carried in enlarged underfuselage weapons bay with associated wire-reel on port fuselage side

■ Auxiliary fuel tank on starboard fuselage side

☐ ASW radar (NATO reporting name 'Big Bulge') under nose
Unidentified electro-optical sensor in fairing below ventral fin
Dipping sonar in compartment immediately aft of standard weapons bay
3×'A-class' sonobuoys in external box on starboard rear fuselage side
4×dye-markers/smoke-floats in pairs mounted on forward fuselage sides

☐ ASST (Anti-Ship Surveillance and Targeting) radar (NATO reporting name 'Short Horn') under nose
Unidentified radar in small underfuselage radome

☐ ASW radar (NATO reporting name 'Big Bulge') under nose
Unidentified Yagi aerials on nose (possibly for autoland or carrier recovery system)
Rescue hoist above cabin door
Searchlight on port fuselage side

■ Auxiliary fuel tanks on fuselage sides

Anti-submarine/shipping, torpedo attack
The enlarged weapons bay fitted to some Kamov 'Hormones' extends aft as far as the tailboom, so that dipping sonar or trailing MAD gear cannot be carried. The standard bay can reportedly accommodate a variety of torpedoes and depth charges, and the enlarged bay is said to be for wire-guided weapons. Some 'Hormone-As' have allegedly been seen carrying pylon-mounted fire-and-forget ASMs.

Anti-submarine, detection
ASW-configured 'Hormone-As' can use a variety of sensors to detect and track their prey before calling in other assets for the kill if they themselves are not carrying depth charges or torpedoes. A towed MAD bird can be carried in place of the dipping sonar.

Mid-course missile guidance and course-correction
'Hormone-B' is tasked with the mid-course guidance of ship-launched surface-to-surface missiles, and has virtually all ASW avionics and equipment removed. Data-link equipment is installed.

'Hormone-C' search-and-rescue
'Hormone-C' is a utility and search and rescue variant of the Ka-25, with all operational equipment removed and used for COD, SAR and planeguard duties. They may be new-build aircraft, but it is more likely that they are conversions of early-production ASW aircraft.

219

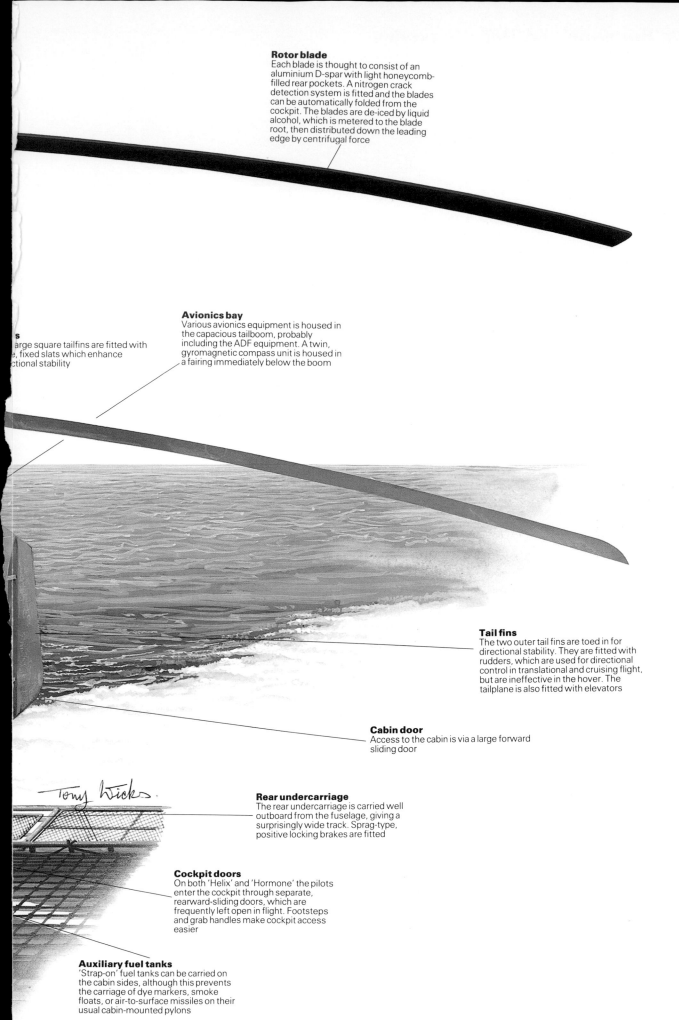

Rotor blade
Each blade is thought to consist of an aluminium D-spar with light honeycomb-filled rear pockets. A nitrogen crack detection system is fitted and the blades can be automatically folded from the cockpit. The blades are de-iced by liquid alcohol, which is metered to the blade root, then distributed down the leading edge by centrifugal force

Avionics bay
Various avionics equipment is housed in the capacious tailboom, probably including the ADF equipment. A twin, gyromagnetic compass unit is housed in a fairing immediately below the boom

s
arge square tailfins are fitted with e, fixed slats which enhance ctional stability

Tail fins
The two outer tail fins are toed in for directional stability. They are fitted with rudders, which are used for directional control in translational and cruising flight, but are ineffective in the hover. The tailplane is also fitted with elevators

Cabin door
Access to the cabin is via a large forward sliding door

Tony Wicks.

Rear undercarriage
The rear undercarriage is carried well outboard from the fuselage, giving a surprisingly wide track. Sprag-type, positive locking brakes are fitted

Cockpit doors
On both 'Helix' and 'Hormone' the pilots enter the cockpit through separate, rearward-sliding doors, which are frequently left open in flight. Footsteps and grab handles make cockpit access easier

Auxiliary fuel tanks
'Strap-on' fuel tanks can be carried on the cabin sides, although this prevents the carriage of dye markers, smoke floats, or air-to-surface missiles on their usual cabin-mounted pylons

Rotor hub
The main hub spiders are of titanium construction, with elastomeric main bearings

Anti-vibration weights
Adjustable/anti-vibration masses are bolted across the rotor blade spars immediately inboard of the aerofoil section of each blade

Rotor head
The rotor head is fully articulated with oil-lubricated flapping and drag hinges. A clumsy hub has a complex system of long push rods which link the two sets of counter-rotating blade roots and swash plates. This does ensure a large clearance between the blades

Contra-rotating main rotors
The two main rotors turn in opposite directions about the same vertical axis, driven by coaxial shafts. The torque produced by each rotor cancels out the torque produced by the other, so no anti-torque tail rotor is needed. On conventional helicopters the tail rotor absorbs much of the engines power output. The rotor area needed can be obtained with a smaller rotor diameter, giving a more compact helicopter

Oil cooler
The fan-driven oil cooler is situated adjacent to the main gearbox

Cabin
The cabin can accommodate 12 passengers on tip-up seats along the cabin sides, 1300 kg of cargo, or three ASW operators

Sla
The
larg
dire

Performance (at normal take-off weight)

Maximum speed	132 kts; 245 km/h	(152 mph)
Cruising or patrol speed	120 kts; 222 km/h	(138 mph)
Hovering ceiling, out of ground effect	11,480 ft	(3500 m)
Normal patrol endurance	4 hours 30 minutes	

Weapon load

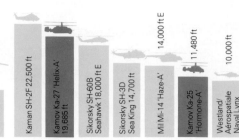

- Mil Mi-14 'Haze-A' 800 kg E
- Kamov Ka-27 'Helix-A' 600 kg E
- Kamov Ka-25 'Hormone-A' 600 kg E
- Naval Lynx 460 kg
- SH-60B Seahawk 460 kg
- Kaman SH-2F 460 kg
- SH-3D Sea King 381 kg

Service ceiling

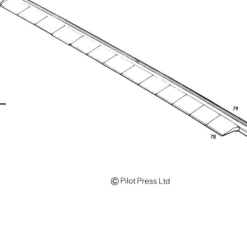

- Kaman SH-2F 22,500 ft
- Kamov Ka-27 'Helix-A' 19,685 ft
- Sikorsky SH-60B Seahawk 18,000 ft E
- Sikorsky SH-3D Sea King 14,700 ft
- Mil Mi-14 'Haze-A' 14,000 ft E
- Kamov Ka-25 'Hormone-A' 11,480 ft
- Westland/Aérospatiale Naval Lynx 10,000 ft

Cruising speed

- Westland/Aérospatiale Naval Lynx 125 kts
- Kamov Ka-27 'Helix-A' 124 kts
- Kaman SH-2F 120 kts
- Sikorsky SH-3D Sea King 118 kts
- Sikorsky SH-60B Seahawk 110 kts E
- Mil Mi-14 'Haze-A' 108 kts
- Kamov Ka-25 'Hormone-A' 104 kts

Maximum speed at optimum altitude

- Sikorsky SH-3D Sea King 144 kts
- Westland/Aérospatiale Naval Lynx 140 kts
- Kamov Ka-27 'Helix-A' 135 kts
- Kaman SH-2F 130 kts
- Sikorsky SH-60B Seahawk 126 kts
- Mil Mi-14 'Haze-A' 124 kts
- Kamov Ka-25 'Hormone-A' 119 kts

Range, internal fuel and typical weapon load

- Sikorsky SH-3D Sea King 1005 km
- Mil Mi-14 'Haze-A' 925 km
- Kamov Ka-27 'Helix-A' 800 km
- Kaman SH-2F 679 km
- Sikorsky SH-60B Seahawk 600 km E
- Westland/Aérospatiale Naval Lynx 593 km
- Kamov Ka-25 'Hormone-A' 400 km

Kamov 'Hormone' and 'Helix' variants

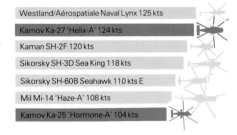

Kamov Ka-20 'Harp': prototype built to meet late 1950s requirement for specialized shipborne ASW helicopter; two 671-kW (900-shp) Glushenkov GTD-3F turboshafts, three-blade co-axial contra-rotating main rotors; assigned ASCC reporting name 'Harp'; demonstrated at Tushino in July 1961, carrying two large missiles (almost certainly dummies); long and troubled gestation

Kamov Ka-25K: civil flying crane version, with undernose gondola for crane operator; displayed at 1967 Paris airshow; believed not to have entered production

Kamov Ka-25 'Hormone-A': initial production version of Ka-20 for AV-MF; production decision almost certainly made late 1962, with first deliveries 1965; first seen on *Moskva* helicopter carrier during 1967; 'Big Bulge' I/J-band search radar undernose, various equipment and armament fits on cabin sides and in underfuselage pannier

Kamov Ka-25 'Hormone-B': electronic warfare and missile guidance/mid-course correction platform; different radar in more spherical radome, and other role-related equipment

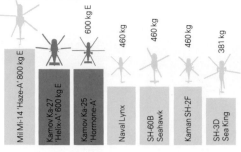

Kamov Ka-25 'Hormone-C': search-and-rescue and utility transport variant of 'Hormone-A' with radar retained, but with all other ASW sensors removed; some have four-pronged Yagi type antennae on nose, serving autoland system

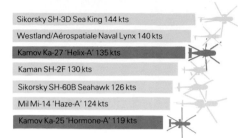

Kamov Ka-27 'Helix-A': basic military version of Ka-32 for AV-MF. Early prototype, in company with Aeroflot Ka-32, seen undergoing trials on the guided missile destroyer *Udaloy* during the 'Zapad-81' exercises in the Baltic during September 1981; operational since 1982, and at least 16 deployed on maiden cruise of *Novorossiysk* in 1983

Kamov Ka-27 'Helix-B': infantry assault transport variant, with 'different undernose equipment' according to US DoD, possibly deletion of undernose radome

Kamov Ka-27 'Helix-C': search-and-rescue and plane guard variant, with 300-kg (661-lb) capacity winch on port side, and usually seen with auxiliary fuel tanks

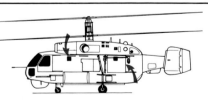

Kamov Ka-32: all-new civil basic transport and flying crane helicopter with 1659-kW (2,225-shp) Isotov TV3-117V turboshafts and larger fuselage, but retaining basic configuration of earlier Ka-25 variants; prototype public displayed at Minsk in late 1981

Kamov Ka-32S: civil maritime version of basic Ka-32, with undernose radar and full IMC avionics for SAR, ice patrol and other duties

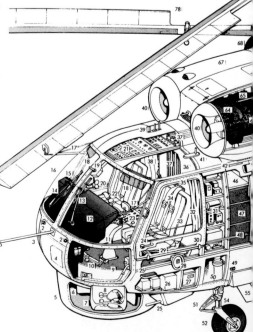

© Pilot Press Ltd

Specification: Ka-27 'Helix A'

Rotors

Diameter, each	15.90 m	(52 ft 2 in)
Total disc area	397.11 m²	(4,274.64 sq ft)

Fuselage and tail unit

Accommodation of three	flight crew of two and mission crew	
Length overall, excluding rotors	11.30 m	(37 ft 0.9 in)
Cabin cross section, width/height	1.32 m	(4 ft 4 in)

Landing gear

Fixed quadricycle type with a single wheel on each unit, and with the facility to be raised out of the radar's line of sight

Wheelbase	3.02 m	(9 ft 10.9 in)
Wheel track,		
nose units	1.40 m	(4 ft 7.1 in)
main units	3.50 m	(11 ft 5.8 in)

Powerplant

Two Isotov TV3-117V turboshafts

Maximum contingency rating, each	1659 KW	(2,225 shp)

Weights

Empty, without ASW equipment	6100 kg	(13,348 lb)
Normal take-off	11000 kg	(24,251 lb)
Maximum take-off	12600 kg	(27,778 lb)

Ka-27 'Helix' recognition features

Each main rotor has three blades

Engines mounted side-by-side on upper fuselage decking

Compact, co-axial contra-rotating main rotors

Tailfins toed in from leading edge

Rear undercarriage units carried on tubular struts well clear of cabin

Short stroke fixed landing gear at corners of fuselage

Extensively glazed flight deck

Long, but rather deep fuselage fairing into stubby tail boom

Small square-cut tail fins

Some variants have chin-mounted radome

Kamov Ka-27 and Ka-32 'Helix' cutaway drawing key

1 Air data sensor probe
2 Forward radar warning antennas
3 Downward vision window
4 Instrumentation access panel
5 Ventral radome
6 360° rotating search radar scanner (Ka-27 'Helix-A' and Ka-32S)
7 Lateral lamp housing
8 Twin remotely-controlled floodlights
9 Cockpit floor level
10 Yaw control rudder pedals
11 Cyclic pitch control column
12 Instrument panel shroud
13 Windscreen wipers
14 Radar display
15 Radar control panel
16 Curved windscreen panels
17 Rear view mirror, port and starboard (Ka-27 'Helix-C' and Ka-32S)
18 Retractable sun visors
19 Air temperature probe
20 Cockpit air circulation fan
21 Overhead switch panel
22 Navigator's swivelling seat

23 Engine power and condition levers
24 Sliding door latch
25 Boarding steps
26 Electrical equipment bay
27 Battery
28 Ground power socket
29 Collective pitch control lever
30 Sliding cockpit door, port and starboard
31 Avionics equipment racks
32 Folding sun blind
33 Pilot's seat
34 Safety harness
35 Bulged side observation window
36 Cockpit rear bulkhead
37 Control rod runs
38 Starboard side observer/ loadmaster/winch operator's swivelling seat

39 Forward 'Odd Rods' IFF aerials
40 Engine air intakes, bleed air de-iced
41 Intake air temperature sensor
42 Sliding cockpit door top rail
43 Cabin fresh air ventilating intakes
44 Handgrip
45 Cabin window panel
46 Cabin wall-mounted passenger seating; 16 passengers in Ka-32

47 Main cabin loading floor
48 Sliding door lower rail
49 Tie-down point
50 Nose undercarriage leg strut
51 Torque scissor links
52 Self-centring castoring nosewheel
53 Nosewheel rebound position
54 Shock absorber strut

55 Position of communications aerial on starboard side
56 Flotation gear pannier, port and starboard (Ka-27 and Ka-32S)
57 Underfloor fuel tank groups, port and starboard
58 Floor hatch for externally-slung load, maximum load 5000 kg (11,023 lb)

59 External long-range fuel tank pannier, port and starboard
60 Lateral engine exhaust port
61 Engine/gearbox coupling shaft
62 Engine turbine section
63 Isotov TV3-117V turboshaft engine
64 Engine accessory equipment gearbox
65 Generator
66 Engine bay fireproof bulkhead

67 Hinged engine cowling/ work platform
68 Starboard engine exhaust duct
69 Rotor head hydraulic actuators
70 Lower rotor swashplate mechanism
71 Articulated rotor hub
72 Blade pitch control rods
73 Upper/lower rotor interconnecting control rods
74 Upper rotor swash plate mechanism
75 Blade pitch control links and rods
76 Upper rotor articulated hub
77 Blade folding hinge joints, manual-folding
78 Three-bladed, co-axial, contra-rotating main rotors
79 Electro-thermal leading edge de-icing
80 Vibration damping pendulum weights, lower rotor only
81 Blade root attachment fittings
82 Communications aerial
83 Maintenance handgrips
84 Cooling air louvres
85 Oil cooler fan
86 Rotor brake
87 Central combining and main reduction gearbox
88 Gearbox mounting struts

89 Engine and gearbox mounting deck
90 Rescue hoist/winch hydraulic motor and gearbox
91 Pannier tank filler cap
92 Main undercarriage shock absorber strut
93 Rescue hoist/winch mounting
94 Main undercarriage wishbone links
95 Mainwheel leg strut
96 Mainwheel forks
97 Port mainwheel
98 Mainwheel rebound position
99 Rescue hoist/winch (Ka-27 'Helix-C' and Ka-32), 300 kg (660 lb) capacity
100 Boarding steps
101 Main cabin sliding door
102 Hoist floodlight
103 Three-abreast rear seat row
104 Sliding door rail
105 Air intake grilles
106 Airborne auxiliary power unit (APU)
107 Cabin heater unit
108 ESM antenna (Ka-27)
109 Upper anti-collision light
110 Engine/gearbox/APU tail fairing
111 Fuselage frame and stringer construction
112 Access panels
113 Pressure refuelling connection
114 Doppler equipment fairing
115 Main rotor blade honeycomb trailing edge pockets
116 Composite skin panels
117 Ground adjustable blade tab
118 Blade tip balance and tracking weight fairing
119 Glass/carbon fibre D-section blade spar
120 Twin gyromagnetic compass unit
121 Tailcone joint frame
122 Rear avionics equipment bay
123 Access door
124 Tailcone construction
125 ADF sense aerial
126 HF aerial cable
127 Tailfin leading edge slat
128 Starboard tailfin
129 Starboard rudder
130 Rudder control linkage
131 Fixed horizontal tailplane
132 Rear radar warning antennas, port and starboard
133 Rear 'Odd Rods' IFF aerials
134 Aft-facing radome
135 Horizontal tailplane construction
136 Tailplane bracing strut
137 Port tailfin leading edge slat
138 Port navigation light
139 Tailfin construction
140 Fin/tailplane joint rib
141 Composite rudder construction
142 Lower rotor blades, folded position
143 Blade locking struts
144 Upper rotor blades, folded

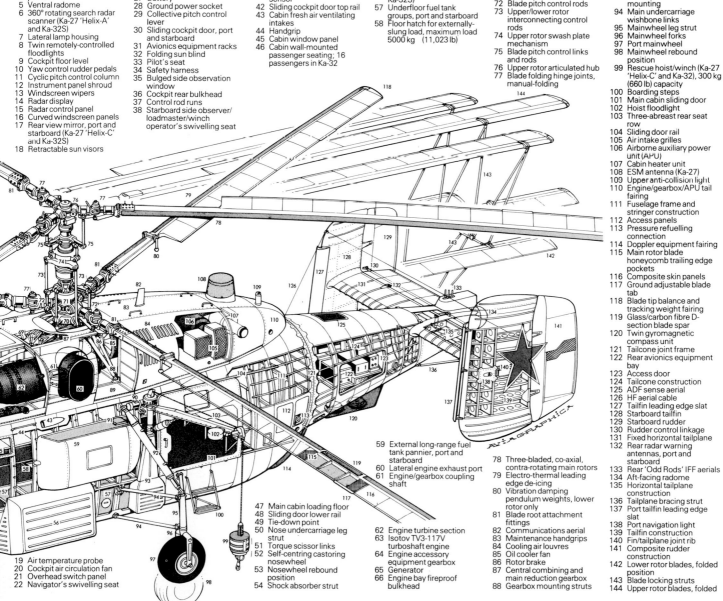

GLOSSARY

AAA	Anti-Aircraft Artillery		**MCAS**	Marine Corps Air Station
AAM	Air-to-Air Missile		**NAS**	Naval Air Station
ACM	Air Combat Manoeuvre		**NAVWAS**	NAVigation and Weapon-Aiming System
AFB	Air-Force Base		**NWDS**	Navigation and Weapons Delivery System
AFRes	Air Force Reserve		**OAS**	Offensive Avionics System
ANG	Air National Guard		**OCU**	Operational Conversion Unit
AHRS	Attitude and Heading Reference System		**OTEAF**	Operational Test and EvaluAtion Force
ALARM	Air-Launched Anti-Radiation Missile		**PGM**	Precision-Guided Munition
ALCM	Air-Launched Cruise Missile		**Photint**	Photographic intelligence
ARM	Anti-Radiation Missile		**QRA**	Quick-Reaction Alert
ASM	Air-to-Surface Missile		**RAAF**	Royal Australian Air Force
ASMP	Air-Sol Moyenne Portee (medium-range surface-to-air)		**RDT&E**	Research, Development, Test and Evaluation
AMRAAM	Advanced Medium-Range Air-to-Air Missile		**RIO**	Radio Intercept Officer
AV-MF	Soviet Naval Aviation		**RNAS**	Royal Naval Air Station
BW	Bomber Wing		**RWR**	Radar Warning Receiver
CBU	Cluster Bomb Unit		**SAC**	Strategic Air Command
CILOP	Conversion In Lieu Of Procurement		**SACEUR**	Supreme Allied Commander EURope
CITS	Central Integrated Test System		**SACLANT**	Supreme Allied Commander AtLANTic
COMED	COmbined Map and Electronic Display		**SAM**	Surface-to-Air Missile
CRT	Cathode Ray Tube		**SAR**	Search And Rescue
DARIN	Display, Attack, Ranging and Inertial Navigation		**SEAM**	Sidewinder Expanded-Acquisition Missile
			SIOP	Single Integrated Operational Plan
DME	Distance Measuring Equipment		**SLEP**	Service Life Extension Program
ECM	Electronic CounterMeasures		**SNOE**	Smart Noise Operation Equipment
Elint	Electronic Intelligence		**SOR**	Specific Operational Requirement
EMP	Electro-Magnetic Pulse		**SRAM**	Short-Range Attack Missile
EO	Electro-Optical		**Tacan**	Tactical air navigation
ESM	Electronic Support Measures		**TAC**	Tactical Air Command
EVS	Electro-optical Viewing System		**TERCOM**	TERrain COntour Matching
EW	Electronic Warfare		**TFR**	Terrain Following Radar
FLIR	Forward-Looking Infra-Red		**TFS**	Tactical Fighter Squadron
GP	General Purpose		**TFW**	Tactical Fighter Wing
GSFG	Group of Soviet Forces in Germany		**TFX**	Tactical Fighter eXperimental
HARM	High-speed Anti-Radiation Missile		**TISL**	Target Indicator System - Laser
HUD	Head-Up Display		**TRAM**	Target Recognition and Attack Multi-sensor
HUDWAS	Head-Up Display and Weapon-Aiming System		**TRIM**	Trails, Roads, Interdiction Multi-sensor
IFF	Identification Friend or Foe		**TTTE**	Trinational Tornado Training Establishment
ILS	Instrument Landing System		**UHF**	Ultra High Frequency
INS	Inertial Navigation System		**VG**	Variable Geometry
IOC	Initial Operational Capability		**VHF**	Very High Frequency
IR	Infra-Red		**VOR**	VHF Omni-directional Range
IRCM	Infra-Red CounterMeasures		**VTAS**	Visual Target-Acquisition System
JATO	Jet-Assisted Take-Off		**VTOL**	Vertical Take-Off and Landing
LID	Lift-Improvement Device		**V-VS**	Soviet air force
LLLTV	Low-Light-Level TV		**WAC**	Weapon-Aiming Computer
LRMTS	Laser Ranger and Marked-Target Seeker		**WSO**	Weapons System Officer